SUBALTERN STU
Writings on South Asian His

Subaltern Studies III

Writings on South Asian History and Society

Edited by
RANAJIT GUHA

DELHI
OXFORD UNIVERSITY PRESS
OXFORD   NEW YORK

Oxford University Press, Walton Street, Oxford OX2 6DP

NEW YORK TORONTO
DELHI BOMBAY CALCUTTA MADRAS KARACHI
KUALA LUMPUR SINGAPORE HONG KONG TOKYO
NAIROBI DAR ES SALAAM
MELBOURNE AUCKLAND

and associates in
BERLIN IBADAN

First published 1984
Paperback edition 1989
Second impression 1992

SBN 0 19 5624823

Typeset by South End Typographics, Pondicherry
Printed by Rekha Printers Pvt. Ltd., New Delhi 110020
Published by S.K. Mookerjee, Oxford University Press,
YMCA Library Building, Jai Singh Road, New Delhi 110001

Contents

Maps

Preface

At the time of this writing, in the spring of 1984, *Subaltern Studies I* has been in print for about two years and *Subaltern Studies II* for half as long. These publications, we are delighted to acknowledge, have not gone unnoticed. Although the big guns of the academic press are yet to open up—that old-fashioned artillery operates with the tardiness of a medieval seige and takes its time to be moved into position—a sufficient number of reviews have already appeared and raised a host of questions relating not only to our own performance but to several issues of a fundamental nature about the scope and manner of studies devoted to South Asian history and society. We shall take up some of the more important of these issues for discussion in the forthcoming volumes of this series and elsewhere. Meanwhile, we wish to thank our readers for their comments on our work. We recognize that for a project like ours, designed as it is to ask questions, nothing can be more rewarding than questions asked.

The questions raised so far in the pages of *Subaltern Studies* are not specialized in theme or limited to any particular phase of the South Asian experience. The contributions have ranged widely indeed in topic and period, as witness the present collection of essays. Yet what binds them together is a critical idiom common to all of them—an idiom self-consciously and systematically critical of elitism in the field of South Asian studies.

One learned reviewer has seized precisely on this point and reproached us for being against all existing schools of historiography. We are indeed opposed to much of the prevailing academic practice in historiography and the social sciences for its failure to acknowledge the subaltern as the maker of his own destiny. This critique lies at the very heart of our project. There is no way in which it can express itself other than as an adversary of that elitist paradigm which is so well entrenched in South Asian studies. Negativity is therefore the very raison d'être as well as the constitutive principle of our project.

It is this negativity, this critical drive, which enables *Subaltern Studies* to disturb the charmed and almost soporific smugness of established scholarship. It prompts us to hold up to doubt orthodoxies cushioned in the self-assurance of final truths (it will no longer be easy to fall back on some of the more facile interpretations of the nationalist movement after Sumit Sarkar's essay, or on their opposite numbers in labour history after Dipesh Chakrabarty's); to take the wrapping off packaged ideologies by reading (as Partha Chatterjee does) hallowed texts with sealed meanings in an altogether new way; to turn class-room sociology on its head (as in David Hardiman's study of an Adivasi cult) in order to identify the element of subaltern protest in reformist campaigns hitherto regarded as merely emulative of upper castes and classes; to challenge the condescending assumption about the passivity of the masses in the face of communal disaster (by describing, as David Arnold does, peasant beliefs and practices during the Madras famine of 1876–8); to give the lie about the alleged want of evidence for the structure and dynamics of subaltern consciousness by locating and interpreting (as Shahid Amin and Gyanendra Pandey have done) hitherto unexplored records of popular discourse both in oral and graphic forms. Taken together, these essays should give readers an idea of the scope and orientation of our effort to interrogate the elitist paradigm which dominates teaching, research and generally academic thinking about South Asian history and society.

Canberra   Ranajit Guha
April 1984

Note on Contributors

SHAHID AMIN is a Reader in History at the Jamia Millia Islamia, New Delhi. He is the author of *Sugarcane and Sugar in Gorakhpur: An Inquiry into Peasant Production for Capitalist Enterprise in Colonial India* (Delhi, 1984).

DAVID ARNOLD is a Lecturer in History at the University of Lancaster. He is the author of *The Congress in Tamilnadu: Nationalist Politics in South India 1919–37* (Delhi, 1977). He has recently completed his work on a history of the police in colonial India.

DIPESH CHAKRABARTY, until recently a Lecturer in Indian Studies at the University of Melbourne, is currently employed as an official in the Public Service of the Government of Australia. His monograph on a history of the jute-mill workers of Bengal is soon due for publication.

PARTHA CHATTERJEE is Professor of Political Science, Centre for Studies in Social Sciences, Calcutta. He has published *Arms, Alliances and Stability: The Development of the Structure of International Politics* (Delhi, London and New York, 1975) and is co-author of *The State of Political Theory: Some Marxist Essays* (Calcutta, 1978). His most recent work, a monograph on nationalist thought, is soon due for publication.

DAVID HARDIMAN has taught political science at the University of Leicester and is currently a Fellow of the Centre for Social Studies, Surat. He is the author of *Peasant Nationalists of Gujarat: Kheda District, 1917–34* (Delhi, 1981).

GYANENDRA PANDEY, a Fellow in History at the Centre for Studies in Social Sciences, Calcutta, is currently a Visiting Fellow at the South Asian History Section of the Research School of Pacific Studies, Australian National University, Canberra. He is the author of *The Ascendancy of the Congress in Uttar Pradesh, 1926–34: A Study in Imperfect Mobilization* (Delhi, 1978).

SUMIT SARKAR is Professor of History, University of Delhi. His publications include *Swadeshi Movement in Bengal, 1903–08* (New Delhi, 1973), *Modern India, 1885–1947* (New Delhi, 1983), and *'Popular Movements' and 'Middle Class' Leadership in Late Colonial India: Problems and Perspectives of a 'History from Below'* (Calcutta, 1983).

Acknowledgement

This volume of *Subaltern Studies* is the product of collective work by a team made up of Shahid Amin, David Arnold, Gautam Bhadra, Dipesh Chakrabarty, Partha Chatterjee, Ranajit Guha, David Hardiman, Gyan Pandey and Sumit Sarkar, all of whom have participated equally in every detail of its planning and editing.

We are grateful to Margaret Hall for typing the manuscript and to the Oxford University Press for their support in publishing this series.

The essays in this volume are revised versions of papers read at the First *Subaltern Studies* Conference on 'Subaltern and Elite in South Asian History and Society', held in November 1982 under the auspices of the South Asian History Section of the Research School of Pacific Studies, Australian National University, Canberra. We wish to put on record our gratitude to all members of the Research School of Pacific Studies and especially to its Director and Business Manager for the material and intellectual support received for that conference and the preparation of this volume.

Gandhi as Mahatma:
Gorakhpur District, Eastern UP, 1921–2[1]

SHAHID AMIN

'Many miracles, were previous to this affair [the riot at Chauri Chaura], sedulously circulated by the designing crowd, and firmly believed by the ignorant crowd, of the Non-co-operation world of this district'.

—M. B. Dixit, Committing Magistrate, Chauri Chaura Trials.

I

Gandhi visited the district of Gorakhpur in eastern UP on 8 February 1921, addressed a monster meeting variously estimated at between 1 lakh and 2.5 lakhs and returned the same evening to Banaras. He was accorded a tumultuous welcome in the district, but unlike in Champaran and Kheda he did not stay in Gorakhpur for any length

[1] Research for this paper was funded by grants from the British Academy and Trinity College, Oxford. I am extremely grateful to Dr Ramachandra Tiwari for letting me consult the back numbers of *Swadesh* in his possession. Without his hospitality and kindness the data used in this paper could not have been gathered. Earlier versions of this essay were discussed at St Stephen's College, Delhi, the Indian Institute of Management, Calcutta, and the Conference on the Subaltern in South Asian History and Society, held at the Australian National University, Canberra, in November 1982. I am grateful to David Arnold, Gautam Bhadra, Dipesh Chakrabarty, Partha Chatterjee, Bernard Cohn, Veena Das, Anjan Ghosh, Ranajit Guha, David Hardiman, Christopher Hill, S. N. Mukherjee, Gyan Pandey, Sumit Sarkar, Abhijit Sen, Savyasaachi and Harish Trivedi for their criticisms and suggestions. My debt to Roland Barthes, 'Introduction to the Structural Analysis of Narratives', in Stephen Heath (ed.), *Image-Music-Test* (Glasgow, 1979), Peter Burke, *Popular Culture in Early Modern Europe* (London, 1979), Ch. 5 and Ranajit Guha, *Elementary Aspects of Peasant Insurgency in Colonial India* (Delhi, 1983), Ch. 6 is too transparent to require detailed acknowledgement.

of time to lead or influence a political movement of the peasantry. Gandhi, the person, was in this particular locality for less than a day, but the 'Mahatma' as an 'idea' was thought out and reworked in popular imagination in subsequent months. Even in the eyes of some local Congressmen this 'deification'—'unofficial canonization' as the *Pioneer* put it—assumed dangerously distended proportions by April-May 1921.

In following the career of the Mahatma in one limited area over a short period, this essay seeks to place the relationship between Gandhi and the peasants in a perspective somewhat different from the view usually taken of this grand subject. We are not concerned with analysing the attributes of his charisma but with how this registered in peasant consciousness. We are also constrained by our primary documentation from looking at the image of Gandhi in Gorakhpur historically—at the ideas and beliefs about the Mahatma that percolated into the region before his visit and the transformations, if any, that image underwent as a result of his visit. Most of the rumours about the Mahatma's *pratap* (power/glory) were reported in the local press between February and May 1921. And as our sample of fifty fairly elaborate 'stories' spans this rather brief period, we cannot fully indicate what happens to the 'deified' image after the rioting at Chauri Chaura in early 1922 and the subsequent withdrawal of the Non-Co-operation movement. The aim of the present exercise is then the limited one of taking a close look at peasant perceptions of Gandhi by focusing on the trail of stories that marked his passage through the district. The location of the Mahatma image within existing patterns of popular beliefs and the way it informed direct action, often at variance with the standard interpretations of the Congress creed, are the two main issues discussed in this essay.

In a number of contemporary nationalist writings peasant perceptions of and beliefs about Gandhi figure as incidents of homage and offering. Touching instances of devotion and childlike manifestations of affection are highlighted in the narratives of his tour in northern India during the winter of 1920–2.[2] And if this spectacle of popular regard gets out of hand, it is read as a sign of the mule-like obstinacy (*hathagraha*) of simple, guileless *kisans*. The sight and sound of

[2] See Mahadev Desai, *Day-to-day with Gandhi* (Secretary's Diary), iii (Varanasi, 1965), pp. 143ff. and 262–6. For a condensed version of the same ideas, see D. G. Tendulkar, *Mahatma: Life of Mohandas Karamchand Gandhi*, ii (Bombay, 1952), p. 78.

uncouth peasants invading the train carrying Gandhi, rending the sky with cries of '*jai*' and demanding *darshan* at an unearthly hour, could be annoying and unnerving. But all was not yet lost because local Congress leaders could be counted on to restrain the militant exuberance of lathi-wielding, torch-bearing enthusiasts.³ A passage titled 'Boundless Love' from the tour diary of his secretary is representative of how peasant attitudes towards Gandhi have been written about in nationalist narratives:

> It is impossible to put in language the exuberance of love which Gandhiji and Shaukat Ali experienced in Bihar. Our train on the B.N.W. Railway line stopped at all stations and there was not a single station which was not crowded with hundreds of people at that time. Even women, who never stir out of their homes, did not fail to present themselves so that they could see and hear him. A huge concourse of students would everywhere smother Gandhiji with their enthusiasm. If at some place a sister would take off her coral necklace and tell him, 'I give this specially for you to wear', at some other, *sanyasis* would come and leave their rosaries on his lap. If beautiful sheets of handspun and hand-woven cloth, many yards long, would be presented at one place, at some other place would turn up a loving villager from the woods, boastful of his trophy, saying, 'Maharaj (an address of reverence) this is my feat of strength. The tiger was a terror to our people; I am giving the skin to you'. At some places, guns normally used as fog-signals were fired in his honour. At some others, we came across railway officers who would not give the green flag, when our train came within their jurisdiction, in order to have and let others have Gandhiji's *darshan*. Not minding the fact that our 'Special' was certain to pass by them in terrific speed, people were seen at some places, standing along the railway lines in distant hope of having just a glimpse of Gandhiji or at least of making their loud shouts of 'Gandhi-Shaukat Ali-ki-jai' reach his ear. We have met with even policemen who had the courage to approach Gandhiji to salute him or touch his hand, and CID's [*sic*] also who would plaintively say, 'We have taken to this dirty work for the sake of the sinning flesh, but please do accept these five rupees'.⁴

Seeking darshan was obviously a fairly visible sign of popular reverence, and no wonder it occupies a prominent place in descriptions of Gandhi's tours. D. G. Tendulkar writes of the Mahatma's 'tour of mass conversions to the new creed' in 1921 as follows:

> Remarkable scenes were witnessed. In a Bihar village when Gandhi and his party were stranded in the train, an old woman came seeking out Gandhi. 'Sire, I am now one hundred and four', she said, 'and my sight has grown dim. I have visited the various holy places. In my own home I have dedicated two temples. Just as we had Rama and Krishna as *avatars*,

³ See below, p. 21.   ⁴ Desai, pp. 142–3.

so also Mahatma Gandhi has appeared as an *avatar*, I hear. Until I have seen him death will not appear'. This simple faith moved India's millions who greeted him everywhere with the cry, 'Mahatma Gandhi-ki-jai'. Prostitutes of Barisal, the Marwari merchants of Calcutta, Oriya coolies, railway strikers, Santals eager to present khadi *chaddars*, all claimed his attention.

From Aligarh to Dibrugarh and then as far as Tinnevelly he went from village to village, from town to town, sometimes speaking in temples and mosques. Wherever he went he had to endure the tyranny of love.[5]

Examples of such darshan-seeking scenes could be multiplied, and we shall come back to them in our account of Gandhi's passage through Gorakhpur. It is worth stressing here that the Gandhi-darshan motif in nationalist discourse reveals a specific attitude towards the subalterns—the *sadharan janta* or ordinary people as they are referred to in the nationalist Hindi press. To behold the Mahatma in person and become his devotees were the only roles assigned to them, while it was for the urban intelligentsia and full-time party activists to convert this groundswell of popular feeling into an organized movement. Thus it would appear that even in the relationship between peasant devotees and *their* Mahatma there was room for political mediation by the economically better off and socially more powerful followers.[6]

The idea of the artifacts of the 'mythopoeic imagination of childlike peasants' being mediated by political intermediaries occurs in anti-nationalist discourse as well. Referring to stories about the power of Gandhi current in Gorakhpur and other districts of eastern UP in the spring of 1921, the *Pioneer* wrote in an editorial:

Mr Gandhi is beginning to reap the penalty of having allowed himself to be unofficially canonized (as we should say in the West) by his adoring countrymen. We say 'reap the penalty', because it is inconceivable that a man of his transparent candour and scrupulous regard for truth should hear without chagrin the myths which are being associated with him as a worker of miracles. *The very simple people in the east and south of the United Provinces afford a fertile soil in which a belief in the powers of the 'Mahatmaji', who is after all little more than a name of power to them, may grow.* In the 'Swadesh', a paper published in Gorakhpur, four miracles were quoted last month as being popularly attributable to Mr Gandhi. Smoke was seen coming from wells and, when water was drunk, it had the fragrance of keora (pandanus odaratissimus) an aloe-like plant which is used in the manufacture of perfume; a copy of the Holy Quran was found in a room which had not been opened for a year; an Ahir who refused alms to a Sadhu begging in Mahatma Gandhi's name, had his gur

---

[5] Tendulkar, p. 78.   [6] Cf. p. 19 below.

and two buffaloes destroyed by fire, and a sceptical Brahmin, who defied Mr Gandhi's authority, went mad and was only cured three days afterwards by the invocation of the saintly name! *All these events admit of an obvious explanation, but they are symptoms of an unhealthy nervous excitement such as often passed through the peasant classes of Europe in the Middle Ages, and to which the Indian villager is particularly prone.* Other rumours current in Ghazipur are that a man suffered the loss of his wife, sons and brothers because he had offended Gandhi, that the 'Mahatma' was seen in Calcutta and Multan on the same day, and that he restored two fallen trees. *In all these instances we see the mythopoeic imagination of the childlike peasant at work, and perhaps nobody is much the worse, but a case reported from Mirzapur would require sooner or later the attention of the police.* The story is told that a young ahirin who had been listening during the day to speeches took a grain of corn in her hands when playing with her companions in the evening, blew on it with an invocation of the name of Gandhi and, lo! the one grain became four. Crowds came to see her in the course of a few days and she quadrupled barley and gram and even common objects like pice. But it is reported that strange coins could not be multiplied. *While this is obviously a mere trick of mouth concealment, the agitator is proclaiming it as a miracle*, and all the neurotic girls of the countryside will be emulating the achievement.[7]

A fuller analysis of some of these stories is presented in another section of this essay. What is important to notice at this point is that while the *Pioneer* locates the *origin* of these stories in a popular imagination fired by 'nervous excitement', their *circulation* is attributed to 'agitators'. There is no room here for the 'deified' Mahatma inspiring popular attitudes and actions independent of élite manipulation and control.

Jacques Pouchepadass' sensitive study of Gandhi in Champaran can be read at one level as an elaboration of this theme.[8] In an extended discussion of Gandhi's presence in this district in 1917, the 'obstinate quest for his *darshan*' is picked out as the initial point of departure. Pouchepadass notes that Gandhi was 'invariably met by throngs of raiyats at railway stations' and elsewhere, and this, combined with the influx of peasants from a large number of villages to Bettiah and Motihari to give evidence against the planters, enlarged the area of agitation in the district. 'The name of god was frequently used to denominate Gandhi' and the 'obstinate quest for his *darshan* gives further evidence about the deification of the Mahatma' in the

---

[7] *Pioneer*, 23 April 1921, p. 1. Italics mine.

[8] Jacques Pouchepadass, 'Local leaders and the intelligentsia in the Champaran satyagraha (1917): a study in peasant mobilization', *Contributions to Indian Sociology* (NS) 8: 1974, esp. pp. 82–5.

district. The peasants' faith in Gandhi's power was indexed by 'fantastic rumours':

> Those rumours . . . reported that Gandhi had been sent into Champaran by the Viceroy, or even the King, to redress all the grievances of the raiyats, and that his mandate overruled all the local officials and the courts. He was said to be about to abolish all the unpopular obligations which the planters imposed on their raiyats, so that there was no need to obey the word of any planter any more. A rumour was also in the air that the administration of Champaran was going to be made over to the Indians themselves, and that the British would be cleared out of the district within a few months.[9]

Not all of these however were the product of popular imagination. Pouchepadass is of the opinion that 'many of these rumours were very consciously spread by the local leaders, who took advantage of Gandhi's charismatic appeal to give additional impetus to the agitation . . . . But what matters is that the peasants believed them because Gandhi's name was associated with them'.[10] This faith also broke the normal ties of deference in the countryside—the *hakims* and the *nilhe sahebs* held no terror for the peasants testifying before the Champaran Enquiry Committee. The implication of all this for direct political action by the peasants is unfortunately left unexplored. In fact a case is made out for the transference of Gandhi's charisma to the authorized local interpreters of his will. Pouchepadass warns against overrating Gandhi's 'personal ascendancy over the humbler classes':

> When he is present, of course, only his own word counts. But once he is gone, the local leaders are apt to retain part of his prestige, and become the authorized interpreters of his will. It is a fact that from 1918 onwards, after Gandhi had left and the planters' influence had begun to fade away, the hold of the rural oligarchy grew more powerful than ever.[11]

---

[9] Ibid., pp. 82–3. It is interesting to note that most of these rumours can be classified under the motif 'redressal of wrongs done to the peasantry', a development of the popular idea that Gandhi had come to Champaran precisely for such a task. In war-time all rumours are concerned with war. Though not each and every one of the thirty rumours collected by J. Prasad after the great Bihar earthquake was about seismic upheaval, all of them were nevertheless concerned with disaster. See J. Prasad, 'The Psychology of Rumour: a study relating to the great Indian earthquake of 1934', *British Journal of Psychology*, 35:1 (July, 1935), p. 10 and *passim*.

[10] Ibid., p. 84; cf. Pandey: 'The belief in an "outside leader" can also be seen as an obverse of a belief in the break-down of the locally recognized structure of authority; and rumour fulfils the function of spreading such a notion as efficiently as the leader from the town'. See Gyan Pandey, 'Peasant Revolt and Indian Nationalism: the peasant movement in Awadh, 1919–22', in R. Guha (ed.), *Subaltern Studies I* (Delhi, 1982), p. 164.

[11] Pouchepadass, p. 85.

However, evidence from north Bihar and eastern UP suggests that no authorized version of the Mahatma could have been handed down to the peasants, either by 'local leaders' or by members of the District Congress Committees. The spate of *haat*-looting incidents in Muzaffarpur, Darbhanga, Rae Bareli and Fyzabad in early 1921 in the name of Gandhi was clear proof of a distinctly independent interpretation of his message.[12] Blaming agent provocateurs for misleading the poor ignorant peasants'[13] into committing these acts would, therefore, be to turn a blind eye to the polysemic nature of the Mahatma myths and rumours, as well as to miss out the stamp these carried of a many-sided response of the masses to current events and their cultural, moral and political concerns.

In existing literature the peasants of eastern UP and Bihar are often portrayed as more superstitious than those of some other regions such as western UP and Punjab. We have seen that according to the editor of the *Pioneer*, 'the very simple people of the east and south of the United Provinces afford[ed] a fertile soil in which a belief in the powers of the "Mahatmaji" . . . [might] grow'. In a recent piece of sociological writing the metaphor of 'fertile soil' seems to have been taken literally. In eastern UP, writes P. C. Joshi, summing up his experience of field work in the area, the 'very fertility of soil had minimized the role of human effort', as a result of which 'religion and magic permeated every sphere and occasion of life'.[14] Whether rice growing areas dependent on monsoon rains are more superstitious than canal-fed wheat growing tracts is a question which need not detain us here. Instead I propose, very briefly, to sketch those features of the political history of Gorakhpur in the late nineteenth and early twentieth centuries which throw some light on the specific response of the area to Gandhi's visit in February 1921.

II

The spread of Gaurakshini Sabhas (Cow Protection Leagues) in the 1890s and the subsequent growth of the Nagri movement, Hindi journalism and Hindu social reform in the 1910s appear to have been

[12] See *Bihar and Orissa Legislative-Assembly Debates*, 28 Feb. 1921, i, p. 279; Stephen Henningham, *Peasant Movements in Colonial India. North Bihar, 1917–42* (Canberra, 1982), pp. 98–9; Kapil Kumar, 'Peasants' Movement in Oudh, 1918–1922' (Ph.D. thesis, Meerut University, 1979), pp. 154–7.

[13] J. Nehru, *An Autobiography* (Delhi, n.d.), p. 61.

[14] P. C. Joshi, 'Fieldwork Experience: Relived and Reconsidered. The Agrarian Society of Uttar Pradesh', *Journal of Peasant Studies*, 8:4 (July 1981), p. 470.

the important landmarks in the political history of Gorakhpur in the period up to 1919–20.[15] These saw the involvement of a wide range of the district's population. Former *pargana* chiefs—rajas and ranis, members of the dominant landed lineages, schoolmasters, postmasters and *naib-tahsildars*, middle-caste Ahir and Kurmi tenants—all 'rallied round the Cow' (although the last two did so with ideas quite different from the rest).[16] The developments in the first twenty years of the present century relied on *rausa* and trader support but drew in the intelligentsia, religious preachers and sections of the rural population as well. Gorakhpur neither witnessed widespread agitation against the Rowlatt Acts, as had happened in the Punjab, nor did a Kisan Sabha movement of the Awadh type develop in this region.

The Gaurakshini Sabhas of Gorakhpur in their attempt at selective social reform anticipated the 'Sewa Samitis' and 'Hitkarini Sabhas'— Social Service Leagues—of the early twentieth century. A mammoth meeting of the Gorakhpur sabha held at Lar on 18 March 1893 laid down rules for different castes regarding the maximum number of *baratis* (members of the bridegroom's party) to be entertained at a wedding and the amount of money to be spent on the *tilak* ceremony—all in an effort to cut down 'foolish expenditure on marriages'. Observance of proper high-caste rituals was also stressed. Thus it was made obligatory for 'all *dwija* castes (i.e. Brahmins, Kshatriyas and Vaishyas) . . . to recite the *gayatri mantra* at the three divisions of the day', and he who failed in this was to 'be expelled from the brotherhood'.[17] Contributions 'for the protection of the Gao Mata' (Mother Cow) were also made compulsory for every Hindu household on pain of exclusion from caste. Rule 4 of the Lar sabha stated that 'each household [should] every day contribute from its food supply one *chutki* [handful], equivalent to one *paisa*, per member', and that 'the eating of food without setting apart the *chutki* [should] be an offence equal to that of eating a cow's flesh'. Women

[15] On the cow-protection movement in eastern UP and Bihar see John R. McLane, *Indian Nationalism and the Early Congress* (Princeton, 1977), Pt iv; Sandria B. Freitag, 'Sacred Symbol as Mobilizing Ideology: The North Indian Search for a "Hindu" Community', *Comparative Studies in Society and History*, 22 (1980), pp. 597–625; Gyan Pandey, 'Rallying Round the Cow: Sectarian Strife in the Bhojpur region, *c.* 1888–1917', in R. Guha (ed.), *Subaltern Studies II* (Delhi, 1983).

[16] Pandey, 'Rallying Round the Cow'.

[17] 'Note on the Cow-protection Agitation in the Gorakhpur District', *c.* 1893, L/P&J/6/365, India Office Records. This document is also discussed in Freitag and Pandey.

were to be 'instructed as to the contribution of *chutki* in proper fashion with due regard to *pardah*'.[18]

Again, the power of panchayats was brought to bear upon 'remorselessly [to] boycott' those who sold cows or bullocks to Muslims or butchers. It seems that these panchayats were of two kinds. In the 'Cow Courts' of Azamgarh 'whose proceedings . . . were a somewhat flattering imitation of the proceedings in the Magistrate's Courts' it was generally the zamindars who acted as judges.[19] In certain other cases, as in that of a 'respectable Hindu farmer' of Sagri pargana of that district in June 1893, a less formal and more militant boycott was undertaken by the peasants themselves. To quote Gyan Pandey:

> Villagers gathered at . . . [the house of Lakshman Paure], pulled down tiles from the roof, smashed his earthern vessels, stopped the irrigation of his sugarcane field, prohibited Kahars from carrying sweets which were needed for his daughter's entry into her bridegroom's house and slapped Lakshman, adding the threat that the house would be looted and he himself killed if he did not get the bullock back.[20]

The 'Gandhi Panchayats' of the early 1920s organized by local volunteers meted out punishment similar to what Lakshman Paure of the village of Pande Kunda had received in 1893. However, in the spring of 1921 when all was charged with magic, any mental or physical affliction (*kasht*) suffered by persons found guilty of violating panchayat decisions adopted in Gorakhpur villages in the Mahatma's name was often perceived as evidence of Gandhi's extraordinary powers, indeed as something providential and supernatural rather than as a form of chastisement devised by a human agency.[21]

Hindi was officially adopted as the language of the courts of law in UP in 1900. Soon after, the *Nagri pracharini* (Hindi propagation) movement began to pick up momentum in Gorakhpur as well. In 1913 the local branch of the sabha agitated successfully for judicial forms to be printed in Hindi, and in September 1914 *Gyan Shakti*, a literary journal devoted to 'Hindi and Hindu *dharma prachar*', was published by a pro-government Sanskrit scholar with financial support

[18] Rules 4 and 16. For analogous alms and subscriptions in the name of Gandhi, see pp. 46–7 below.

[19] Offg. Commr. Banaras to Chief Sec., NWP & Oudh, 29 Sept. 1893, cited in McLane, p. 311.

[20] Pandey, 'Rallying Round the Cow'.

[21] For a detailed discussion, see section VI below.

from the rajas of Padrauna, Tamkuhi and Majhauli, as well as some
from the prominent rausa of Gorakhpur.[22] In the following year
Gauri Shankar Misra, who was later to be an important figure in the
UP Kisan Sabha, brought out a new monthly—*Prabhakar*—from
Gorakhpur. Its object was to 'serve the cause (*sewa*) of Hindi, Hindu
and Hindustan'. However, the journal ceased publication within a
year;[23] only *Gyan Skakti* remained, and even this closed down
between August 1916 and June 1917. The full impact of Hindi
journalism was not felt in Gorakhpur until 1919. In April and August
of that year two important papers—the weekly *Swadesh* and the
monthly *Kavi*—made their appearance.[24] These, especially Dasrath
Dwivedi's *Swadesh*, were to exercize an important influence in
spreading the message of Gandhi over the region.

In the 1910s movements and organizations of Hindi, Hindu culture
and social reform—'nagri sabhas', 'pathshalas' (vernacular schools),
'gaushalas' (asylums for cattle), 'sewa samitis' (social service leagues)
and 'sudharak sabhas' (reform associations) of various sorts provided
the support and cover for nationalist activity in Gorakhpur. Each
type of these socio-political movements served nationalism in its own
way; but there was a considerable amount of overlapping in their
functions and interests. In August 1919 a branch of the Bhartiya Sewa
Samiti which had M. M. Malaviya for its head was established in
Deoria.[25] A number of 'sudharak' and 'gram hitkarini sabhas' (village
betterment societies) and subsidiary branches of the sewa samitis
were established in the smaller towns and bigger villages of the region
during 1919–20. The inspiration usually came from the local notables
and pleaders at the tahsil and pargana headquarters, though sometimes
appeals in the *Swadesh* for the setting up of community organizations
also bore fruit. At these sabhas, heads of Hindu religious trusts
(*mahants*) and celibates (*brahmcharis*) from nearby *ashrams* or
itinerant preachers (*pracharaks*) from neighbouring districts and from
Banaras discoursed on the Hindu way of life and its rituals. *Yagya*

---

[22] Arjun Tiwari, 'Poorvi Uttar Pradesh mein Hindi Patrakarita ka Udbhav aur
vikas' (Ph.D. thesis, Gorakhpur University, 1978), pp. 37, 49–50; *Statement of
Newspapers and Periodicals Published in U.P. during 1920 and 1921*, entry under
Gyan Shakti.

[23] Tiwari, pp. 107–8.

[24] *Statement of Newspapers and Periodicals . . . U.P.*, 1920, 1921.

[25] See Note on 'The Sewa Samiti Movement in the United Provinces', by
P. Biggane of the CID, dated 18 Dec. 1919, GAD File 604 of 1920, UP, State Archives,
Lucknow.

(sacrifice) was performed; a Sanskrit pathshala and a gaushala endowed with financial support from traders, arrangements made for the orderly running of Ramlilas and *melas*, and panchayats set up for the arbitration of disputes.[26]

Thus, the fourth annual convention of the Sanskrit Pathshala, 'supported by the zamindars and peasants' of *tappa* Belhar in Basti district, was the occasion for launching a 'Belhar tappa Hindu Sabha' for which more than 300 Hindus from some twenty-five neighbouring villages had gathered at *mauza* Kotiya on 23 October 1920. The proceedings started with the chanting of Vedic sacrificial mantras, and after deliberating on the progress of Sanskrit education in the locality, Pragyachakshu Dhan Raj Shastri discoursed on *samskar*, especially *upanayan samskar*. A Brahmchari from Ballia who for the past five months had been 'reciting continuously' from the Mahabharata, the Bhagavad Gita, etc. followed with a powerful speech on cow protection. It was resolved that only those who were prepared properly to look after the welfare of Brahmani bulls (*sand*) should get them branded; those unable to do so should, as an alternative, contribute to the sabha for other religious deeds on a scale ranging from Rs 1.5 to 5 according to their means. The 'most important and topical resolution' passed at this sabha was 'that in every village of Belhar tappa, a . . . panchayat consisting of five persons [should] be established and a big panchayat . . . set up for the tappa as a whole'.[27]

The evolution of the Pipraich Sudharak Sabha at about the same time indicates how those who were active in the promotion of Hindu culture could also be promptly induced to espouse the cause of Non-Co-operation. Pipraich was the seat of an important market town owned by the pro-government Jawwad Ali Shah of Gorakhpur city. A railway town, it was an important centre of the grain and sugar trade which was mostly in the hands of Hindu traders.[28] A sudharak sabha was formed on 21 October 1920 at a meeting of 300 presided over by the local *raees*, Babu Munni Lal. The Sabha handled the arrangements for the Dussehra *mela* (fair) and the subsequent festivities of Bharat-milap (based on the story of the exiled Rama's

[26] Details of these activities are scattered through the 1920 volume of the *Swadesh*.

[27] Notice by Chandra Bali Visharad, B.A., in *Swadesh*, 14 Nov. 1920, p. 9. Unless stated otherwise, translations from the local Hindi journals are my own. *Tappa* is a grouping of villages, with the chief village as the seat of the dominant local landed lineage.

[28] See Statement of Bazar Collections at Pipraich, File I-A13-1917, Gkp. Collector's Rec. Room.

reunion with his brother, Bharat). After ten days of activity during the Dussehra fortnight, yet another meeting was held. Again presided over by the local raees, it was attended by 1,500 people including the *babus* of nearby Balua. However, on this occasion speakers from Gorakhpur town gave a different direction to the deliberations. The editor of *Swadesh* spoke on council boycott, and others on sewa dharma and commercial matters. A decision was taken unanimously to open a 'swatantra pathshala'—an independent school unaffiliated to the government—with the spinning of *khaddar* yarn specified as an important part of its curriculum.[29]

Traditional Hindu religious discourses addressed to large congregations lasting several days at a time were also put to a similar use on some occasions:

> In mauza Gointha, Post Office Dohrighat (Azamgarh) the discourse of Pt Ramanugraha Sharma, *dharmopdeshak*, went on for ten days. Many thousands turned up for these lectures. After the last lecture he organized a Vedic yagya and many indigents and Brahmins were feasted. He also established a Bharat Hitaishi Sabha to which both Hindus and Muslims have contributed 5 *panches* and 2 *sarpanches* each . . . . Many cases have been settled [out of regular courts].[30]

Caste sabhas could undergo interesting transformations as well. Thus on 12 December 1920 a Bhumihar Ramlila Mandal was established at Bhiti village in the Bansgaon tahsil of Gorakhpur; its 'object was to encourage unity and propagate satyagraha by revealing the [true] character of Sri Ramchandraji'.[31] Similarly, in a great many cases lower and middle-caste panchayats imposed novel dietary taboos as a part of the widespread movement of self-assertion which was also exemplified by acts such as the refusal of their women to work as housemaids or the witholding of *begar* (forced labour) both from the *sarkar* and the zamindar. A correspondent from Naugarh in Basti district wrote to the *Swadesh:*

> The sweepers, washermen and barbers of this place met in panchayats of their various *biradaris* on 27 January 1921. They have decided that anyone who partakes of meat, fish and liquor would be punished by the biradari

[29] *Swadesh*, 31 Oct., 7 Nov., and 19 Dec. 1920. *Babus*: members of the dominant local lineage of a tappa.

[30] *Swadesh*, 11 Sept. 1919, p. 11. Ramanugraha Sharma, resident of Bhelia (Rasra), Ballia district had followed this procedure in Shahabad, Pipraich and Paina, near Barhaj in present day Deoria district. See *Swadesh*, 4 July 1920, p. 8, 1 Aug, pp. 10–11, 30 Oct. 1920, p. 7. *Panch*: member of a panchayat; *Sarpanch*: head of a panchayat.

[31] *Swadesh*, 19 Dec. 1920, p. 8.

(brotherhood) and would have to donate Rs 51 to the gaushala. The Dhobis and Barbers have also decided not to wash the clothes and cut the hair of any of their patrons who partakes of meat, fish and liquor.[32]

A widespread boycott of meat and liquor 'due to the efforts of a Bengali sadhu' was reported from Padrauna in Gorakhpur in early 1921, though caste panchayats played a role in this instance as well.[33]

It must be emphasized that the very act of self-purification on the part of the ritually impure amounted, in some instances, to a reversal of the signs of subordination. 'All low caste Hindus, except those who are Bhagats or vegetarians by vow, almost without exception eat meat', observed a local ethnographer of Gorakhpur in the late nineteenth century.[34] For them, especially the sweepers, washermen and untouchable agricultural labourers, to give up meat in 1920 was not simply an instance of 'Sanskritization'. Thus at a sabha held in October 1920 the Chamars of Bareilly (central UP) had decided to forsake meat as well as liquor and other intoxicants; but they were also very forthright in their refusal to do begar for the district officials on tour. As they said in a petition addressed to the Governor on that occasion: 'We are ready to perform any legitimate services required of us appertaining to our profession but inhuman treatment, meted out to a Chamar every day, by petty servants of the thana and tahsil is nothing short of a festering sore'.[35]

By early 1922 indications of a 'growing restlessness among the . . . [Chamars] . . . arising out of the general spirit of revolt' were reaching the police headquarters in the districts. The movement for 'self-reform' now revealed 'a tendency to forsake hereditary callings' as well.[36] The eight resolutions passed at a large meeting of the Chamars of Azamgarh in January 1922 followed the standard pattern of caste reform in their concern about the prevalence of child marriage and co-habitation out of wedlock, and in the interdictions they imposed on toddy, liquor and animal sacrifice. What is perhaps equally significant

[32] *Swadesh*, 6 Feb. 1921, p. 8.

[33] *Idem.*

[34] Note by Ram Gharib Chaube on 'Eating Meat', William Crooke Papers, MS 131, Museum of Mankind, London.

[35] Extracted in Harcourt Butler to Chief Sec., UP, 26 Oct. 1920, GAD File 694 of 1920; *Swadesh*, 10 Oct. 1920, p. 1. For a discussion of the assertive nature of middle-caste movements in early twentieth century eastern UP, see Pandey, 'Rallying Round the Cow'. See also David Hardiman's essay on the Devi movement in the present volume.

[36] UP Police Abstracts of Intelligence (PAI), 1 April 1922.

is that members of this caste of leather workers also pledged themselves not to trade in hides and skins and to discourage young boys from taking up their ancestral profession.[37] In western and central UP, Chamars were refusing to skin carcasses and perform begar for the landlords and were 'allowing their women less liberty of movement',[38] an euphemism for the withdrawal of female labour from the homes of the upper castes.

III

Gorakhpur in 1920 was no stronghold of the Congress or the independent Kisan Sabhas. In fact the relative backwardness of the entire region comprising Gorakhpur, Basti and Azamgarh districts was lamented repeatedly by the editor of the Congress weekly, *Swadesh*, and the main reason for this was thought to be the absence of an effective and dedicated leadership.[39] Political meetings in Gorakhpur city and in important market towns like Deoria and Barhaj Bazar picked up from July–August 1920, as the campaign for council elections by the rajas, rausa and *vakla* was sought to be countered by challenging the bona fides of 'oppressive landlords' and 'self-seeking pleaders'. Open letters appeared in the columns of *Swadesh* highlighting the oppression suffered by peasants in the bigger zamindaris and challenging the presumption of the rajas to be the natural spokesmen of their *praja* (subjects). At a public meeting of the newly-formed Voters' Association in Deoria the representative of a landlord candidate was faced with the charge that his patron's command of English was inadequate for him to follow the proceedings of the legislative council.[40] But increasingly, the boycott of council elections and, after the Nagpur Congress (December 1920) the propagation of Non-Co-operation, was being written up and broadcast as a part of the spiritual biography of Mahatma Gandhi. In a powerful editorial, prominently displayed by *Swadesh* on the front page on 11 November and reprinted the next week, Dasrath Dwivedi appealed to the local electorate in bold typeface:

[37] Report of the Chamar conference held at Gopalpur village, thana Madhuban, district Azamgarh, *Swadesh*, 8 Jan. 1922, p. 6.
[38] PAI, 1 April 1922.
[39] See *Swadesh*, 18 April 1920, pp. 13–14, 23 May, p. 9, 15 Aug., p. 14.
[40] See *Swadesh*, 16 May, 6 June, 4 and 18 July 1920.

OH YOU VOTERS OF THE GORAKHPUR DIVISION! HAVE
SOME SELF RESPECT. BEWARE OF THE OBSEQUIOUS
STOOGES! BE SURE WHO IS YOUR GENUINE WELLWISHER!
MAHATMA GANDHI, PT MOTILAL NEHRU, PT MALVIYAJI or
those who are now running after you, begging for your votes? Think for
yourself; what good have the latter done for you so far that you may now
expect them to help remove your sorrows and sufferings from inside the
Council. Now cast your eyes towards Mahatma Gandhi. This pure soul
(*pavitra murti*) has sacrificed everything for you (*tan-man-dhan . . . arpan
kar diya hai*). It is for your good that he has taken the vow of renunciation
(*sanyas-vrat*), gone to jail and encountered many a difficulty and suffering.
Despite being ill, he is at this moment wandering all over [the country] in
the service of your cause. It is the *updesh* of this same Mahatma Gandhi
that you should not vote. And you should not vote, because approximately
thirty thousand of your unarmed Punjabi brethren were fired upon in
Amritsar, people were made to crawl on their bellies, and despite the hue
and cry for justice you were shoed away like dogs (*tumhen dutkar diya
gaya tha*). And no heed was paid whatsoever. Look out. Beware.
DO NOT VOTE FOR ANYBODY.[41]

In this text, which may be regarded as representative of the local
nationalist discourse on council boycott,[42] the 'Punjab Wrongs' and
the callous indifference of the British are no doubt mentioned as
reasons for not voting; but it is hard to miss the person of a saintly
Gandhi, resplendent in his suffering for the people and, in turn,
requiring and even demanding their obedience to his injunctions.
Perceived thus the boycott of elections and the rejection of loyalist
candidates appear as a kind of religiously prescribed abstinence from
the polling booth, analogous to the observance of proper Hindu
rituals and self-purification which was being propagated by many of
the nationalist religious preachers and taken up by certain low-caste
panchayats as well. It was to such a region, which was not unaware of
the peasant rioting in southern Awadh in January 1921 but had not
yet developed any comparable peasant movement of its own, that
Gandhi came on 8 February 1921.

The decision to invite Gandhi was taken at a public meeting held in
Gorakhpur city on 17 October 1920. Maulvi Maqsood Ali Fyzabadi

[41] *Swadesh*, 11 Nov. 1920, p. 1.

[42] In all likelihood the Congress volunteers who were to tour the district for a
fortnight, spreading 'Gandhiji's message of council boycott', would have taken the
above editorial as their central text. It seems that voting was thin in Bansgaon tahsil and
at Siswa Bazar, Bridgmanganj, Pipraich and Parwapar in Maharajganj and Padrauna
tahsils. See *Swadesh*, 14 Nov. 1920, p. 12, 12 Dec. 1920, p. 12.

presided over it and Gauri Shankar Misra was the main speaker. The meeting resolved to support the cause of those arrested in connection with the Khilafat agitation, pronounced *asahyog* (Non-Co-operation) to the *uchit* (proper) and decided to send a telegraphic invitation to Gandhi and the Ali brothers to visit Gorakhpur at an early date.[43] Gandhi was also approached by the Gorakhpur delegates (prominent amongst whom was Baba Raghav Das, successor to the spiritual *gaddi* (seat) of Anant Mahaprabhu and founder of the Paramhans Ashram, Barhaj) at the Nagpur Congress and he told them that he would visit the district sometime in late January or early February.[44] To the creed of *asahyog* that Raghav Das and Dasrath Dwivedi brought with them from Nagpur was added mounting excitement at the prospect of its author's advent. Propagation of the politics of Non-Co-operation in the Gorakhpur countryside in early 1921 had elements of a celebratory exordium, a preparing of the district for the Big Event. The peregrinations of Raghav Das and his brahmachari followers around their ashram in Barhaj, the 'melodious Gandhi-*bhajans*' sung by Changur Tripathi to a peasant assembly at Kuin nearby[45] and the 'poetical effusions' in the first issue of a rejuvenated *Kavi* magazine—'written with the set purpose of arousing in the masses and classes alike a yearning for the quick descent of Krishna, the Messiah'[46]—are the few surviving fragments of this picture of enthusiasm and expectation in Gorakhpur at that time.

An index of this popular expectation was the increase in the number of rumours which assigned various imaginary dates to Gandhi's visit. By the first week of January the news of his arrival had 'spread like wild fire'. Dasrath Dwivedi, the editor of *Swadesh*, was bombarded with hundreds of letters asking for the exact dates. To allay anxiety on this score the journal printed a column on its front page on 9 January assuring its readers that the date of Gandhi's arrival would be announced in the *Aaj* (Banaras), *Pratap* (Kanpur), *Bhavishya* (Prayag), *Vartman* (Kanpur); the *Leader* and *Independent* would also publish the news, while the *Swadesh* press would ensure that notices, posters and letters carried the word to all six tahsils of the district.

[43] *Swadesh*, 24 Oct. 1920: p. 11.

[44] Amodnath Tripathi, 'Poorvi Uttar Pradesh ke Jan-jeevan mein Baba Raghav Das ka Yogdaan' (Ph.D. thesis, Allahabad University, 1981), pp. 62–7, 77; *Swadesh*, 2 Jan. 1921.   [45] Tripathi, p. 78; *Swadesh*, 6 Feb. 1921, p. 9.
[46] *Statement of Newspapers and Periodicals, U.P.*, 1921, p. 33.

Meanwhile the District Congress Committee (DCC) geared itself into action. It had been decided to get a national school inaugurated by Gandhi, and the DCC was active on this front. Advance parties of lecturers (*vyakhyandata*) announcing his arrival were to be dispatched to the tahsil headquarters and to Barhalganj, Dhakwa and Gola in the densely populated southern tahsil of Bansgaon; to Rudarpur and Captainganj in the central tract of Hata; to the railway towns and marts of Deoria, Salempur, Majhauli, Lar, Bhatpar and Barhaj Bazar to the south-east, and to Padrauna in the north-east. Within the sparsely populated northern tahsil of Maharajganj, Peppéganj and Campierganj—seats of European zamindaris—and Siswa Bazar, the important entrepôt of gur and rice, were to be the target points. At meetings held at these places, the visiting lecturers were to preach the doctrine of the Congress and ask for contributions to the National School Fund. In their turn the local residents were to ensure that people within a radius of ten miles attended these public discourses on the philosophy and advent of Gandhi.[47] The massive attendance at the Gorakhpur sabha on 8 February and the crowds that thronged the five stations on the fifty mile railway strip between Bhatni and Gorakhpur city suggest that the news had spread widely enough.

On 30 January the *Swadesh* announced that the probable date was now 8 February and requested the people of Gorakhpur to seek the Mahatma's darshan and bring their donations with them. It also wrote about the need for more Congress workers to come forward and help in supervising the arrangements.[48]

An editorial which appeared in the columns of that newspaper on 6 February announcing the impending arrival is a significant text and is reproduced in Appendix I. Besides illustrating how the image of the distinguished visitor was projected in Gorakhpur by local Congress-men, it is also representative of nationalist understanding of the relationship between the subaltern masses, the élite leadership and Gandhi himself. Dasrath Dwivedi, the young author of this text, had been trained as a journalist on the staff of the *Pratap* in Kanpur and on Ganesh Vidyarthi's advice had come back to his home district in 1919 to start his own *Swadesh*.[49] The editorial, 'The Great Fortune of

[47] *Swadesh*, 9 Jan. 1921, p. 11; see also Appx II below.
[48] *Swadesh*, 30 Jan. 1921.
[49] The circulation of the paper in early 1921 was 3,500, though according to official estimates it dropped to 2,300 in the course of that year. See Tiwari, p. 558; *Statement of Newspapers etc.*, *U.P.*, 1921, entry under *Swadesh*.

Gorakhpur', was written by one who was obviously an ardent
nationalist disappointed at the political stupor prevailing in the region,
and who felt as if his dream of Gandhi bringing about a transformation
was soon to be fulfilled. Addressed basically to lawyers and students
whom it urges to cast off sloth, it is also significant in its attitude
towards the common people:

> Our plea is that the common people (*sadharan janta*) of Gorakhpur are
> only anxiously awaiting for the darshan of the Mahatma. The Mahatma
> will arrive, the public will have darshan and will be eternally grateful for
> it. There will be no end to the joy of the people when they are able to feast
> their eyes on the Mahatma.
>   But what about those who are openly co-operating with the government
> . . . don't they have some duty at this juncture . . .? A voice from the heart
> says 'Of course! . . . *They should kneel before Mahatma Gandhi and pray
> to the Almighty for courage to enable them to row their boats out of the
> present whirlpool and into safety . . . . For Mahatma Gandhi to appear
> [avteern:* from *avtar] before us in these difficult times is a tremendous
> boon, for us, our society and our country . . . .* Don't vacillate, arise now to
> serve the oppressed brothers of your district. Blow the *shankh* (conch-
> shell) of Swaraj . . . . This movement is an elixir (*amrit-bati*) for you.
> Mahatma Gandhi is offering it to you.[50]

How the common people and the élite should respond to Gandhi's
visit is thus clearly laid out. The task of the janta is to congregate in
large numbers, 'feast their eyes on the Mahatma', count themselves
lucky, and after such brief taste of bliss return to their inert and
oppressed existence. So far as they are concerned the Mahatma is to
be in Gorakhpur for no other purpose than to offer them darshan.
They are not expected to proclaim the cause of *swaraj* on their own.
The clarion call (written metaphorically, as *shankhnaad*, after the
blast of conch-shells used for Hindu sacred rituals) of swaraj in
villages requires only the power of élite lungs: for that rallying blast
the 'oppressed brothers' of Gorakhpur must rely on the initiative of
the élite followers of the Mahatma. The implication is that the
peasants' pilgrimage to Gorakhpur and the mufassil stations will be
useless from a nationalist perspective unless 'leaders' step in to channel
the goodwill generated in the villages as a result of Gandhi's darshan.
That such a journey, made often in defiance of landlord opposition,
could in itself be a political act and that Gandhi's message might be
decoded by the common villager on his own, without prompting by
outsiders, were possibilities not entertained by Dasrath Dwivedi at

---

[50] 'Gorakhpur ka Ahobhagya', *Swadesh*, 6 Feb. 1921. Emphasis mine.

this time. Yet a perusal of local news published by him in subsequent months shows that these were the lines along which popular response to the Mahatma's visit expressed itself.

Apart from this the imagery, feeling and metaphors used by Dwivedi to convince educated waverers about the greatness of Gandhi and convert them to his cause are of interest in themselves. At this level there is no significant difference between the religiosity informing the peasants and the attitude Dwivedi wants the intelligentsia to adopt towards Gandhi; the language of belief seems to be the same in both instances with merely some variations in tone and accent. The italicized portions of the extract quoted above testify to the religious, indeed devotional nature of Dwivedi's writings. The boat and boatman imagery occurs frequently in rural and urban devotional songs. As Susan Wadley notes in her study of popular religion in a village in western UP, 'many . . . devotional songs use the whirlpool analogy for a crisis situation, along with other nautical imagery (the ocean of existence, boat, boatman, ferry across, the far side, etc.)'.[51]

Gandhi's visit to Gorakhpur was well organized and the gatherings of people on that occasion were truly phenomenal. An advance party of Gorakhpur Congressmen had been sent to Bhatni junction at the south-eastern edge of the district, and the train by which he travelled made its way very slowly through, stopping at every railway station where people had assembled for darshan. As Shyam Dhar Misra who led the reception party reported in *Swadesh*:

> At Bhatni Gandhiji addressed *(updesh diya)* the local public and then the train started for Gorakhpur. There were not less than 15 to 20,000 people at Nunkhar, Deoria, Gauri Bazar, Chauri Chaura and Kusmhi [stations] . . . . At Deoria there were about 35–40,000 people. Mahatmaji was very pleased to witness the scene at Kusmhi, as despite the fact that the station is in the middle of a jungle there were not less than 10,000 people even here. Some, overcome with their love, were seen to be crying. At Deoria people wanted to give *bhent* [donations] to Gandhiji, but he asked them to give these at Gorakhpur. But at Chauri Chaura one Marwari gentleman managed to hand something over to him. Then there was no stopping. A sheet was spread and currency notes and coins started raining. It was a sight . . . . Outside the Gorakhpur station the Mahatma was stood on a high carriage and people had a good darshan of him for a couple of minutes.[52]

[51] Susan Wadley, 'Power in Hindu Ideology and Practice', in K. David (ed.), *The New Wind: Changing Identities in South Asia* (The Hague: Paris, 1977), p. 144, n. 17.
[52] *Swadesh*, 13 Feb. 1921, p. 3.

Among the peasants who had come all the way from their villages for Gandhi-darshan on this occasion, there were many who would again in a year's time—in February 1922—march past the Chauri Chaura railway station to the adjacent thana as participants in another fateful event. Indeed, at the trial of the peasant-rioters of Chauri Chaura, some of those who acted as witnesses for the prosecution found it necessary to try and offer an innocuous explanation of their presence among the crowd at the station on 8 February 1921. As Shankar Dayal Rae, a prosperous contractor of the locality, put it to the Sessions Judge in June 1922: 'I never before went to the station to meet any *rajnaitik* (political) leader—to Gorakhpur or Chaura—except that I went to pay my respects to Gandhiji when he passed through Chaura in the train.'[53] The devotion of the Gorakhpuri peasants to the Mahatma seems to have acquired a militant edge. According to Mahadev Desai's account of the return journey from Gorakhpur, darshan was now demanded almost as a right:

> The train started from Gorakhpur at 8.30 p.m. at night . . . . It was a train that halted at every station . . . . Hordes and hordes of people began to rush upon our compartment . . . . At every station peasants with long long lathis and torches in their hands would come to us and raise cries loud enough to split the very drums of our ears. Of course, all of us in the compartment were making as many appeals for quiet as we possibly could. But whoever would care to listen to us? . . .
>
> Many of these devotees do not even know how their 'Mahatma Gandhi' looks like. A few of them thrust themselves into our compartment, and began to bawl out, 'Who is Mahatma Gandhiji?' 'Who is Mahatma Gandhiji?' I got desperate and said 'I'. They were satisfied, bowed down to me and left the compartment! What a difference between my presumptuousness and these people's untainted love! But it was no use getting enchanted with that guileless love . . . .
>
> Any sleep for Gandhiji in the midst of this uproar was out of question . . . . The people's *hathagraha* (mule-like obstinacy) was repeated at each and every station that came after Bhatni: At last even Gandhiji's endurance and tolerance was exhausted . . . . He began to entreat the people 'Please go away. Why do you harass us at this dark hour?' He was answered only by sky-rending shouts of victory to him! . . . That was the height of the people's love-mad insolence . . . .[54]

IV

If this was the way in which the peasants reacted to Gandhi, how was his message understood by them? Were there any ambiguities in what

[53] Evidence of Shankar Dayal Rae, Chauri Chaura Trials (Sessions Judge), p. 508.
[54] Desai, pp. 263–6.

Gandhi said or was believed to have said? If so, what implications did these have for peasant beliefs about Gandhi as revealed in the 'stories' about his power?

The main thrust of Gandhi's speeches at the 'massive gatherings of peasants' in Fyzabad and Gorakhpur was to condemn the recent acts of peasant violence and rioting in southern Awadh. As Mahadev Desai recounts in his diaries of this period:

> Gandhiji had only one message to give them, viz. those big sticks [lathis] were not to be used for killing or injuring anybody. The same thing was preached at Fyzabad also. Gandhiji's utterances were devoted exclusively to the outbreaks of robbery, villainy and rioting that had taken place in the United Provinces.[55]

This was indeed so, but a close reading of his speech at Gorakhpur suggests that it had enough ambiguity in it to cause semantic slides. After a laudatory poem written by the Hindi poet 'Trishul' and read by Dasrath Dwivedi, Gandhi started his speech to a mammoth gathering of over 1.5 lakhs, which included a 'fairly large number of illiterates and rustics',[56] as follows:

> This gathering is not the occasion for a long speech. This gathering shows that there is a commonality of purpose amongst us. The poem that was recited just now did not mention Mohammad Ali . . . . Now brother Shaukat Ali, Mohammad Ali and I are saying the same thing . . . .

After stressing the need for Hindu-Muslim unity, he warmed up to a condemnation of peasant violence in Awadh:

> What happened in Fyzabad? What happened in Rae Bareli? We should know these things. By doing what we have done with our own hands we have committed a wrong, a great wrong. By raising the *lakri* [i.e. lathi] we have done a bad thing. By looting haats and shops we have committed a wrong. We can't get swaraj by using the lakri. We cannot get swaraj by pitting our own devilishness (*shaitaniyat*) against the satanic government. Our 30 crore lakris are no match against their aeroplanes and guns; even if they are, even then we shall not raise our lakris. The Quran says so. Brother Mohammad Ali tells me that [according to the Quran] as long as the raising of the stick is unnecessary we cannot do so . . . .
> Our kisan brothers have committed a mistake. They have caused great anguish to my brother Jawahar Lal. If further difficulties [of this sort] are put in our way then you shall see that that very day it would become impossible for Gandhi to live in Hindustan. I shall have to do penance—this

[55] Ibid., p. 267. For a detailed discussion of Gandhi's 'Instructions' to the peasants at Fyzabad, see Pandey, 'Peasant Revolt and Indian Nationalism'.
[56] *Gyan Shakti*, Feb. 1921, p. 407.

is a peaceful struggle. Only after I retire to the Himalayas can it become a violent struggle. Our fight should be like the one put up by our Sikh brethren in Taran Taran . . . . They did not seek revenge against their oppressors . . . . This is our way, this the *asahyog dharma*, this is real *Brahmacharya*. This is *kshatriya dharma*. And today this is the dharma of the Musalmans. To go against it is to commit a sin . . . .

Right now we should forget about 'social boycott'. The time has not yet arrived for such actions. Nobody should prevent any brother from going to the burial ground, nobody is to prevent anybody from the use of the services of barbers or to have *chilum* [i.e. ganja] and liquor. In fact we want to rid everybody of chilum and booze (*daru*).[57] If all of you give up [these things] today then we shall attain swaraj straightaway . . . .

[Congratulating Gorakhpur on its organization of this meeting Gandhi continued] The real result of your organizational abilities and your work would be seen when in Gorakhpur lawyers give up their practice, schools no longer remain sarkari [i.e. affiliated to the government], titles are given up, no drinkers, no whoremongers, no gamblers remain in your district. When every house has a *charkha* and all the *julahas* of Gorakhpur start weaving [hand-spun yarn] . . . . You should produce so much khaddar in Gorakhpur that you people don't have to go to Ahmedabad, to Bombay or Kanpur [for your cloth] . . . .

I would request you to be patient and listen to Maulana Mohammad Ali's speech and carry on donating money to the volunteers. Please refrain from being noisy. I want to tell you, if you follow my programme—I want to assure [you] if you do as I tell you, we shall get swaraj by the end of September. We could also get the Khilafat and the Punjab Wrongs undone by the sarkar. But this is the right [task] of only those who accept the things discussed at the Nagpur Congress. This is not the business of those who are not with us in our work . . . . From those who are not with us, but still come to our meetings, I expect that they will at least keep the peace—we can attain swaraj by end September if God grants us peace; if all of us Indians have the spirit of self-sacrifice and self-purification then 30 crore people can achieve just about anything.[58]

The main constitutive elements—*baat* in the indigenous parlance—of Gandhi's message to the Gorakhpur kisans could be arranged as follows:

1. Hindu-Muslims unity or *ekta*.
2. What people should *not* do on their own: use lathis; loot bazaars and haats; enforce social boycott ('*naudhobi band*').

[57] The words used were 'Koi kisi bhai ko kabristan jane se na roke, koi kisi ko hajjam, chilum aur daru se na roke'. *Chilum* is an earthen bowl for smoking tobacco, but is understood in popular parlance to refer to *ganja* smoking. It seems that Gandhi is here using the word chilum to refer to ganja, but this can also be understood to be an injunction against smoking as such.

[58] Translated from the verbatim report published in *Swadesh*, 13 Feb. 1921, p. 6.

3. What the Mahatma wants his true followers to do: stop gambling, ganja-smoking, drinking and whoring.
4. Lawyers should give up their practice; government schools should be boycotted; official titles should be given up.
5. People should take up spinning and weavers should accept hand-spun yarn.
6. Imminence of swaraj: its realization conditional on innate strength of numbers when matched with peace, grace of God, self-sacrifice and self-purification.

This sequential summary of Gandhi's speech is an attempt to reconstruct the way in which his utterances might have been discussed in the villages of Gorakhpur. It is reasonable to assume that such discussions would proceed by breaking up his message into its major ideological constituents.[59] If the practice, which is current even today, of communicating printed news in the countryside is any guide, then in all likelihood the main points of that speech summarized from the version published in *Swadesh* was conveyed to the illiterate peasants in the local dialect.

It will be seen that baat no. 4 does not greatly concern the peasants. No. 1 is very general and figures only marginally in the Gandhi 'stories'. Baat no. 5 is, in part, far too specific as an instruction addressed exclusively to weavers, while the advice in favour of spinning might have sounded rather too general, lacking as it did an infrastructure to make it feasible at this stage. It is the conflation of baats no. 3 and no. 6, and its contexualization within the existing ideas about 'power' and magic, which lay at the root of some of the 'stories' relating to the Mahatma in Gorakhpur. It seems that the complimentarity of his negative advice with regard to popular militancy (baat no. 2) and the positive actions enjoined on the 'true followers' (baat no. 3)—the complimentarity, so to say, of the do's and don'ts in these particular messages, was (*pace* Mahadev Desai) largely lost on his rustic audience. On the other hand baats no. 3 and 6 came to be associated in the popular mind as a linked set of spiritual command-ments issued by a god-like personage. As such these were consistent with those legends about his 'divinity' which circulated at the time.

[59] For an example of one such breaking up of Gandhi's message to the peasants into main (*mukhya*) baats, see 'Kisanon ko Mahatma Gandhi ka amritmay sandesh', *Abhyudaya*, 18 Feb. 1931, p. 19. For an extended use of the term baat, and its use as an organizing principle in the narrative of Bhojpuri fables, see George A. Grierson, *Seven Grammars of the Dialects and Subdialects of the Bihari Language etc.*, Pt. II (Calcutta, 1884), pp. 102ff.

The enforcement of social boycott was not widespread yet; it was to pick up only from late 1921. Meanwhile, that is immediately in the wake of Gandhi's visit, people, acting on their own or through their panchayats and sabhas, were still involved in efforts at self-purification, extending and transforming his message on this theme. It is with the intervention of the supernatural in this process and the Mahatma's role in it that most of the Gorakhpur 'stories' are concerned. To these we now turn.

V

The feeling of devotion towards Gandhi in Gorakhpur was commented on in glowing terms in the nationalist press. Dasrath Dwivedi wrote in an editorial about the 'fantastic flow of *bhakti*' (devotion) caused by the Mahatma's visit. Mahavir Prasad Poddar, a Gorakhpuri merchant resident in Calcutta and a popular retailer of Swadeshi-sugar of yesteryears,[60] elaborated on this theme thus in the columns of the *Swadesh*:

> It had not occurred to us in our wildest dreams that the same Gorakhpur which was politically dormant would suddenly wake up like this. A crowd of 2–2½ lakhs for the darshan of Gandhiji is no ordinary thing. It can probably be said that this is the biggest crowd that has ever gathered for the darshan of the Mahatma . . . . But let no one think that this vast multitude came like sheep, inspired by blind faith (*andhbhakti*) and went back empty handed. Those with eyes can see that the darshan of 'Gandhi Mahatam' (this is the phrase used in villages) have not been in vain. The janta came with devotion (*bhakti*) in their hearts and returned with feelings and ideas (*bhav*). The name of Guru-Gandhi has now spread in all four corners of the district . . . .
>
> But roses have thorns as well . . . . A zamindar of the city had it proclaimed in his *ilaqa* that anyone going for Gandhi's darshan would be fined Rs 25 and receive twenty-five shoe-beatings to boot . . . . The people of this area wrung their hands in despair . . . . A Ramlila procession goes in front of the house with so much fanfare and the children are locked up in the attic! . . . I know there are other creatures like the above-mentioned raees in this district.[61]

Here is a far better understanding of the impact of that visit than we have so far encountered in nationalist prose. The janta does not just have bhakti; seeing and hearing the Mahatma also inspires *bhav*, a word suggestive not merely of feelings and ideas but of urge to action as well.[62] The laudatory poem read as a welcome address to Gandhi had ended on the note:

[60] *Swadesh*, 20 April 1919, p. 4.   [61] *Swadesh*, 27 Feb. 1921.
[62] I am grateful to Veena Das for this suggestion.

jaan dalega yahan aap ka aana ab to; log dekhenge ki badla hai
   zamana ab to . . .
aap aye hain yahan jaan hi aae samjho, goya Gorakh ne dhuni phir
   hai ramai samjho.[63]

By February 1921 times had indeed changed, beyond the 'wildest dreams' of Poddar: a new life was already infused into a 'politically dormant' Gorakhpur—a regeneration brought about by, as it were, the powerful *tapasya* of Gorakhnath, the eponymous founder of the city. Gandhi's advent was perceived as a major event by the zamindars who had sought forcibly to prevent their peasants from seeking his darshan. It was for them an event which stood out of the flow of quotidian existence and as such threatened to bring about displacements in the local power structures. The analogy of eager children being denied the joy of participation in an important religious procession was apt, for it suggests in the landlords a cruel paternalism designed to prevent any subversion of the relationships of dominance and subordination which constituted the stuff of everyday life in the countryside. The enthusiasm Gandhi generated, the expectations he aroused and the attack he launched on British authority had all combined to initiate the very first moments of a process which, given other factors, could help the peasant to conceptualize the turning of his world upside down. This was an incipient political consciousness called upon, for the very first time, to reflect—albeit vaguely and intermittently—on the possibility of an inversion of many of those power relations deemed inviolable until then, such as British/Indian, landlord/peasant, high-caste/low-caste, etc. This process of conceptualization was set in train that spring in Gorakhpur by a clash between the ordinary and the extraordinary, between the habitual and the contingent—a clash triggered off directly by the Mahatma's visit.[64]

IV

Stories about Gandhi's occult powers first appeared in the local press in late January 1921. An issue of *Swadesh* which announced his arrival in the district also carried a report under the heading: 'Gandhi in dream: Englishmen run away naked'. A loco-driver—presumably

[63] *Swadesh*, 13 Feb. 1921, p. 5.
[64] The argument in this paragraph owes a lot to discussions with Bernard Cohn and Ranajit Guha.

an Anglo-Indian—who had dozed off while reading a newspaper at Kasganj railway station in Etah district woke up from a nightmare at 11 p.m. and ran towards a cluster of bungalows occupied by the English and some Indian railway officers shouting: 'Man, run, man! Gandhi is marching at the head of several strong Indians decimating the English'. This caused a panic and all the local white population emerged from their bedrooms in a state of undress and ran towards the station. The key to the armoury at the station was asked for, but could not be found as the officer-in-charge was away. English women were locked up in boxes and almirahs, and some Englishmen were heard saying, 'Man! The cries of "jai jai" are still reaching our ears. We shall not go back to our bungalows'. In the morning Indians who heard of this incident in the city had a good laugh at this example of English self-confidence (*atmik-bal*).[65] This story, first published in the Banaras daily *Aaj* and then in *Swadesh*, is illustrative of the wider tendency of the times to berate British power and boost Indian prowess by contrast.[66] The British emerge in tales of this kind as a weak-kneed race, mortally afraid of the non-violent Mahatma.

Other stories to appear in the press just prior to and immediately after his arrival were about a lawyer of Deoria who was cursed by a follower of Gandhi for going back on his promise to give up legal practice and had his house polluted with shit; about a high-caste woman who suffered the same polluting fate after she had denied a young boy a blanket to protect him from the cold when he wanted to go to the station at night to seek darshan; about a Kahar who tried to test the Mahatma's power with a foolish wish and came out the worse for it; and about a Pandit who sought to defy Gandhi by insisting on eating fish only to find it crawling with worms. These stories have the same sequential and structural characteristics as many others reported

[65] 'Swapn mein Mahatma Gandhi: Angrez nange bhage', writer Banwari Lal Sewak, *Swadesh*, 30 Jan. 1921 (extracted from *Aaj*).

[66] Thus Mohammad Ali addressing the Gorakhpur meeting on 8 February after Gandhi, concluded his speech with the following exhortation: 'We should only be afraid of Allah, and no one else. No Deputy Commissioner was sent saddled with his office from the house of God. No midwife ever said that the child-to-be-born would become a Commissioner, or a Viceroy. Even the Collector and Commissioner of Gorakhpur, even Sir Harcourt Butler must have emerged from their mothers' wombs as innocent babes, like the rest of us. Therefore [don't be afraid], have faith in Allah, keep the peace, all thirty crores work the charkha—you shall get swaraj in six month's time'. Reported in *Swadesh*, 13 Feb. 1921, p. 8.

from Gorakhpur. Taken together and classified according to their motifs, they may be said to fall into four fairly distinct groups:[67]

A. Testing the power of the Mahatma.

B. Opposing the Mahatma.

C. Opposing the Gandhian creed in general and with respect to dietary, drinking and smoking taboos.

D. Boons granted and/or miracles performed in the form of recovery of things lost and regeneration of trees and wells.

A. Testing the Power of the Mahatma

1. Sikandar Sahu of *thana* Mansurganj, *mauza* Mahuawa (Dist. Basti) said on 15 February that he would believe in the Mahatmaji when the *karah* (boiling pan) full of cane-juice in his *karkhana* split into two. The karah split in two in the middle![68]

2. On 18 February a Kahar (domestic servant; palanquin bearer) from Basantpur said that he would be prepared to believe in Mahatmaji's authenticity (*sacha manoonga*) only when the thatched roof of his house was raised. The roof lifted ten cubits above the wall, and fell back to its original position only when he cried and folded his hands in surrender and submission.[69]

3. On 15 March a cultivator in mauza Sohraghat (Azamgarh) said that he would believe in the Mahatmaji's authenticity (*sacha jaane*) if sesamum sprouted on 1.5 *bighas* of his field. Next day all the wheat in that field became sesamum. 'I have seen this with my own eyes at the house of Pt Brijwasi Vakil', wrote a correspondent. 'The ears look like that of wheat, but on rubbing with hand, grains of sesamum come out of them'.[70]

4. Babu Bir Bahadur Sahi of mauza Reaon was getting his fields harvested on 15 March. In order to test the Mahatma's powers he wished for some sweets. Suddenly sweets fell on his body. Half of the sweets he distributed among the labourers and the rest he kept for himself.

[67] These stories, unless otherwise stated, are taken from *Swadesh*, 27 Feb., p. 11; 6 March, p. 9; 13 March, p. 5; 10 April, pp. 1, 11; 17 April, p. 4; 24 April: pp. 11–2; 1 May, p. 7 and 8 May 1921, p. 2. I am aware that these stories can well be classified differently, and that a particular story can be grouped under more than one category. However, I have found the above classification useful for the purposes of the present discussion.

[68] These stories have been translated from the Hindi versions reported in *Swadesh*.

[69] 'These news items (*samachar*) have been sent in by Sri Sant Raj Chaudhuri of Rajpur. He maintains that all of these incidents are true'. *Swadesh*, 27 Feb. 1921, p. 11.

[70] Reported by Shyamnand Lal.

5. On 13 April a *karahi* was being set up as an offering to the Mahatma. The wife of one thakur saheb said that she would offer karahi to the Mahatmaji only if there were some miracles performed. Suddenly a dhoti hanging on a peg caught fire and was reduced to ashes, although there was no smell of burning whatsoever. 'I have seen this with my own eyes'.[71]

6. A reader of *Swadesh* from Barhaj wrote: 'Two chamars while digging were having a discussion about the *murti* (idol, image) that had emerged in Bhore village (Saran). One of them . . . said . . . "only if a murti emerges at that site as well will I accept that the one at Bhore is calling out for Gandhi". By a coincidence, while digging, a murti of Mahadev came out. On hearing the news people rushed for darshan, and *puja-paath* was done and offerings made. People are of the opinion that the cash offered should be sent to the National School [fund]'.

7. A similar incident was reported to have happened at the well of Babu Shiv Pratap Singh of Gaura [adjacent to Barhaj]. But it was said that as soon as people rushed to get the murti out of the well, it disappeared.

8. A Brahman of mauza Rudrapur (Post Office Kamasi) had the habit of stealing grass. People tried their best to convince him that Mahatma Gandhi had forbidden such evil deeds. He replied, 'I shall believe in Gandhiji if when I go stealing grass at night someone catches me, or I fall ill, go mad, or start eating *gobar* (cow dung)'. Strange are the ways of God: all these things happened. While stealing grass he started shouting that someone was coming to catch him. He fainted. He ran a high fever. People got hold of him and took him to his house. Soon after he ran out and started eating gobar. When after three days his family members took the *manauti* [i.e. pledged to propitiate Gandhi if the patient recovered], he started feeling better. 'As a result of this people in the village and its neighbourhood have given up theft etc. completely'.[72]

9. Shri Balram Das of the Gorakhpur School reported, 'On February 26th I had gone to the Rudrapur village in Maharajganj

[71] Reported by Jaikumar Singh. For the practice of karahi-offering see p. 47 below.

[72] Reported in Sarju Singh. *Manauti*: from *minnat*: taking of a vow; a promise to offer something (normally cash) in return for the fulfilment of a wish or the granting of a boon.

tahsil to give a lecture. Everybody agreed to follow the ways of
Mahatma Gandhi. But one character did not give up his [old]
habit and went to cut grass. On his return he went mad. He
broke and smashed things around him. When he offered Rs 5 in
the name of Mahatmaji he quietened down (*shanti hui*)'.[73]

Even a cursory reading of these 'stories' suggests that two obvious
processes are at work here. First, the rumours are indicative of a
considerable discussion about Gandhi in the villages of Gorakhpur in
spring 1921. The recurring phrase, 'I shall believe in Mahatmaji only
in the event of such an extraordinary happening', should be read as an
index of a dialogue between sceptics and firm believers. It makes
sense only in the context of such a discussion.

Secondly, this crucial phrase also suggests that what people thought
of the Mahatma were projections of the existing patterns of popular
beliefs about the 'worship of the worthies' in rural north India.[74] As
William Crooke has observed, the deification of such 'worthies' was
based among other things, on the purity of the life they had led and
on 'approved thaumaturgic powers'.[75] The first of these conditions
Gandhi amply satisfied by all those signs of saintliness which a
god-fearing rural populace was prone to recognize in his appearance
as well as in his public conduct. As for thaumaturgy, the stories
mentioned above attribute to him magical and miraculous powers
which, in the eyes of villagers nurtured on the lore of Sālim Chishti
and Sheikh Burhan, put him on a par with other mortals on whom
peasant imagination had conferred godliness.

Turning to the stories themselves we find that they are developments of the basic idea of the genuineness of the Mahatma as revealed
through various tests. In its simple version a test is set in the context
of the immediate activity or environment of the person concerned, or
there is the fulfilment of an expressed wish. The conditions are met
and the story or the rumour connected with it goes no further.
Examples of this are to be found in Nos. 1, 3 and 4, and to a lesser
degree in No. 5 as well. In some of the other instances a further
development takes place: the person who sets the test submits to the
Mahatma's power. Thus the Kahar of Basantpur in No. 2 gets the
roof of his hut back in position only after he makes amends for
questioning the saint's authority by tearful repentance.

[73] *Swadesh*, 1 May 1921, p. 7.
[74] W. Crooke, *The Popular Religion and Folklore of Northern India*, i (London,
1896), pp. 183–96. We are not concerned with the deification of those 'who have died
in a miraculous way', discussed by Crooke under this category.   [75] Ibid., p. 191.

A clearer example of the power of rumours in spreading the name of Gandhi in villages and reorienting normal ritual actions towards nationalist goals is contained in story No. 6. Of the two Chamars, one evidently believed in the rumour from Saran district in Bihar. But the other made his acceptance conditional on an extraordinary occurrence taking place in the context of his immediate activity—digging. When as a result of coincidence[76] his spade brought out a murti from the ground, the Chamar (perhaps convinced of the power of the Mahatma) retired as the subject of the narrative. Now others, who also had heard this particular rumour (further proof of which had been unearthed in their own area), entered the scene and propitiated the image of Mahadev in the usual way by having darshan and making offerings of flowers and money. But it is significant that the money which would otherwise have gone towards the construction of a concrete platform at that site was earmarked as a contribution to the National School Fund, a project with which Gandhi was directly associated in Gorakhpur.[77]

The story about finding a murti in Barhaj (No. 7) follows the line of popular interpretation adopted for the previous anecdote. That this particular rumour might have been spread deliberately by someone, and that the idol had 'disappeared' by the time people rushed to the scene, is immaterial for the purposes of the present discussion. What is important is that a series of 'extraordinary occurrences' in the villages of Gorakhpur were being read in a familiar way, that is according to the conventions of reading the episodes in a sacred text but with their religiosity overdetermined by an incipient political consciousness.

There is an element which story No. 2 shares with No. 5—where the *thakurain* makes her offering to the Mahatma conditional on the occurrence of a miracle and where this happens in the form of a dhoti bursting into flames. In both stories it is fear which imposes faith on non-believers. This penal motif recurs frequently in many religious ballads in eastern India. The doubting woman and the sceptical Kahar are persuaded to join the devotees—and do so ritually in the karahi episode—in the same way as a forceful display of an offended

[76] Phrases like 'by a coincidence', or 'strangely enough', which would otherwise qualify these miracles, occur very seldom in these stories. Besides, these should be read more as reflecting the viewpoint of the person reporting these occurrences to the press rather than as indicating a sceptical attitude on the part of the people as a whole.

[77] The fund was launched by the DCC in late 1920 so that Gandhi on his visit could open a National School at Gorakhpur.

godling's wrathful power breaks the resistance of a non-conformist in a *vratkatha* or *panchali*.

This motif is made explicit in No. 8 and its variation, No. 9, by the challenge to the Mahatma's power and the manner in which the latter is seen to triumph. The Brahman thief of Rudrapur village is representative not just of the ordinary village sceptic but of high-caste opposition to the Gandhian creed. His resistance questions by implication the conformism of the rest of the village (see the modified version in No. 9). But he pays for this by being subjected to physical and mental suffering. Only when his family relents on his behalf, joins the Mahatma's devotees by taking a vow in the latter's name and makes an offering does the man's condition improve. It is hard to miss the similarity between this and many other stories of opposition to the Gandhian creed, and between their predictable outcomes. (See Nos. 12, 21 and 23 below). The ending—'as a result of this particular occurrence people in the village and its neighbourhood have given up theft/drinking/gambling, etc.'—announces in each instance the victory of the new moral authority which is made all the more resplendent by the fact of having been deified at the outset.

B. *Opposing the Mahatma*

This theme of personal suffering (*kasht*) and pollution recur in many other stories expressly concerned with incidents of direct opposition to Gandhi. Thus:

10. Pt Damodar Pandey from mauza Gayaghat, PO Uska Bazar (Dist. Basti) reported that a man in mauza Dumariya near his village had called Gandhi names, as a result of which his eyelids had got stuck . . .

11. In Unchava village, one mile from Chara Ghat, four seer of ghee belonging to Abhilakh Ahir had gone bad. The reason for this was that he had made some sarcastic remarks (*vyang vachan*) about Gandhiji.

12. Mauni Baba Ramugraha Das of mauza Benuakuti (Benuatikur?) had slandered Mahatmaji on several occasions. As a result of this his body began to stink of its own (*khud-ba-khud*). After some exertion in the right direction (*kuch yatn karne par*) things improved somewhat. Mauniji then made arrangements for a *lakshaad ahuti* (sacrifice).

13. Sri Murlidhar Gupt from Majhauli reported, 'When Mahatma Gandhi was going back on the night of 8 February from

Gorakhpur to Banaras there was a huge gathering at
Salempur station to have his darshan. There was a lad of a
Barai (betel-leaf grower) in that gathering as well. It is said
that he had asked a Mishrain (wife of a Misr, a high caste
Brahman) for a wrapper to come to the station. She repri-
manded him and refused to give him the blanket. The poor
soul came shivering to the station, had darshan of the
Mahatma and went back home. In the morning I heard a
rumour in the village that she suffered the same fate as befell
the household of Babu Bhagavan Prasad, vakil of Deoria [i.e.
shit rained all over, see Nos. 17 & 18]. In the end, only when
she kept a fast, not even touching water for a day and a night
and did *aradhana* (ritual praying) of the Mahatma, did peace
finally return to her.'

14. In qasba Hariharpur, tahsil Khalilabad (District Basti) a big
raees was getting a *mandir* (temple) constructed after the
wishes of his deceased father. Babu Gyan Pal Dev—the
raees—had been against Gandhiji, and had threatened his
praja with a fine of Rs 5 if anyone even talked of Gandhiji or
became his follower. On 4 April at 11.30 p.m. a huge figure
with four hands appeared on the scene and announced aloud
before a large gathering, 'I am a follower of Siva. All of you
should do puja to him. Babu sahab give up your wrong
policies (*aniti ko chor do*). Speak the Truth. Follow the
Dharma; forsake *adharma*.' After this it assumed a diminutive
form and disappeared. 'This is a factual and eye-witness
account'.

In the first four stories (Nos. 10–13), physical ailment and pollution
are seen as supernatural punishments meted out to those who opposed
Gandhi or (as in No. 13) any of his devotees in word or deed. In No.
14 the idea of physical punishment is replaced by a divine warning
which, since it was delivered in front of a crowd which included
presumably his social inferiors, hurt the prestige of the anti-Gandhian
raees of Hariharpur.

The story (No. 12) of the holy man of Banuatikur (Mauni Baba)
who seems to have broken his vow of silence to criticize Gandhi, puts
the usual image of religious preachers and peasant audiences in a
slightly different light. It is generally believed that the manipulation
of popular religious idiom by renouncers—babas, *sanyasis* and the
like—was conducive to the spread of the nationalist message in the

countryside.[78] The peregrinations of *dharmopdeshak* Pandit Ramanugraha Sharma in eastern UP and western Bihar and the career of the *Ramayana*-reciting Baba Ramchandra in Awadh were clear examples of this process at work.[79] However, the rumour about the Mauni Baba's criticism of Gandhi and the afflictions it caused suggest that the word of the local sadhu was not always taken at its face value in the villages of Gorakhpur. His suffering was interpreted in Benuatikur and broadcast through rumour over a wide area as an obvious punishment for his anti-Gandhian stance. Apparently the holy man himself found this explanation convincing enough to repent and make amends in an appropriate manner. We do not know whether it was a local Congressman or the common people who first thought up this explanation. Even if the former did, the wide currency of this and similar stories structured around the theme of physical suffering caused by opposition to Gandhi and his creed indicates that in these we have a moment representative of a very general idea.

Nos. 13 and 14 provide additional insights into the widespread phenomenon of Gandhi-darshan. In the first of these the resolve of the true darshan-seeker enables him to withstand personal discomfiture while bringing suffering and pollution to an opponent of Mahatmaji. Here fasting and puja add up to an act of penance; in other instances, to 'worship' the Mahatma would appear to be a part of the customary female ritual of *vrat* and aradhana, which were not necessarily linked with the notion of penance or *prayschit*.[80] The text of the story is also suggestive of the power and spread of rumour: the alleged pollution of the Mishrain's household as a divine retribution provoked by her anti-Gandhian attitude is identical to the terms of a

[78] The following description in a pro-government newspaper is illustrative of the crude view which projects the peasants as objects of their manipulation: 'The special correspondent of an Indian contemporary [newspaper] throws considerable light on the methods of certain politico-religious preachers professing to be followers of Mr Gandhi who have been carrying on active propaganda in the Rae Bareli district. They settle in a village, . . . dress themselves in saffron-coloured clothes, and in the beginning of their career refuse to take food for many days. The village people think that their saviour has come. The disciple of the Mahatma next takes to preaching, and gathers round him a great following of persons . . .'. *Pioneer Mail*, 28 Jan. 1921.

[79] For Ramanugraha Sharma, see p. 12 above. For Baba Ramchandra and his use of the Ramayana and the religious cry 'Sita Ram' in mobilizing peasants in Awadh, see M. H. Siddiqi, *Agrarian Unrest in North India: the United Provinces, 1918–22* (Delhi, 1978); S. K. Mittal and Kapil Kumar, 'Baba Ramchandra and the Peasant Upsurge in Oudh', *Social Scientist*, 10:71 (June 1978); Gyan Pandey, 'Peasant Revolt and Indian Nationalism'. [80] See p. 46 below.

similar report received from Deoria twenty miles away a couple of
days ago. (See Nos. 18 and 19 below).

The Mishrain from Salempur only rebuked the Barai lad for seeking
darshan; there were landlords like Rai Kishore Chand (raees of
Sarheri estate in northern Gorakhpur) and Babu Gyan Pal Dev (of
Hariharpur in Basti) who sought to restrain their praja (tenants) in a
more forthright fashion.[81] The supernatural occurrence at a mandir
in Khalilabad tahsil on 4 April, timed by our correspondent for 11.30
p.m. and attested as factual, once again shows how such phenomena
lent themselves to very different interpretations. Both Jamuna Prasad
Tripathi who contributed this story to *Swadesh* and Babu Gyan Pal
Dev agreed that a *daitya* (ogre) had appeared on the scene, but while
the former understood this as a divine rebuke for the landlord's
anti-Gandhian actions the latter denied the charge in a rejoinder and
claimed that the apparition was merely a signal for the promotion of
the Siva cult. How the assembled peasants read this supernatural sign
we do no know for certain, but it is unlikely that they would have
failed to identify in it an element of divine rebuke to landlord
oppression.

C. *Opposing the Gandhian creed in general*

15. A gentleman from Gorakhpur city wrote that a *mukhtar* of
    Alinagar *mohalla* had asked the women of the house to ply
    charkha. They said that they were not short of anything, so
    why should they ply the charkha? By a coincidence a trunk in
    the house caught fire in a strange way. 'The whole city was
    talking about this incident'.

16. There was a criminal case in mauza Bistauli. When the police
    arrived, both the accused and the aggrieved started telling lies.
    Someone, invoking the name of Mahatmaji (*Mahatmaji ka
    pratap batla kar*), told them not to tell lies. As soon as the
    evidence was taken down, the culprit's daughter-in-law died.

17. 'Sri Tilakdhari Rai from Dhoki (Azamgarh) writes that it was
    decided on 18 February at a sabha in mauza Ghaziapur that no
    one was to let his cattle loose. Qadir chaukidar had also
    pledged (*pratigya*) not to let his cattle loose, but later he broke
    his pledge. People reminded him of his solemn promise. He
    replied, "I shall let my cattle astray, let's see what your

---

[81] One of the zamindars referred to on p. 25 was Rai Kishore Chand Raees, a
resident of Gorakhpur town and member of the District Board.

panchayat and Gandhiji can do?" An hour later his leg started
to swell up and pain. Even now the swelling has not stopped'.

18. 'A special correspondent writes from Deoria that Babu
Bhagvan Prasad vakil is in a strange predicament; shit is to be
found all over his house. Suddenly a murti that was kept in a
trunk fell down from the roof of his house. Even when he left
the house, the same predicament prevailed. The illiterates of
the town are of the opinion that this is due to the fact that the
vakil sahab had got into an argument with a speaker who was
discoursing on Non-Co-operation'.

19. 'The wife of the famous vakil, Babu Bhagvan Prasad of Deoria
has been in a strange predicament for the past few days.
Wherever she sits, she sees a bit of *vishtha* (shit) kept at a
distance from her. Sometimes she sees shit kept in a leaf-
container (*dona*) for food. There is a murti in the house. When
she keeps it back after puja it either disappears or is to be found
on the roof, or falls down from there. If she serves *poori* (a
type of fried bread) to someone, four of these become two; if
she serves five then they are reduced to three.

But it is absolutely false that she has been cursed by a
disciple of Gandhiji. People say that the vakil sahab had gone
to the Calcutta [Congress] and had agreed there to give up his
practice, but went back on his word. Subsequently a disciple
(*shishya*) of Gandhiji cursed him. Now wherever the vakil
sahab goes he encounters shit, and even his food, when served,
is transformed into shit. All this is untrue. Vakil sahab is
healthy, he does not see these things; neither did he go to
Calcutta nor did he promise to give up his practice, and
nobody has cursed him. Whatever his wife sees in the house,
people say, is the work of a ghost (*bhoot-leela*)'.[82]

20. 'On 11 April some people were gambling in the village of
Parasia Ahir. I told them not to. People accepted my advice.
Only one person did not listen to me and started abusing
Gandhiji. The next day his goat was bitten by four of his own
dogs, as a result of which he is now very unhappy and has
accepted his *qusoor* (fault)'.[83]

[82] *Gyan Shakti*, Feb. 1921, p. 407.
[83] Reported by Kasinath Tiwari, *Swadesh*, 1 May 1921, p. 7. Some other stories in
which Gandhi is not directly mentioned have been gathered together in Appendix III
and serialized as Nos. 42–50.

Opposing the Gandhian creed with respect to dietary, drinking and smoking taboos.

21. 'Rao Chokri Prasad writes, "The sons of a Tamoli (betel-leaf grower and seller) in the Tamoli neighbourhood of Lalchak near Bhatni station killed a goat and ate it up. Some people tried to dissuade them but they paid no heed. Later, all of them started vomiting and got very worried. In the end when they vowed in the name of Mahatmaji never to eat meat again their condition improved" '.

22. A Pandit of Rampur village, thana Mansurganj (Basti) was repeatedly told by many to give up his habit of eating fish, but he did not listen to anybody. He said—'I shall eat fish, let's see what the Mahatmaji can do.' When he sat down to eat [the fish] it was crawling with worms!

23. Babu Bhagirath Singh of Paisia, thana Naikot, district Gorakhpur wrote—'On 21 February the *riyaya* (peasants) of Babu Chandrika Prasad Singh promised to give up liquor as a result of his persuasion. But one Kalwar (of the caste of distillers) did not keep his solemn promise. As soon as he started for the liquor shop, brick-bats started to rain in his path. When he spoke the name of Gandhiji from the core of his heart the brick-bats stopped flying.'

24. On 22 February a sadhu came to Godhbal village and began puffing at his ganja pipe. People tried to reason with him, but he started abusing Mahatmaji. In the morning his entire body was seen covered with shit.

25. Pandit Krishnanand Misr from Paharipur village, PO Rampur, District Azamgarh wrote: 'It was decided at a sabha in mauza Kamal Sagar that nobody was to partake of any kind of intoxicant. Later a couple of persons, hiding from general view, started rubbing *surti* (tobacco-leaf, chewing-tobacco) on their palms. Suddenly the leg of a calf fell near the house of a Chaturvedi sahab. As a result of this strange occurrence everybody has given up tobacco, *surti*, etc. [as well]'.

26. A man in a sabha in mauza Majhwa had vowed not to smoke, but he took to smoking once again. Suddenly he was hemmed in by worms and insects from all sides. Because of this incident people in villages far away from Majhwa have also given up intoxicants.

27. In mauza Davani a Tambolin who used to smoke tobacco

dreamt that she was smoking and the pipe had got stuck to her mouth. She got afraid and has vowed not to smoke tobacco again.

In a sense these stories are variations on Nos. 10–13. The movement of the narrative as a sequence of personal suffering and/or pollution followed by repentance which, in its turn, generates a social impac., remains as of before. However, in the present series the punishments are seen to be meted out to those defying popular decisions taken in accordance with generally accepted tenets of the Mahatma. Nearly all rumours about the ill effects of breaking dietary and other taboos are indicative of a local elaboration of what was believed to be Gandhian ethics. Even Nos. 16–20 and No. 42 (in Appx III), not concerned with such taboos, suggest that an imbrication of popular attitudes and Gandhian ideas of self-purification was under way in the villages of Gorakhpur.

The story (No. 15) from the Alinagar ward of Gorakhpur city is the only one concerned with the refusal to ply charkha, while No. 20 about gambling refers to an activity specifically denounced by Gandhi on his visit there. Nos. 15 and 16 deal with truthfulness and attempts to regulate by a formal pledge the anti-social practice of letting one's cattle loose on other people's fields. The two variations of the story about the Deoria vakil and his wife (Nos. 18 and 19) draw on the familiar themes of pollution through human excreta and the breach of a solemn promise—that of Babu Bhagvan Prasad to give up his legal practice in accordance with the Non-Co-operation creed. It may be worth our while to pause for a closer look at these two versions.

The special correspondent of the *Swadesh* sought to distance himself from the popular interpretation of this story—'it is the opinion of the illiterates of the town'—without providing an alternative explanation. This mild disclaimer notwithstanding, he in effect gave currency to what had been thought up by the 'illiterates' of Deoria. The editor of the pro-government *Gyan Shakti* (whose pamphlet against Gandhi and Non-Co-operation was the standard text used by the district's loyalists),[84] provided a fuller account of the rumour, rebutting each and every ideological element of this popular story. In his account, which accepted the pollution of the house as a fact, it was the wife rather than the lawyer-husband who was the object of

[84] See for example the eleven-page pamphlet, *Hoshiyar ho jao* ('Beware'), written by Shiv Kumar Shastri and printed by him at the Gyan Shakti press for the Aman Sabha, Gorakhpur.

retribution. Any suggestion of the woman suffering for her husband's misdemeanour was rejected by the demonstration of all the rumours as being untrue, including the one about the lady having been cursed by a disciple of Gandhiji. The lawyer who, according to this report, had not broken any promise (made to the Congress), remained healthy in mind and body. Having taken the politics out of this rumour, the editor of *Gyan Shakti* offers an alternative explanation of this episode. The strange occurrence was not itself in doubt, it was just the reading of the signs which was problematic. In the popular version the rumour appears as a moment in the march of nationalist politics in the district. In the columns of the loyalist *Gyan Shakti* it loses that particular function: the empirical refutation put forward by the editor results in the spirit of Mahatma Gandhi being replaced by the activity of apolitical spirits (*bhoot-leela*)!

However, it is the stories in the next series which are truly illustrative of the way Gandhi's message was being decoded and amplified in terms of the popularly accepted notions of pollution, with coincidence and temporal sequence being read as indicators of casuality. Gandhi did not press his Gorakhpur audiences to forsake fish and meat, yet Nos. 21–2 reproduced above and Nos. 43–6 in Appendix III suggest that a considerable amount of discussion, ending sometimes in a collective resolve (e.g. No. 46), was going on in the villages on the subject of vegetarianism. In these texts Gandhi's name is not explicitly associated with any *pratigya* (vow) to give up fish, meat, liquor or ganja. However, as in Nos. 21, 22 and 24, the image and 'power' of Gandhi are the essential turning points in the progress of the narrative: they imbue what precedes and follows with a particular set of meanings. The defiant phrase, 'I shall eat meat/fish, smoke ganja, drink toddy/liquor, let's see what Mahatmaji can do' is crucial to the construction and progress of these rumours. It suggests an interlocution between persons for and against abstinence and the use of Gandhi's name as a part of the argument. A calamity befalling a non-conformist, its social impact and his repentance are then connected in popular imagination with the unpracticability and undesirability of going against locally imposed decisions in these matters.

Again, the absence of the Mahatma from the texts supplied in Appendix III (see Nos. 43–6, 48) suggests that he has been so fully internalized in this kind of discourse as to require no mention. It would indeed be a narrowly empirical reading which would see in these rumours no trace whatsoever of the popularly accepted notions of dietary taboos associated with the Mahatma in Gorakhpur. A comparison of the stories in which he figures explicitly (e.g. Nos. 21, 22) with those from which he is missing would suggest much affinity in the ordering of the two sets of texts. The sequence: interdiction-violation-consequence in Nos. 43, 46 and 48 is the same as in No. 21. In No. 44, the first step, interdiction, is absent (for no one warns Shankar Kandu against eating fish), but the follow-up—worms emerging from fried fish and the village giving up consumption of fish and fowl—is suggestive of the notice being taken of such evils as might result from transgressions of this kind, and of the tailoring of popular behaviour in accordance with them.

Why this concern for dietary purity? We have no evidence to enable us fully to answer this question. However, some plausible explanations may perhaps be suggested. We have already seen that conforming to the drive for ritual purity in the 1910s, a movement in favour of giving up not only liquor but also meat and fish had picked up momentum in the towns and bazaars of Gorakhpur and Basti districts.[85] Religious preachers were not alone in their advocacy of vegetarianism. Even the low-caste panchayats of Dhobis, Bhangis and barbers were insisting on heavy fines as a penalty for breaking the newly-imposed dietary taboos within their respective communities. This particular emphasis on purity in the spring of 1921 may therefore be seen as an extension of the Gandhian idea of self-purification (through abstinence from ganja and liquor) to a context where the prohibition enlarged its scope to include meat and fish and could be regarded as indicative of religiosity and lower-caste self-assertion at the same time. It is worth recalling in this connection that caste panchayats in northern Basti had decreed in January 1921 that fines imposed at a standard rate of Rs 51 for each violation of this taboo would have to be donated to the gaushala (asylum for cows).[86]

An example of this extension from one banned item to another is provided by the widening of the scope of interdiction against ganja to smoking and even chewing tobacco. It has been noticed above that Gandhi's injunction against smoking chilum, by which he meant ganja, could be regarded as applicable to smoking in general.[87] Nos. 25–27 of our stories show how this process was worked out in popular imagination. In No. 25 the ban on intoxicants (*maadak vastuven*) by which is generally meant liquor, toddy and ganja is already extended to surti—chewing tobacco. In that story divine

---

[85] See pp. 12–13 above.   [86] *Idem*   [87] See n. 57 above.

retribution helps to reform not only the culprit, but also the entire village. In No. 26 the violation, and the punishment which follows, has an impact not only on the village concerned but far beyond it. The story from mauza Dewani (No. 27) about a tobacco-addict frightened out of her wits in a dream may perhaps be read as a measure of the way in which the interdiction against the use of tobacco in any form had already been internalized.

In some cases (Nos. 22, 23, 43, 44) transgressors of dietary rules suffer physical harm and pollution of various sorts. The notion of pollution is articulated in a multi-faceted way, and for good reasons. In popular Hinduism, as Lawrence Babb has argued recently . . .

> . . . Pollution has certain physical embodiments. All body effluvia are polluting, especially faeces, urine, body saliva, menstrual flow and after-birth. Products of dead cattle, especially beef and leather, are highly polluting. Decaying things are polluting (a common rationale for considering liquor to be mildly polluting: 'It's a rotten thing'). Corpses, or anything having to do with death, are sources of extremely powerful pollution.[88]

In our collection of stories the same polluting agents—worms (as an embodiment of the idea of decay) or human faeces—are often associated with rather different acts or items of food. Thus faeces is associated in No. 19 with a curse for breaking a solemn promise, in No. 24 it is the consequence for abusing Gandhi and not conforming to the local advice against smoking ganja, and in No. 45 it is seen as a proof of and punishment for animal slaughter. Worms as polluting agents are associated with fish (Nos. 22, 44), though the idea of a miracle—live worms emerging from fish that had been fried or roasted—is also present. However, in No. 26 worms figure as a kind of calamity, while the frying of fish in No. 48 leads to the burning of huts.

Punishments for wrongs done could be (as in No. 42 below) visited on persons other than the actual wrong-doer. Thus in No. 46 the spread of an epidemic is associated with violating the generally accepted taboo against eating fish in a village near Pipraich. The gratuitous suffering by a high-caste person for the sin committed by another—the defilement of a Chaturvedi's house because of an attempt at surti-eating by others (No. 25)—is a theme that is encountered in other contexts as well. Thus Kashi Nath Tiwari of mauza Asiya Ahir

[88] Lawrence A. Babb, *Divine Hierarchy: Popular Hinduism in Central India* (New York, 1975), p. 48.

wrote to the *Swadesh* in early April that in his village 'one person had mixed water in milk, as a result of which the *dahi* (yoghurt) of several notable persons was infested with worms'. One can hardly miss here the echoes of a Brahmanical tradition going back to antiquity.[89]

D. *Boons granted and/or miracles performed in the form of manauti and the recovery of things lost*

28. Pandit Jiwnandan Pathak from mauza Devkali, PO Bhagalpur wrote, 'As a result of manauti of Mahatmaji a vessel of a Musalman which had fallen into a well six months ago came up on its own'.

29. In Naipura village (Azamgarh), the long-lost calf of Dalku Ahir returned to its peg as a result of the manauti of Mahatmaji. Dalku Ahir has contributed the one rupee of the manauti to the Swaraj Fund.

30. A gentleman from Ballia district wrote, 'In mauza Rustampur a *thaili* (purse) of a gwala-sadhu containing Rs 90 had disappeared from his hut. When he took manauti of Mahatmaji, he found it back in his hut, and the money was intact'.

31. A well-known zamindar of mauza Samogar (tahsil Deoria) had taken a *minnat* [manauti] of Bhagwatiji and offered a goat as a sacrifice. Many took the meat as *prasad*. After some time the son of the zamindar found his hands stuck to his chest and his wife went mad. It was only when the zamindar vowed to contribute the price of the sacrificial goat to the National School Fund and feast Brahmans that both the son and the daughter-in-law began to feel well.

Boons granted and/or miracles performed in the form of regeneration of trees and wells

32. 'In mohalla Humayunpur, Gorakhpur city, two dead trees which had fallen in the garden of Babu Yugul Kishore, vakil, have planted themselves back! Many believe that this is due to the grace of Mahatmaji. This, because the person who cut the trees said that if the pratap (spiritual power) of Mahatmaji was

---

[89] *Swadesh*, 10 April 1921. The idea of the sins of the lower castes visiting the higher castes is represented in its classic form in the Ramayana story of a Brahman child's death caused by a Sudra's insistence on engaging in the purificatory rituals of *tapasya* in order to attain a high degree of spiritual merit. For a Sudra to do so was to commit a sin. So a Brahman had to pay for it.

saccha (genuine) the trees would stand up on their own! Thousands gather at this site everyday and *batashas* (a kind of sweetmeat), money and ornaments are offered by men and women alike. It is said that the proceeds will be donated to the Swarajya ashram and the Tilak Swaraj Fund'.[90]

33. 'A frail mango tree had been bent by a storm. As a matter of fact its roots were not strong enough to withstand the weight of its branches . . . Because of the storm some of the roots were uprooted, but a part remained embedded in the ground. The tree dried up in a few days. People began cutting its branches and taking them home for fuel. As the weight of its branches was now reduced, the tree straightened up either on its own, or with the aid of some person. People proclaimed that [the] fallen tree [had] planted itself back. A crowd soon gathered, assuming the proportions of a *mela* (fair). They are now offering flowers, batashas and money to the tree. It is said that the tree has stood up because of the pratap of Gandhiji. The educated are laughing at the mela, and this particular exemplification of Indian beliefs'.[91]

34. A respected person from Basti district reported to the *Swadesh* the following incidents: 'Two saplings have sprouted from the *khunta* (peg) of a Mahua tree in Chakdehi village, two miles from the Khalilabad station. This khunta had been fixed in the month of Kartik (October-November), and every day the bullocks of one Pandeji used to be tied to it. It is also rumoured that a Chamar had seen a sapling coming out of the peg on an earlier occasion, but his wife had plucked it out. Subsequently, the Chamar was rebuked by some people. He then prayed to the Mahatma: "Oh! Mahatmaji, if you are a true Mahatma, then let another sapling sprout". And so it happened. Now every day crowds of men and women are coming to the spot to see the peg'.

35. 'In Basti town there lives a widow of Sri Raghubar Kasaudhan. She had a son who died three years ago. Her late husband had planted two mango trees; one was cut down some time back and the other dried up a year ago. Fifteen days ago it began sprouting fresh leaves. The old woman maintains that she had taken a manauti of Mahatmaji: "This tree is the only *nishani*

---

[90] *Batsha:* A light sweet-meat, in appearance like ratafia cakes.
[91] *Gyan Shakti,* April 1921, p. 34.

(sign) of my late husband, let this tree live". A large crowd gathers at this site as well'.

36. 'Last Saturday smoke started coming out of four or five wells in Gorakhpur city. People exclaimed that the water had caught fire. The whole city rushed to the spot. Some people drew water from one well: it had the fragrance of keora (*pandanus odaratissimus*). It is believed that this is also due to the 'pratap' of the Mahatma! Some money etc. has also been offered to the well'.[92]

37. 'Some days ago a major fire broke out in a village near the Gorakhpur Civil Courts. The entire village was burnt down. There is a *nala* (open drain) nearby. People started digging a *chaunra* (*katcha* well) in the nala to get some wet clay and water, but water was not struck even after digging several cubits. It is said that in the end one person took the manauti of the Mahatma. After this such a huge jet of water gushed out that not only was the 16–17 cubit deep well filled up, but the two adjacent *garhas* (depressions) were also submerged. Since then thousands of men and women gather at the site. Flowers, batashas and money are offered, they bathe and wash their faces there and some even carry the water back to their homes'.[93]

38. 'There is a big depression (garha) to the south of Bulandpur village [on the outskirts of Gorakhpur]. This garha is not less than twenty-three feet deep. The water level in Gorakhpur is around twenty-one feet. In some cases water is struck even before this depth is reached. An eleven cubit rope is normally used in these parts [to raise water from wells]. The present well from which water gushed out was dug in this deep depression. When water was struck it filled the chaunra to the brim. Now a mela is taking place here. When a chaunra is dug in a deep depression such an occurrence is only natural. The water level in Gorakhpur is eleven cubits; if you so desire you may measure it. We have seen scores of such wells which, when dug in a depression have been filled with water to the brim. People are offering flowers, batashas and money at the [above mentioned] well. They say that even this is an example of the grace of Gandhiji. This well is now called "Gandhi Chaunra" . . . Does one require this kind of intelligence for the attainment of swaraj?'[94]

---

[92] *Swadesh*, 13 March 1921, p. 5.   [93] *Swadesh*, 10 April 1921, p. 11.
[94] *Gyan Shakti*, April 1921, p. 34.

39. 'The *bhakts* (devotees) have . . . offered Rs 23-8-12 in Mirzapur Bazaar where water had come out on its own. Sri Chedi Lal has arranged for this sum to be sent to the Gorakhpur Swaraj Fund'.

40. The water of a well in Bikramjit Bazaar, tappa Belwa (Basti) had a very foul smell. Two *mahajans* took a manauti of the Mahatmaji. By morning the water had become pure.

41. 'Plague was raging through Sonaura village. People were living in [outlying] huts. The water in a well at this place was so shallow on 27 April that even a small drinking vessel (*lota*) could not be fully submerged in it. Seeing this, one Misrji offered to distribute Rs 5 in the name of Gandhiji. Subsequently, water began to rise slowly. By the afternoon of 28 April the well had filled up to five cubits, the next day it was eleven cubits deep'.

Once again we have in these stories the suggestion that the Mahatma's image takes form within pre-existing patterns of popular belief, and ritual action corresponding to these. In Nos. 28–30, Gandhi is fitted into the widespread practice of taking a vow (manuati) addressed to a god, a local godling or a saint on condition of the removal of an affliction or the fulfilment of a wish. In No. 31 we have an interesting development of this idea. Here the sacrifice of a goat in accordance with a manauti to Bhagwatiji boomerangs—it brings physical and mental suffering to the high-caste household of the zamindar of Samogar. The penance required is not limited to the traditional feasting of Brahmans; it now includes the donation of an amount equivalent to the cost of the sacrificial goat to the National School Fund.

The rational, if politically insensitive, explanations offered by the anti-Congress *Gyan Shatki* with regard to the regeneration of trees and wells (see Nos. 33 and 38) indicate the material basis for belief in these miracles. On the other hand, a couple of stories (Nos. 49 and 50 in Appx III) not strictly connected with Gandhi point once again to the existing stereotype of 'strange occurrences' in which the Mahatma's name figures so very often. It is thus that the traditional offerings made at the appearance of an image (No. 6) or at the site of a miraculous tree (Nos. 32 and 33) or a well can so easily be transferred to a nationalist fund.

The stories connected with wells (Nos. 36–41) which underline their importance for irrigation and even more for supplies of drinking water, call for some additional comments. The two major themes here are, first, the taking of a manauti by a banker or a high-caste person (usually a landlord) for the purification of drinking water (Nos. 40 and 41), and secondly, the more common offering of flowers, batasha and money to wells where water has appeared miraculously. Both these are readily understandable once it is realized that it was generally the bigger zamindars and bankers who invested in the expensive construction of pukka (masonry) wells. This was a highly ritualized activity in Gorakhpur and was described thus by a local ethnographer towards the end of the nineteenth century:

> When a man intends to sink a well he enquires an auspicious moment from the Pandit to commence it. When that hour comes, he worships Gauri, Ganesh, Shesh Nag, earth, the *kudari* (spade), and the nine planets. After worshipping these deities the person himself begins to dig with the *kudari* five times, facing the direction the Pandit has prescribed. Then the labourers begin their work. When they have sunk, so far as to make water appear, an auspicious moment is obtained to put the *jamuat* or wooden support on whom [sic] the brick structure of the well rests in the well. At the auspicious moment the person to whom the well belongs smears the *jamuat* with red powder in five places and ties grass (*dub*) and thread (*raksha*) on it, and then it is lowered down in the well. On this occasion a fire sacrifice (*homa/hawan*) is performed and Brahmans are fed. When the well has been sunk, cow-dung, cow-milk, cow-urine, cow-ghee, Ganges water, leaves of tulsi plant and honey are put in it before its water is made use of. Then a fire sacrifice (*homa*) is performed and Brahmans are fed.[95]

In Gorakhpur, according to the same informant, a mango tree was usually 'married' to a well.[96] Accounts from neighbouring Basti district suggest that the construction of a pukka well was both a communal and a ritual act. Neighbouring zamindars sent men, women and children to collect wood for the firing and baking of bricks, and the *sattu*, gur and liquor received by them were regarded 'in the light rather of a marriage feast than of remuneration'.[97] The 'marriage' of the well to an image (*jalotsarg*) was preceded by the carpenter spreading a *chaddar* (sheet) on the wooden frame. Into this the members of the brotherhood would throw coins of various denomination ranging from one paisa to one rupee, depending on their means and liberality. It was a measure of the importance of ritual in the consecration of pukka wells in this region that the

[95] Note by Ram Gharib Chaube, *North Indian Notes and Queries*, 3:12 (March 1894), no. 437.

[96] *North Indian Notes and Queries*, 4:12 (March 1895), no. 437.

[97] *Statistical, Descriptive and Historial Account of the North Western Provinces*, vi (Allahabad, 1881), p. 595.

'regular cost' of constructing a well, eight feet wide and nineteen feet deep, was reckoned to have been Rs 43 in the 1860s, while nearly twice as much was spent on ceremonial expenses.[98] As the settlement officer reported from Rasulpur Ghaus, Basti, 'On account of the expense the ceremony is often delayed one or two years, during which time the family of the builder makes no use of the water'.[99]

With this kind of worshipful attitude towards the construction of masonry wells, the offerings of flowers and money to those spots where water had appeared miraculously in the spring of 1921 and the transference of these offerings to a nationalist fund appear as an elaboration of existing ideas in a novel context. The practice of Gandhi manauti, of his vrat and aradhana (fast and worship), and of women begging alms in his name and making offerings of cooked food (*karahi charana*), as noticed in some of the earlier stories, can all be adduced as further instances of this process at work.[100]

[98] The break-up was as follows:

	Rs	annas
Offering to family god	1	0
Given to Brahmins: 5 dhotees and 5 rupees	9	0
Given to head beldar, 1 dhoty and 1 rupee	1	12
Liquor for remaining beldars	0	4
Feast to Brahmins (5 to 20)	11	0
Given to Brahmins and workmen, 5 rupees and 5 dhotees	9	0
Marriage ceremony from 10 rupees to an unlimited amount	50	0
	82	0
Total:	125	0

See Report on Pegunnah Rassolpore Ghaus, Appx L, in *Gorakhpur-Bustee Settlement Report*, i (Allahabad, 1871), p. 48.

[99] *Idem*

[100] In a study of popular religion in a north Indian village it has been suggested that the relationship between the devotees (*bhakts*) and the power-wielding deified beings moves along the grid of *Bhakti/Sewa: Krpa/Vardan*. Faith (bhakti) leads to the mercy (krpa) of the gods, while the sewa (service) of the devotees results in the granting of boon (vardan). On the other hand, the mercy of the gods leads to faith, and the accompanying boon results in further service (sewa) through the ritual of vrat (fast, puja and bhakti). Powerful deities have the ability not only to remove immediate distress, but are distinguished by their power to provide long-term shelter (*sharan*) and even *moksha* (salvation). See Wadley.

While the idea of boons and removal of distress is present in the stories collected above, the notion of the Mahatma providing sharan to his devotees seems to be absent, probably because Gandhi has not been constructed yet as a full-fledged deity in his own right. Rather, we have the suggestion that Gandhi, because of the fluidity of his 'powers', can stand in place of existing powerful beings and appropriate ritual actions connected with their worship, without upsetting the existing hierarchy of the divine and the deified.

The editor of *Swadesh* reported in April 1921 that 'news [had] been received from several places of women begging in the name of Gandhiji as they did for Devi Bhawani and offering karahi [to him]'. Women were also going round the threshing-floors, where the rabi crop had just been gathered, and asking for donations of grain, again to make offerings of karahi to the Mahatma.[101] The contemporary significance of the karahi ritual is somewhat unclear, though it appears to have been associated with propitation and the bringing of luck.[102] What is significant, in any case, is that this was an extension of a practice related to the worship of Devi Bhawani and that begging at the threshing-floor put the peasants under a moral obligation to donate some grain in the name of the Mahatma at a time when a surplus was readily available at the very site where it was being processed. In fact a similar obligation was placed on peasants manufacturing gur at the *kolhuar* as well: to turn a beggar away from a place where so much raw sugar was being made was an undesirable act which would seldom go unpunished.[103] It is hardly surprising, then, that the refusal of an Ahir in Nanusakh village (Azamgarh) to offer some gur to a hungry sadhu who came begging to his kolhuar (on 1 March 1921) was rumoured to have resulted within half an hour in the gur and the two buffaloes of the Ahir being destroyed by fire.[104] The version of this story, as reported in the *Swadesh*, did not mention Gandhi, although the *Pioneer* suggested that the sadhu was asking for alms in the Mahatma's name. True or not, it is possible that the Lucknow journal was not alone in associating him with this particular episode.

[101] *Swadesh*, 10 April 1921.

[102] Prof. A. N. Pandeya (IIT, Delhi) informs me that the phrase '*karahi charana*' refers in his part of the district (Padrauna tahsil) to the practice of women offering cake-like cooked food, prepared at the site of the local godling (usually female) in the open under a tree. Devi Bhawani, according to Crooke, is a north Indian mother goddess.

[103] Grierson's account of the worship of Makkar or Makar Bir in Bihar by the workmen of the kolhuar is worth recalling in this context. 'Near the place where the cane is cut into slips the men make a round idol of the deity called *makar bir* . . . He is said to have been originally a Dom, who once came to a sugar manufactory in the olden time and asked for juice, which the people refused to give to him. Thereupon he jumped into the boiler and was boiled to death. His spirit became deified, and is now worshipped by the workmen . . .'. G. A. Grierson, *Bihar Peasant Life* (1885: reprint, Delhi, 1975), pp. 55–6. The theme of suicide leading to the wrongdoer accepting his fault and then propitating and worshipping the spirit of the deceased is a recurring one in Indian folklore. See Crooke, pp. 191–5.   [104] *Swadesh*, 13 March 1921, p. 5.

VII

Taken together, these stories indicate how ideas about Gandhi's *pratap* and the appreciation of his message derived from popular Hindu beliefs and practices and the material culture of the peasantry. Does not the fact of the reporting of these rumours in the local nationalist weekly suggest that these were actively spread by interested parties? It is true that such rumours enter our sources at the point where a correspondent communicates them to the *Swadesh*. But that need not be taken to mean that these did not exist prior to and independent of their publication. Their generalized circulation in the villages of Gorakhpur is also attested by their being reported and denied in the local anti-nationalist monthly, *Gyan Shakti*.

There can be no doubt that the reporting of these rumours in the local paper, *Swadesh*, must have added to their circulation and even to their authenticity. Lefebvre in his study of rural panic in revolutionary France observes how journalists imbued rumours 'with a new strength by putting . . . them into print'.[105] However, it seems unlikely that printing could have changed the character of these rumours to any significant degree; it merely increased their effectiveness as oral and unauthored speech.[106] People in the Gorakhpur countryside believed in these not out of any unquestioning trust in the weekly newspaper but because they accorded with existing beliefs about marvels and miracles, about right and wrong.

In Indian villages even printed texts often revert to their oral characteristics in the very process of communication. It has been noted that newspapers, pamphlets, etc. are made intelligible to the illiterate population in the countryside by reading aloud, paraphrasing the text in the rustic dialect and commenting on it.[107] In 'advanced cultural communities', Vachek notes, written texts are taken 'as a sign of the first order (i.e. the sign of an outside world)', the deciphering of which requires 'no detour by way of spoken language'.[108] It seems that one of the reasons for the reading aloud of newspapers in

[105] Georges Lefebvre, *The Great Fear of 1789: Rural Panic in Revolutionary France* (London, 1973), p. 74.

[106] For the characterization of rumour as oral and unauthored speech, see Ranajit Guha, *Elementary Aspects of Peasant Insurgency in Colonial India* (Delhi, 1983), Ch. 6.

[107] 'Language Problem in the Rural Development of North India', in *Language in Social Groups: Essays by John J. Gumperz* (California, 1971), p. 19.

[108] Josef Vachek, 'Some Remarks on Writing and Phonetic Transcriptions', in Eric Hamp *et al.* (eds.), *Readings in Linguistics*, ii (Chicago, 1966), p. 155.

Indian villages is that even for a large part of the technically literate population printed texts can be deciphered only by a detour through the spoken language. In such readings, it seems reasonable to suggest, a story acquires its authentication from its motif and the name of its place of origin rather than from the authority of the correspondent. It then spreads by word of mouth, and derives its credibility from any association, real or imaginary, it might have with place-names familiar to the local population.[109]

How did the local Congress leadership react to the spread of these stories? Maulvi Subhanullah, the DCC President, while recounting some of these to the Sessions Judge in June 1922, admitted that 'no attempt was made by the Congress or Khilafat to prevent [the] public from believing in them'.[110] *Swadesh*, the newspaper which published these stories under the sanctimonious rubric *bhakton ki bhavnain*— 'beliefs of the devotees'—adopted a double-edged policy in this regard.[111] On the one hand it published a note every now and then debunking some of the more fanciful stories and also let its satirist, Mannan Dwivedi, poke fun at them. On the other hand when attacked by the *Pioneer*, it came up with a spirited defence of its policy of printing these stories.

In March 1921 some people used the services of public criers to announce that 'Mahatmaji had emerged from fire [unhurt] and that Swaraj had been established'. They went so far as to swear by the truth of such statements. The editor of *Swadesh* promptly denounced this as an irresponsible act which had no sanction from the Mahatma. However, the same issue of the journal contained two columns of Gandhi stories under the heading 'strange happenings'. Elsewhere in the same issue Mannan Dwivedi, writing under the pen-name Shriyut Muchandar Nath, satirized some of these as follows:

> It is true that a felled tree in the front of Babu Yugal Kishore's garden has planted itself back and even sprouted leaves due to the grace of Mahatmaji. [See No. 32 above]. Every day lakhs of people come to see this [miracle],

[109] Thus in Satyajit Ray's film, *Ashani Sanket*, the foreign place-name Singapore is made meaningful to the peasants in a Bengal village by the suggestion that it is somewhere near Midnapore!

[110] Evidence, Chauri Chaura Trials, p. 556.

[111] Dwivedi, when queried by the Court about these miracles, proffered little information, and in fact maintained that in his paper he had 'given a summary . . . of the teaching of Mahatma Gandhi that he [was] not a god'. An extract from *Navjivan* in which Gandhi disclaimed to be an avtar was printed by *Swadesh* on the front page of its issue of 4 September 1921. See Evidence, Chauri Chaura Trials, p. 569.

as a result of which crores of rupees are being collected. Therefore, due to
the efforts of Babu Krishna Prasad, neither will postal rates go up nor will
there be a deficit in the budget this year . . .

It was rumoured that a well in Gorakhpur was smelling of keora. [See
No. 36]. Now it has been confirmed by the Khilafat Committee that Sri
Shiv Mangal Gundhi had emptied his karahs full of keora into the well, as
it is said that he is going to perform the last rites for his Sundar Shringar
Karyalay [a perfumary in the city] and is shortly to take up the running of
a [nationalist] press.[112]

It is doubtful how many outside the city of Gorakhpur would have
understood Mannan Dwivedi's allusions or allowed satire to get the
better of belief. Even the editor of *Swadesh*, when pressed, could
write an impassioned defence of the peasant's acceptance of these
stories:

> We do not consider . . . *Swadesh* to be the property (*miras*) of its editor.
> Therefore, we consider it as part of our duty to report the thoughts and
> feelings current among the people (janta), whether right or wrong, in our
> paper . . . . It is possible that some people might doubt these strange
> happenings, but the janta does not consider them so [improbable]. And
> there is a reason for this. It is because Hinduism has placed faith and belief
> (*shraddha aur vishwas*) on a high footing. It is because of this that those
> who worship stone images have their prayers answered. It is because of
> this that people take a dip in the holy waters of Gangaji and think that
> their sins have been washed away. In every age and country, every now
> and then, such things have happened. Even in the time of the Buddha,
> Mohammad and Christ such miracles were supposed to have taken place.
> Then we see no reason why miracles (*chamatkar*) should not be associated
> with Mahatma Gandhi whose name is perhaps even better known in India
> than that of Ram and Sita. It has been said: '*Vishwaso* [sic] *phaldayakah*':
> faith yields fruit.
> '*jaki rahi bhavana jaisi,*
> *prabhu moorat dekhi tin taisi*'.[113]

The editor of *Swadesh*, who had himself sought to inculcate an
attitude of devotion in the district towards the Mahatma,[114] had thus
no hesitation in printing rumours about the latter's pratap. It was
only when these appeared to instigate dangerous beliefs and actions,
such as those concerning demands for the abolition of zamindari,
reduction of rents or enforcement of just price at the bazaars, that the
journal came out with prompt disclaimers.[115]

[112] *Swadesh*, 10 April 1921, p. 5.
[113] 'Bhakton ki Bhavnain', editorial note, *Swadesh*, 1 May 1921.
[114] Cf. pp. 17–18 above.
[115] See *Swadesh*, 18 Sept. 1921, p. 8; 6 March 1921, p. 12.

VIII

Just as the Mahatma was associated in Gorakhpur with a variety of miraculous occurrences, so did his name lend itself as a label for all sorts of public meetings, pamphlets—and of course for that polysemic word Swaraj. Surveying the background to the Chauri Chaura riot, the judges of the Allahabad High Court found it 'remarkable . . . how this name of "Swaraj" was linked, in the minds of the peasantry of Gorakhpur, with the name of Mr Gandhi. Everywhere in the evidence and in statements made . . . by various accused persons', they found that 'it was "Gandhiji's Swaraj", or the "Mahatmaji's Swaraj" for which they [i.e. the peasants] were looking'.[116] 'Announcements in Urdu' were sold by Lal Mohammad, one of the principal accused in the Chauri Chaura case, as 'Gandhi papers' which were to be preserved and produced 'when Gandhiji asked for . . . [them]'. The receipt for donations to the Khilafat fund, which bore a superficial resemblance to a one-rupee bank note, was referred to as a 'Gandhi note' by the peasants of Gorakhpur. The editor of *Gyan Shakti*, to whom we owe this information, alleged that villagers interpreted its non-acceptance (as legal tender?) as an act of opposition to the Mahatma.[117] Whether peasants genuinely failed to recognize the difference (as officials in some Awadh districts implied),[118] or whether this was just a conscious manipulation of an ambiguous printed paper to force non-believers into acceptance, we do not know for certain. What is clear, however, is that we have in the 'Gandhi note' an index of the popular tendency to look upon the Mahatma as an alternative source of authority. We have it on local testimony that peasant volunteers proceeding to a *sabha* at Dumri on the morning of 4 February 1922 (hours before the historic clash with the police was to occur at the Chaura thana a couple of miles away), claimed that they were 'going to hold a Gandhi Mahatma Sabha' which would bring about 'Gandhi Swaraj'.[119]

The popular notion of 'Gandhiji's Swaraj' in Gorakhpur appears to have taken shape quite independently of the district leadership of

---

[116] Appeal No. 51 of 1923: King Emperor vs. Abdullah and others. Judgement of the Allahabad High Court, dated 30 April 1923, p. 9, High Court Archives, Allahabad. The evidence about Lal Mohammad in the next sentence comes from the testimony of Shikari before the Sessions Judge, p. 1.

[117] *Gyan Shakti*, Feb. 1921, p. 404.

[118] See for instance the official handbill 'Khabardar', issued by the Dy. Commr. of Rae Bareli, encl. in Jawaharlal Nehru Papers, Pt II, File 120, NMML.

[119] Evidence of Mindhai, cultivator of Mahadeva, and Birda, cultivator of Bale, Chauri Chaura Trials, pp. 512–13.

the Congress party. As the High Court judges observed, the local peasantry 'perceived of it [Swaraj] as a millenium in which taxation would be limited to the collection of small cash contributions or dues in kind from fields and threshing floors, and [in] which the cultivators would hold their lands at little more than nominal rents'.[120] During the course of the trial the district Congress and Khilafat leadership repeatedly denied having propagated any such ideas in the villages. In fact there is evidence that as early as March 1921 public proclamations about the advent of Swaraj were being made in the Gorakhpur countryside. These, as we have noted above, were denounced by the Congress paper *Swadesh*. The pro-landlord *Gyan Shakti* drew pointed attention to such occurrences as ominous signs which boded ill for all concerned:

> One night people from all the villages [!] kept awake and roamed over five villages each. That night it was impossible to get any sleep. They were shouting 'Gandhiji ki jai'. They had *dhol, tasa, jhal, majiras* (kettledrums and cymbals) with them. The din thus caused was unbearable. People were shouting, this is the drum of swaraj (*swaraj ka danka*). Swaraj has been attained. The English had taken a bet with Gandhiji that they would grant Swaraj if Gandhiji could come out of fire [unhurt]. Gandhiji took hold of the tail of a calf and went through fire. Now Swaraj has been attained. It was also announced that now only four annas or eight annas a bigha would have to be paid in rent. We have also heard that some peasants are insisting that they will not pay more than eight annas a bigha as rent.
>
> These rumours are signs of an impending clash between the peasants and the landlords. As a result of this both parties shall suffer. Sensible (*parhe-likhe*) peasants, landlords and the government should refute such rumours. Remember this! If ordinary people retain their belief in such rumours and persist in their quest for the chimerical then the attainment of Swaraj will become increasingly distant. Peasants are now refusing to obey their landlords, or work for them. This is not a good sign for the country.[121]

Quite clearly this was a miracle (Gandhi's passage through fire) consistent with the existing level of peasant consciousness and its foil in utopian hopes for a world free of rents—a far cry these from

[120] Judgement, Allahabad High Court, p. 9.

[121] 'Swaraj ka Danka: Char Anna Malguzari: Zamindaron ki Chinta', *Gyan Shakti*, April 1921, pp. 34–5. This rumour, which had originated in the villages of the south-eastern tahsil of Deoria, spread to the neighbouring district of north Bihar and underwent a transformation in the process. It was rumoured here that Gandhi Baba, a cow, a Brahman and an Englishman had been put to an ordeal by fire, and only the Englishman had got burned. People were to pass on this story to five other villages on pain of incurring the sin of killing five cows. Cited in Henningham, p. 100.

official Congress policy—which marked the irruption of Swaraj that night in Gorakhpur villages.[122] However, as local-level volunteer activity entered a more militant phase in late 1921, the coming of Swaraj was perceived—contrary to anything the Congress stood for at that time—in terms of the direct supplanting of the authority of the police[123] (just as the earlier notion of divine punishment for opposition to the Gandhian creed was replaced by the idea that it was for the panchayats themselves to dispense justice in such cases). Thus Sarju Kahar, the personal servant of the murdered *thanedar* of Chaura, testified that 'two or four days before the affair [he] had heard that Gandhi Mahatma's Swaraj had been established, that the Chaura thana would be abolished, and that the volunteers would set up their own thana'.[124] According to Harbans Kurmi of Mangapatti, Narayan, Baleshar and Chamru of his village said on their return from the riot that 'they had burnt and thrown away and Swaraj had come'.[125] Or as Phenku Chamar told the Sessions Judge in August 1922:

> Bipat Kahar, Sarup Bhar and Mahadeo Bhuj were coming along calling out 'Gandhi Maharaj Gandhi Maharaj' from the north, the direction of Chaura, to [the] south, the direction of Barhampur. I asked why they were calling out 'Gandhi Maharaj' and they said the thana of Chaura had been burnt and razed to the ground [by them] and the Maharaj's swaraj had come.[126]

IX

Corresponding to this dramatic change in the manifestation of 'Gandhiji's Swaraj', there was for the peasant volunteers of Chauri Chaura a transformation in the spirit of that ubiquitous cry, 'Gandhi Maharaj ki jai', as well. We have noticed how this cry had assumed an audacious overtone during Gandhi's return journey from Gorakhpur in February 1921.[127] Within a month, as the 'Swaraj ka danka' episode suggests, the *jaikar* of Gandhi had become a militant avowal of the organized strength of peasant volunteers, a cry which mobilized

[122] The belief in an impending Swaraj was no doubt related to Gandhi's utterances on this point, though its signs were far from Gandhian.

[123] See 'Some Instances of the highhanded methods of Non-Cooperation Volunteers', encl. to Bihar Govt. letter dated, 5 Dec. 1921, Home Poll. File 327/I/ 1922, NAI.

[124] *Tajwiz Awwal*, Chauri Chaura Trials, p. 358.

[125] Chauri Chaura Trials, p. 525.

[126] Chauri Chaura Trials, p. 516.

[127] See pp. 19–20 above.

and struck terror in the hearts of waverers and enemies alike.[128] For
the peasants of north India this had ceased in effect to be a Gandhian
cry; it was now a cry with which an attack on a market or a thana was
announced. 'Mahatma Gandhi ki jai' had, in this context, assumed
the function of such traditional war cries as 'Jai Mahabir' or 'Bam
Bam Mahadeo'. An interesting case of such a transformation is
provided by the following intelligence report from Bara Banki:

> The big Mahadeo Fair near Ramnagar passed off quietly, though the
> extensive substitution of Gandhi ki jai for the orthodox Bam Bam Mahadeo
> was noticeable even when there were no government officer[s] present.[129]

The crowd of Badhiks (a so-called 'criminal tribe') that looted the
Tinkonia Bazaar in Gorakhpur on 15 February 1921, did so to the cry of
'Mahatma Gandhi ki jai'. In a small fair at Auraneshwarghat in Bara
Banki a dispute with *halwais* (confectioners) on 22 February 1922 led to
the upsetting and looting of sweatmeat and other stalls 'to the accom-
paniments of shouts of *Mahatma Gandhi ki jai aur mithai le leu*'.[130]

Thus a 'jaikar' of adoration and adulation had become the rallying
cry for direct action. While such action sought to justify itself by a
reference to the Mahatma, the Gandhi of its rustic protagonists was
not as he really was, but as they had thought him up. Though deriving
their legitimacy from the supposed orders of Gandhi, peasant actions
in such cases were framed in terms of what was popularly regarded to
be just, fair and possible. As an official reply to the question of
haat-looting in north Bihar in the winter of 1921 stated:

> The evidence in the possession of the Government leaves no doubt that
> the haat-looting was directly connected with the state of excitement and
> unrest produced by the non-co-operation agitation. The persons who
> started the loot first of all asked the price of rice, or cloth or vegetables or
> whatever the particular article might be, and when the price was mentioned,
> alleged that Gandhi had given the order that the price should be so much,
> usually a quarter of the current market rate. When the shopkeepers
> refused to sell at lower prices, they were abused and beaten and their
> shops were looted.[131]

---

[128] This transformation was similar to what the cry 'Sita Ram' had been undergoing
in the villages of Awadh at about the same time. See Pandey, 'Peasant Revolt and
Indian Nationalism', pp. 169–70.   [129] PAI, 1 March 1922.

[130] *Idem*; King Emperor vs. Badloo Badhik and others, Trial no. 25 of 1921,
Judgement by the Sessions Judge, Gorakhpur, 30 April 1921.

[131] *Bihar and Orissa Legislative Council Debates*, 8 March 1921, i, p. 293. There
was a rumour current in Gorakhpur villages as well, that wheat, rice and cloth would
become cheaper because of the 'order of Mahatma Gandhi'. See *Gyan Shakti*, Feb.
1921, p. 405.

There was thus no single authorized version of the Mahatma to which the peasants of eastern UP and north Bihar may be said to have subscribed in 1921. Indeed their ideas about Gandhi's 'orders' and 'powers' were often at variance with those of the local Congress-Khilafat leadership and clashed with the basic tenets of Gandhism itself. The violence at Chauri Chaura was rooted in this paradox.

Appendix I

'गोरखपुर का अहोभाग्य'

प्रार्थना यह है कि गोरखपुर की साधारण जनता तो केवल महात्मा जी के दर्शन को बेतरह उत्सुक है. महात्मा जी आयेंगे; अपना दर्शन देकर उसे कृतार्थ करेंगे. लोग भी अपने त्राता को, अपने सामने, भर आँख देखकर, फूले नहीं समायेंगे. परन्तु, हम पूछते हैं कि वे लोग, जो प्रत्यक्ष रूप से सरकार के साथ सहयोग कर रहे हैं ... उनका भी ऐसे अवसर पर कुछ कर्त्तव्य है या नहीं ? हृदय से आवाज़ उठती है "बेशक" .... उनका कर्त्तव्यपथ निश्चित हो चुका है, वे कार्यक्षेत्र में आबें, अपने देश को गुलामी से छुटकारा दिलाने के लिए, अपनी मान-मर्यादा कायम करने के लिए और अपने को अपने देश पर न्यौछावर करने के लिए कमर कस कर तैयार हो जायें. महात्मा जी के सामने अपने घुटने टेक दें और जगदाधार जगतियन्ता से प्रार्थना करें कि वह उन्हें बल दे कि वो अपनी किश्ती को इस मझधार में से पार कर ले जावें. परन्तु अगर उनका हृदय डावाँडोल हो, उन्हें दुनिया की दुनियादारी अपनी ओर घसीट रही है और अगर उन्हें अपने उज्ज्वल भविष्य पर सन्देह है तो वे कृपा करके अपने हृदय पर हाथ रखकर अपने ही दिल से पूछें कि महात्मा गाँधी के प्रति उनके हृदय में कितना सम्मान है ? और, अगर महात्मा गाँधी के प्रति उनके हृदय में कोई सम्मान है, तो ... किसलिए ? क्या इसलिए कि वो बहुत दुबले-पतले हैं ? क्या इसलिए कि वे गाढ़े-गजी की वस्तुएँ व्यवहार में लाते हैं ? नहीं, यह और इस प्रकार की कोई भी बात नहीं है. इस बात को समझने के लिए ज़रा महात्मा गाँधी के जीवन इतिहास की ओर नज़र दौड़ाइये, उसकी तह तक जाइये, गोते-पर-गोते लगाइये; आपको मालूम होगा कि महात्मा गाँधी का ऐसे कठिन अवसर पर हमारे बीच अवतीर्ण होना हमारे समाज और हमारे देश के लिए कितना कल्याणप्रद है. यही उपयुक्त अवसर है कि जबकि हम या तो दो बल्ले में पल्ले पार हो जायेंगे या बीच धारा में डूब कर डुबकियाँ लगाते रह जायेंगे. . . . अधिक कहना फ़जूल है. आगा-पीछा छोड़ो. अपने

जिले के पीड़ित भाइयों की सेवा करने के लिए उठ खड़े हो. गाँव-गाँव और घर-
घर में स्वराज्य का शंख फूक दो . . . . यह आन्दोलन तुम्हारे लिए अमृतबटी है.
महात्मा गाँधी तुम्हारे सामने इसे पेश कर रहे हैं. यह तुम्हारी सूझ-बूझ और
दानिशमन्दी पर मुनहसर है कि तुम इसे ग्रहण करो या छोड़ दो. कम-से-कम
महात्मा गाँधी ने तो जो बीड़ा उठाया है उसे वो पूरा करके रहेंगे, पर कहीं ऐसा
न हो कि विजय के समय तुम यह कहते नज़र आओ कि—

जिन खोजा तिन पाइयाँ गहरे पानी पैठ,
मैं बौरी ढूँढन गई रही किनारे बैठ.

—स्वदेश, 6 फरवरी 1921

Appendix II

from NEPAL

Uska Bazar (Basti)

Thuthibari

Nautanwan

Nichlaul

R. Gandak

Bridgmanganj Stn.

Lehra Stn.

Dhani

MAHARAJGANJ

Siswa Stn.

Stn.

Khada

Pharenda Stn.

Ghughli Stn.

Little Gandak

Naurangia

Campierganj Stn.

Partawal

Peppeganj Stn.

Captainganj

Ramkola

PADRAUNA

Khalilabad

Pipraich

Paikauli

Pakri

Sandi

BASTI

from Basti

GORAKHPUR

Jagdispur

Keotali

HATA

Kasia

Mahua

Babhnauli

Tiwaripatti

Sahjanwa

Saraia

Turkaulia
or Sahibganj

Bhauapar

Chauri Chaura

Bakhra

Shahjahanpur

Gazipur

Taria Sujan

Unaula

BANSGAON

Gauri Bzr.

Tarkulwa

To Chapra

Dhakwa

Gagaha

Silhat

DEORIA

Dhuriapar

Rudarpur

R. Ghaghra

Gola

Bhatni Stn.

Bhatpar Stn.

Barhalganj

Chillupar

Gaura

Majhauli

To Chapra

Barhaj

Salempur

Sohanpur

Lar

	River
	Railway Line
	Unmetalled Road
	Metalled Road
	Tehsil Boundary

● Places from where volunteers came to Gorakhpur on 8 February 1921 to help with the organization of the meeting.

● Approximate locale of Gandhi-stories reported in *Swadesh*.

△ Places where lecturers were sent to announce the arrival of Gandhi.

Gorakhpur District, *circa* 1909

Notes to the Map

Legend

† Places where lecturers were sent to announce the arrival of Gandhi.
● Places from where volunteers came to Gorakhpur on 8 February 1921 to help with the organization of the meeting.
* Approximate locale of Gandhi-stories reported in *Swadesh*.

Note

This is a rough and tentative sketch map which makes no claim to be entirely accurate. Not all the unmetalled roads as they existed in 1921 have been shown. In a majority of cases it has been possible to locate the villages by checking place-names mentioned in *Swadesh* with the *Village Directory of the North-Western Provinces, xxi, Gorakhpur* (Allahabad, 1893), compiled by the Postmaster-General NWP. Where the village concerned does not appear in the district and tahsil maps, I have hypothetically situated it near the Post Office which served it. However, in spite of my best efforts I must inevitably have fallen into a degree of error in those instances where, for instance, the text does not mention either the tappa or the Post Office, especially if its name was identical with that of any other village or villages. However, it seems to me that even if the marking of villages from which a particular 'story' originated may not be cartographically accurate in all cases, a rough placement may be of some use in indicating the locale of a story and the territory generally traversed by a rumour. The geographical coverage of rumours outside Gorakhpur district has not been indicated, except by a rough marking for some of the places in Basti district.

Appendix III

Some 'extraordinary occurrences' in Gorakhpur,
1921, other than those ostensibly related to
Mahatma Gandhi.

Motif: *Opposing the Gandhian creed*

42. 'A Koiri of mauza Tandwa forcibly brought a woman to a village and kept her in his house. Far from reprimanding and punishing him the men of the village offered their congratulations. Consequently, the harvested crops of the villagers kept at a common threshing-floor caught fire and were reduced to ashes'.

43. 'Pandit Madho Shukl of Kakarahi village (tahsil Bansgaon) continued to eat meat despite the attempts by his family to dissuade him. One day a trunk kept between two others in the house caught fire. Seeing this his wife raised an alarm and people from the village rushed to the house. Now Panditji has promised not to touch meat again'.

44. 'In Sinhanjori village (PO Kasia) hundreds of live worms emerged out of the fish fried by Shankar Kandu. Seeing this the entire village has given up meat and fish (*mans-machli*)'.

45. 'In Kurabal village shit rained in the house of a Bari (caste of domestic servants) for a whole day, and he is now living in another's house. On enquiry he has confessed to his crime (*dosh*) of slaughtering a goat'.

46. 'A gentleman from mauza Patra (PO Pipraich) writes that people of the village had given up the practice of eating meat and fish. However, on the instigation of a *karinda* some people caught fish in a shallow ditch and ate it up. Since then an epidemic has spread here; ten people have been swallowed by death (*kaal ke graas ho gaye*) in five days'.

47. 'A Muslim toddy-tapper of Padrauna was told by a Master sahab to give up this practice. One day he fell down from the tree. As a result of this incident all the Muslims are giving up toddy-tapping'.

48. 'The building of the Punjab Sugar Mill, Ghughli was being constructed. On 4 March, a few of the *memars* (construction workers) went to the bazaar of the Mahant and despite the attempt by some people to prevent them, they bought fish and drank toddy. When they sat down at night to fry the fish their huts caught fire. They had to sleep out in the open, with dew falling on them. That very night it rained and hail fell as well. In the morning the news came that their homes had also caught fire. What could they do? Crying and repenting they went back to their respective homes'.

Motif: *Boons and Miracles*

49. 'In mauza Surdahi (PO Sahjanwa), a branch has come out at one end of a dead-and-cut pipal tree. Huge crowds are gathering at this sight'.
50. 'In Padrauna on 29 April, two new springs sprouted in a well three feet above the water level. Now the source of the spring has gone down because of the rise in the water level. For the past three days large crowds have been gathering at the site'.

Famine in Peasant Consciousness and Peasant Action: Madras 1876–8

DAVID ARNOLD

In India's recent history famine has occurred on so vast a scale, with such frequency and involved the loss of so many millions of lives that it has been impossible to ignore. Indeed few aspects of modern India have attracted such a voluminous and rapidly growing literature. And yet, in a fashion familiar from élitist approaches to other areas of India's history and society, peasant experience of dearth and famine has with rare exceptions been subordinated to the description of state policy and relief administration. That peasants in their millions were involved in famines could hardly be overlooked. But in reducing the peasants to arithmetical abstractions—statistics of mortality, the number of relief recipients, and so forth—the character of the peasants' own perception of famine and of their actions in response to it has largely been ignored. This neglect of the peasant or, more widely, subaltern domain of dearth and famine is not difficult to explain. Administrators, policy-makers and scholars, reacting to the immensity of human suffering and economic dislocation caused by famine, have sought to make it intelligible to themselves by trying to discover the causes of famine, to assess its social and economic effects and to suggest how it might be averted or its impact lessened in the future. In so doing they have imposed their own perceptions on our understanding of the human experience of famine. Peasant consciousness and peasant action, where they have impinged on the outsiders' awareness at all, have been regarded mainly in the light of inconvenient obstacles to the implementation of effective relief measures or the creation of a more satisfactorily famine-proof agricultural system.

A further discouragement to interest in subaltern attitudes and responses to famine has been the widely prevalent view that peasants are the passive, fatalistic and powerless victims of such a major disaster. They are thought of as having neither the will nor the capacity to resist or to lessen its onslaught. In part this view is simply a projection onto the famine situation of the common belief that peasants are, as a rule, inert and passive and that they have, in Barrington Moore's words, no alternative but to 'accept a society of whose working they are no more than victims'.[1] But the notion of peasants as famine victims has also acquired a more politically and culturally specific significance. As, over the course of the past 150 years or so, famine (like most major epidemic diseases) has come to be eliminated in the West and geographically regionalized in the Third World, so has it become in the eyes of the West (and of Western-oriented élites in Asia and Africa) a stigma of backwardness and inferiority. Famine, along with such diseases as cholera and smallpox, is associated with Europe's now distant past: that it should continue to afflict the Third World is perceived as a mark of the cultural obscurantism, technological inadequacy and political ineptitude of the countries affected. The West by contrast feels assured of its own superiority. The giving of famine relief aid has often exemplified this attitude, as was apparent even in the 1870s when substantial privately-donated funds first began to be sent from the West to famine 'victims' in India and China. In order to press their claims for funds upon the Western public, present-day relief agencies project an emotionally powerful image of what famine means—the matchstick limbs, the protruding ribs, the great sad eyes, the large and lolling head. This image serves to confirm and perpetuate the notion of powerless victims. It achieves a maximum emotional impact by presenting the famine-sufferer as an isolated individual (or at most an adult and a child) devoid of any social, cultural or political context: powerlessness and dependence upon outside aid is therefore seen to be absolute.

This essay does not presume to try to establish the causes or the long-term consequences of famine in India. Nor is it an account of state policy except in so far as that has a significant bearing on peasant attitudes and actions. The objective is to determine how peasants perceived and responded to the crisis created by drought, dearth and famine. The focus is on the South Indian famine of 1876–8 and, even

---

[1] Barrington Moore, *Social Origins of Dictatorship and Democracy: Lord and Peasant in the Making of the Modern World* (Harmondsworth, 1973), p. 204.

more narrowly, on the areas of the Madras Presidency affected: no attempt has been made to draw on material relating to the parts of the Bombay Presidency and the princely states of Hyderabad and Mysore that were also subject to the famine. Selecting a single famine episode may have certain disadvantages. Any one famine is bound to be untypical in various ways, including in its immediate causes, extent and duration. It might be contended too that examination of a single famine fails to take into account significant changes that were taking place over time, particularly through the advent of colonialism and the development of rural capitalism. These objections are not without validity. But in defence of the approach adopted here it can be said that concentrating upon a single event allows greater sensitivity to the complexities of a specific historical situation. It can be argued too that in peasant perceptions and responses one famine was in certain general respects much like another. This is borne out by the similarity of many of the beliefs and actions discussed here with those attributed to peasants not only in previous and subsequent Indian famines but also in famines in China, Africa and pre-industrial Europe.

The essay has a further objective—to use the crisis of the famine as a window onto subaltern consciousness and action. It might be objected that a famine is, by its very nature, untypical, a calamity that forces the suspension or dissolution of normal human activity and which is, therefore, unsuitable for this purpose. Instead, it might be argued, the need is to study the everyday life and material conditions of subaltern groups. This objection is largely unjustified. There is first of all a practical problem. Much of what peasants and other subalterns did and thought has passed unrecorded in any form and is therefore inaccessible. It is often only when, as in a famine or a rebellion, subaltern activities and beliefs entered élite discourse that some record, however patchy and partisan, becomes available. Secondly and from a theoretical standpoint more substantially, an event like a riot or a famine may tell us more about the reality of social relations and subaltern consciousness than everyday life. The repetition of day-to-day activities and the requirements of everyday survival tend to foster apparent acceptance and conformity to patterns of domination. A crisis like that constituted by a famine throws into sharper relief (for those involved as well as for outside observers like ourselves) loyalties, identities and conflicts obscured by the dust of daily existence. A crisis is a time of testing—of religious beliefs, of social relations and of institutions. Crises heighten social realities: they rarely negate them.

The Meaning of Famine

Definitions of famine abound, most of them centring on food scarcity leading to mass hunger and death.[2] It has sometimes been suggested that famine can be said to exist when the food intake of a substantial number of people has fallen below a specified calorific minimum. But by this criterion a large percentage of the population of India and elsewhere could be said to be almost permanently in a state of famine. While this might serve to dramatize the enduring problem of malnutrition, poverty and the maldistribution of food resources, it does not help to identify the specific nature of famine as it was generally known in India.

It has been common to identify famine further by referring to two main types of causation—natural and man-made—or to some combination of the two. In a characteristic statement of natural causation the Indian Famine Commission in its report of 1880 declared that the famines which periodically affected India were 'in all cases to be traced directly to the occurrence of seasons of unusual drought, the failure of customary rainfall leading to the failure of the food crops on which the subsistence of the population depends'.[3] The Madras government in its survey of the 1876–8 crisis attributed famines in general to 'a complete or very extensive and general failure of food or water, or both, over a very large area of the country'.[4] The colonial regime also came to recognize the possibility of 'price famines' in which human agency was the main cause in forcing up prices beyond the paying capacity of would-be customers, even though there might be adequate food stocks in reserve. War, conquest, political upheaval and administrative mismanagement have also been included among the man-made causes of the onset or intensification of famine.

One can go beyond this conventional two-fold classification of famine to suggest that it was inherent in the nature of peasant society. Because peasants as a rule did not possess any substantial reserves or resources, they were necessarily poorly equipped to protect themselves from flood, drought and other environmental calamities. As a subordinate class they were denied, through the exploitation and depredations of superordinate groups, the chance to establish more than a slender margin of subsistence. Colonial rule, as in India, might

[2] For a recent review of famine definitions, see William A. Dando, *The Geography of Famine* (London, 1980), pp. 57–65.

[3] *Report of the Indian Famine Commission*, Pt. 1 (Cmd. 2591) (London, 1880), p. 7.

[4] [Government of Madras] *Review of the Madras Famine, 1876–1878* (Madras, 1881), p. 73.

further weaken the peasant's capacity to cope with natural disasters by enhancing tax demands or promoting the cultivation of cash rather than subsistence crops. A blight, a flood, a drought or a war might provide the immediate cause for a famine, but the underlying reasons lay deep in the social, economic and political subordination of the peasantry.

Some writers on dearth and famine introduce a further factor into their discussion, identifying in panic a subjective element to set alongside the objective fact of diminished rainfall or blighted harvest. In colonial phraseology the term 'panic' was used to signify supposedly irrational and irresponsible behaviour on the part of subaltern groups. It often in fact indicated the observer's own incomprehension or served to register his disapproval. But shorn of its imputation of subaltern irrationality the notion of panic is of some use in reminding us of the acute tension and sense of crisis that accompanied the arrival, or even threat, of famine. Richard Cobb has drawn attention to this aspect of dearth and famine in late eighteenth and early nineteenth century France, though he wavers uncertainly between identifying it as the excessive volatility of the lower classes and their legitimate alarm. Hence at one point he asserts that 'the fear of dearth was permanent, especially at the lower levels of society, and it took very little at any time for this fear to become hysterical and to develop into the proportions of panic'. But elsewhere he comments that the fear of dearth was a 'central theme in all forms of popular political expression. Nor were the common people living solely in a world of myth and panic fear; for dearth and famine were in fact the greatest single threat to their existence . . .'[5] In India the perennial problem of subsistence for the poor was intensified by the extreme dependence of agriculture on the arrival of adequate monsoon rains. The consequences of even a few weeks' delay or a partial failure of the monsoon were well-known from experience. It was not therefore from blind and irrational panic that the prospect of drought and dearth caused alarm and generated such widespread suspicion, anxiety and fear.

If famine is to be classed as a species of disaster, it was disaster of a peculiar kind. It did not usually come entirely without warning, as might an earthquake or tidal wave. Often as in 1876–7 famine was the cumulative result of a run of poor harvests, during which time

[5] R. C. Cobb, *The Police and the People: French Popular Protest, 1789–1820* (London, 1970), pp. xvii–xviii, 215.

anxiety steadily mounted. Nor was famine a socially indiscriminate catastrophe (few in practice are!). It was highly selective, felling the rural poor with its double-edged axe of starvation and disease, but leaving many of the richer villagers and town-dwellers relatively unscathed. Indeed there were many among the latter who prospered from the high prices and acute shortages. Famine was not the great leveller. It tended on the contrary to accentuate social and economic divisions.

Famine also informed peasant consciousness in other ways and at other levels of perception. Hindu myths and legends, like those of many other peasant and tribal societies, made frequent reference to drought and famine as the cause of severe trials for kings, sages and common people. They were linked too with the cataclysm that was to engulf the world at the end of the corrupt Kali Age and, through the arrival of Kalki, the final incarnation of Vishnu, would usher in a new Golden Age.[6] The memory of past famines was deeply entrenched in the collective consciousness of the Indian peasantry. They were too awesome and significant to readily forget. A particularly severe famine in the Deccan in 1396 was long remembered as Durgadevi, a title that recalled its heavy mortality by associating it with the destructive power of the goddess Durga.[7] Inhabitants at Ongole in coastal Andhra in 1876 remembered the famine forty years earlier when 'men ate men'.[8] Because famines and other major disasters were such conspicuous landmarks in peasant experience they served as a folk calendar, a series of markers stretching back into the distant past by which other events could be ordered and recalled. The threat of famine stirred up these ancient fears and folk memories and imbued them with fresh meaning and vitality.

For the peasants therefore famine was both an extension and intensification of familiar anxieties and hardships, and an event charged with exceptional religious significance and destructive potency. Peasant attitudes and actions were a product of the complex interplay of these two sometimes opposing but more often mutually reinforcing elements.

[6] Wendy Doniger O'Flaherty, *The Origins of Evil in Hindu Mythology* (Berkeley, 1976), pp. 35–40, 291–5; cf. Stephen P. Cohen and C. V. Raghavulu, *The Andhra Cyclone of 1977: Individual and Institutional Responses to Mass Death* (New Delhi, 1979), pp. 1–2.

[7] A. Appadorai, *Economic conditions in Southern India (1000–1500 A.D.)* (Madras, 1936), Vol. 2, pp. 748–9.

[8] Emma R. Clough, *While Sewing Sandals* (London, 1899), p. 272. Clough gives the date as 1836 but presumably the 'Guntur' famine of 1833–4 was the one remembered.

Famine was no stranger to Madras. In the course of the previous 150 years there had been several major famines—in 1729–33, 1781–2, 1807, 1833–4, 1854, 1866—and more were to follow in the quarter century after 1878. Few areas of the province were wholly immune, though the failure of the monsoon rains was least common (and thus famine least likely) in the west coast districts of Malabar and South Kanara. The inland belt from Tirunelveli district in the extreme south of Tamil Nadu to Krishna in Andhra had the lowest average rainfall—30 to 40 inches—and was most vulnerable to famine. In good years however these 'dry' districts produced commercial cash crops like cotton, sugar and indigo, as well as the millets *ragi, cholam* and *cambu* that formed the staple foodgrains of the area.

The famine of 1876–8 had its immediate origins in a series of deficient monsoons. The middle and late 1870s appear to have been a period of widespread rainfall irregularity with droughts and famines occurring as far apart as Brazil, Morocco and northern China. In Madras difficulties began in 1875 when half the districts in the province suffered a partial failure of the southwest monsoon. In normal years this brought rain to most areas between June and September, and provided the water needed for the year's main grain crop. Late rain in August and September saved cultivators from more acute distress in 1875, but the low yield left stocks depleted for the following year. When the south-west monsoon of 1876 failed (except on the west coast and in the far northeast) signs of hardship and distress were soon apparent. By July and August reports of drought conditions were reaching the government from Bellary, Cuddapah and Kurnool, the three driest and most vulnerable of the interior districts. In many years the northeast monsoon, falling between October and December and heaviest along the eastern seaboard, gave cultivators a second crop or, if the first monsoon had failed, a second chance. But it too failed in 1876. 1877 at first promised no better, and only with satisfactory rains in September and October did the drought end and the famine begin to wane.

The 1876–8 famine was unusually widespread as well as exceptionally persistent. Of the 21 Madras districts, 14 were badly affected: they represented 83,000 square miles and (according to the 1871 Census) a population of 19 million. It was officially estimated that at least 3.5 million people died in the famine in Madras.

If the famine-affected areas of Bombay, Hyderabad and Mysore are included as well the tally was a loss of more than 5.25 million lives.[9]

The Rites of Drought and Famine

In the official mind famine began when its existence could no longer be denied and when its effects could be empirically demonstrated and quantified—by the inches of rain that had fallen, by the percentage of crops that had withered and died, by the price of grain in the bazaars. Peasants, however, did not wait for such empirical confirmation of their fears before they began to show alarm and respond to the prospect of drought and famine.

Vernacular prognostics and proverbs gave abundant expression to peasant anxieties about the season and crop prospects. Some were reassuring: 'If it rains in Chittirai [the Tamil month April–May] you may till with a golden ploughshare', promised one; 'If there is rain in Aruda [the Telugu astral period 23 June to 4 July]', advised another, 'there will be no scarcity'. But others urged caution: 'Wait till Kartigai [the Tamil month November–December] to sell your grain', or were grimly foreboding, 'If there is no rain in Chitta [the Telugu astral 9–22 October], even an ant will suffer from the heat', and even more starkly, 'If the sky fails, the earth will fail'. Astrological signs and conjunctions were also used to predict the wheather—'If Jupiter sets at the rising of Venus, there will be rain'—or to foretell disasters. More immediate auguries were insects, birds, animals and plants. Dragonflies were a portent of rain; tamarinds were supposedly plentiful in a good year, mangoes in a bad one. Familiarity with the annual cycle of the monsoons bred an acute appreciation of the importance of their timing: 'Rain will cease after the lamp-lighting festival in Kartigai [November–December]', ran another Tamil saying.[10] Outsiders might dismiss such agricultural predictions as mere superstition. Certainly some contradicted others or drew

---

[9] *Report of the Indian Famine Commission*, Pt. 1, p. 28. For a recent study of the famine and its demographic effects, see Roland Lardinois, 'La Famine de 1876–1878 en Inde du Sud: Étude des Conséquences Démographiques d'une Crise de Subsistence sur le Mouvement et la Structure d'une Population', unpublished thesis, Institute de Démographie, Paris, 1980.

[10] *Tamil Sayings on Agriculture* (Department of Land Records and Agriculture: bulletin no. 34) (Madras, 1896), pp. 33–47; C. Benson, *A Collection of Telugu Sayings and Proverbs bearing on Agriculture* (Department of Agriculture: bulletin no. 22) (Madras, 1891), pp. 181–99.

improbable conclusions from chance connections. But, as some colonial officials admitted, they were based on generations of experience and observation, and peasants were often remarkably successful at predicting the weather.[11]

But peasant expectations and attitudes concerning the weather and crops had to do with more than observation and inherited wisdom. For the peasants religion was an essential and integral part of their everyday lives; it also mediated between themselves and those forces, for good and evil, that appeared to lie beyond their control. The arrival of timely and adequate rains, the fertility of the soil, and the abundance of the harvest were matters determined more by divine disposition than human skill or endeavour. Extreme dependence upon the monsoon and the unpredictability of the seasons and crops made the belief in capricious, vengeful or neglectful deities all the more compelling. Peasants sought to ward off malevolent forces and secure the blessings of beneficent ones by saying prayers and performing appropriate rituals before commencing important agricultural operations such as ploughing and harvesting. They also participated in the annual cycle of village and local festivals, many of which (like Pongal, falling shortly after the year's main harvest) were closely linked with the agrarian calendar.[12]

Drought, famine and related disasters like cholera, smallpox, or crop blight might be attributed to a failure to perform the normal rites and celebrations correctly, or to the sinfulness of individuals and whole villages. Peasants in the neighbourhood of Hampi, an important festival centre in Bellary, attributed the drought of 1876–7 to the failure of pilgrims at the annual celebration in March 1876 to pull the main temple car or to draw even the smaller one more than half-way round its customary circuits.[13] Coimbatore's Hindus were said to ascribe their distress to the displeasure of the local goddess.[14] 'As to the cause of the famine', wrote a representative of the London Missionary Society in Salem in 1877, 'there are various opinions prevalent, but they all agree in attributing it to some kind of

[11] Arthur F. Cox, *A Manual of the North Arcot District* (Madras, 1881), p. 319.

[12] Brenda E. F. Beck, *Peasant Society in Konku: A study of Right and Left Subcastes in South India* (Vancouver, 1972), pp. 52–5.

[13] V. Venkatachellum Pantulu, Deputy Collector, to Collector, Bellary, 17 Apr. 1877, G[overnment] O[rder] 622, Public, 3 May 1877. All archival sources cited in this essay are located in the India Office Records, London.

[14] *Madras Standard*, 28 Feb. 1877, p. 2f.

sin'.[15] Some villagers identified causes that were apparently without direct religious connotations, such as a perceived decline in the soil's productivity in recent years. But others linked divine causation to their own unease at the technological, ecological and administrative changes and innovations associated with British rule. The Americans of the Madura Mission heard the famine attributed to the disturbing effect of the survey department's operations and to the railway which had stopped the rain by 'the skies taking fright at the thundering noises of the locomotive'.[16] Telegraph wires and recent forest clearing were also blamed.[17]

Interesting though these sentiments are as indicators of peasants' suspicion of (and indirect antipathy to) colonialism, it was probably more common for drought and other disasters to be attributed to the intrinsic nature of the deities, particularly the villages goddesses Whitehead describes.[18] It was their *dharma* to spread disease and affliction from time to time; once aroused, their appetite for human lives could only be satiated by offering sacrifices and performing special ceremonies. Thus the initial response of the villagers to the onset of drought or the visitation of cholera was not the fatalistic inertia Western observers often attributed to them but, on the contrary, the active performance of rites and rituals to satisfy the deities' wrath or hunger and so bring an end to the period of sickness and suffering. Not to act in this way was likely to invite still greater calamities. Thus although the relationship of villagers to their gods was clearly thought of as one of extreme subordination, the villagers were not wholly incapable of influencing their own destiny. Through their ceremonies, prayers and devotion they hoped to assuage the deities' malevolence and move them to relent. There existed an expectation of divine response,[19] an expectation which had, as will be seen subsequently, close parallels in other subordinate/superordinate relations in the famine situation. Interpreting the ultimate cause of drought and famine in religious terms thus not only enabled the peasants to give the disaster a meaning intelligible to themselves, but

[15] 'Report of the London Mission, Salem, 1877', p. 8, in *Reports of the Stations in Connection with the South India District Committee of the London Missionary Society, 1877* (Madras, 1878).

[16] *Madras Standard*, 27 Apr. 1877, p. 2d.

[17] Cox, p. 315.

[18] Henry Whitehead, *The Village Gods of South India* (2nd edn., Calcutta, 1921).

[19] Cf. Susan Wadley, 'Power in Hindu Ideology and Practice', in Kenneth David (ed.), *The New Wind: Changing Identities in South Asia* (The Hague, 1977), p. 143.

also provided them with appropriate cultural responses through which they could seek to end their affliction.

Village religiosity was matched initially by village solidarity and collective self-mobilization. Because drought was seen as a threat to the village as a whole the response to it had to come from the village collectively, regardless of caste and differences of economic standing. Moses noted that in the Ceded Districts (Bellary, Kurnool and Cuddapah) all agrarian castes—from the Kapus, the leading peasant caste, down to the Malas, untouchable labourers—participated in rain-making ceremonies.[20] These rites were organized by the villagers themselves, sometimes helped by donations from wealthier households, and a perambulation of the village, calling at each house in turn, was commonly made by a procession of women and children. The participation of women was significant as it gave symbolic expression to the association of human fertility with that of nature and to *shakti*, the principle of female energy that gave the village goddesses their potency. Water and creatures associated with water, particularly frogs, also featured prominently in these village ceremonies.

Moses describes how in Bellary women tied a live female frog to a winnowing-fan (in this context presumably symbolic of the grain harvest) and almost covered it with the sacred leaves of the margosa tree. The fan and frog were then taken in procession by women and children singing 'Mother frog should have her bath. The tanks are all full [ironic in view of the drought]. Give water, O Rain God!' At each house the procession stopped for a woman of the household to bring out water, mixed with a little turmeric, to pour over the frog. The ceremony was performed with variations in most parts of the Presidency. In Vishakhapatnam the women's chant was 'Lady frog must have her bath. O Rain God, give a little water for her at least'. In other places the unfortunate frog was suspended or tortured so that its pitiful cries would move the god, variously described as Indra or Varuna, to relent and send down rain.[21]

Other rain-making ceremonies of which there are accounts from Madras and elsewhere in India made use of sympathetic magic. Idols were washed and the water run off into the fields in emulation of the deities' customary watering of the fields with rain. Tom-toms were beaten loudly to simulate the thunder clouds that would bring the

[20] S. T. Moses, 'Frog Folk-lore', *Quarterly Journal of the Mythic Society*, 30: 1 (July 1939), p. 18.   [21] Ibid., pp. 17–19.

monsoon showers. Children, especially girls, their hair loosened, danced and whirled, perhaps in imitation of torrential rain.[22] Some rituals were intended to shame or to provoke the gods into sending rain. Mock ploughing ceremonies were held with women instead of men to wash and hold the plough. The reversal of normal sex roles again reflected the female fertility motif and, by stressing the abnormality of the drought situation, it was hoped that the gods would be moved to relent. This can be seen in a Bihari women's song addressed to the Rain God:

> A wonder has taken place, O Lord!
> The male is grinding millet and the female is ploughing fields.
> Is not your heart moved with pity, O God!
> The widow Brahmani is ploughing the field.[23]

When these rites failed to bring results villagers might turn to cursing and slandering the gods so that they would be provoked into sending rain.[24]

Village rain-making rites expressed a collective recognition of the threatening crisis of drought and famine and the need for collective action. But peasants also expected the *sarkar* (the state) or the local zamindar (landed proprietor) to arrange and pay for the holding of special ceremonies. During the early colonial period officials of the English East India Company complied with these expectations. The ceremonies were accepted as part of the customary responsibilities of government the British had inherited; they also saw practical advantages in complying. The Collector of Tirunelveli paid 600 'chucrums' in December 1811 for rain-making ceremonies to be performed in the principal temples of the district 'with the view of inspiring the people with confidence and encouring them to proceed with their preparations for cultivation . . .'[25] In the same month Cuddapah's Collector paid 150 star pagodas for rain-making ceremonies 'with a view of satisfying the ryots [*raiyats*: peasants] and convincing them that the Sirkar is not an indifferent spectator of the present calamity'.[26] By the

---

[22] J. Abbott, *The Keys of Power: A Study of Indian Ritual and Belief* (London, 1932), pp. 342, 347–8.

[23] Piyush Kanti Mahapatra, 'Rain-compelling Ceremonies in West Bengal', *Indian Folk-Lore*, 1: 3 (July-Sept. 1958), p. 79.   [24] Ibid., p. 78; Abbott, p. 347.

[25] James Hepburn, Collector, Tirunelveli, to Board Revenue, 10 Dec. 1811, extract Board of Revenue Proceedings (hereafter BRP), 19 Dec. 1811, India Office Records, Board's Collections, F/4/383.

[26] C. R. Ross, Collector, Cuddapah, to Board of Revenue, 3 Dec. 1811, extract BRP, 9 Dec. 1811, ibid.

1870s however the colonial state had long abandoned such responsibilities. Whether the peasants resented this is not recorded, but there
were complaints from other Hindus that the British were neglecting
an ancient and important duty.[27]

The persistence of drought and famine despite these rites and
ceremonies could be explained in terms of a failure to perform them
properly or by the intensity of the deities' displeasure. More ceremonies might be called for; but in some instances a crisis like that of
1876–8 might severely test the villagers' traditional beliefs and open
them to the persuasions of another faith. Writing from a mission
station in Bellary in January 1877 the Reverend Edwin Lewis reported
that the local weavers, already hard-hit by the decline of their markets
before the drought, now went into 'most violent tirade against the
god who had been so merciless, so untrustworthy, as to send them
this great distress'. This was the first time he said he had heard
Hindus, 'suffer what they may, abuse their god'.[28] Perhaps Lewis
was witnessing little more than the kind of ritual cursing and abusing
of deities already described and not a genuine loss of faith. But other
missionaries in the famine districts also reported what they saw (not
without hope for their own religion) as the 'bewilderment' of villagers
at the unresponsiveness of the heavens.[29]

The 1876–8 famine marked the beginning of a mass conversion
movement among Madiga and Mala untouchable labourers in the
southern Telugu districts. It has been argued that this movement had
its origins before the famine in the changing ideas and attitudes of the
untouchables to their position of extreme subordination in rural
society: the impact of colonialism and missionary activity may have
encouraged the Madigas and Malas to question their customary roles.
But the famine seems to have provided the essential impetus through
the failure or inability of higher castes to help the labourers in their
distress, and the contrasting readiness of the English and American
missionaries to do so.[30] According to census reports the number of

[27] 'Report of the London Mission, Salem, 1877', p. 9.
[28] 'Report of the London Mission, Bellary', p. 16, in *Reports on the Stations in
Connection with the South India District Committee of the London Missionary Society,
1876* (Bangalore, 1877).
[29] E. G., 'Report of the London Mission, Belgaum, 1876', pp. 6–7, in ibid.; 'Report
of the London Mission, Salem, 1877', pp. 8–9 in *Reports . . . . 1877*.
[30] Clough, pp. 271–95. For a recent interpretation, see Duncan B. Forrester, 'The
Depressed Classes and Conversion to Christianity, 1860–1960', in Geoffrey A. Oddie
(ed.), *Religion in South Asia: Studies in Conversion and Revival Movements in
Medieval and Modern Times* (London, 1977), pp. 41–8.

the Indian Christians in Nellore rose from 3,012 in 1871 to 20,794 in 1881, and in Kurnool from 3,855 to 11,464. There were significant but not such spectacular increases in other famine districts.[31] Not all those converted remained attached to the Church after the famine. The 1891 Census suggested that 'many of those converted during the [1876–8] famine gave only such allegiance to their new faith as would secure them the material advantages which the missionaries were able and willing to offer'; as grain prices returned to normal, the initial material incentives lost their attraction.[32] But a great many of the famine converts remained Christians. The crisis had brought about a lasting severance from their old religion.

Divisions within the Peasantry

As fears of famine grew, village solidarity began to break down. While ultimate responsibility for the drought and distress continued to be laid at the feet of unappeased deities, human culpability for exploiting the situation and profiting from the hardship of others assumed more and more importance, especially in the minds of subordinate villagers. One of the first and most significant lines of division that opened up was between the peasant proprietors or raiyats and their landless labourers.

Only about a fifth of the Madras Presidency in the 1870s lay under zamindari estates. Where these were to be found, especially in Nellore, North Arcot and Madurai, within the famine zone, distressed raiyats addressed their pleas for remissions and requests for loans to the zamindars. But over most of the province and over the greater part of the famine tract of 1876–8 the *raiyatwari* (ryotwari) system prevailed. This brought the raiyats into direct subordination to the state to the exclusion of zamindars and other intermediaries. In consequence the critical agrarian relationship in the raiyatwari areas was not between landlord and tenant, but between peasants, i.e. between those who held their own land titles (*pattas*) and paid their revenue directly to the state, and the subordinate labourers who were largely landless and possessed no such relationship to the state. Contemporary official sources referred to these two classes as 'ryots' and 'coolies'; today we might prefer to describe the one as middle and rich peasants and the other as poor peasants or simply landless labourers.

[31] *Census of India, 1881: Madras* (Madras, 1883), Vol. I, p. 45.
[32] *Census of India, 1891: Madras* (Madras, 1893), Vol. XIII, p. 69.

In some respects this is a rather crude categorization of a complex and locally varying agrarian system. It does not adequately take into account the position of sharecroppers or of those who in other ways straddled the line between 'ryot' and 'coolie'. But the distinction was supported not only by economic activity and relationship to the land and the state, but also by caste. The raiyats belonged to Sudra peasant castes—such as the Vellalas and Kapus—that stood high in the local caste hierarchy and which through their numbers, economic strength and political power generally constituted the dominant village stratum. By contrast the labourers were drawn either from low-ranking caste Hindus such as the Vanniyars (Pallis) and Kaikolans (who were weavers as well as labourers), or from untouchable castes like the Tamil Paraiyas and Pallars and the Telugu Malas and Madigas. The division was not absolute but relatively few of the main peasant castes were to be found below the line and even fewer of the low castes and untouchables above it. Villages also included members of artisan and service castes (such as weavers, fishermen, potters and washermen), but many of these were also part-time labourers or petty cultivators and fell broadly within the poor peasant-labourer category. Calculations of the size of the 'coolie class' varied, but it was generally estimated that in most dry districts agricultural labourers formed between a third and a quarter of the rural population. The apparent slenderness of the dividing line between the two peasant classes was emphasized by the smallness of many raiyat holdings. In Kurnool district on the eve of the 1876–8 famine roughly a third of the 914,000 inhabitants were classed as labourers. But of the 85,000 raiyats some 50,000 (nearly 60 per cent) had holdings of six acres or less and only 4,000 held lands that could be termed 'very considerable'.[33] It would seem however that even raiyats with relatively small holdings made some use, if only during the harvest season, of non-family labour. A survey of Coimbatore district forty years earlier indicated that 60 per cent of the raiyats cultivated their own lands: the rest used hired labour.[34]

[33] 'Memorandum on Kurnool District', *Correspondence between the Secretary of State for India and the Government of India on the Subject of the Threatened Famine in Western and Southern India*, Pt. 2 (Cmd. 1754), (London, 1877), p. 34.

[34] 'Replies to the Governor-General Lord William Bentinck's Queries respecting the Ryotwar System of Revenue Administration', Sept. 1834, p. 10, India Office Records V/27/310/40.

The division between 'ryots' and 'coolies' was further expressed through the former's firm conviction that it would be degrading for them to perform manual labour in the service of others. So strong was the raiyats' antipathy to 'coolie' labour that, even at the height of the 1876–8 famine when all but the wealthiest were suffering the effects of drought and food shortages, many refused to undertake labouring work on public relief schemes. An official was told by village headmen in South Arcot in October 1876 that 'under no circumstances would a putta [patta] ryot come forward to work for cooly [hire] in the road or tank. He would rather incur debts and keep himself up'.[35] Two months later the Collector also noted that 'in this district the poorest puttahdar [*pattadar*, patta-holder] considers it disgraceful to work for hire at earthwork, even to keep himself alive'. Some professed that they 'did not understand such work, being cultivators'.[36] South Arcot's raiyats were not alone in their aversion. By contrast peasant proprietors took great pride in their ownership and cultivation of the land. Vernacular sayings extolled the virtues of living by tillage rather than by service for others. Some celebrated leading peasant castes by name, as in one that proclaimed, 'A Vellala is a proper husbandman'. Conversely proverbs sneered at the labouring castes' landlessness and lack of agricultural expertise.[37]

Possession of land and control of labour were primary factors in the raiyats' dominance over the labourers. In times of hardship land could be sold or, more often, mortgaged or used as security for a loan. Other than this labour the field hand had virtually nothing to sell or use to raise a loan, and demand for his labour was one of the first casualties of drought and incipient famine. In the 1870s most tied farm servants (*pannaiyals* in Tamil) and hired labourers (*patiyals*) were paid in grain, the quantity varying with place, time and seasonal demand.[38] Permanent hands might also receive a small plot of land as a hut site and to grow a few grains or vegetables of their own. But this did little to lesson the labourer's dependence on the raiyat's grain payments and indeed served as a reminder of the labourer's obligations

---

[35] C. Sribaliah, Deputy Collector, to Collector, S. Arcot, 14 Oct. 1876, BRP 2685, 27 Oct. 1876.

[36] J. H. Garstin, to Sec., Board of Revenue, 18 Dec. 1876, BRP 3340, 30 Dec. 1876.

[37] *Tamil Sayings on Agriculture*, pp. 23–7.

[38] For details, see C. Benson, *An Account of the Kurnool District* (Madras, 1889), p. 116; Cox, p. 319; F. A. Nicholson, *Manual of the Coimbatore District* (Madras, 1887), pp. 270–1.

to the raiyat. In similar fashion the raiyat also gave advances of grain to help the labourer survive the dry season and trifling presents on ceremonial occasions and festival days.

The relationship of agrarian labourers to peasant proprietors and landlords is now often expressed in terms of 'reciprocity' and seen as part of a rural 'moral economy'. It is held that rural 'patrons' accepted a moral obligation to assist their 'clients' in times of hardship and distress. However according to this view in years of extreme drought and crop failure the leading raiyats and landlords were themselves too hard hit to be able to provide for the subsistence needs of the poor: the mechanism of reciprocity was accordingly suspended until the return of more normal conditions.[39]

The reciprocity and moral economy argument as it is applied to peasant societies is an attempt to deny the relevance of class identities and class conflict to agrarian relations in Asia until a very recent date.[40] But it fails to look deeply enough at the underlying relationship between different sections of rural society or to examine critically enough the way in which the relationship was perceived by the 'clients'. There was no reciprocity in any meaningful sense because the relationship was founded on inequality between the two sides. It was a relationship of superordination and subordination, not of mutual and equal exchange. The interest of the 'patron', whether peasant proprietor or landlords, was in securing and retaining for his own use the labour and other services of the poor peasant, labourer or artisan, or in other ways (socially and culturally as well as materially) demonstrating his superior power over other villagers. It was a relationship of power, of command and control. This was recognized by Crole in the 1870s while discussing the practice of landlords and rich peasants in Chingleput of advancing loans to their labourers: 'The master is quite willing to pay this, as he thereby gets the labourer into the clutches of debt, which prevents his leaving his service, and which is increased by further loans on the occasion of marriages or

---

[39] James C. Scott, *The Moral Economy of the Peasant: Rebellion and Subsistence in Southeast Asia* (New Haven, 1976); Paul R. Greenough, 'Indian Famines and Peasant Victims: The Case of Bengal in 1943–44', *Modern Asian Studies*, 14:2 (Apr. 1980), pp. 205–35; Scarlett Epstein, 'Productive Efficiency and Customary Systems of Rewards in Rural South India', in Raymond Firth (ed.), *Themes in Economic Anthropology* (London, 1967), pp. 229–52.

[40] Note, for example, Greenough's concluding remarks, p. 235, and Scott's earlier article, 'Patron-Client Politics and Political Change in Southeast Asia', *American Political Science Review*, 66:1 (Mar. 1972), p. 91

deaths in the labourer's family'.[41] It is also indicative of the nature of raiyat-labourer relations that as late as 1918 the present of cloth given to labourers at the Pongal festival was known to the donors as 'slave money'.[42] There is not much evidence here of a sense of reciprocity among the rural élite.

For their part the labourers had little choice but to recognize their dependence on the raiyats, but that did not mean that they were without certain expectations from those who held power over them or entirely without the ability to remind the raiyats, from time to time, of those expectations. One expression of this took a ritualized, but not for that reason any the less significant, form. It was reported from Chingleput in the late eighteenth and early nineteenth centuries that at the beginning of the agricultural year in June-July the Paraiya labourers collectively withdrew from the fields until the raiyats had made promises of good treatment and customary payments. The agreement was then sealed by the labourers' acceptance of betel from the raiyats.[43] Such episodes serve to remind us that labourers and raiyats were not unaware of their different, often divergent, interests, but that there were certain recognized forms and customary exchanges through which direct confrontation was avoided and economic and social antagonism mediated and contained.

In a situation like that of 1876 where crop failure and famine appeared imminent many raiyats were tempted to abandon these customary relationships. Their self-interest lay in not employing or feeding labourers for whom they had no work. There does not appear to be anything particularly new about such a response—it can be seen in many earlier famines in the region—though it may have been encouraged by a growing capitalistic attitude among wealthier raiyats to regard labour as merely a commodity to be hired or dispensed with as required. But the employment of tied labourers in particular often reached back many generations in the same families, and such ties were not lightly discarded in village society. Future labour requirements after the drought and famine had also to be

[41] Charles Stewart Crole, *Chingleput: A Manual* (Madras, 1879), p. 50.

[42] Benedicte Hjejle, 'Slavery and Agricultural Bondage in South India in the Nineteenth Century', *Scandinavian Economic History Review* 15: 1–2 (1967), p. 123.

[43] Lionel Place, Collector of the Jagir (Chingleput), to President, Board of Revenue, 6 Oct. 1795, extract BRP, 25 Jan. 1796, Board's Collection, India Office Records, F/4/31/854; see also Eugene F. Irschick, 'Peasant Survival Strategies and Rehearsals for Rebellion in Eighteenth-Century South India', *Peasant Studies*, 9: 4 (Summer 1982), p. 237.

considered. The raiyats' response was therefore at first a mixed and
uncertain one, hardening as conditions deteriorated. Some raiyats
took to cultivating their fields themselves rather than pay labourers
to assist them.[44] But others not wishing to narrow their options too
soon continued until the end of 1876 to pay out small doles to the tied
labourers to keep them alive and on hand in case work in the fields
became possible. In Madurai district where thousands of unemployed
labourers were already corssing to Sri Lanka in search of work,
raiyats were paying farm servants 'a pittance to prevent their
emigration'.[45] Others ádopted a different expedient, paying labourers
either a lower grain wage than was usual to keep their services or a
cash sum instead of grain. This conserved the raiyat's own grain stock
but, with prices in the bazaars rising rapidly, it bought the labourer
only a fraction of the normal grain equivalent.[46]

Where agricultural prospects appeared completely hopeless raiyats
seem to have no compunction about withdrawing their support from
farm labourers. Paraiyas in Chingleput in January 1877 were said to
have been 'turned off with a little food by the ryots who could no
longer support them'.[47] In Guntur taluk, Krishna district, untouchable
labourers were told by caste villagers in November 1876 that their
services were no longer needed and the sooner they left the village the
better.[48] The action of the state may also have had an effect in
encouraging this casting off of rural labour. Once relief works were
opened in a locality the raiyats stopped any doles they might have
been giving and directed the labourers to seek their subsistence from
the state until the famine was over. Village headmen sometimes urged
officials to open relief works with this objective specifically in mind.[49]

The labourers and poorer villagers generally did not accept this
self-interested response on the part of the village élite without

[44] 'Memorandum on North Arcot', *Correspondence . . . on the Famine in Western
and Southern India*, Pt. 3 (Cmd. 1879) (London, 1877), p. 232 Major E. W. Shaw,
Special Relief Officer, to Collector, N. Arcot, 27 Apr. 1878, G.O. 1124, Revenue
(Famine) (hereafter Rev. (Fam.)), 15 May 1878.

[45] F. A. Nicholson, Head Assistant Collector, to Collector, Madurai, 25 Nov.
1876, BRP 3040, 1 Dec. 1876.

[46] C. J. Crosthwaite, Subcollector, to Collector, Bellary, 29 Sept. 1876, BRP 2486,
2 Oct. 1876.

[47] 'Memorandum on Chingleput', *Correspondence on . . . the Famine*, Pt. 3, p. 42.

[48] *Madras Times*, 30 Nov. 1876, p. 2e. A *taluk* is an administrative sub division of a
district.

[49] C. Sribaliah, Deputy Collector, to Collector, S. Arcot, 14 Oct. 1876, BRP 2685,
27 Oct. 1876.

complaint, especially when they knew that raiyats and traders had large quantities of grain stored in their houses and grain pits. The raiyats' action ran counter to the labourers' perception of the collective character of the subsistence crisis and of the raiyats' responsibilities towards them. Visiting villages in the Jammalamadugu taluk of northwest Cuddapah in early September 1876, an Indian Deputy Collector was approached by labourers protesting at the withholding of grain from them by raiyats and Komatis (Telugu traders). He arrived at the hamlet of Chinna Venuthurla the day after labourers had tried to loot grain from a Komati, but managed to persuade a raiyat to open his grain store to feed needy villagers. The Deputy Collector remarked that the raiyats were most reluctant to feed the labourers who had also ceased to be able to obtain grain on credit.[50] Similar observations were made about other villages. Yedavalli in Kurnool district was reputedly a relatively rich village for the dry zone, producing twice as much grain as was needed to feed all its inhabitants. But the rich raiyats, fearing famine, refused to help the poorer villagers and buried their grain 'in very deep holes on account of fear of robbers'. This caused the Head Assistant Collector to observe that Yedavalli was a village 'divided against itself; those who have resources prey upon those who have none, and will not give any assistance when relief works are started'.[51]

The famine crisis thus quickly produced a deepening division between raiyats and labourers, but it was a division that reflected their separate class interests. Few raiyats appear to have felt any obligations, moral or otherwise, to feed those for whom they had no employment. On the contrary their response was to conserve as much grain as they could for their own consumption. By discarding the labourers they shifted much of the initial burden of famine from their shoulders onto those of the subordinate class. But the raiyats themselves were not entirely free agents and their response to the onset of drought and famine was in turn affected by other classes, by the state and by their own customary outlook and practices.

Almost alone among recent writers on famine in India, Morris D. Morris has argued that peasants' responses to frequent drought and famine have been not passivity and fatalistic acceptance, but flexibility and initiative. He claims that India's cultivators have responded to

[50] A. Krishna Row, to Collector, Cuddapah, 13 Sept. 1875, BRP 2412, 22 Sept. 1876.

[51] H. R. Farmer to Collector, Kurnool, 5 Nov. 1876, BRP 2863, 17 Nov. 1876.

the uncertainties of the monsoons by making 'rational adaptations' within the perceived context of a market economy in order to survive. Farmers he points out were likely to profit, even when their own crops were deficient, from the resultant high prices. They could respond to inadequate or tardy rainfall by switching to crops that required less water or which could be sown later than usual. Even in a situation of total drought they would have reserves to fall back on—grain, livestock, jewelry and so forth—which had been accumulated in more prosperous times and could now be traded in for food and other necessities. The Indian cultivator is thus seen to act according to a 'calculating rationality' born of long experience of subsistence crises.[52]

Morris is referring primarily to contemporary India, a context in which the language of capitalist decision-making and responsiveness to market forces is perhaps appropriate. For Madras in the 1870s however his approach is open to question for two main reasons. Firstly although rural capitalism was clearly making inroads into the peasant economy—in terms of the sale and purchase of land, for example,—capitalistic attitudes and relationships had not fully matured. Peasants could participate in crop production for the market without necessarily altering their inherited attitudes to the land, their crops and other possessions. For the great majority subsistence continued to be the primary concern. They preferred, especially when famine threatened, to play safe rather than to play a market over which they had no control and of whose mechanics, most likely, they had little understanding. Similarly, for them land, cattle or their wives' jewelry were not merely resources that could be turned into cash or food when necessity pressed. Cultural values and peasant self-esteem and standing in the village community stood in the way of such a purely economic valuation of their worth and importance.

Secondly peasants were not free, even if they wished to be, to act with the flexibility and freedom of choice which Morris, from a capitalistic viewpoint, calls 'rationality'. One of the foremost constraints was the drying up of rural credit when drought threatened. Rural indebtedness was already well advanced in Madras by the 1870s: so much so that creditors often claimed a share of the harvest as soon as it was gathered or had reduced the peasant proprietors

[52] Morris D. Morris, 'What is a Famine?', *Economic and Political Weekly*, IX, 2 Nov. 1974, pp. 1855–64.

virtually to the level of cultivating tenants.[53] In normal years money-lenders saw it to their profit to extend loans and credit at the beginning of the agricultural seasons in expectation of a substantial share of the harvest. But when the rains failed, as in July and August 1876, they refused to risk their money by extending credit to the raiyats. Even land, usually the most reliable form of security, temporarily lost its value as a means of raising loans. This 'credit-squeeze' left many raiyats in 1876–7 without the means even to commence cultivation, so great had their dependence become.[54]

For raiyats with the funds to begin cultivation one way of reducing their normal outlay (apart from shedding labour) was to abandon part of their holding so as to concentrate on a smaller, perhaps better-watered or more fertile, area. The raiyatwari system enabled raiyats to do this. As a result marginal land taken on during recent decades was abandoned. Some 3.25 million acres in the province passed out of cultivation in 1876–7.[55] A related response was a switch to food grains from special cash crops, produced for the market and not for the peasant's own consumption, such as indigo, sugar and cotton. In part this change-over can be accounted for in terms of peasants' response to changing market conditions: in times of shortage food prices rose sharply and thus promised the greatest financial reward to the producers. But it appears more generally to have been a peasant retreat from commercial to subsistence agriculture in the face of incipient dearth and famine.[56] Even in the worst famine districts there were some raiyats with access to dependable irrigation water who were able to raise crops and profit handsomely from the general scarcity.[57] But many raiyats relied upon keeping such grain as they already had, whether for their own consumption or in order to sell when market prices were irresistibly high.[58] In consequence most

[53] Benson, *Kurnool*, p. 116; C. J. Crosthwaite, Subcollector, to Collector, Bellary, 21 Sept. 1876, BRP 2486, 2 Oct. 1876.

[54] Crosthwaite to Collector, Bellary, 5 Aug. 1876, BRP 2055, 12 Aug. 1876; J. R. Daniel, Collector, Cuddapah, to Sec., Board of Revenue, 19 Sept. 1876, BRP 2412, 22 Sept. 1876.

[55] Nicholson, p. 281; Benson, *Kurnool*, p. 36; cultivation reports in BRP 3322, 29 Dec. 1876; *Report of the Indian Famine Commission*, Pt. 3 (Cmd. 3086) (London, 1885), p. 209.

[56] Revenue Administration Report, 1877–8, BRP, 12 Nov. 1878.

[57] Nicholson, p. 274.

[58] W. S. Whiteside, Collector, N. Arcot, to Chief Sec., 18 Nov. 1876, BRP 3092, 6 Dec. 1876; F. R. H. Sharp, Collector, Nellore, to Sec., Board of Revenue, 15 Dec. 1876, BRP 3262, 22 Dec. 1876.

grain in the villages quickly went 'to ground' and was not sent to market, with the result that shortages in the bazaar grew rapidly more acute.

As the immediate subordinates of the state the peasant proprietors looked to the government to recognize the disastrous nature of the season and to respond by granting the reduction, suspension or remission of the revenue demand. Through petitions and personal requests to touring officials the raiyats also sought permission to cultivate tank beds, where enough moisture remained to raise a few vegetables, or to have access to canal water at reduced cost.[59] But the state was seldom as responsive or as benevolent as the raiyats wished. It was reluctant to grant remissions, being anxious to maintain its revenues and suspicious that villagers were exaggerating their losses in order to defraud the state. Raiyats' petitions were often not answered (and then not always favourably) until after the critical moment had passed for sowing or watering crops.

Thus although some raiyats were able to respond in the manner Morris suggests, many more were unable to do so or were more concerned with risks and losses than possible profits. Without credit or food reserves poorer peasants had to consume their seed grain, leaving them none to chance in a later sowing. Others felt that it would be folly to gamble remaining seed on the dwindling possibility of late rains. There was some sense in this. The Collector of Chingleput noted in November 1876 that those who had not tried to plant a wet crop that year were now better off than those who had, for they still had their seed grain left.[60] Away from the famine zone some raiyats tried to compensate for the deficiencies of the southwest monsoon in 1876 by planting more extensively for the northeast. Cultivation figures for Coimbatore for example showed a decline for the southwest monsoon period in 1876, but for October to December 1876 the area under cultivation rose from the recent years' average of 810,957 acres to 830,695.[61]

In the districts more severely affected by drought even this degree of flexibility was rare. The conventions of the peasant calendar were often more powerful determinants of attitudes towards cultivation than the market economy. Precise directions were laid down about

[59] R. W. Barlow, Collector, Chingleput, to Sec., Board of Revenue, 4 Nov. 1876, BRP 2788, 9 Nov. 1876; *Madras Times*, 23 Oct. 1876, p. 2f.

[60] Barlow to Sec., Board of Revenue, 4 Nov. 1876, BRP 2788, 9 Nov. 1876.

[61] BRP 518, 7 Feb. 1877.

when to expect rain and when to sow. It was 'better not to sow at all than sow in Pubba [the Tamil astral 30 August to 11 September]', the peasant was warned. Even more emphatically, one Telugu saying insisted that 'even in dreams the seed should be sown in the proper season'.[62] As the Madras Board of Revenue observed in November 1876 of peasants in the Ceded Districts, 'the ryots, as a rule, grow particular crops only on particular soils, and are reluctant to break through custom or to commence cultivation operations after the usual season has expired'.[63] Tradition and conventional wisdom thus discouraged individual risk-taking and contributed to the 'comparative inflexibility'[64] of peasant agriculture in Madras.

Peasants and the Market

Two kinds of expectation lay behind the demands and actions of the rural and urban poor in Madras in 1876–7. Firstly there was a material demand for a basic subsistence. The belief was prevalent among the subaltern classes that those who had grain should not withhold it, charge excessive prices for it, or export it from the locality, but must make it available to feed those threatened by hunger and starvation. As long as there was food to be had, the poor should have enough to eat to keep them alive. If the holders of grain failed to respond to such demands, subalterns felt themselves entitled to appropriate what they needed for themselves. The second expectation related to subaltern perceptions of power and its use. In a situation of crisis and extreme need, like that created by drought and incipient famine, subaltern classes believed that those who held power over them, whether moneylenders, grain traders, landholders or officials, should not abuse their power but be responsive to subaltern needs. Power in their view connoted responsibility. Protest was accordingly directed not to overturning the superordinate classes but to reminding them of the proper use of their power. This might be achieved by a direct demonstration of collective anger or by invoking the intervention of another superordinate group, such as the state officials. Foodgrain availability was central to both these expectations in 1876–7 for food was simultaneously an issue of power and subsistence.

Subaltern expectations and demands arose primarily from their

---

[62] Benson, *Telugu Sayings*, pp. 197, 199.
[63] BRP 2766, 7 Nov. 1876.
[64] Benson, *Kurnool*, p. 64.

own needs and consciousness and from customary practice in such matters as standard grain payments to labourers, normal availability of credit from traders, and so forth. They might also, as Thompson indicates in his account of the eighteenth-century food protesters in England,[65] derive an additional sense of legitimacy and authority from élite ideology and élite action. For their part élites were likely to respond to subaltern demands for two interrelated reasons. There were cultural values, present among the élite and perhaps common to society as a whole, that attached merit to charity and a philanthropic attitude towards the poor, sick and needy. But even this cultural approbation had political significance, for displays of charitable munificence served as demonstrations and reminders of the wealth and power of the donor and the subordination of the recipients. Charity and other related élite responses to subaltern expectations often also had more immediately material and political motives. They arose from a fear of or anxiety to forestall greater unrest on the part of the subalterns and to ensure the safety of élite lives and property.

The issue of subsistance and the various expectations and attitudes relating to it was partly fought out, as we have seen, in the villages. But the primary battlefield was the weekly market held in many towns and larger villages. The market place or bazaar provided an arena peculiarly favourable to the collective expression of the subsistence demands of the rural (and urban) poor. It was a powerful attraction to the labourer or petty raiyat who had neither work nor food, who went to the market to buy (or obtain on credit) whatever grain he could, or who went simply in a desperate hope that somehow something would turn up to save him from the looming prospect of hunger. The bazaar was a conducive environment for the incubation and dissemination of rumour; it provided the occasion for contact, communication and collective action on a larger scale, and often with greater chance of anonymity, than in the village. Moreover it was in the market town or weekly bazaar that the traders and their grain were to be found, the targets that concentrated and focused subaltern anger and anxiety. It was there too that the intervention of officials could be most actively sought to redress the traders' profiteering and their seeming indifference to the subsistence needs of the poor.

The grain sellers and dealers contributed to the escalating mood of crisis in the bazaars by doubling and trebling prices in September and

[65] E. P. Thompson, 'The Moral Economy of the English Crowd in the Eighteenth Century', *Past and Present*, 50 (Feb. 1971), pp. 76–136.

October 1876. In May of that year a rupee would have bought 28 seers of ragi or cholam in Kurnool; by September it would buy little more than half that amount, and by the end of October barely a quarter.[66] In Cuddapah, where the quantity of ragi that could be purchased for a rupee had dropped from 13.5 seers on 1 October to 8 seers a fortnight later, traders were said to be making six times their usual profit on a sack of grain.[67] Worse still, as far as the grain-buying public was concerned, traders were beginning to refuse to sell at all, holding out for higher prices later or withdrawing their grain to export elsewhere where prices and profits ran even higher.

The consequence was a series of disturbances, or threatened disturbances, in many parts of the Presidency, concentrated between September 1876 and January 1877, the period of steeply rising prices and alarm following the failure of the monsoons. The English-language press in Madras reported about twenty incidents during this period though it seems likely that there were many more smaller occurrences that passed unrecorded.

In some of these incidents subordinate groups other than peasants were involved—town labourers, railway workers and, in a later incident in Vishakhapatnam in August 1877, Indian soldiers. But in many of the small town disturbances rural labourers (often untouchables) joined with other subalterns in looting grain stores or threatening to pillage the bazaars. Grain carts travelling to market and canal boats carrying grain were other targets of attack. In one of the largest disturbances four to five hundred people, including a large number of women, were said to have taken part in the looting of grain shops in the market town of Kalladaikurichi in Tirunelveli district on 17 December 1876.[68] Many incidents did not develop beyond the stage of unrest, rumour and the gathering of discontented crowds in the bazaars on market day. Rumour was a particularly potent force in drawing the poor together on these occasions. It gave them a collective yet anonymous voice. Sometimes, if the authorities had not first intervened, it provided the final impetus to drive the would-be

[66] Benson, *Kurnool*, p. 34; *Review of the Madras Famine*, pp. 10, 15; Lardinois, pp. 80f. A seer is equal to 2.057 lbs.

[67] R. S. Benson, Head Assistant Collector, to Collector, Cuddapah, 16 Oct. 1876, BRP 2621, 20 Oct. 1876.

[68] J. F. Smith, Joint Magistrate, Tirunelveli, to District Magistrate, 24 Dec. 1876, Judicial Proceedings, 17, 4 Jan. 1877. For a further discussion of the character of food riots in Madras, see David Arnold, 'Looting, Grain Riots and Government Policy in South India, 1918', *Past and Present*, 84 (Aug. 1979), pp. 111–45.

purchasers or discontented to loot and riot. During October and November 1876 the *Madras Times*, a European paper, testified several times to the power of rumour in the bazaars. On 19 October it commented on 'the great dearth that forms the staple conversation of the bazaars', and four days later on the popular belief that, though prices were abnormally high, traders held two or three years' grain in stock. In a further week the paper reported from Coimbatore a rumour that the Collector was about to order the release of grain which merchants intended to export from the district: crowds gathered at the railway yards in expectation, only to be disappointed. The same rumour stiffened by threats of looting circulated in Coimbatore again in the first week of November.[69]

Once drawn to the bazaars, mobilized by rumour, anger and the fear that soon food would be totally unavailable, it took only a small incident to ignite discontented crowds. Looting in the town of Madras on 16 October began when a few young men ran through the bazaars shouting '*kollai, kollai*' ('loot, loot'). In Kalladaikurichi traders themselves sparked off the looting by closing their shops on reports of looting elsewhere in the province: the crowd was so angered at their refusal to sell that it resorted to precisely the plundering that the traders had feared. Anger against the traders and determination to resist high prices, speculation and the export of grain were often greatest away from the main famine area. Thus many of the incidents recorded were in districts like Coimbatore, Thanjavur, Godavari and Tirunelveli where some rain had fallen but from which grain stocks were rapidly being drained to be sold for higher prices elsewhere. This created a powerful sentiment that the locality was being robbed of what local conditions justified and it was feared that no grain would be left for the district's own consumption.[70] An additional factor in the geographical distribution of the disturbances may have been the response of the authorities. While they could not hope to anticipate, even to check, disturbances occurring seemingly without warning throughout most of the province, in Bellary, Kurnool and Cuddapah police reinforcements were quickly posted to discourage and quell any signs of unrest and officials were on the look-out for possible incidents.

[69] *Madras Times*, 19 Oct. 1876, p. 2a; ibid., 23 Oct. 1876, p. 3a; ibid., 30 Oct. 1876, p. 2f; ibid., 9 Nov. 1876, p. 2f.

[70] F. Wilkinson, Subcollector, to Collector, Salem, 18 Oct. 1878, BRP 2650-A, 24 Oct. 1876.

The rural and urban poor expected the state to respond sympathetically to their difficulty in obtaining food. On many occasions they turned first to the Collector or to any other government servant they could find to protest at the high prices, the export of grain and the traders' profiteering. Such appeals were not altogether without effect. Although the Board of Revenue in Madras clung resolutely to its laissez faire orthodoxy and opposed state interference in the grain trade, local officials were apt to waver. Faced with the petitions of the poor, concerned at the unrest high prices were causing and sharing something of the crowd's distaste for the traders' greediness, officials communicated their sympathy while stressing that they were unable to intervene to regulate prices or release stocks. It is not difficult to see how in such circumstances the protesters returned to the bazaars convinced that their cause had the approval of the government. The rumour noted earlier that the Collector of Coimbatore would order the release of grain held ready for export at the railway yards was one demonstration of the popular belief that officialdom was on the side of the poor.

But even without any putative official support the rural and urban poor were adamant in their convictions. C. J. Crosthwaite, Sub collector of Bellary, reported in September 1876 that

> The feeling against merchants is very bitter in some parts. It is common thing to be told by the poor that the sowcars [*sahukars*, here meaning traders as well as moneylenders] are cheating them, by which they mean that they pretend to have no grain and are reluctant to sell even when they cannot deny they have it. The poor ryots consider that, as they have helped to enrich the sowcar, the latter should not fail them in their time of need, and that Government should step in and prohibit sowcars from selling at more than what they call a fair rate of profit.[71]

Crosthwaite added that the opinion that the 'sowcars should not make the ryots' distress their own opportunity' was shared by Indian officials as well as the poor.[72] The European editor of the *Madras Times*, while personally defending the principle of a free market economy, acknowledged that it found no support among the bulk of the Indian population. There was he wrote, 'not a native of the lower orders in India who is not fully assured of the preventability of famines' through government intervention to control grain prices and supplies. They regarded he said, 'the grain-dealers, and their

[71] Crosthwaite to Collector, Bellary, 21 Sept. 1876, BRP 2486, 2 Oct. 1876.
[72] Ibid.

great accumulation of corn, as the real authors of the distresses that oppress them'.[73]

But Indian or European, the official who, like the Collector of Nellore, favoured intervention and proposed to 'set aside theories of political economy which will lead only to starvation and riot', was quickly rebuked by the Board of Revenue and reminded that any violation of the free trade in grain could not 'for a moment be entertained'.[74] Withheld from coercing the traders as the poor expected, state power was, on the contrary, deployed to protect the traders from threats of looting and rioting. Open protest and disturbances in the bazaars were deterred or quashed, but the grievances that had given rise to these forms of protest remained to find expression in other ways. Violence and crime were among these.

Subaltern Appropriation and Violence

The early phases of drought and famine drew from the peasantry responses that were active rather than passive and involved a large measure of collective as opposed to individual action. During that time there were significant shifts. In particular the collectivities changed from whole villages participating in rain-making rites to the poorer villagers (by themselves or in temporary association with other subalterns) taking part in food riots and protests while the village élite opposed them or pressed their separate demands (for revenue remissions and the like) upon the government. Elements of subaltern collectivity were sustained in the acts of appropriation and violence that burgeoned during the famine period in Madras, for they constituted a continuing form of protest by poorer peasants, acting together in small bands, against richer villagers, moneylenders and traders. But as the drought intensified and the effects of famine became more widespread, subaltern collectivity began to break down still further until appropriation and violence became expressions of individual frustration, desperation and despair.

For the poorer villagers, especially the untouchables and low-caste labourers, petty theft, even dacoity, was a familiar means of surviving the dry season when there was little work or food. Raiyats and village headmen often connived at this: it lessened labourers' dependence on them and their grain stores at a critical time of the year; it brought them, as the labourers' protectors, windfall profits; and it diverted to

73 *Madras Times*, 10 Nov. 1876, p. 2c.
74 BRP 277, 30 Oct. 1876.

more distant targets energies that might otherwise be directed against the village leaders. In the dry districts in particular the hot weather months from February to June were the 'dacoity season'. With the arrival of the monsoon field work resumed and crime rapidly dwindled.[75] But when the monsoon failed and there was no work to return to, then inevitably crime assumed even greater importance than normal in the labourers' struggle for survival.[76] Nor were the targets of famine-crime, initially at least, arbitrarily selected. They were often, unlike in normal circumstances, traders, moneylenders and rich raiyats within the village or locality itself. Finding the bazaars closed or grain prices beyond their means, or harbouring resentment at the unresponsiveness of those who held grain to the subsistence needs of the poor, the labourers plundered and stole what they had been unable to acquire by other means. Arson as well as theft registered their indignation at the selfishness of others.[77] In one such case in Tirunelveli district a trader refused to give credit for peasants to buy cambu from him. The villagers quitely returned later to loot his grain store and left him promissory notes as payment.[78] Theft in such circumstances was a means both of punishing a trader and of satisfying the subalterns' immediate subsistence needs.

The famine placed unprecedented demands on the control machinery of the colonial state. Although by the end of 1876 over 3,000 extra police had been sanctioned for the three main famine districts, many policemen were deployed to escort grain convoys, patrol bazaars and guard grain stores and so were not available to protect wealthier villagers. Normally village watchmen were charged with guarding the standing crops, but many of them, hit by the famine and epidemics of cholera and smallpox, could no longer carry out their customary duties. The system of village administration, like the cohesion of the village community itself, was beginning to disintegrate as village servants died from hunger and disease or joined the drift to the towns and relief works. Where crops could be raised they were a powerful attraction for hungry villagers and wanderers.

[75] W. Francis, *Madras District Gazetteers: Bellary* (Madras, 1904), pp. 185–6; C. F. Brackenbury, *Madras District Gazetteers: Cuddapah* (Madras, 1915), p. 169.

[76] *Madras Times*, 30 Nov. 1876, p. 2e. For a further discussion of 'famine crime', see David Arnold, 'Dacoity and Rural Crime in Madras, 1860–1940', *Journal of Peasant Studies*, 6: 2 (Jan. 1979), pp. 145–9.

[77] *Madras Times*, 12 Sept. 1876; ibid., 14 Oct. 1876, p. 2f; *Madras Standard*, 22 Jan. 1877, p. 2c.

[78] *Madras Mail*, 4 Jan. 1877, p. 2f.

Desperate to save their crops, especially after losing others through drought, raiyats reacted with great ferocity against anyone they caught pilfering from their fields. When the owner of a cholam field near Korlakanta village, Cuddapah, discovered five people cutting his grain at night he gave chase and clubbed one of them to death.[79] 'The people grow savage', the government remarked, 'in the protection of their property'.[80] It was a measure of the intensity of the conflict dearth created between those who grew and possessed grain and those who had to buy, steal or beg for it.

The severity, duration and scale of the 1876–8 famine resulted in the highest recorded level of crime in Madras between the 1850s and the 1940s. Official figures are unreliable (for much rural crime went unreported at any time), but they do give some indication of the trend. Dacoity, defined as robbery by five or more people and those broad enough to encompass bazaar looting as well as the depredations of armed gangs, was dubbed the 'special famine crime' by the Inspector-General of Police.[81] From 229 cases in 1875, the lowest recorded total since the 1850s, dacoities shot up to 980 in 1876 and 1,695 in 1877, before falling back to 639 in 1878. In the main famine zone the rise was even more dramatically linked with the failure of the monsoon. Bellary's tally of dacoities increased more than tenfold (from 15 to 159) from 1875 to 1876 and almost doubled again in 1877 (to 273). North Arcot, though less severely affected by the famine itself, lay on the wanderers' route to Madras and incorporated several zamindari estates where government control was weak. It recorded 164 dacoities in 1876 as against 22 in the previous year and 317 in 1877.[82] More than half of the dacoities committed in the famine zone in 1876 fell within the last two months of the year after the monsoons had finally failed.[83]

Despite official optimism that crime rates would drop as soon as famine relief works came into operation, levels remained exceptionally high for every category of recorded crime during the early months of 1877. By April there was a slight falling off, but when the southwest monsoon failed once more the prospect of another year's drought

---

[79] *Madras Standard*, 21 Feb. 1877, p. 3c.

[80] *Report on Criminal Justice and Criminal Judicial Statistics of the Madras Presidency, 1879* (Madras, 1880), p. 5.

[81] *Administration Report of the Madras Police, 1877* (Madras, 1878), p. 1.

[82] *Administration Report of the Madras Police, 1876* (Madras, 1877), pp. 23–9; ibid, *1877*, pp. 19–20; ibid., *1878*, p. 25.   [83] *Madras Standard*, 7 Feb. 1877, p. 3b.

and hunger sent crime rates soaring again. There were 154 dacoities in June 1877, 276 in July, 295 in August. Only with heavy rains in September 1877 did a lasting decline begin. The 265 dacoities in September were followed by 117 in October and 76 in November. Districts like Salem, Coimbatore and Madurai, which had not suffered the first brunt of famine in 1876, were high in the lists of serious crime in 1877 and 1878 as conditions worsened.[84]

Other official statistics registered however inaccurately the trend of social disintegration and individual desperation. The number of murders recorded rose from 295 in 1875 to 309 in 1876 and 538 in 1877. Suicides, reported as 1,723 and 1,621 in 1876, rose to 2,308 in 1877, 3,054 in 1878 and 2,481 in 1879. Accidental deaths, a category that included many unproven murders and suicides, totalled 7,641 in 1875, but 10,900 in 1876, 13,503 in 1877 and 10,244 in 1878.[85] These deaths do not appear to conform to any pattern of 'victimization' such as that Greenough attributes to famine-struck peasants during the Bengal famine of 1943.[86] In desperation parents drowned or strangled children they saw no prospect of being able to feed. Other adults, especially women, committed suicide to escape from their hunger and exhaustion. There were no confirmed reports of cannibalism from Madras, as there had been in earlier famines, but there were accounts in the press of parents going without food (and so sacrificing their own chances of survival) so that their children could eat.[87] The longer famine persisted the less crime and acts of violence bore the mark of collective protest and appropriation, and the more they assumed the bitterness of personal anguish, desolation and despair.

The Means of Survival

Rain-making ceremonies, bazaar disturbances, even violence and crime, represented outwardly directed responses to drought and famine. They were intended to remind, coerce or punish those who failed to answer the prayers, entreaties and demands of the rural poor. But peasants did not rely solely upon trying to persuade others to recognize and respond to their subsistence needs, or even upon seizing what they felt was wrongly denied or taken away from them. They also resorted to changes within their own lifestyle and livelihood

---

[84] *Administration Report of the Madras Police, 1877*, p. lxxv.
[85] Ibid., for 1875–9.   [86] See Greenough.
[87] *Madras Times*, 21 Oct. 1876, p. 2e; ibid., 24 Sept. 1877, p. 2f.

in an attempt to survive the famine. Not a few of these adjustments can be seen as the extension to the famine situation of survival techniques already familiar to the peasants from their poverty, indebtedness and the annual struggle to stay alive until the next harvest.

One obvious area of adjustment was in the quantity and nature of food consumed. An adult peasant who could afford and obtain such a quantity might eat as much as 1.5 to 2 lbs of grain a day and supplement this with pulses, vegetables and, more rarely, meat and fish. At festivals and weddings he might eat rice, the prestigious food of the Brahmins and well-to-do. But in the dry interior districts the staple food of the rural population was millet, principally the locally grown varieties known as ragi, cholam and cambu. In actuality, peasants rarely consumed as much as 1.5 lbs of grain a day. During the hot summer months especially, when grain was scarce and dear, they might subsist on no more than one main meal a day of millet, boilded or made into flour cakes. Others might be reduced to consuming only *Kanji* (gruel).[88] As famine began to stalk the province in 1876 many peasant households had no choice but to further reduce their daily food intake. 'Four people', it was said in Kurnool in November 1876, 'were glad to be able to get between them for a meal what one man would not consider sufficient in ordinary times'.[89] The landless labourers were particularly vulnerable. As Clough remarked of the Madigas of coastal Andhra, a great many of them lived 'so close to the starvation point all the year round that the first failure of crops brought hunger to their door . . . '[90]

Although their consumption might not be publicly acknowledged because of the social stigma attached to the eating of such items, poorer peasants, especially the untouchable labourers, were accustomed to supplement their meagre income of grain with whatever vegetable and animal foodstuffs they could find. These included roots, leaves, wild fruits, rodents, insects and birds.[91] Being permitted to eat the flesh of dead cattle was part of the customary reward of Madigas for their services to the caste Hindu raiyats.[92] As the drought and dearth intensified in 1876–7 the rural poor were driven into

---

[88] William R. Cornish, *Reports on the Nature of the Food of the Inhabitants of the Madras Presidency* (Madras, 1863), p. 3.

[89] H. R. Farmer, Head Assistant Collector, to Collector, Kurnool, 5 Nov. 1876, BRP 2863, 17 Nov. 1876.

[90] Clough, p. 273.   [91] Cornish, p. 67.   [92] Clough, p. 41.

increased dependence upon these supplementary or surrogate food-stuffs. The fact that they had names for a great number of edible, or barely tolerable, leaves and roots is indicative of the peasants' familiarity with them and their properties.[93] As famine persisted however the more accessible and palatable roots, seeds and leaves disappeared and peasants were driven to eat those that, while they might temporarily allay hunger, caused vomiting and diarrhoea. This and the drinking of contaminated water contributed to sickness and disease among the weakened rural population. From Bellary in August 1876 one official reported that village labourers were eating a leaf known as 'dhevadaru' which, he understood, was not used to any great extent in normal times. By mid-October another noted that villagers had virtually exhausted roots like 'kunkaragadda' that were 'tolerably pleasant' (as if he knew!) and were reduced to eating 'thitagadda', 'which is not nutritious, and causes great irritation [to the bowels]'.[94] Towards the end of the famine the process was reversed. Labourers rapidly deserted the government relief works and camps as soon as adequate rain began to fall in September 1877. They kept themselves alive on the wild vegetables and leaves that sprang up with the rains until the raiyats were ready to hire them and pay them in grain.[95]

The first onset of drought brought the labourers one windfall that eased the immediate problem of survival. Apart from such grain as they were able to beg, pilfer or plunder, untouchable labourers consumed the flesh of dead cattle and other animals. Some of these animals had died from thirst and hunger but many must have strayed away from their owners in search of food and water or been stolen and killed. Cattle theft was one of the crime categories in the police files that rose most dramatically in the famine years—from 2,856 reported cases in 1875 and 4,347 in 1876 to 18,704 in 1877 and 10,289 in 1878.[96] Because of their consumption of cattle flesh, Malas, Madigas and Boyas in the southern Telugu famine districts were sometimes reported to be surprisingly well-fed and healthy. Ironically they were for this reason excluded from state relief works. Flesh-eating

[93] G.O. 739, Public, 29 May 1877.

[94] C. J. Crosthwaite, Subcollector, to Collector, Bellary, 5 Aug. 1876, BRP 2055, 12 Aug. 1876; H. T. Ross, Head Assistant Collector, to Collector, Bellary, 16 Oct. 1876, BRP 2649, 24 Oct. 1876.

[95] F. A. Nicholson, Head Assistant Collector, to Collector, Madurai, 22 Nov. 1877, G.O. 3068, Rev. (Fam.), 8 Dec. 1877; G. A. Ballard, Third Member, Board of Revenue, to Sec., Revenue, 10 Nov. 1877, G.O. 3078, Rev. (Fam.), 8 Dec. 1877.

[96] *Administration Reports of the Madras Police*, 1875–78.

had other drawbacks in the quest for survival, for putrid and diseased carcases brought sickness and death to a great many labourers.[97]

Very few caste Hindu raiyats, even when on the verge of starvation and death, would violate the powerful taboo against eating the flesh of their cattle. They adopted various expedients in a desperate attempt to keep the animals alive. Raiyats in Nellore, Cuddapah, Bellary and Kurnool sent large numbers of cattle to the Nallamallai hills where some grazing was still to be had. A similar migration to the hill tracts occurred in other parts of the province. But the price of fodder and pasturage rose steeply and the concentration of so many animals favoured the spread of fatal cattle diseases.[98] Other raiyats in desperation tore the thatch from their roofs to feed to the cattle or, responding with some reluctance to official persuasion, prepared the pulp of the prickly pear cactus for them to eat. But for most raiyats there was no hope of saving their animals and they tried to sell them to buy food for themselves. The cattle markets and fairs were full of cheap cows and bullocks. In Bellary in January 1877 bullocks fetched only one rupee a head or eight seers of cholam.[99] Others left without food and water wandered off and died of starvation in a sad semblance of human migration and suffering. By July 1877 cattle mortality was running as high as 60 per cent in Coimbatore's Kollegal taluk, one of the foremost cattle-raising areas of the province, and by the end of the famine the toll in two hard-hit taluks of Kurnool was around 80 per cent.[100] For the raiyats the loss of their cattle was a multiple tragedy, depriving them of their plough and haulage beasts, costing them one of their principal investments, and making their eventual recovery from famine infinitely harder. Since too the possession of cattle was an important mark of peasants' pride and status, their loss brought the tragic consequences of famine measurably closer to the raiyats: 'the death of the plough cattle and the death of one's wife', according to a vernacular saying, 'are equal calamities'.[101]

[97] W. R. Cornish to Chief Sec., 31 Mar. 1877, in *Madras Sanitary Commissioner's Proceedings*, XIV, pp. 162–3; Cornish to Sec., Revenue, 8 May 1877, ibid., XIV, p. 81; *Madras Mail*, 24 Feb. 1877, p. 2d.

[98] Benson, *Kurnool*, p. 6; H. T. Ross, Head Assistant Collector, to Collector, Bellary, 16 Oct. 1876, BRP 2649, 24 Oct. 1876; F. R. H. Sharp, Collector, Nellore, to Sec., Board of Revenue, 24 Oct. 1876, BRP 2688, 27 Oct. 1876.

[99] 'Memorandum on Bellary District', in *Correspondence . . . on the Famine*, Pt. 2, p. 44; *Madras Times*, 8 Nov. 1876, p. 2g; *Madras Standard*, 19 Jan. 1877, p. 2e; ibid., 22 Jan. 1877, p. 2b.

[100] C. A. MacKenzie, Deputy Collector, Coimbatore, to Collector, 16 July 1877, G.O. 2477-A, Rev. (Fam.), 10 Aug. 1877; Benson, *Kurnool*, p. 6.

[101] *Tamil Sayings*, p. 86.

From the sale and loss of their cattle peasants were driven to the sale and surrender of their remaining possessions. For sums far below their normal worth they sold the timber from their doors and window frames, agricultural implements, 'brass pots and utensils, clothes, gold ornaments, silver and jewelry, even their wives' wedding necklaces, the very symbol of married honour. Traders and money-lenders bought them up at bargain rates, an action which increased raiyats' resentment at their humiliation.[102]

From desperation too women and children were sold or gave themselves up to prostitution. In part this was a further aspect of the hierarchy of rural subordination. Men preserved their own chances of survival by sacrificing their women and children. But women themselves might see no other prospect. A woman in Bellary who sold her child for 12 annas in June 1877 declined, when pressed, to take it back: she could not find the food to feed it. A tank-digger in Krishna district sold his three daughters to a 'Dancing Girl Society', the thinly-veiled façade for a prostitution agency.[103] The *Madras Times* reported in August 1877 that in Bellary raiyats were so destitute that in some cases 'even their wives and children have passed away into the hands of the hard and grasping money-lender'.[104] Famine brought not only an intensification of the peasants' struggle for survival, but also an enhanced awareness of their exploitation by others.

Famine Migration

As immediate sources of food and water disappeared, as employment vanished and local charity failed, peasants, individually, in family groups, or in gangs, set out in search of work and subsistence elsewhere. For some this may have been no more than flight, a desperate bid to escape from destitution and starvation. For those weakened by hunger and sickness evacuating the villages might lead only to confused and aimless wandering, exhaustion and a wayside death. Whatever its motivation the 'wandering instinct' was a powerful one, as colonial officials discovered when they tried to counter it. When Coimbatore's Assistant Collector intercepted wanderers

---

[102] F. A. Nicholson, Head Assistant Collector, to Collector, Madurai, 10 July 1877, Revenue Proceedings, 557-C, 30 July 1877; G. MacKenzie, Head Assistant Collector, to Collector, Coimbatore, 12 Aug. 1877, G.O. 2680-A, Rev. (Fam.), 8 Sept. 1877.

[103] *Madras Times*, 30 Nov. 1876, p. 2e.   [104] Ibid., 4 Aug. 1877, p. 2f.

ascending the ghats to the Nilgiris and urged them to go back to relief
houses in the plains they refused to listen, scattering into the jungle
until he had gone and they could continue their journey. They
were convinced he wrote that they would find 'an el Dorado on
the hills'.[105]

But in the main these mass movements, involving perhaps several
million people over the course of the Madras famine, were more than
irrational or purposeless flight from a famine-stricken countryside.
They were directed towards places where from past experience or
hearsay peasants believed that they could find relief from their distress.
Towns were an obvious objective. The temple towns of the region
were renowned as places of charity for pilgrims and the mendicant
poor. Towns were reservoirs of the precious grain that had vanished
from the countryside, the haunts of merchants and officials. Railway
junctions and sea ports, where grain was stored and imported or
trans-shipped, were similarly magnetic attractions for the migrant
peasants. In the hills, in the irrigated coastal plains and even abroad
there was the hope of escaping from drought and dearth to find food
and work. Some peasants had relatives in the towns or in less affected
areas with whose help they hoped to survive the famine period.

Despite three-quarters of a century of British rule in the province
(indeed partly because the colonial government's response was seen
to be so niggardly and tardy), the rural poor turned to traditional
sources of charity. Among these were the petty princelings and
zamindars. The response of the zamindars was actually very mixed.
Many were too engrossed in their own affairs or too burdened with
debt to be able or willing to assist even the raiyats on their own
estates: it was left to the government to pester them to accept responsibility for destitute tenants and to initiate relief measures. But
other zamindaras saw it as part of their traditional *raja dharma*, their
duty as rulers, to provide for their subjects in times of distress. In
North Arcot the zamindar of Karvetnagar was in financial difficulties
and could do virtually nothing, while the zamindar of Kalahasti was
said to be 'well-disposed but not wealthy' and his initial charitable
distribution of food to the poor could not be sustained.[106] The zamindar

---

[105] A. Martindale to Collector, Coimbatore, 9 Aug. 1877, G.O. 2624-B, Rev.
(Fam.), 1 Sept. 1877.

[106] Board of Revenue's review of N. Arcot, BRP, 24 Feb. 1877; R. K. Puckle,
Director of Revenue Settlement, to Sec., Board of Revenue, 2 Apr. 1877, *Madras
Sanitary Commissioner's Proceedings*, XIV, 1877, pp. 187–9.

of Punganur asked the British for a loan of Rs 50,000 to provide relief for his raiyats. From a sense of his traditional responsibility as a ruler, rather than (it would seem) merely a wish to be in the good books of the colonial power, he wrote in November 1876: 'I am aware that the giving of relief to my ryots is a duty which should fall on me, and my wish to relieve them is great, as it grieves me to see them starving whilst the poor in the adjoining district have work given to them'.[107]

In the towns wealthy merchants, sometimes in association with Indian officials and professional men, organized the distribution of rice and kanji. Motives for this charity were mixed. For some it was a humanitarian as well as religious duty to feed the poor regardless of their caste or creed. Others gave food selectively to members of their own caste, and to needy Brahmins alone, or in the case of Muslims to the destitute of their own religion.[108] But among the merchants self-interest was not absent. With looting and rioting threatened or already in evidence, merchants sought to buy off public (and official) animosity and criticism by offering food free or at reduced rates rather than be plundered and suffer greater loss and ignominy. Charity was a convenient form of insurance. It was no accident for example that four days after the outbreak of food riots in Madras town a group of Chetti merchants announced a scheme to sell rice at below market rates. They covered themselves from too great a loss by calling for public subscriptions to meet the expenses involved.[109]

The numbers fed by private charity could be very large. In the town of Thanjavur and its environs fifteen *choultries* were reported to have fed over half a million 'foreign paupers' between October 1876 and May 1877 at a cost of Rs 25,000.[110] In Vishakhapatnam district in the north-east, where scarcity was induced by high prices elsewhere rather than by conditions locally, the Maharaja of Vizianagaram authorized the feeding of not less than 7,000 people a day.[111] In the

---

[107] Zamindar of Punganur to Collector, N. Arcot, 6 Nov. 1876, BRP 2810, 11 Nov. 1876. In Vishakhapatnam district it was noted that those zamindars who had acquired their titles and estates since the advent of British rule 'were far less disposed to liberality towards their tenants' than the 'ancient zamindars': Memorandum, H. Goodrich, Collector, 1 Aug. 1878, G.O. 1806, Rev. (Fam.), 19 Aug. 1878.

[108] For example, see the reference to the feeding of 'needy Brahmins' in *Madras Mail*, 9 Jan. 1877, p. 3a.   [109] *Madras Times*, 26 Oct. 1876, p. 2e.

[110] H. S. Thomas, Collector, to Additional Sec., Rev. (Fam.), 21 Dec. 1877, G.O. 114, Rev. (Fam.), 14 Jan. 1878.

[111] Memorandum, H. Goodrich, Collector, 1 Aug. 1878, G.O. 1806, Rev. (Fam.), 19 Aug. 1878.

town of Madras in January 1877 private charity was provided for 10,000 daily.[112] Charity on this scale, matched in other major famines in the province in the nineteenth century,[113] was not significant only in terms of the substantial contribution it made to relief. Without their having to reach back to a now-distant era of pre-British rule, peasants were presented with an alternative, indigenous system of support and relief during subsistence crises, one which, for all its limitations in European eyes, operated without the regimentation and tests that characterized the state's own system. The existence of private charity must also have heightened peasant indignation at rich raiyats, landlords, merchants and officials who did not respond to their needs. Not surprisingly therefore private charity in the towns was a major stimulus to rural migration.

In North Arcot peasants headed for Vellore, the district town, and for other commercial and administrative centres. With a population formerly around 38,000, Vellore was swollen by a further 7,000 as the famine-stricken flowed in during December 1876 and January 1877. Others flocked to Kalahasti when news of the zamindar's charity spread, and to Tiruttani, a pilgrimage centre where there were temples and choultries to provide alms, food and shelter.[114] From Salem, Coimbatore and Madurai peasants and artisans (mainly weavers) moved into Tiruchirappalli and Thanjavur, whose irrigated ricelands held out the prospect of food and work and whose centuries of agricultural prosperity were reflected in the wealth and number of temples and choultries. By the end of November 1876 the poor of rural Salem and Madurai were said to be arriving at the rate of 50 to 100 a day to be fed at the choultries of the former rajas of Thanjavur, and in the town itself there were thought to be nearly 3,000 beggars by the end of July 1877.[115] There was a similar exodus from the interior Telugu country to the irrigated deltas of the Krishna and

[112] R. K. Puckle, Director of Revenue Settlement, to Sec., Board of Revenue, 17 Jan. 1877, BRP 268, 23 Jan. 1877.

[113] R. A. Dalyell, *Memorandum on the Madras Famine of 1866* (Madras, 1867), pp. 89, 114–15; (Madras Government) *Report of the Famine in the Madras Presidency during 1896 and 1897* (Madras, 1898), pp. 47–8.

[114] W. S. Whiteside, Collector, N. Arcot, to Sec., Board of Revenue, 29 Jan. 1877, BRP 592, 15 Feb. 1877; R. K. Puckle, Director, Revenue Settlement, to Sec., Board of Revenue, 2 Apr. 1877, *Madras Sanitary Commissioner's Proceedings*, XIV, 1877, pp. 187–9.

[115] H. S. Thomas, Collector, Thanjavur, to Sec., Board of Revenue, 30 Nov. 1876, BRP 3074, 5 Dec. 1876; Thomas to Chief Sec., 27 July 1877, G.O. 2501, Rev. (Fam.), 14 Aug. 1877.

Godavari rivers,[116] while many thousands of destitutes crossed the Tungabhadra into Bellary and Kurnool from Hyderabad where the Nizam's administration was even more inadequate in its relief measures than the Government of Madras.[117] But the greatest movement was towards the Presidency town itself. In two weeks at the end of November and early December 1876 an estimated 12,000 people flooded into Madras. It was there that the first officially acknowledged deaths from starvation occurred—a raiyat and two of his children, part of a family from a village a few miles to the west that had set out four or five days earlier in search of food.[118] In the months that followed tens of thousands of destitutes crowded towards the town: some seventy to eighty thousand arrived during the course of the famine, mainly poor raiyats and labourers from Chingleput, North Arcot and Nellore.[119]

While movements of this kind and the charitable distribution of food by rajas, zamindars and merchants had long been a feature of famine in the region, the migration of labourers to hill plantations and to Sri Lanka dated only from the opening of coffee estates in these areas since the late 1830s. Significantly during the famine this form of migration attracted only those individuals and communities that were already accustomed to short-term labour migration. Despite the intensity of the famine in the central districts from Salem to Kurnool very few peasants volunteered themselves as migrant labourers. A scheme devised by the Government of Burma to solve its own labour shortage by inviting large numbers of starving Madrasis to work in Burma had to be abandoned in June 1878 after no more than 800 men, women and children had applied.[120] Most of the labourers for the coffee estates along the Western Ghats from the Nilgiris to Travancore came either from Mysore or the adjacent plains of Madurai and Tirunelveli. This was the normal pattern of recruitment but, with famine pressing at home, many more than

---

[116] G. D. Leman, Collector, Krishna, to Sec., Board of Revenue, 29 Nov. 1876, BRP 3087, 5 Dec. 1876; W. J. Tate, Assistant Collector, to Collector, Godavari, 30 Aug. 1877, G.O. 2398, 17 Oct. 1877.

[117] W. B. Oldham, Taluk Officer, Advani, to Collector, Bellary, 16 June 1877, G.O. 2438-B, Rev. (Fam.), 3 Aug. 1877.

[118] *Madras Times*, 4 Dec. 1876, p. 3d–e; ibid., 6 Dec. 1876, p. 2c–d.

[119] Minute, Sir William Robinson, 27 May 1878, G.O. 1858, Public, 27 Sept. 1878.

[120] Sec. to Chief Commissioner, Burma, to Sec., Revenue, Agriculture and Commerce, Government of India, 3 Mar. 1877, India Emigration Proceedings, 3–4, Mar. 1877; India Emigration Proceedings, 15–17, June 1878.

usual brought their wives and children with them to the hills and were reluctant to return to the plains at the end of the coffee-picking season.[121]

Labourers for Sri Lanka came almost exclusively from the dry taluks to Thanjavur and from the southeast of Madurai district. Proximity to the island was one obvious reason for this but the poverty of agriculture, particularly in Madurai's zamindari estates of Ramanathapuram and Sivaganga, also contributed. The onset of the famine induced greater numbers than usual to leave for Sri Lanka. In August 1877 it was reported that in the dry areas of Thanjavur so many had left that the 'habitations of the poor have in places a deserted appearance'.[122] From southeastern Madurai the scale of emigration was said to have been so great by early 1877 as to have 'saved the Government from the necessity of commencing heavy expenditure on relief works . . . '[123] By February a third of the able-bodied population had gone: 'In some cases, one member of a family is left with the women and children; in other cases the houses are shut up and all are gone'.[124] By September an estimated 20,000 were believed to have left Sivaganga zamindari alone. No caste census of migrants was kept but it was clear that the great majority were untouchable and low-caste labourers—Paraiyas, Pallars, Chakkilyas— or the poorer sub-tenants and raiyats—Valaiyas, Maravas and Kallas.[125]

The number of labourers arriving in Sri Lanka from India, almost entirely from Madras districts, roughly doubled as a result of the famine. This had been running at about 80,000 to 90,000 a year since 1871, but in 1876 it rose to 164,497 and 167,196 in 1877 before falling again to 101,093 in 1878 and 76,897 in 1879.[126] There was also a corresponding fall in the number returning from Sri Lanka during the famine years. Migration to more distant places like Mauritius, Natal and the West Indies also increased, though not very substantially. In view of the severe and protracted nature of the famine it might be asked why the exodus from Madras was not even greater.

[121] W. Logan, Collector, Malabar, to Chief Sec., 29 Nov. 1876, BRP, 14 Dec. 1876.

[122] H. S. Thomas, Collector, Thanjavur, to Sec., Board of Revenue, 1 Aug. 1877, G.O. 2332, Rev. (Fam.), 15 Oct. 1877.

[123] W. McQuhae, Collector, Madurai, to Sec., Board of Revenue, 28 Dec. 1876, BRP 96, 9 Jan. 1877.

[124] McQuhae to Sec., Board of Revenue, 3 Feb. 1877, BRP 585, 12 Feb. 1877.

[125] F. A. Nicholson, Head Assistant Collector, to Collector, Madurai, 9 Sept. 1877, G.O. 2461, Rev. (Fam.), 19 Oct. 1877.

[126] *Ceylon Administration Reports for the Year 1896* (Colombo, 1897), p. F1.

As already pointed out one major reason was that migration did not appeal to those communities not already accustomed to labouring in the hill estates or abroad. The restricted scale of labour migration is indicative of the limited extent to which rural labour in Madras had ceased to be tied to the land and villages and become a more mobile wage-earning proletariat. Only in the longer term as a result of repeated famine, persistent hardship and the further advance of rural capitalism were others drawn to overseas migration. Another powerful factor in limiting migration in 1876–8 was the raiyats' prejudice against 'coolie' labour, reinforced by a great reluctance to move far away from their fields and remaining possessions. Landless and virtually propertyless the labourers had neither the raiyat's antipathy to manual labour for others nor his material inducements to stay put. Finally not all those who might have wanted to migrate were able to do so. Many would-be migrants were rejected at the embarkation ports as too sick, feeble or old, and even the planters of Sri Lanka, greedy though they were for as much cheap labour as possible, could not employ and feed an indefinite number. Unable to migrate overseas or reach the hills, many turned back home or sought charity in the towns. Thousands must have died from hunger and exhaustion even before reaching their destinations. The number who actually reached Sir Lanka may thus represent only a fraction of those who sought that avenue to survival.

State Relief

At first, from financial considerations backed by a non-interventionist philosophy, it suited the British to leave the burden of shouldering the famine to peasant adaptability and private charity. Although small relief works were sanctioned for Bellary as early as August 1875 the government was opposed to any rapid expansion of relief measures. Towards the end of 1876 it was forced to revise its attitude but the failure of the monsoons and the unmistakable evidence of widespread distress and incipient mass starvation were only two of the factors prompting a change of policy.

Such private charity as existed in the towns and zamindaris was increasingly felt by the government to be unsatisfactory. It fed too much to some, too little to others; it encouraged 'indolence' and the 'demoralization' of the poor by not obliging them to work if they possibly could; and it encouraged mass migration from the country-side. The colonial state's conception of relief was thus at variance with that of Indian donors and recipients. High crime rates too were a powerful inducement to government intervention: to this degree crime as a form of protest and a demand for state action had some effect. A month after it had rejected a proposal for relief works for North Arcot as hasty and unnecessary, the Board of Revenue in Madras authorized the opening of relief measures in the district as it was (it informed the Collector) now 'anxious that sufficient works be established to prevent crime'.[127] Looting too helped to draw official attention to the hardships of the poor, though partly as a consequence relief works were deliberately located away from the towns where they might result in 'mischief to [the] property of merchants with whom the poorer classes are displeased'.[128] Apart from crime and looting the influx of the poor in their thousands into small towns like Vellore and Bellary, and on a greater scale into Madras, placed a great strain on sanitary and medical services that were already less than adequate. The fear of an army of the mobile poor, unregulated and unchecked, thieving and pilfering as they went, spreading alarm and disease to towns and districts otherwise untouched by dearth and drought, at last drove the government to admit that there was a serious famine and that it must assume active responsibility for relief.

Early in December 1876 the government authorized the opening of depots in Madras town to feed those who had already arrived from the drought-affected districts. Others were to be intercepted before reaching Madras and taken to special relief camps a few miles from the town. State support for private relief was withdrawn and instead officially organized relief works were opened in fourteen of the province's twenty-one districts. These soon attracted nearly a million people, three-quarters of them in the worst-hit districts of Bellary, Kurnool and Cuddapah.[129] But following the arrival in mid-January 1877 of the Government of India's special emissary, Sir Richard Temple, state relief measures were again constricted. Temple was outraged to find a third of the population of Bellary and Kurnool dependent on state support and, accusing the Madras government of unacceptable extravagance in its relief provisions, directed that only those in the most extreme state of destitution should be admitted to

[127] Revenue Proceedings, 146-B, 10 Nov. 1876.
[128] W. S. Foster, Collector, Kurnool, to Sec., Board of Revenue, 6 Oct. 1876, Revenue Proceedings. 196, 17 Oct. 1876.
[129] *Review of the Madras Famine*, pp. 25–6, 35, 49–50; *Report of the Indian Famine Commission*, Pt. 3, p. 205.

gratuitous relief. Wages for labourers on relief works were also cut despite protests from Madras officials and medical experts.[130]

For its part the Government of Madras was increasingly anxious to deter further migration from the countryside to the towns and less drought-affected districts. It was felt that the provision of relief only through special camps and works had failed to meet the still expanding scale of the famine by May 1877 and that this had 'tended to foster wandering and unhomely habits among the distressed, which rendered their distress more difficult to detect and costly to relieve'.[131] It was concerned too in looking forward to the expected monsoons of 1877 to operate relief measures that would 'keep the people at their homes, where they are known and where they will be on the spot to take advantage of any opportunities for cultivation which may arise . . .'[132] Accordingly in May 1877 it authorized the issue through village headmen of money doles to those who were 'fit objects for relief' but who could not, or would not, go to the relief camps. By mid-August 1877, at the high point of the famine, gratuitous relief was being provided for 1,131,000 people while, despite Temple's intervention, the number on relief works had reached around one million. Once rain in September of that year made the resumption of agricultural operations at last possible, numbers dropped sharply. By December 1877 there were only 470,000 on relief works. But the final run-down was protracted. In July 1878 relief was still being provided for 200,000 people and the works were not finally closed and gratuitous relief terminated until December 1878.[133]

Drought and famine occasioned unparalleled contact between the peasantry and the colonial state. This was particularly so of the subordinate stratum of the peasantry which in normal times rarely had any direct communication with the state. The patta-holding peasant proprietors under the raiyatwari system had more frequent contact, but even for them drought and famine created greater inter-action with, or new expectations of, the state. In the main however the encounter between peasant and state was marked by a high degree of mutual suspicion and misunderstanding.

As we have already seen there was a widespread expectation on the

[130] *Madras Sanitary Commissioner's Proceedings*, XIV, 1877, pp. 49–86.
[131] G.O. 1830, Rev. (Fam.), 28 May 1877.
[132] G.O. 2443, Rev. (Fam.), 4 Aug. 1877.
[133] *Report of the Indian Famine Commission*, Pt. 3, pp. 205–7; G.O. 2485, Rev. (Fam.), 6 Dec. 1878.

part of the poorer peasantry that the government would intervene on its behalf to curb the profiteering of grain traders and exercise control over the hoarding, pricing and distribution of food. Raiyats looked to the government to grant remissions on failed or deficient crops and to liberalize normal restrictions on irrigation water and tank cultivation. The expectation was of an interventionist, sympathetic state. But the government's actual response was based upon different principles. It adhered to a policy of free trade in grain movements and sales (which may well have pleased the richest raiyats); it was reluctant to grant remissions or loans; and when it did respond to the needs of the destitute it demanded labour wherever possible in exchange for food, and enforced its measures with a resort to coercion, regimentation and incarceration in camps that was uncongenial to the peasantry. A Hindu, presumably from the middle classes but expressing a subaltern viewpoint many peasants must have shared, wrote to the *Madras Mail* in February 1877 to protest at the force policemen in Madras used to get destitute women and children to go to relief houses and police stations. The latter, he remarked, 'the unfortunate women from the country look upon as prisons, and are most reluctant to enter, and do enter only with bitter cries'.[134]

Objections to their treatment at the hands of police and officials, and protests at the conditions and regulations in the camps, were also voiced by the peasants themselves. Inmates at a camp in Krishna district complained in July 1877: 'We are not prisoners that you should compel us to work'.[135] Some destitutes threatened to commit suicide rather than be dragged off to the camps intended for their benefit.[136] It was not therefore surprising that desertions from the camps and works occurred on a large scale. Out of 4,000 labourers sent to a construction site in Gooty taluk, Bellary, in December 1877, 600 had fled by the following morning.[137] Many of the famine poor were said to prefer 'liberty and the chance of picking up a scant living by begging and pilfering a little grain in the fields to the confinement and discipline of a closed camp'.[138] In Madurai district it

[134] *Madras Mail*, 9 Feb. 1877, p. 3e.

[135] S. M. Tyrell, Zillah Surgeon, Guntur, to Deputy Surgeon-General, Madras, 11 July 1877, G.O. 2440-A, Rev. (Fam.), 3 Aug. 1877.

[136] R. K. Puckle, Third Member, Board of Revenue, Memorandum, 4 Aug. 1877, G.O. 2443, Rev. (Fam.), 4 Aug. 1878.

[137] Lt. R. E. Wilson, Taluk Relief Officer, Gooty, to Subcollector, Bellary, 14 Dec. 1877, G.O. 120, Rev. (Fam.), 14 Jan. 1878.

[138] J. F. Price, Collector, Cuddapah, to Sec., Board of Revenue, 26 Oct. 1877, G.O. 3060, Rev. (Fam.), 8 Dec. 1877.

was remarked that as soon as a family has saved enough food for the road, 'they preferred to emigrate to easy labour in Ceylon to continuing to work here [on relief works]'.[139] Suspicion of the government's motives was easily aroused. Rumours circulated that people had been brought together in such large numbers so that they could be converted to Christianity or sacrificed to the Christian god. It was feared that they would be sent to work in some strange and distant place or that they were being made to lose caste by eating ritually impure food and by association with ritually polluting castes.[140] Twenty years later (another reminder of the lasting impression famine experience left on peasants' consciousness) at the time of the 1896–7 famine in the Presidency it was still widely believed that the camps of 1876–8 had been set up deliberately to poison the the inmates: why else it was reasoned had so many people died in them?[141] Famine thus brought out the ambiguity in peasant attitudes to the colonial state: the expectation of a sympathetic response tempered by resentment at official harassment and restrictions and by deep suspicion of the state's motives.

Government relief measures also met with other forms of cultural resistance on the part of the peasantry. Despite the destitution to which the famine had reduced many raiyats by the second half of 1877, they remained most reluctant to join the relief works and camps because of their disdain for 'coolie' labour and for taking charity from others. They were also suspicious of being forced into polluting contact with untouchable castes or made to lose caste by accepting food prepared by cooks from ritually inferior castes. As a result the poorer of the caste-proud raiyats, like the Gounders of Coimbatore, began to suffer severely during the later stages of the famine, though some it would appear were willing to set aside their scruples to the extent of attending kanji-houses or accepting village doles.[142] The government tried to satisfy the raiyats that caste sentiments were being respected by the provision of appropriate cooks

[139] J. Lee-Warner, Special Assistant Collector, to Collector, Madurai, n.d., G.O. 2284, Rev. (Fam.), 11 Oct. 1877.

[140] Major E. W. Shaw, Special Relief Officer, Punganur, to Collector, N. Arcot, 23 Feb. 1878, G.O. 633, Rev. (Fam.), 9 Mar. 1878; *Madras Times*, 10 Nov. 1877, p. 3a.

[141] *Report of the Famine . . . 1896–97*, I, pp. 147–8.

[142] A. Wedderburn, Collector, Appendix to Fortnightly Report, 13 Oct. 1877, G.O. 2610, Rev. (Fam.), 29 Oct. 1877; G. MacKenzie, Head Assistant Collector, to Collector, Coimbatore, 12 Aug. 1877, G.O. 2680-A, Rev. (Fam.), 8 Sept. 1877; Wedderburn to Sec., Board of Revenue, 24 July 1877, G.O. 2522, Rev. (Fam.), 17 Aug. 1877.

and of separate eating and sleeping areas for the different communities. But the raiyats remained aloof for as long as they could possibly do so. Partly for this reason the great majority of labourers on the relief works and inmates in the camps were from the poorest and lowest-ranking sections of rural society. They included a very large proportion of untouchables, as well as members of itinerant and tribal communities, poor raiyats, shepherds, village artisans and members of service castes.[143] Weavers were also badly affected by the famine but were treated by the government as a special case and not obliged to labour on relief works for their living.

A second striking feature of the composition of the famine labourers and camp inmates was the high proportion of women and children. In Kurnool district in July 1877 for example women formed 39 per cent and children 35 per cent of the 10,366 people in relief camps, and 34 and 40 per cent respectively of those on village relief.[144] Of the 1,141 inmates of two camps in Cuddapah in June 1877, 34.4 per cent were women and 33.4 per cent children compared to only 32.3 per cent men, while of the 2,888 labourers on road works in Nellore in December 1877, 46.6 per cent were women, 29.2 children and 24.2 men.[145] In the southern Tamil districts the low proportion of men on relief might be explained by the fact that it was mainly men who left to work in Sri Lanka or in the hills, while women and children remained at home or drifted to the relief camps. But cultural factors might also be involved. Among low-caste and untouchable communities it was common even in normal times for women and children to perform manual work in the fields and on earthworks and roads. Since a large proportion of those on relief came from these communities it was not surprising that their women and children were well represented among those seeking work and food. Among the caste-conscious raiyats however their extreme reluctance to accept state charity or enter relief works appears to have been partially overcome by sending the women and children instead. As the official report on

[143] W. R. Cornish to Sec., Revenue, 1 Aug. 1877, G.O. 2492, Rev. (Fam.), 13 Aug. 1877; A. J. B. Atkinson, Head Assistant Collector, to Collector, Nellore, 10 Dec. 1877, Rev. (Fam.), G.O. 3237, 27 Dec. 1877.

[144] C. J. Knox, Special Assistant Collector, Kurnool, to Sec., Board of Revenue, 18 July 1877, G.O. 2488-A, Rev. (Fam.), 11 Aug. 1877.

[145] R. S. Benson, Head Assistant Collector, to Collector, Cuddapah, 22 June 1877, Rev. (Fam.), Proceedings, 19-A, 1 Aug. 1877; A. J. B. Atkinson, Head Assistant Collector, to Collector, Nellore, 10 Dec. 1877, G.O. 3237, Rev. (Fam.), 27 Dec. 1877.

the 1896–7 famine remarked (somewhat condescendingly) on the same phenomenon, the raiyats preferred to send their wives and children 'to bear the brunt of the disgrace—and the hard work incident to it' rather than go themselves.[146] If this was so then it represents another example of the way in which raiyats transferred part of the burden of the famine to subordinate social groups, in this case women and children. One other possible explanation is that men were more likely than women to be able to take advantage of any work opportunities that arose, whether on their own land or on others', and that the raiyats wanted to stay as close to their land for as long as they could.

It would seem too that many of the children that arrived at relief camps claiming to be famine orphans were actually sent by parents or other relatives as a temporary expedient while the crisis lasted. Once the drought was over the great majority were quickly reclaimed by relatives: by the end of 1878 only 760 orphans were still in state hands, by the end of 1879 a mere 69.[147] The young were welcomed back to replace those who had died, and as productive family members. There was greater reluctance to reassume the responsibility of the old, the infirm, and widows who had also been abandoned to the state during the famine. Along with 'habitual paupers', these constituted a large part of the social residue that remained in the relief camps after September 1877.[148]

The Aftermath

Slowly, painfully, peasant society in south India began to recover from the ravages of famine. Those who survived returned to their homes—from Sri Lanka, from hills, from the towns, the relief works and the famine camps. But many districts, above all Bellary, Kurnool and Cuddapah where the famine had been most intense and protracted, showed the scars for many years afterwards. The devastating combi-

---

[146] *Report of the Famine . . . 1896–97*, I, p. 148.

[147] *Review of the Madras Famine*, p. 76; E. Gibson, Special Assistant Collector, to Collector, Kurnool, 10 Dec. 1877, G.O. 9, Rev. (Fam.), 3 Jan. 1878. In Kipling's fictionalized account of the Madras famine, mothers tied beads and rags round their children's wrists a l necks before entrusting them to the relief camps so that they would know them to reclaim them after the famine: 'William the Conqueror', *The Day's Work* (London, 1898), p. 192.

[148] Col. W. S. Drever, Commissioner of Police, to Sec., Revenue, 19 Nov. 1877, G.O. 2881, Rev. (Fam.), 23 Nov. 1877; Major C. D. Barnes, to Collector, Salem, 6 Jan. 1878, G.O. 316, Rev. (Fam.), 7 Feb. 1878.

nation of drought, dearth and disease aggravated by mass migration and inadequate relief measures left many areas with depleted, exhausted populations, with villages half-empty or abandoned.

It is impossible to calculate the extent of the mortality with any accuracy and this essay will not try to do so. A toll of 3.5 million dead for the Madras Presidency seemed even to many contemporaries an underestimate. The 1881 provincial Census, despite attempts to minimize the famine's impact, gave some indication of the scale of the disaster. The recorded population was almost half-a-million less than the 31.6 million given in the 1871 Census, itself probably too low a figure. Age profiles showed the heavy mortality that had struck in particular the old and very young and the slow recovery of human fertility. In several districts the number of occupied houses and inhabited villages had fallen significantly. Bellary, Kurnool, Cuddapah and Salem together had lost 19.8 per cent of their 1871 recorded populations and 18.5 per cent of their occupied houses.[149] The Census gave some indication too of the far greater mortality among the labourers, poorer raiyats and village artisan castes than among the higher and more prosperous communities. In Coimbatore for example the number of raiyats and labourers from the Gounder caste was calculated to have fallen by no more than 1.9 per cent of their 1871 population while Vanniyar labourers and sub-tenants had suffered a loss of 23.6 per cent, Kaikilan weavers and labourers 10.1 per cent and Paraiya untouchable labourers 8.4 per cent.[150]

Having lost crops and cattle, having consumed their seed grain and sold their remaining possessions, raiyats saw no alternative but to mortgage their land to richer raiyats, landlords and moneylenders in order to obtain the plough bullocks, seed and implements they needed to resume agricultural activity. With the rains in September 1877 rural credit began to flow again, albeit at even higher rates of interest than formerly. Creditors took the opportunity to profit from the first satisfactory crops for two years and to strengthen their hold over the cultivators. Raiyats who could afford not to sell their grain as soon as it ripened were chary about putting it on the market, fearing that drought and famine might return. In consequence prices remained high despite the adequate harvest, though this did not necessarily have an adverse effect on the labourers who were again being employed and paid in grain.

[149] *Census of India, 1881: Madras*, Vol. I, p. 18.
[150] Nicholson, p. 273; *Census, 1881, Madras*, pp. 114–15.

The government too had an interest in seeing agricultural production resumed as quickly as possible. The famine was estimated to have cost 191 lakhs of rupees in lost revenues and a further 630 lakhs in relief expenditure.[151] In order to stimulate agriculture while trying to recover some of its losses, the government advanced loans to peasants and granted limited remissions for lost or deficient harvests. Between 1876 and 1878 it gave Rs 3,80,903 in advances for seed grain and made Rs 14,19,533 available under the Land Improvement Act. The largest share of this assistance went to Bellary.[152] But loans had to be repaid and fresh revenue demands met. Good harvests aided recovery but the continuing financial burden was too great for many cultivators. As the administration itself acknowledged in 1881, 'The large increase in the number of forced sales and other severe processes, and the decreased area under occupation in Salem and other districts, point to the difficulty the Madras ryot encountered in satisfying the demands of the state'.[153] In Kurnool district, where the famine was said to have set back agriculture by twenty-five years, the revenue arrears for which coercion was used rose from a little over 1 lakh of rupees in 1876–7 to 4.5 lakhs in 1877–8, 7.7 lakhs in 1878–9, and 11.2 in 1879–80 before falling back to 7.3 in 1880–1 and 3.1 in 1881–2. Property valued at 2.9 lakhs in 1879–80 and 1.9 lakhs in 1880–1 was sold in Kurnool to meet arrears.[154] The famine was over but its economic as well as social consequences lasted for many years afterwards.

Assistance of a more generous nature came from the Mansion House Fund, set up on the initiative of Europeans in Madras but collected mainly in Britain. Launched at the end of July 1877 the fund had raised Rs 81,45,829 by the time that it closed in November 1877. Two-thirds of this was distributed to raiyats to buy plough bullocks and seed grain and to repair houses. The scale of this aid and the fact that it was given without a demand for eventual repayment made it a valuable contribution to the famine-ravaged economy.[155] But the opportunity was not lost to impress upon the recipients the magnanimity of the ruling race: there was a clear message that it was

[151] *Report of the Indian Famine Commission*, Pt. 3, p. 208. A lakh is 100,000.
[152] *Review of the Madras Famine*, pp. 294–5.
[153] *Report of the Indian Famine Commission*, Pt. 3, p. 209.
[154] Benson, *Kurnool*, pp. 20, 34.
[155] W. Digby, 'Memorandum on Private Relief', 22 Jan. 1879, *Report of the Indian Famine Commission*, Pt. 3, pp. 121–7.

the superior civilization of the West that made possible charity on
such a scale and from so great a distance.

Famine provided a temporary stimulus to increased labour mobility
but it had little lasting effect. Planters and public works contractors
welcomed the sudden plenitude of cheap labour, but their requirements were small and Madras at this date had little modern industry
to provide employment for those who had fled to the towns in search
of food and work. When the famine was over the great majority of
the survivors returned home to their villages and no substantial
urbanization and proletarianization can be seen to have resulted
directly from the famine. In some districts, notably Coimbatore, a
shortage of labour in the towns and in the countryside led to a
temporary increase in the wages of labourers, but in the Ceded
Districts wage levels appear to have remained low because of the
raiyats' poverty and the slowness of agricultural recovery.[156] Without
a significant pull to the towns, with little immediate increase in
overseas migration, the peasants turned back to the soil for their
livelihood. Despite the hardships famine had engendered, despite the
conflicts and disappointed expectations it had made apparent, peasants
had little practical alternative but to resume their old way of life with
all its anxieties and frustrations, its oppressions and exactions.

Conclusion

What do the attitudes and actions of peasants confronted by a major
crisis of subsistence and survival, like that of the Madras famine of
1876–8, tell us about peasant consciousness?

It is no accident that many aspects of the peasants' response to
drought, dearth and famine have close parallels in peasant insurrection.[157] As was remarked at the outset, subsistence crises, like
rebellions, bring into prominence attitudes and identities that lay
dormant or half-concealed in more normal times: both gave rise to a
form of heightened reality. Certain specific actions, especially the
pillaging of grain bazaars or dacoity and theft directed against traders
and moneylenders, were in themselves enactments of rebellion on a
minor scale and in transitory form. But more fundamentally, peasant
action in famine as in rebellion reflected a single underlying consciousness, employed a single vocabulary of expression and drew

[156] Revenue Administration Report, 1877–8, BRP, 12 Nov. 1878.
[157] Cf. Ranajit Guha, *Elementary Aspects of Peasant Insurgency in Colonial India*
(Delhi, 1983).

upon a basic, limited store of beliefs and symbols. Rumour for example was a powerful agent in the self-mobilization of the poorer peasantry in the face of threatened food shortages and famine as it was in situations of incipient insurrection. Attacks on bazaar traders, moneylenders and grain hoarders often also showed a sense of discrimination only against those whom the poorer peasantry saw as greedy, selfish and exploitative. One might see evidence too of a peasant sense of territoriality in the attachment to village identities and opposition to the export of local grain, though famine migration showed that some peasants were prepared, in such crises of subsistence, to travel far beyond their home territory in search of food and work.

The two most central aspects of peasant consciousness that emerge from the Madras famine situation are peasant solidarity or collectivity, and peasant attitudes towards power.

The rain-making ceremonies described at the beginning of this essay gave expression, through ritual forms, to a congruity between ideal and actual village solidarity. The impending disaster of drought and famine was seen as one that threatened the entire village community, and all members of that community regardless of caste or economic position were required to participate and contribute to the joint endeavour to avert the crisis by seeking divine assistance. While perceptions of village collectivity or peasant solidarity remained, it could not in actuality be sustained in the face of deepening drought and famine. Different sections of rural society had different interests or divergent views of where the collective interest lay. The labourers, though without work, demanded food; the raiyats sought to conserve their grain for their families or in order to sell it; the moneylenders withdrew their credit; the traders raised their prices or refused to sell. The growth of a market-oriented economy may have accentuated the nature of divergent or conflicting interests in the countryside, though it is unlikely that colonialism and capitalism had created a self-interest that was formerly entirely absent.

Peasant collectivity became fragmented but it did not suddenly disappear. Raiyats made collective attempts, sometimes through the agency of the village headman, to secure remission of revenue payments or other concessions from the state. Poorer villagers strove to maintain a collectivity that would ensure them a share of remaining grain stores and sought to punish those who, from self-interest, denied it to them. Only gradually did the possibilities of collective action disintergrate to be replaced by individual desperation. The conventional image of famine 'victims', of isolated and powerless supplicants, relates only to the final process of disintegration and even then perhaps fails to reflect the enduring perception of the crisis as a collective one.

Collectivity informed peasant action at several levels. It lent individual peasants an anonymity and strength of numbers that compensated to some degree from their separate weakness and vulnerability. This was evident when they pressed demands upon village élites and officials or when they engaged in looting and collective theft. The strength of their numbers gave peasants not only greater coercive power, but also greater confidence in the legitimacy of their action. Collectivity was therefore as fundamental to peasant action as it was to peasant consciousness. It was important in one further way, too. Because the experience of famine was, like rebellion, a collective one, it lived on in the collective memory of the peasantry: it was a historical marker that rose above personal tragedy and the annual seasonal cycle as an event of enduring religious and social significance for the peasant community as a whole.

While peasants saw themselves as a collectivity, they were also conscious of the relationships of power and function that operated within and beyond the peasant community. In normal times these relationships were seldom questioned, partly because peasants were preoccupied with the immediate problems of production and survival but also because they saw themselves as occupying a relatively fixed position within the social order. But their acceptance of that order entailed a belief that superordinate groups had certain responsibilities toward the peasants by virtue of the latter's labour and services, from which superordinates had benefitted by virtue of their very possession of power. When in the face of a major subsistence crisis superordinates ignored peasant needs or failed to respond with an appropriate exercize of their power, peasants believed themselves entitled to act—through petitions, entreaties, riots and appropriations—to remind them of their responsibilities or to punish their neglect. The peasants were far from being aspiring revolutionaries seeking to overturn the existing order. On the contrary they were in effect reaffirming that order by requiring that it function in the ways in which, from custom and collective need, they believed it should. They did not see themselves as without power to at least partially achieve this objective, just as in the religious context they believed in the efficacy of their prayers and rituals to move the gods and produce the rain they needed for their crops.

The irony of the famine situation, not unlike that of insurrection, was that peasant solidarity and peasant power were seldom sufficient or sustained enough to do more than produce a limited response. Local and temporary concessions might be won from traders and officials; starvation and loss might be avoided through theft, migration or other expedients. But the net effect of the famine was to render even more emphatic the peasant's subordination to the moneylender, the trader, the landholder and the state.*

---

* In reworking this essay from an earlier draft I am greatly indebted to suggestions and critical comments made by Shahid Amin, Dipesh Chakrabarty, Partha Chatterjee, Bernard Cohn, Ranajit Guha, David Hardiman, Gyan Pandey, Sumit Sarkar and other paritcipants at the Conference on the Subaltern in South Asian History and Society at Canberra in November 1982.

Trade Unions in a Hierarchical Culture
The Jute Workers of Calcutta, 1920–50.[1]

DIPESH CHAKRABARTY

I

In the 1920s and '30s most observers of labour conditions in the jute industry of Calcutta agreed that there was an urgent need for working-class organization. Even the Government of Bengal, which could hardly be suspected of pro-labour sympathies, was moved to remark in 1929 that the industry was 'full of anomalies, which could never exist were there a properly organized jute workers' union'.[2] Besides, with the jute mills situated in very close proximity to one another, the industry often seemed to provide an ideal basis for a strong trade union movement. The government described this labour force in 1933 as 'perhaps the largest and the most compact group of workers with identical interests in the world'.[3] The Bengal Labour Commissioner also wrote in the same vein in 1935: 'Nowhere in the world are there better territorial conditions for labour organization than round about Calcutta. The jute mills are concentrated in a narrow range of, say, 20 miles north and south of Calcutta . . . [and] employ about 300,000 persons'.[4]

[1] This is a part of a larger study that I have recently completed. Some of my statements here are substantiated in more detail in that study. I am grateful to the editor and other contributors of this volume, as well as to the participants at the Canberra seminar on *Subaltern Studies* held in November 1982 for criticisms of an earlier draft.

[2] *Report of the Royal Commission on Labour in India* (London, 1931) [hereafter *R.C.L.I.*] Vol. 5, Pt. 1, p. 159.

[3] West Bengal State Archives [hereafter, W.B.S.A.] Com[merce] Dept. Com[merce] Br. Dec. 1933 A14–39.

[4] W.B.S.A., Home Political [Poll] Confidential [Confdl]. no. 392(1–3)/1935.

Yet a striking feature of the history of the jute workers' movement was the absence, relatively speaking, of strong and enduring trade unions. A government enquiry in 1945 revealed that only about 18 per cent of the workers—some 47,697 of a total of 267,193—were members of any unions.[5] This was an uncertain estimate; 'it is important to remember', cautioned the author of the report, 'that membership figures of Trade Unions are not always very reliable'.[6] An important trade union leader was to sound an even more cautionary note a few years later. Speaking to a convention of the All India Trade Union Congress (A.I.T.U.C.) held in Calcutta in 1952, Indrajit Gupta, the General Secretary of the Communist-dominated Bengal Chatkal Mazdoor Union, reminded his comrades of 'the harsh reality that the *overwhelming majority* of them [the jute mill workers], perhaps 95%, [were] not organized in any trade union' at all.[7] Both Gupta's conclusion and that drawn in the official report of 1946 were the same. 'There is no doubt', the latter said, 'that Trade Unionism in the jute mill industry . . . is in an extremely weak condition'.[8] 'No healthy tradition of trade unionism has yet developed among the jute workers', was the view put forward by Gupta.[9]

II

The persistent weakness of jute workers' organization has been seen as somewhat paradoxical, given the history of their long-standing grievances and their tradition of militant and sometimes well-organized strikes.[10] This militancy was especially marked in the 1920s and afterwards when strikes became much more frequent than before. In analysing some eighty-nine strikes—twenty-seven of them in jute mills alone—that occurred in the Calcutta industrial area during the

[5] S. R. Deshpande, *Report on an Enquiry into Conditions of Labour in the Jute Mill Industry of India* (Delhi, 1946), pp. 6, 34–5. [6] ibid., p. 34.
[7] Indrajit Gupta, *Capital and Labour in the Jute Industry* (Bombay, 1953), p. 50. Emphasis in original. [8] Deshpande, *Report*, p. 35.
[9] Gupta, *Capital and Labour*, p. 51.
[10] This is how the problem has been formulated in a recent study of left politics in Bengal. See Tanika Sarkar, 'National Movement and Popular Protest in Bengal, 1928–1934' (Ph.D. thesis, University of Delhi, 1980). The 'paradox in working-class organization' is seen here in 'the absence of regular unions and the workers' indifference to long-standing joint work on the one hand and the remarkable discipline and organizational ability in the face of tremendous odds of the short-term strike committees on the other' (pp. 155–6). It is also said in this work that the 'conditions of jute workers explain the long tradition of militancy and conflict with the management' (pp. 144–5).

second half of 1920, the Committee on Industrial Unrest did not think it necessary 'to go back further than the 1st July 1920' as strikes were much less common in the past. 'Before that time [1920]', said the Committee, 'a certain amount of industrial unrest had been evident in Bengal as in other parts of India, but in Bengal strikes had not been resorted to on any large scale as a means of enforcing the demands of the workers'.[11] Their opinion was echoed by the Director of Industries, Bengal, in an article he wrote in 1921. He described the 'epidemic of strikes' that broke out in Bengal in 1920 as 'unprecedented in the history of the province', as strikes 'had appeared only in isolated cases' in the earlier period when 'the demands had more commonly been non-economic in character'.[12] Between 1921 and 30 June 1929 there were 201 recorded strikes in the jute industry, far surpassing the numbers in the preceding decades.[13]

It was not just the higher frequency of strikes however that made the authorities take notice of them; the authorities were also sometimes worried by their longer duration. A strike in the Fort Gloster Jute Mills in 1928 was described by the government as 'the most protracted strike in the industry' till then. It lasted from 17 July to 31 December 1928 and was soon followed by a general strike that began in July 1929 and ran till the end of September. One 'notable' feature of this strike, the government thought, was its 'magnitude': 'never before in the history of the jute mills in Bengal had anything of the nature of a general strike been attempted'.[14] The strike presaged the shape of things to come. After a temporary period of lull—1930 to 1933—working-class militancy reached a peak once again in the mid-1930s, culminating in a second general strike in 1937.

What this militancy reflected in the first place was certainly a heightened sense of grievance on the part of the jute mill worker. The Royal Commission on Labour (1929) was told by a jute mill manager who had been around for about thirty years that 'there was not so much discontent [before] as there is today'.[15] A. C. Roy Chowdhury, who carried out on behalf of the Commission an enquiry into the standard of living of the jute mill workers, reported that he had heard 'much discontented talk on the subject of low wages and lack of

[11] W.B.S.A., Com. Dept. Com. Br. July 1921 A40–42.
[12] (D. B. Meek?), 'Trade Disputes in Bengal', *Journal of Indian Industries and Labour*, Pt. 1, Feb. 1921, p. 71.
[13] *R.C.L.I.*, Vol. 5, Pt. 1, p. 126.   [14] ibid.
[15] ibid., Vol. 5, Pt. 2, p. 188.

accommodation'.[16] Further the Commission itself came across some particularly sharp expressions of workers' grievances over wages and living conditions. 'Upon this [wage]' said Kamala, an Oriya woman employed by the Howrah Jute Mill, '. . . two people cannot live'.[17] Mangrul, a young boy from Patna working at the Titaghur Jute Mill, was equally forthright. 'Formerly I was well fleshed', he said, 'but now I am weak as I do not get enough food'.[18]

What made for such 'discontented talk' by the workers? Partly no doubt their conditions, which seem to have taken a turn for the worse in the late 'twenties and 'thirties. From about the mid-1920s, as the industry experienced the beginnings of a trade depression, it moved towards a policy of reducing its wage-bill. An early 'sign of the change' was the decision of the Reliance Jute Mill in 1923 to switch over to the single-shift system of work, resulting in the dismissal of 'over 2,000 workmen' and an important strike. 'There is no doubt whatsoever', wrote R. N. Gilchrist, the Labour Intelligence Officer of Bengal, 'that the condition of the industry at the moment is giving the Managing Agents furiously to think', and some of them were now 'coming round to the view that perhaps it would be more economical to work 5 or 5½ days a week on the single shift in preference to the multiple shift system'.[19] By 1927 the workers had begun to feel the pinch of the employers' policies. About one-third of the recorded strikes in the jute mills that year were due to 'the recently introduced change in the system of shifts'. The Government of Bengal informed the Government of India that 'in each of these disputes there invariably was a complaint on the part of the workmen concerned that the change, which was accompanied by the lengthening of the working week, resulted in a decrease in their weekly earnings'.[20] The same complaint provided the 'economic basis' to the general strike of 1929. When the employers tried to explain the strike away by attributing it to 'the machinations of [political] agitators financed by Marwari "Hessian" merchants', Sir David Petrie of the Government of India's Intelligence Bureau retorted by pointing to the 'economic basis' of the strike, which 'did not seem to be disputed by anyone'; this basis lay, in Petrie's words, in 'an increase in the weekly

[16] W.B.S.A., Com. Dept. Com. Br. April 1931 A8–13.
[17] *R.C.L.I.*, Vol. 11, p. 361.
[18] ibid., Vol. 5, Pt. 1, p. 77.
[19] National Archives of India [N.A.I.], Industries [Ind.] and Labour [Lab.] no. L-881(4) of 1923.   [20] N.A.I., Ind. and Lab. no. L-881(18) of 1927.

working hours without any corresponding adjustment of wages'.[21] To these grievances were added those of unemployment and actual reduction in the wage-rates in the 1930s. About 60,000 workers were laid off in 1930–1,[22] and this was followed by wage-cuts. As one government official wrote in August 1932—

> The majority of the mills are working for 40 hours a week spread over four or five days. Many operatives are now paid as little as from Re 1–10 Rs 2–1 a week. In the present economic depression of the industry there is no possibility of any increase in the rates of wages . . .[23]

The decline in the bargaining position of the working class in these years is reflected in the stagnant money-wage figures for the industry. They are in strong contrast to an apparent increase in productivity. In addition the figures for the remittances (money-orders) sent by the workers to their villages suggest a significant drop in their earnings. The average value of such money-orders fell by 17 per cent in the 1930s compared to the average for 1922–9.

There was thus enough in the jute mill workers' conditions to make them feel discontented. But we should not fall into the trap of thinking that working-class militancy was rooted in conditions alone or that the conditions by themselves were sufficient to generate such militancy. The persistence and volume of labour unrest in the 1920s and '30s have also to be understood as signalling a growing propensity on the part of the workers to protest and challenge the employer's authority. The 1929 general strike for instance surprised the government by the 'apparent ease with which the jute mill workers were brought out' by the organizers of the strike.[24] 'One thing is certain', Sir Edward Benthall of Bird and Company privately remarked in his diary immediately after the strike, 'the best paid labour struck as easily as the less well paid'.[25] It is indeed this growing presence among the workers of a will to resist the employer that makes their lack of organization seem truly paradoxical.

Given the problems of documenting the consciousness of the jute mill workers, their will to resist and question the authority of their

[21] N.A.I., Home Poll Confdl. no. 257/I and K.W. of 1930. I owe this reference to Mridula Mahajan.

[22] See W.B.S.A., Home Poll Confdl. no. 150/1931.

[23] W.B.S.A., Com. Dept. Com. Br., Feb. 1933 A5–37. See also Com. Dept. Com. Br. June 1935 A35–48. [24] *R.C.L.I.*, Vol. 5, Pt. 1, p. 126.

[25] Centre for South Asian Studies, Cambridge [hereafter, C.S.A.S.] Benthall Papers [hereafter B.P.] Box 7, Diary for 1929–33, entry for 10 Sept. 1929.

employers can be read only in terms of the sense of crisis it produced among the people in authority. 'Labour has come to a dim realization of its own importance', discerned a concerned government official as early as 1924. 'This is not yet overt', he said, 'yet, as every mill manager will bear out, labour cannot be handled as it was in the old days. It now requires delicate management. Brutality, bullying, unfairness, all quickly lead to trouble—usually strikes'.[26] The old argument of the government—that the strike was 'a private matter between the masters and the men'[27]—was found no longer tenable as the force and magnitude of the general strike of 1929 compelled the government to abandon such fine considerations and intervene in settling the dispute.[28]

In the 1930s the 'private' authority of the individual mill manager was increasingly viewed as an inadequate agency for controlling working-class unrest. This may be seen in the direct and enlarged role given to the Labour Commissioner of the Bengal government in 1937 in monitoring labour disputes in individual jute mills.[29] The institution of Labour Officers that the Indian Jute Mills Association (I.J.M.A.) created in 1937 was another attempt to create a new means of control.[30] In addition, the I.J.M.A. now set up its own Intelligence Service to receive timely 'warnings of developments and of the general trend of opinion' among labourers.[31] 'The idea . . . [was] to have paid spies in every mill or group of mills who [would] give information to the Intelligence Officers'.[32] Some individual companies even created their own labour officers and Benthall's description of the physical construction of the office proposed for their own man, Col. Spain, bears a distinct imprint of the wariness with which the employers now viewed the mood of the workers. Spain's office was to be given a 'bolt hole at the back in case labour control[led] him instead of the reverse'.[33]

[26] R. N. Gilchrist, *The Payment of Wages and Profit-Sharing* (Calcutta, 1924), pp. 236–7. See also my article 'On Deifying and Defying Authority: Managers and Workers In the Jute Mills of Bengal, 1890–1940', forthcoming in *Past and Present*.

[27] W.B.S.A., Com. Dept. Com. Br. Aug. 1925 A7–8.

[28] See *R.C.L.I.*, Vol. 5, Pt. 1, p. 133; N.A.I., Home Poll Confdl. no. 257/1 and K.W. of 1930.

[29] C.S.A.S., B.P., Box 12, confidential record of an interview of the I.J.M.A. Chairman with H. S. Suhrawardy, Labour Minister, with A. Hughes, Labour Commissioner, present, on 28 July 1937 at the Writers Buildings.

[30] *I.J.M.A. Report for 1937* (Calcutta, 1938), pp. 43, 132.

[31] C.S.A.S., B.P., Box 12, 'Paul' to Benthall, 11 Aug. 1937.

[32] C.S.A.S., B.P., Box 13, 'Paul' to Benthall, 1 Sept. 1937.

[33] C.S.A.S., B.P., Box 13, Benthall to 'Paul', 28 Sept. 1937.

We intend to provide him with an office in Titaghur Bazar on a piece of
Kinnison land with an unobtrusive means of entry through the back into
Titaghur [Mill] compound in case at any time a hasty retreat becomes
desirable.[34]

'The average cooly', wrote an angry jute mill manager in 1937, 'has
his point of view and thinks we are exploiting him all the time, which
is borne out by the fact that they believe the most ridiculous things
told to them by the outside agitators in spite of all we have done to try
and convince them of the truth of affairs'.[35] This naive but important
statement can serve as a measure of the growing sense of hostility and
distance that formed an important element of capital-labour relations
in the 1930s. The intensity of this hostility is inscribed in the currency
that the word 'dalal' (an agent or stooge of the employer) acquired in
the 1930s as a working-class term of abuse and in the strong emotions
it aroused. Some of the Muslim League trade unionists and workers
who tried to combat the influence of the Communist leader A. M. A.
Zaman among the jute mill workers of Hooghly in 1937 learned this
at much cost to themselves. Mohiuddin Khan, one of their leaders,
bitterly complained to his mentor, H. S. Suhrawardy, how labourers
belonging to his union had been 'intimidated, threatened [and]
molested' by the followers of Zaman. One of his 'Dalhousie [Mill]
Union worker[s]', he said, had been 'assaulted by one Subhan of the
Dalhousie Jute Mills'; his supporter, Mati Sardar of the Northbrook
Jute Mills, had been 'chased [away] by some mill-hands'; and his
follower Syed Habibur Rahman's life was in such danger that 'the
poor man . . . slept inside [his] room bolted from within and was
literally boiled in this oppressive weather'. At the Champdani Jute
Mill an effigy of yet another worker of his union, Nurie, was 'taken
round the mill by the partisans of Mr Zaman . . . [and was] spat on
and beaten with shoes'.[36] Interestingly Khan's own explanation of
what caused such working-class hatred and anger to be unleashed
against his men suggests the strongly negative appeal of the word
'dalal' to at least some of the labourers in the mills:

> The supporters of Mr Zaman . . . abused and insulted us. [They] shouted
> that the Dallals had come and that nobody should listen to them [us] . . .
> [Zaman] incited the mob to beat the dallals if they ever set their feet in
> Champdany.[37]

[34] C.S.A.S., B.P., Box 13, 'Paul' to Benthall, 20 Sept. 1937.
[35] C.S.A.S., B.P., Box 12, 'Paul' to Benthall, 21 July 1937, enclosures.
[36] W.B.S.A., Home Poll Confdl. no. 326/1937.   [37] ibid.

If the mere labelling of someone as a 'dalal' (i.e. as an agent of the employer) could trigger off such a violent response towards him, we can imagine how charged with a spirit of hostility the atmosphere must have been towards the owners and the managers of the mills, alongside a cordial hatred of anyone seen acting in their interests. To be sure this does not fully describe the consciousness of the workers—a pro-employer, Suhrawardy, would otherwise not have had any followers at all; but for any understanding of the history of jute workers' organization this aspect of the workers' consciousness cannot be overlooked.

III

We can now formulate more clearly the apparent paradox in the history of the jute workers' trade union movement: so much militancy, yet so little organization! The 'harsh reality' was not simply that the 'overwhelming majority' of the workers had not been unionized. An even greater problem was that the unions that had been formed appeared inherently unstable. Throughout the 1920s and '30s the government continued to describe trade unionism in the jute mills as being 'still in its infancy'.[38] Or to slightly vary the metaphor the trade union movement in the jute mills appeared to have been born spastic.

One important symptom of this 'spasticity' was the spasmodic nature of jute-mill unions. Each outburst of labour protest, especially from the 1920s, resulted in some kind of organization. Once the outburst spent itself, however, the organization as a rule disintegrated. As the Government of Bengal put it to the Royal Commission on Labour, 'in almost every strike some sort of labour body was formed, usually after the strike broke out', but such unions remained entirely ephemeral.[39] The Kankinarrah Labour Union, one of the oldest (1922) in the jute industry, complained in its submission to the Commission that while membership of the union 'grew very rapidly during strikes or temporary excitements', it also fell 'equally rapidly after the termination of disputes'.[40]

The pattern can be traced for the entire period under study. The 'widespread unrest' among the jute workers during the anti-partition 'Swadeshi' movement in Bengal (1905–8) coincided with the founding of the Indian Mill-Hands' Union organized by the Swadeshi leader

[38] W.B.S.A., Com. Dept. Com. Br. August 1922 A32–51; Jan. 1925 A183–227; Dec. 1933 A14–39; Feb. 1937 A50–81.

[39] *R.C.L.I.*, Vol. 5, Pt. 1, p. 143.   [40] ibid., p. 273.

A. C. Banerjee. As the unrest continued the union 'gradually extended the field of its activities, and by the end of 1907 . . . was coming to be known by the more ambitious name of Indian Labour Union'.[41] The enthusiasm it generated among the workers is revealed in the letters they wrote to Banerjee during these years. In these letters they expressed their feelings of 'undying gratitude' to Banerjee for the 'infinite good' he had done them by establishing this trade union.[42] But the organization faded away once the period of working-class unrest came to an end. To quote the historian of the Swadeshi movement: 'When the labour movement [in Bengal] revived immediately after the [1914] war, it was led by men of a new generation, and its Swadeshi pre-history was hardly ever recalled'.[43]

An idea of 'progress' obviously stirs within that optimistic word 'pre-history', but we would be wrong to suppose that the Swadeshi experience of trade unionism was superseded and made irrelevant by a future that embodied 'progress'. A longer view of jute workers' trade unionism would produce a distinctly contrary impression. The Swadeshi experience would then appear to have only foreshadowed the future developments. For example some twenty odd jute mill unions were formed by the Khilafatists during the industrial unrest of 1920–1; six of these were 'abolished' outright within a few months of their formation,[44] while the rest were described by the government in August 1921 as 'rather nebulous concerns'.[45] The newly-formed Bengal Labour Federation which controlled some of these unions was stated to be 'collapsing' by the middle of 1921.[46] The Howrah Labour Union and the Central Jute Mill Association (Howrah) were two unions whose 'existence and activities [had been] deposed to by their respective Secretaries before the recent [1921] Committee on Industrial Unrest', yet in a few months' time the District Magistrate advised the government that 'the local police report that the associations [were] both dead and [had] no members [was] correct'.[47] Trade

[41] Sumit Sarkar, *The Swadeshi Movement in Bengal 1903–1908* (Delhi, 1973), pp. 227, 234.

[42] Sumit Sarkar, 'Swadeshi Yuger Sramik Andolon: Kayekti Aprakashita Dalil', *Itihas*, Vol. 4, No. 2, Bhadra-Agrahayan 1376 (1969), pp. 113–15; also *Swadeshi Movement*, pp. 233–5.

[43] Sarkar, *Swadeshi Movement*, p. 241.

[44] W.B.S.A., Com. Dept Com. Br. July 1921 A34–72.

[45] W.B.S.A., Com. Dept Com. Br. Sept. 1921 A54–55.

[46] W.B.S.A., Com. Dept Com. Br. July 1921 A34–72.

[47] W.B.S.A., Com. Dept Com. Br. Sept. 1921 A54–55.

unions had also been established among the jute workers of Barrack-pore and Garden Reach (24 Parganas) in 1920. In 1921 the police described them as being 'in a moribund state' and Donald Gladding, an official in the Industries Department of the Government of Bengal, was reluctant to include them in his list of trade unions for that year 'because they are almost certainly of a very frail and nebulous character'.[48]

The groundswell of labour protest in the jute industry during the two general strikes of 1929 and 1937 was accompanied by the same phenomenon: quick flourishing and wilting of trade union organiza-tion. The strike of 1929 was preceded, as we have seen, by a growing volume of unrest in the mills over changes in working hours and wages.[49] This unrest surely helped in the establishment of trade unions in some of the jute mills in the Chengail-Bauria region of the Howrah district. It also helped to revitalize the Bengal Jute Workers' Association at Bhatpara (24 Parganas) that had been formed in 1925.[50] In both these areas the leadership of the unions was in the hands of a group of young Bengalis, committed by their ideology to the cause of the working class. With the strike movement gathering momentum in the jute mills—

the organizations at Bhatpara under Kali[das] Bhattacharjee and Gopen Chakravarti and those at Chengail and Bauria under Radharaman Mitra, Bankim Mukherjee and later Kishori[lal] Ghose amalgamated under a central organization called the Bengal Jute Workers' Union with its head office in Calcutta.[51]

The Bengal Jute Workers' Union (B.J.W.U.) gave leadership to the general strike of 1929. As the strike began and while it lasted, the organization of B.J.W.U. 'began to extend' and branches were opened at Bhatpara, Champdani, Shibpore, Chengail, Budge Budge and Titagarh.[52] The popularity and fame of the union spread fast among the working classes of Calcutta. In the words of one of the organizers of the union:

The Bengal Jute Workers' Union stood right at the centre of working-class movement in Bengal at this time [April 1930]. Its success in leading the general strike of three and a half lakhs of jute mill workers in 1929

[48] ibid.
[49] For details, see W.B.S.A., Com. Dept Com. Br. July 1927 A6–8.
[50] For details, see Gautam Chattopadhyay, *Communism and Bengal's Freedom Movement*, I (Delhi, 1970). [51] W.B.S.A., Home Poll Confdl. no. 161(29–67)/1934.
[52] ibid.; *R.C.L.I.*, Vol. 1. 5, Pt. 1, p. 161.

had awakened the entire working class to a new state of consciousness and generated a new enthusiasm among them . . . it [B.J.W.U.] enjoyed such fame that workers from any factory would rush to this union to seek advice regarding their own struggles. It was under the leadership of the organizers of this union [B.J.W.U.] that strikes were conducted by the workers of the ice factories in Calcutta, of the Gramophone Company and of Stuart Motor Company.[53]

Such popularity and spread notwithstanding, the B.J.W.U. was to lose its vitality very soon. An intelligence report of 1934 said:

After the strike [of 1929] a split occurred between Miss Prabhabati Das Gupta [the acknowledged leader of the strike] on the one hand and Kali Sen on the other . . . Two unions came into existence; one controlled by Miss Prabhabati Das Gupta which *gradually died out* and the other controlled by the communists under Bankim Mukherjee and Kali Sen . . . *It is not a powerful organization.*[54]

When some 60,000 jute mill workers were 'rendered idle' (to use the euphemism of the I.J.M.A.) in 1930–1, the jute workers' lack of any organization strong enough to resist the onslaught was painfully clear. The most that the retrenched workers could do was to go back to their villages.[55]

The thirties too do not fall outside the pattern. The police authorities of Calcutta reported in 1934 'a steady flow' of communist teaching . . . by leaders of trade unions', many of whom were now using 'Communist slogans and . . . language characteristic of that movement'.[56] In May the next year the Labour Commissioner of Bengal drew the attention of the government to 'the rapid development of labour organizations in the last few months'.[57] The following few years saw another round of confrontation between labour and capital in the jute industry, the high point of which was the general strike of 1937 that lasted from 'early February until the middle of May' and that involved a good majority of the workforce—at least some 77 per cent.[58]

Once again trade union organization flourished dramatically and sixty-seven jute mill unions were registered with the government in

---

[53] Abdul Momin, 'Kolkatay Gadowan Dharmaghater Chardin', *Mulyayan*, Pous-Magh (1977), pp. 11–12.
[54] W.B.S.A., Home Poll Confdl. no. 161(29–67)/1934. Emphasis added.
[55] See W.B.S.A., Home Poll Confdl. no. 150/1931.
[56] W.B.S.A., Home Poll Confdl. no. 161 (13–16)/1934.
[57] W.B.S.A., Home Poll Confdl. no. 392(1–3)/1935.
[58] *I.J.M.A. Report for 1937* (Calcutta, 1938), p. 41.

the years 1937–8.[59] During the general strike of 1937 many of these unions formed themselves into one central executive body, the Bengal Chatkal Mazdoor Union, which was affiliated to the A.I.T.U.C.[60] While the outburst of trade union activity of the 1930s may look like a 'definite advance' over the previous situation,[61] the similarities with the past are too strong to be ignored. The Bengal Chatkal Mazdoor Union, formed to function as 'a single, centralized union', was described by one of its organizers in 1952 as 'never [having] functioned as such'.[62] When the A.I.T.U.C. leaders returned to trade union work among jute workers in 1943 they had only sixteen unions with a meagre strength of 3,000 members altogether, an insubstantial minority in a 250,000-strong labour force. Abdul Momin, an important Communist trade union leader to whom we owe this information, admitted to his comrades in 1943 that none of the communist-led trade unions formed 'before the war' could be considered 'powerful'.[63] The situation remained unchanged for some time to come. Both Gupta and Deshpande as we have seen have discussed the languishing state of the trade union movement among the jute workers even after the war and the coming of independence.

IV

The paradox of 'strong militancy but weak organization' has been usually resolved by an implicit or explicit argument about the workers' lack of education. Organization was weak, or so the argument has run, because the structural and other features of the workers' conditions deprived them of any opportunity to acquire an understanding of trade union discipline and functioning. The effort therefore has been to understand why the workers remained 'ignorant', and persistently so in spite of two or three decades of attempts to educate and organize them. Depending on their convictions different authors have emphasized different factors—economic, social or political—to explain this 'ignorance'. Obviously the answers differ in terms of their ideological contents and emphases, but one broad fundamental

[59] W.B.S.A., Com. and Labour, April 1939 A14–16.
[60] Gupta, *Capital and Labour*, p. 45.
[61] See Tanika Sarkar, 'National Movement', pp. 161–2.
[62] Gupta, *Capital and Labour*, p. 45.
[63] Abdul Momin, *Bharater Communist Partir Bangla Pradesher Tritiya Sammelanne Grihita Pradeshik Trade Union Front Report* (Report on the Trade Union Front, accepted at the Third Bengal Provincial Conference of the Communist Party of India), Calcutta, 18–21 March 1943, pp. 7–8, 30.

agreement runs through the entire body of the existing discourse on jute workers' organization: that to organize was to educate.

To the politically conservative trade unionist this was simply a question of making the workers literate. K. C. Roy Chowdhury, the President of the Kankinarrah Labour Union, once cited the 'widespread illiteracy of the [Indian] working class' as an important reason why 'unions [had] failed to satisfy'.[64] His union told the Royal Commission on Labour that 'illiteracy [was] the main cause of labour's helplessness':

> It is the conviction of the organizers of this union . . . that the plant of constructive trade unionism will not take root for many years to come until and unless the soil is weeded and workers receive primary instruction.[65]

Almost identical were the views of government officials. If 'the Indian labourer' was 'notoriously difficult to organize in trade unions', as R. N. Gilchrist put it in 1924, the reason lay in their lack of education, without which no permanent unity of the working men was ever possible. 'Only education', wrote Gilchrist, 'and the mutual tolerance bred of education will soften the differences [of language, religion, etc.]'. 'Living in close contiguity in circumscribed areas, and service under one master, may lead to temporary unity . . . but continuous and sustained common action is as yet out of the question'.[66] The Government of Bengal pointed to the same relationship between education and organization in their memorandum to the Royal Commission in 1929:

> On the [jute mill] employees' side, the organization at present is in an infantile stage, and little more can be expected till the workers have some measure of education . . . With education and proper guidance he [the mill worker] will inevitably build up an organ to express his obvious community of interest with his fellows . . . It is in the interest of employers and community at large that the basis of this organization should be well and truly laid.[67]

To the more radical authors however 'education' has meant the 'political education' of the worker and not simply the question of his literacy. One of the earliest Bengali-language tracts on trade unionism,

---

[64] K. C. Roy Chowdh[u]ry, 'Some Thoughts on Indian Labour', *Journal of Indian Industries and Labour*, Feb. 1923, pp. 23–8.

[65] *R.C.L.I.*, Vol. 5, Pt. 1, pp. 262–3.

[66] R. N. Gilchrist, *The Payment of Wages*, pp. 232, 250.

[67] *R.C.L.I.*, Vol. 5, Pt. 1, pp. 153–4.

Trade Unioner Godar Katha (The Fundamentals of Trade Unionism) published in 1934, had as its aim the correction and improvement of the prevalent ideas of the labouring classes. 'So many rival ideas have now entered the field of trade unionism [in Bengal] that the workers have problems in discovering the correct path, and the friends of the rich can come along and put all kinds of ideas into their heads'. Hence the author said

> Every worker must read this book and explain its contents to ten others. He should organize his friends into a study-circle and meet three times a week to discuss in depth such issues as the sufferings of the labourers, the ways of the exploiters etc.[68]

True to this spirit the Bengali communists who went about organizing jute workers in the 1920s, '30s and '40s told them stories about Lenin and the Russian revolution,[69] read out to them radical journals[70] and started conducting 'study circles' among them.[71] Imparting 'political education' to the worker was seen as the key to a strong trade union movement. Indrajit Gupta's suggestion in 1952 that 'serious attention' be given by communists 'to cultural and social activity' among jute mill workers 'through libraries, night schools, schools for workers' children, drama and music groups' was inspired by the same consideration.[72]

The figure of the 'ignorant' worker (even if this 'ignorance' is defined in strictly political terms) has thus been central to all existing explanations of the problems of working-class organization in the jute mills. Factors such as the 'linguistic heterogeneity' of the jute workers (or the absence of 'a single means of communication' among them),[73] their 'linguistic separation' from the Bengali community,[74] the 'structural peculiarities' of this labour force, their 'amorphous, undefined and generally unskilled nature',[75] their 'half-pastoralist,

[68] Saroj Mukherjee (ed.), *Trade Unioner Godar Katha* (Calcutta, 1934), p. 3.

[69] See W.B.S.A., Home Poll Confdl. nos. 161(29–67)/1934 and 33/1940.

[70] See Chattopadhyay, *Communism*, p. 135.

[71] W.B.S.A., Home Poll Confdl. nos. W–40/1940.

[72] Gupta, *Capital and Labour*, p. 61.

[73] See A. K. Bagchi, *Private Investment in India* (Cambridge, 1972) p. 142; *R.C.L.I.*, Vol. 5, Pt. 1, p. 154; S. R. Deshpande, *Report*, p. 35 and Gupta, *Capital and Labour*, p. 142; Sarkar, 'National Movement', pp. 156–7, 161–2.

[74] Bagchi, *Private Investment*, p. 142; Gupta, *Capital and Labour*, p. 42.

[75] Sarkar, 'National Movement', pp. 156, 158.

half-proletarian' outlook[76] and, of course, the suppression of left-wing trade unions by the state[77] have all been mentioned with varying degrees of justification to explain why the jute mill workers never grew out of their 'ignorance', political or otherwise.

It is not our purpose to contest the validity of these individual propositions, though some are obviously more true than others. The 'linguistic separation of the majority of workers from the surrounding Bengali community' for instance was indeed a problem that trade unionists had to reckon with. Abdul Momin writes in his reminiscences of the 1929 general strike that even when the strike spread from Alambazar to Titagarh with 'lightning speed' and several people volunteered to help in the organization of the strike, language remained an important problem: 'Not all our volunteers could speak Hindi and in no other language could propaganda in favour of the strike be carried out in most of the [mill] areas'.[78] Given the necessary will however a solution was soon found to the problem. Before long many trade unionists mastered the art of speaking Hindi. Momin mentions the following among the leaders of the 1929 strike who could make speeches in fluent Hindi—Bankim Mukherjee, Kali Sen, Bakr Ali Mirza, Prabhabati Das Gupta, Sachidananda Chatterjee, Moni Singh, Swami Biswanand, Shroff Nand Kishore Sharma and himself.[79] Besides we should also remember that the leaflets distributed by the B.J.W.U. during the strike were after all printed in 'several languages'.[80]

A more seriously crippling factor for the left-wing trade unions was the repressive measures that the state often adopted in dealing with them. The frequent use by the government of section 144 of the Indian Penal Code to extern leftist leaders from their areas of activity was clearly aimed at minimizing the level of their contact with the working class. The common sense of purpose that united the mill managers and government officials in this effort proved a particularly formidable obstacle to trade union activity. P. D. Martyn of the Indian Civil Service saw 'something of life as it [was] lived in the huge jute mill suburbs' when he served as a Sub-Divisional Officer at Barrackpore early in the 1930s.

[76] Gupta, *Capital and Labour*, pp. 56–7; K. C. Chowdh[u]ry, 'Thoughts', pp. 23–8, and his letter of 10 Nov. 1924 in W.B.S.A., Com. Dept. Com. Br. Jan. 1925 A183–227.   [77] Momin, *Report*, p. 8; Sarkar, 'National Movement', p. 159.
[78] Abdul Momin, 'Chatkal Sramiker Prathan Sadharan Dharmaghat', *Kalantar*, 11 August 1970.   [79] ibid.
[80] *R.C.L.I.*, Vol. 5, Pt. 1, p. 144.

While there [he wrote] I played my part in coping with a strike with 60,000 operatives out of work. Coping with the situation included the passing of orders prohibiting the entry of certain agitators from Calcutta into the area. What struck me at the time was how helpful the jute mill managers (Scots to a man) were during these troubles.[81]

For us then the question is not one of disputing the statements made by individual scholars who have attempted to explain the weakness of jute workers' organization. Taken by themselves these statements contain a certain measure of truth and many of them do point to important factors that may have retarded the growth of unions in the jute industry. What we are concerned with here is the point at which these different and apparently dispersed statements meet. In the final analysis they all seek to explain why the workers remained ignorant of 'trade union discipline and functioning' and enumerate the factors that supposedly deprived them of such education. The task of organizing is then seen in this entire discussion as essentially an exercise in making certain types of knowledge (literacy, self-awareness, etc.) available to the workers, i.e. in educating them.

It is here that I feel we can use the existing statement of the 'paradox' of jute workers' organization to open up a deeper paradox that this one already contains. There is something fundamentally problematic about viewing organization simply as a matter of political education for the worker. To do this is to sidestep certain important issues of culture and consciousness that are raised when we examine more closely the problem of working-class organization. Even within the framework of Marxist theory it is now recognized that the Leninist project of inserting a body of 'intellectuals' between the working class and the 'theory' is fraught with ambiguities.[82] This is only more so in a society entangled in a variety of pre-capitalist relationships. Besides it would surely be a very élitist view of working-class history that did not ask if the 'educator' himself needed some educating as well!

V

The cultural issues alluded to in the previous paragraph relate to questions of power and authority. Indeed it may be argued that to

[81] India Office Library, London (hereafter I.O.L.) Mss. Eur. F180/13, Memoirs of P. D. Martyn, p. 6.

[82] Q. Hoare and G. N. Smiths, ed. and trans., *Selections from the Prison Notebooks of Antonio Gramsci* (New York, 1973), pp. 9, 198–9; Christine Buci-Glucksmann, *Gramsci and the State* (London, 1980), pp. 29–30.

raise the point about the jute mill worker's ignorance of 'trade union functioning and discipline' is to raise these issues. For what is 'organizational discipline' if not a way of resolving questions of power and authority within organizations?

For the purpose of analysis here the important point is that there are certain assumptions about culture—not just of the workers' alone but of their leaders as well—inherent in the concept of 'trade union discipline'. Ideally speaking the proper functioning of a stable, broadbased trade union requires a bourgeois culture. As Gramsci once said, trade unions are organizations based on 'voluntary' and 'contractual' relationships; their emphasis on membership, subscription and other procedures of organizational discipline is based on the assumed existence of such relations.[83] Trade unions also embody a principle of representation that manifests itself in elections. The trade union properly conceived is thus a bourgeois-democratic organization and is organized in the image of the bourgeois-democratic government. In the same way as the latter represents the 'people'—through 'voluntary' and 'contractual' relationships—the trade union represents its members, and through them the class. Gramsci made the point clearly and forcefully while discussing the nature of trade unions and political parties: 'These are organizations born on the terrain of bourgeois democracy and political liberty, as an affirmation and development of political freedom . . . They do not supersede the bourgeois state'.[84]

In theory then the elected representative of the worker is his equal and is chosen as a representative precisely because he stands in a relationship of 'equality'—the equality of the 'contract'—to those represented. He does not owe his capacity to represent to any prior position of privilege and authority; his is not, in other words, the figure of the master. This is the crucial question on which trade union democracy turns and it must be set in contrast to that other kind of political representation that Marx once talked about with respect to the peasantry: 'They cannot represent themselves, they must be represented. Their representative must at the same time appear as their master, as an authority over them . . .'[85]

[83] A. Gramsci, 'The Turin Workers' Council' (trans. from the *Ordine Nuovo*, 1919–20) in Robin Blackburn (ed.), *Revolution and Class Struggle: A Reader in Marxist Politics* (Glasgow, 1977), p. 378.   [84] ibid.
[85] K. Marx, 'The Eighteenth Brumaire of Louis Bonaparte' in K. Marx and F. Engels, *Selected Works I* (Moscow, 1969), p. 479.

If all this seems too theoretical and too much to expect in concrete historical situations, let me make two points. The model is always a useful measure of the reality. Secondly, and this is perhaps a more important point for the historian, the concept of trade-union democracy explained above was precisely what all organizers of labour aspired to realize. The notion of democratic representation was fundamental to all discussions on the question of organizing the jute workers. Listen for example to the anti-communist, pro-employer Labour Minister H. S. Suhrawardy arguing to the jute mill owners in 1937 that the 'mere availability' of mill managers was not enough to ensure sufficient contact with the working class:

> Contact between employer and employee should be made through the medium of the *elected* representative of *organized* labour and so that this might be possible the existence of trade unions was absolutely necessary.[86]

And now to the Communist Indrajit Gupta in 1952:

> Of course, organization [of jute workers] must mean something more than mere formal enrolment of union membership . . . The point is to function the unions democratically.

and

> the essence of trade union democracy . . . means, concretely, that the executive committee of the unions must be regularly functioning bodies, *properly elected* by the members, participating in the day to day life of the union.
>   Democratic functioning ensures that the unions will never suffer from a 'shortage' of cadres, nor become dependent on a handful of leading officials or 'organizers'. On the contrary, it will encourage a regular flow of rank and file militants to come forward to discharge the multifarious jobs, ranging from manning the union office and collecting subscriptions to distributing leaflets, pasting up posters, addressing meetings etc.[87]

This ideal however was hardly ever approximated in reality. Trade union organization in the jute mills remained extremely inchoate all through the years under consideration. By 'inchoateness' I do not simply mean the 'traditional gap' or tension that exists in 'every political party or trade-union . . . between the rank-and-file . . . and the leaders'.[88] Such tension existed in the jute mill unions too. For

---

[86] C.S.A.S., B.P., Box 12. Confidential record of an interview between the I.J.M.A., Chairman and H. S. Suhrawardy, Labour Minister, on 28 July 1937, at the Writers' Buildings. Emphasis added.

[87] Gupta, *Capital and Labour*, pp. 51, 55. Emphasis added.

[88] Frantz Fanon, *The Wretched of the Earth* (Harmondsworth, 1974), p. 85.

example despite their claims 'to represent all jute mill workers on the river', the Bengal Jute Workers' Union 'was unable [in 1929] to control workers in some important areas'.[89] The 'excellent intelligence service and organization' that the 'agitators' displayed during the general strike of 1937 was impressive enough to win praise in the most unlikely places,[90] but the leaders nevertheless found it difficult to contain the militancy of their followers in every case. 'The result was', wrote a government official, 'that the Shibpore Mills came out much earlier than . . . was wanted and proved a great embarrassment to the plans [of the leaders]'.[91]

By themselves these cases do not exhaust the definition of 'inchoateness' since it is possible for organizations to maintain a certain degree of coherence and discipline in spite of such tension between the leaders and the rank-and-file. In our case the problem of incoherence went much deeper, for even at their liveliest unions of jute mill labour were never organizations based on a relatively disciplined body of workers subject to such institutional controls as membership rights and obligations, subscription rules, union consti-tutions or even regular meetings. 'The very sight of a subscription book', wrote K. C. Roy Chowdhury in his diary, made the workers feel 'uneasy and suspicious'.[92] In his submission to the Royal Commission in 1929 as President of the Kankinarrah Labour Union he further added that 'the constitution[al] aspect of the union [was] unknown to them [the workers]'.[93] Roy Chowdhury's comments are confirmed in a report by Thomas Johnston and John F. Sime who visited the Calcutta mills in 1925 on behalf of the Joint Committee of Dundee Jute Trade Unions to 'enquire into the conditions of the Jute Workers in India'. The authors found the Calcutta jute mill unions seriously crippled by acute financial and other problems of organization.

> There are, on paper, some three or four Unions among the [Calcutta] jute workers, but with one exception they are quite useless, have no paying membership, and serve no purpose unless to advertise some politician as honorary president. The honorary presidents, we believe, pay for the notepaper and headings, and that is all there is to the Unions.[94]

[89] *R.C.L.I.*, Vol. 5, Pt. 1, p. 127.

[90] C.S.A.S., B.P., Box 11, M. P. Thomas to Benthall, 30 June 1937.

[91] W.B.S.A., Home Poll Confdl. no. 60/1937.

[92] Papers of K. C. Roy Chowdhury (hereafter K.C.R.P.), Diary No. 3, entry for 25.8.1929. These papers are in my possession.   [93] *R.C.L.I.*, Vol. 5, Pt. 1, p. 273.

[94] Thomas Johnston and John F. Sime, *Exploitation in India* (Dundee, [1926?]), p. 15.

The 'one exception' that Johnston and Sime mentioned was the Jute Workers' Association founded at Bhatpara by Kalidas Bhattacharya. Bhattacharya was a Bengali *bhadralok* with terrorist connections who had lost his employment with a jute mill for organizing and encouraging strikes.[95] He was described by the Dundee delegation as 'an able, intelligent workman who . . . [had] the root of the matter [trade unionism] in him', and his Association, it was said, was 'definitely making an effort to remedy workers' grievances'.[96] Yet of a nominal membership of 'only 3000' not more than 400 to 500 paid any subscriptions and, despite low union fees, the organization suffered from severe 'monetary limitations'. It was 'largely financed and inspired . . . by an interesting and self-sacrificing little lady, Mrs Santosh Kumari Gupta'.[97] The monetary problems of the Bengal Jute Workers' Association were to continue in the future when the union reportedly received financial aid 'in the shape of a monthly donation of Rs 100 from the Dundee Jute Workers Association' up to 1927 and perhaps even a bit later.[98] In the 1920s Sime often received letters from trade unionists in India requesting monetary help during strikes in the jute mills. 'We had an appeal from Kalidas Bhattacharji in November last year and sent a donation of thirty pounds (£30) to him', mentioned Sime while responding to another request for help during a 'prolonged stoppage in the Howrah district' in February 1929.[99] That this 'appeal' from Bhattacharya in November 1928 was not the first one of its kind is further suggested by the following letter that Sime wrote to him in June that year:

> Your cablegram duly received was placed before my Committee and I am instructed to cable at once a grant of Twenty five pounds (£25) towards the Wellington Jute Mills strike fund . . . Enclosed please find copy of the 'Dundee Free Press' to which I gave the contents of your cablegram thereby giving the matter publicity.[100]

This persisting problem of finances, caused partly by the absence of a subscription-paying rank-and-file, was only an index—though

[95] Sibnath Banerjee, 'Labour Problems in Jute Industry', unpublished typescript, p. 3.
[96] Johnston and Sime, *Exploitation*, p. 15.　　　　　　　　　　　　[97] ibid.
[98] David Petrie, *Communism in India 1924–1927* (Delhi, 1927; reprint, Calcutta, 1972), p. 130.
[99] J. F. Sime to N. M. Joshi, 26 Feb. 1929, in Sime's letter-book captioned 'India', preserved in the archives of the Dundee and District Union of Jute and Flax Workers, Dundee. I am grateful to Dr William Walker of the University of Dundee for bringing to my attention this letter-book.
[100] ibid., Sime to Kalidas Bhattacharya, 13 June 1928.

perhaps the most obvious one—of the deep organizational maladies that afflicted the nature of trade unionism in the jute mills of Calcutta. After all it is remarkable how the general strike of 1929 was conducted without the executive committee of the Bengal Jute Workers' Union meeting even once during the strike.[101] Moreover no worker was ever a subscription-paying member of the u⁻ ⁻n as its leader, Prabhabati Das Gupta, was to admit later. She called it 'a peculiar labour movement' as the union 'never had any subscription or anything'.[102] B.J.W.U. however was not unique in this respect; the Government of Bengal thus summed up the experience of trade unionism in the 1920s:

> After the war, unions of some kind developed with almost bewildering rapidity, because in every strike some sort of a labour body was formed . . . Such bodies had no constitution, no regular membership, and their power to control workers . . . was extremely problematical.[103]

While the thirties and later decades marked some advance in certain directions—seen mainly in the growing popularity of radical ideas in the political circles of Calcutta—a crucial problem remained unresolved. It was the trade-union leaders' 'failure', to use Indrajit Gupta's words, 'to translate their growing mass influence into organizational terms'.[104] This 'failure' is well illustrated by the case of A. M. A. Zaman, the Communist labour organizer of Hooghly whose growing 'mass influence' we have had occasion to document before. During the industrial unrest of 1936–7 Zaman formed a jute-mill union which got itself registered in 1936. In September 1937 however the General Secretary of the union went to court to complain of severe organizational irregularities. He described the union as a 'great fraud' and said that while as the General Secretary he was responsible for 'all correspondence', subscriptions, and for depositing the subscriptions raised in some bank 'in the name of the union', he found that in practice all these rules were honoured only in their violation. 'Offices were opened and subscriptions . . . raised through collectors but never deposited in any Bank'. He was 'shocked' to see 'receipts being granted' by unauthorized persons while he was kept

---

[101] *R.C.L.I.*, Vol. 5, Pt. 1, p. 149.
[102] Nehru Memorial Museum and Library, Delhi (hereafter N.M.M.L.), Prabhabati Mirza (née Das Gupta), interviewed by K. P. Rangachary, 24 April 1968, Delhi. Transcript, pp. 10–11, 18–19.
[103] *R.C.L.I.*, Vol. 5, Pt. 1, p. 143.
[104] Gupta, *Capital and Labour*, p. 51.

'in the dark'. And when he 'insisted on accounts and explanation', 'the accused No.1 [i.e. Zaman] . . . put it off on flimsy pretext from day to day . . . and . . . wanted your petitioner to resign from the post of the General Secretary giving a back date'.[105] Such inchoateness of organization was to plague jute workers' trade unionism for a long time to come. To quote Indrajit Gupta once again, as he put it in his report of 1952:

> With one or two exceptions, the organizational structure of our unions also [i.e. in addition to those of other political parties] is most unsatisfactory. The pattern is common to jute—periodical mass meetings and bustee or gate propaganda, *irregular* collection of subscriptions, and *very nominal* office work.[106]

If the organization of jute workers' trade unions was so inchoate, how did they resolve questions of power and authority without the aid of organizational discipline? Or to put the question in another way, if it was not submission to organizational discipline that bound the rank-and-file of a union to itself, what did? The answer would seem to be: the power of the leader, the so-called 'representative' who, as in Marx's description of the French peasantry, always turned out to be the 'master' himself. The specific form in which this power expressed itself was to be seen in the personal loyalty, often temporary, that trade union organizers could elicit from the ordinary mill-hands. In contemporary trade union parlance, the word used to describe this style of leadership was 'zamindari'. Apparently the style was endemic; Momin mentioned it to be so in a report to the Communist Party in 1943.[107] Of the different political parties that came together to form one A.I.T.U.C. union for the jute mills in 1937—'Congress, Socialist, Communist, Forward Bloc and other left labour workers'—it was said that 'a sort of territorial division of "spheres of influence" existed, with a particular leader exercising, as it were, "zamindari rights" in his particular trade union area'.[108]

One important characteristic of such power was of course its capacity to render organizational discipline redundant because it was by nature independent of the niceties and rigours of any such discipline. This sometimes created serious problems for organizational unity, as factionalism at the top could easily split the followers.

[105] W.B.S.A., Home Poll Confdl. no. 326/1937.
[106] Gupta, *Capital and Labour*, p. 50. Emphasis added.
[107] Momin, *Report*, pp. 7–8.
[108] Gupta, *Capital and Labour*, p. 45.

The Congress-sponsored Indian National Trade Union Congress (I.N.T.U.C.) experienced this in the early fifties when they failed to set up 'a single central Congress-led [jute workers'] union because of the rivalries of the different groups within the West Bengal Congress itself'. Their 'individual unions (area-wise, mill-wise, and even more than one in the same mill) remained', wrote Gupta, 'as the "zamin-daries" of different leaders and groups', and could only be 'loosely put together into the Jute Workers' Federation'.[109]

Sometimes however the same force of loyalty allowed a particular leader to be influential even if that influence took no firm organiza-tional shape. A good case in point is again that of Zaman, if only because it is easier to document. As we have seen, Zaman's organization among the mill-hands of Hooghly went to pieces at the height of his popularity. But in no way did this diminish his influence. In July 1937 Zaman was convicted 'on charge of rioting during . . . [a] strike at the Wellington Jute Mill in Rishra'. The workers, 'about 4,800 in number', risked their employment and 'came out on receipt of the news', such was Zaman's popularity with them.[110] Even in September 1937 when Zaman's union had suffered splits, mill managers it was said were 'afraid of proceedings being drawn up against the miscreants [i.e. Zaman's followers] as they believe that under such circumstances their respective mills might go on strike'.[111] The personal nature of Zaman's control over workers comes out in the following description of events:

> On 1.7.37 . . . a worker was surrounded in his house by Mr Zaman's partisans who would have assaulted him had he not given in to . . . their demands. That very evening a meeting of Zaman's partisans was held and orders for getting all shops closed to those who had obeyed the orders of the Manager, Angus Jute Works, were passed as it was announced [that] *such was Mr Zaman's wish.*[112]

Or consider the case of Sibnath Banerjee, the Socialist leader of workers in the Shibpur-Ghusury Salkea areas of Howrah. After some fifteen years of trade-union work his authority still derived, according to Indrajit Gupta in 1952, from a display of 'considerable personal initiative' and an exercise of 'direct leadership'.

[109] ibid., pp. 45–6.
[110] W.B.S.A., Home Poll Confdl. no. 484/1937.
[111] W.B.S.A., Home Poll Confdl. no. 326/1937.
[112] ibid. Emphasis added.

They have one central union—the Howrah Zilla Chatkal Mazdoor Union which has *no* organizational form. Its activities revolve entirely around the person of Sri Sibnath Banerjee, whose claim to renown rests on his long years of labour activity in Howrah. It is out and out a one man show.[113]

We must not see these as isolated examples or cases of individual failures. The tradition of 'zamindari' leadership was strong and old. A. C. Banerjee, the Swadeshi trade unionist active around 1905, was a good example of this spirit. Even though his trade union activity spanned only two or three years Banerjee felt that his 'influence with the millhands was so great and discipline so complete that he could make them do whatever he liked'.[114] During the 1929 strike a 'Barrackpore pleader, Babu Narendra Chatterjee . . . very quickly gained ascendancy over the workers' of the Alliance, Craig, Waverley and Meghna mills. 'The managing agents . . . said that after they had granted the concessions which the workers had demanded, the workers refused to go back to work, unless they received a definite order from this pleader'.[115] Chatterjee was soon made the Vice-President of the Bengal Jute Workers' Union even though 'his name had never previously been mentioned in any labour connection whatsoever'.

> He had no knowledge of the jute industry and had never previously been known to have any business connections in Bhatpara, yet certainly for no [ascertainable] reason . . . and without any official position in any union . . . he seemed to get control over a considerable body of men.[116]

The 'Naren Babu incident', the government pointed out, 'is not uncommon in local labour politics'. Not infrequently it happened that 'some persons entirely unknown . . . even to the majority of workers suddenly assume[d] leadership during a dispute'.[117]

The truth of the government's statement is borne out by the case of Prabhabati Das Gupta, the most important leader of the 1929 strike. When the strike began, 'Miss Das Gupta was entirely unknown' to the 'average jute mill worker'.[118] Soon afterwards however the government described her control over workers as 'absolute'. The workers called her 'Mataji' or 'Maiji' (Mother) and would go entirely by her wishes. Das Gupta herself was only too aware of this. As she once

---

[113] Gupta, *Capital and Labour*, pp. 47, 48. Emphasis added.
[114] Sarkar, *Swadeshi Movement*, p. 237.
[115] *R.C.L.I.*, Vol. 5, Pt. 1, p. 144.   [116] ibid., pp. 144, 149, 276.
[117] ibid., p. 144.   [118] ibid., p. 150.

put it to the government, 'she only has to lift her little finger and the workers would obey'. The government had 'no doubt' that this was true.[119] Das Gupta herself later recalled that 'wherever I went I was welcomed by the slogan *Mataji ki jai, Mataji ki jai* [hail the mother]. That was my reward'.[120] And her rival trade unionist K. C. Chowdhury admitted in his diary that—

> Both male and female workers—at least those living in Kankinara, Titagarh and Champdany—looked upon Miss Das Gupta as their 'Maiji' [mother]. They would do anything to carry out her orders, and would not even listen to any other organisers of her union.[121]

Mark how independent such authority was of 'discipline' or organization; they would appear to be irrelevant to its mode of functioning. Indeed one of the aphorisms that Das Gupta's friends sought to popularize among mill workers was, 'unions may come and unions may go but Dr Prabhabati will remain for ever'.[122] This is the important point for us—that what has so far been viewed simply as an absence of trade union discipline or training reveals on closer inspection the presence of alternative systems of power and authority.

VI

The ideal democratic principle of representation based on 'voluntary' and 'contractual' relationships was thus never realized in the trade unions of the Calcutta jute mill workers, and representatives instead became masters. Unions were run as though they were the leaders' 'zamindaries'. One could in fact go further and argue that in the eyes of the millworkers, being a master was a condition of being a representative. Only masters could represent. To see this purely as a function of the worker's ignorance is to overlook the necessarily two-sided character of the relationship. One is reminded of Hegel's discussion (in his *Phenomenology*) of the master-slave relationship, where the master's dominance is dependent on the slave recognizing him as the master, that is to say, on the slave's will to serve. In referring to the bhadralok trade union leaders as 'masters', then, we do not intend to portray the working class as a passive instrument of the leaders' will. At issue is the question of the worker's own will, his own consciousness, his shrewd realization that under the circumstances

---

119 ibid., p. 149.
120 Prabhabati Mirza (née Das Gupta), 'Interview', p. 19.
121 K.C.R.P., Diary No. 3, entry under 25.8.29 to 28.11.29.
122 *R.C.L.I.*, Vol. 5, Pt. 1, p. 148.

he could sometimes best exercize his power by choosing to serve. The relation therefore was pregnant with tension and had its own moments of resistance as well. One only has to remember that for all the loyalty the leaders could elicit from the workers, Prabhabati Das Gupta was once 'abused and insulted' by a number of jute workers towards the end of the first general strike, that Latafat Hossain once had his union-office burned down by a group of angry workers, and that Sibnath Banerjee was greeted by the workers in Howrah with suspicion and insults when he first approached them for votes in 1937[123]—to give but three instances of overt tension between the workers and their leaders.

Sumit Sarkar has rescued from the private papers of the Swadeshi labour organizer, A. C. Banerjee, a very instructive letter that gives us some insight into the nature of the leader-worker relationship and tells us how the workers perceived the 'oppression' they faced at work. Some twenty-eight workers of the Budge Budge Jute Mills wrote this letter to Banerjee in December 1906.[124] They had to 'pay bribes to the babu and the *sardar* . . . every month and when the Durga Puja season approached'; refusal to pay bribes led to unjust fines or dismissal 'on false charges of bad workmanship'.

> Till recently [they added] we felt compelled to meet their unreasonable demands. But as prices ran very high at the time of Durga Puja last year, we expressed our intention to pay them a little less than in earlier years. At this the Head Sardar Haricharan Khanra has been going around instigating the Assistant Babu Atul Chandra Chattopadhyay to collect even more *parbani* [customary dues] than usual. The two of them have even advised the in-charge Panchanan Ghose, a nice gentleman otherwise, to force us to pay a much larger *parbani* this year. When [in protest] we stopped paying any *parbani* whatsoever, they got the Sahib to fine us on cooked up charges . . . But, in truth, we are not guilty.

An interesting aspect of this letter lies in its collection of concrete details. It is obviously a long and detailed list of sufferings. Significantly however the workers who wrote the letter called it only 'a brief description' and expressed their 'desire to describe in even greater detail' their sufferings to Banerjee if and when they met him in person. We must understand this 'desire', for in it lay the nature of the relationship we are seeking to explore. Why did the workers want

---

[123] See *R.C.L.I.*, Vol. 5, Pt. 1, p. 132; Momin, 'Chatkal Sramiker', *Kalantar*, 12 August 1970; Sibnath Banerjee, unpublished memoirs.

[124] Sumit Sarkar, 'Swadeshi Yuger Sramik Andolon', pp. 113–15.

to display their sufferings to men like Banerjee, to give such 'cruel publicity' to the pains their bosses inflicted on them? Or perhaps I should rephrase the question: what could be the relationship that permitted of pain being made into an object of display?

Michel Foucault has discussed this problem in a different but relevant context. 'Can pain be a spectacle?' he asks, and answers:

> Not only can it be, but it must be, by virtue of a subtle right that resides in the fact that no one is alone, the poor man less so than others, so that he can obtain assistance only through the mediation of the rich . . . if others intervene with their knowledge, their resources, their pity.[125]

The poor man making a spectacle of his sufferings was, and still is, a familiar sight in societies marked by pre-capitalist cultures. In explaining the quality of life in medieval Europe the Dutch historian Huizinga said: 'Then, again, all things in life were of a proud or cruel publicity. Lepers sounded their rattles and went about in procession, beggars exhibited their deformities . . .'.[126] He could have written this of Calcutta today. 'Every time I emerged from my hotel in Calcutta . . .', wrote Claude Lévi-Strauss of his brief stay in that city in the 1950s, 'I became the central figure in a ballet which would have seemed funny to me, had it not been so pathetic. The various accomplished performers made their entries in turn: a shoeblack flung himself at my feet, a small boy rushed up to me; whining, 'One anna, papa, one anna!', a cripple displayed his stumps, having bared himself to give a better view . . .'.[127]

To see in all this only a 'single obsession', hunger—as Lévi-Strauss did at first—is to miss the essential element of power in this relationship between the rich and the poor. The relationship involved the will of both and this was what allowed such culturally-defined elements as supplication, pity, compassion, etc. to circulate within the relationship. If the uninviting sight of a beggar in Calcutta made Lévi-Strauss shrink away from it, this was because he could feel the 'acute tension' (mark the metaphor of force!) that instantly developed between him and the beggar. Lévi-Strauss' language here clearly refers to power and not to the physical fact of hunger alone. By his supplication, says Lévi-Strauss, the beggar 'willed' him 'to be even more impressive and

---

[125] M. Foucault, *The Birth of the Clinic: An Archeology of Medical Perception* (New York, 1975), p. 84.

[126] H. Huizinga, *The Waning of the Middle Ages* (London, 1949), p. 1.

[127] Claude Lévi-Strauss, *Tristes Tropiques* (Harmondsworth, 1973) pp. 169–70.

powerful' than he knew he was.[128] Supplication thus acted as an instrument of power by working on the material of compassion and pity.

Once we grasp this we understand why the Budge Budge Jute Mill workers desired to describe their sufferings in 'even greater detail' than they had in their letter. They saw Aswini Banerjee, a barrister and trade-unionist, as a resourceful 'babu' who would respond to the plight of the 'coolie' only if his compassion was sufficiently aroused. 'We write to you about the oppressive acts of our superiors at work and pray for an urgent redress. We hope you will save us soon from their despotism', was how the letter ended.

One is indeed struck by the number of times the babu-coolie relationship surfaces in the middle of working-class protest and trade union activities. The terrain is admittedly difficult for the historian, and not only because the jute workers were predominantly non-literate. The written word that the historian relies on is in itself a rather poor conveyor of this relationship as it usually presents only a fragment of reality.[129] In real life, however, as any Bengali would know, the babu-coolie relationship would have been represented many times over in many different ways—in manners of speech and dress, in body language expressive of hierarchy, indeed in the entire range of the semiotics of domination and subordination (and hence resistance) that the culture would have made available to both the jute mill worker and his bhadralok trade union representative. While much of this would normally escape the historian's attention, a careful interrogation of the available documents yields considerable evidence of the existence of this feudal bond between the babu and the coolie.

The historian for instance does not have to strain his ears to catch 'the voice of the poor' in the clamour of protests that went up in the Calcutta jute mills from time to time. Echoes reverberate even in the most élitist of sources. 'In those days, i.e. about 1922–23', writes K. C. Roy Chowdhury in his diaries,

> the workers preferred rich people as their [trade union] leaders. They were pleased to see the leaders come to meetings in their own motor cars.

[128] Ibid., p. 173.

[129] 'Writing is inescapably distinct', is how Roland Barthes put it in his *Image-Music-Text* (trans. S. Heath; Glasgow, 1979), p. 89, n. 2. See also the interesting discussion on analog and digital processes of communication in Anthony Wilden, *System and Structure: Essays in Communication and Exchange* (London, 1972).

They had the mistaken idea that only the rich could successfully fight [for them] with the wealthy and big millowners. The *sardars* thought that trade union leaders who were themselves big advocates or barristers would fight for them in the court of law, free of charge.[130]

K. C. Roy Chowdhury called himself in his diaries 'A Friend of the Workers', but it is interesting to see how in his imagination the figure of the worker merged with that of the poor. For all his enthusiasm for socialism and strikes[131] the working class is often transformed in his prose into *daridra Narayan*, the Hindu god Narayan in the shape of the poor.[132] The working class or even 'socialism' could all be served from notions of 'pity'. The sentiment was well expressed by a fictitious character called Mrs Guha (presumably modelled on the contemporary trade unionist Santosh Kumari Gupta) in Roy Chowdhury's play *Dharmaghat (The Strike)* when she remarked, 'Poor workers! There is not a single soul to listen to their complaints and tales of woe'.[133]

'After all it was helping the poor people', said Prabhabati Das Gupta reminiscing in old age about the first general strike of jute mill workers, which forced the mill owners and the state alike in 1929 to recognize her as the workers' representative. 'We were not doing trade union movement, we were helping the poor people'. 'So', asked she, explaining the absence of trade union membership and subscription, 'why should we have money from them?'[134] One may choose to dismiss this evidence as rationalization with hindsight or see it only as an instance of the mellowing with age of a once-radical spirit. But what does one do when the babu-coolie relationship comes refracting through the practice of trade unionism even at the height of working-class protest? The leaflets put out by the leaders of the Bengal Jute Workers' Union during the 1929 strike illustrate the point. True they spoke of 'oppression in the jute mills', of the worker's labour filling 'the bellies of the rich', described 'truth and right' as being on the worker's side, and recommended organization and unity.[135] Yet their

[130] K.C.R.P., Bengali diary No. 3, entry under 7.4.1923.

[131] Roy Chowdhury wrote a Bengali play called *Dharmaghat (The Strike)* in 1926 and thus described it in its old age when he considered making it into a film: 'Kindly read it and note its objective—Socialistic propaganda, 21 years before Independence when very few people had any idea of the subject'. K.C.R.P., letter to J. P. Banerjee, 27 June 1959.

[132] Even a casual reading of his diaries would confirm this point.

[133] K. C. Roy Chowdhury, *Dharmaghat* (Calcutta, 1926), p. 45.

[134] Prabhabati Mirza (née Das Gupta), 'Interview', pp. 18–19.

[135] *R.C.L.I.*, Vol. 5, Pt. 1, pp. 159–60.

language was densely inhabited by the babu's stereotype and assumptions regarding the coolie's helplessness and ignorance.

> Brethren—This is a very critical time . . . So beware! It is said that some pleader has advised to the effect that your wages would be realized by action in the court. You are very simple folks, so you have been enmeshed in the plan of an ordinary pleader . . . Ask the pleader to mention this matter to us, we shall give him the right answer.[136]

Necessarily then at the other end of the relationship stood the leader in her larger-than-life-size appearance—'Mother Provabati', 'Mataji', 'the father and mother of the poor', as she was described in her union's pamphlets.[137] And wherever she went she was 'welcomed by the slogan *Mataji ki jai* . . .'. 'That was my reward', she said, the reward of the dominant: 'Practically, the whole of labour was under *my* control'.[138] By now we know this voice: the representative invariably turned out to be a master, as only masters could represent.

VII

'Invariably?', one may still object. 'Your examples so far have been A. C. Banerjee, K. C. Roy Chowdhury and Prabhabati Das Gupta— people who were themselves somewhat élitist in their own minds. What about the generation of socialists and communists who followed them, men who tried to become one with the workers instead of wanting to dominate them, men who won the leadership of the jute workers' struggles in the 1930s and the '40s, and whose faith in socialist ideologies remained unflinching to the very end of their lives?'.

Before proceeding to answer our hypothetical interlocutor, let us fully acknowledge the transformation that socialist ideologies brought about in the Bengali bhadralok's understanding of the problems of the working classes in Bengal. In the nineteenth century the bhadralok viewed the working classes as a problem of morality, and the blame for some of the social problems created by the growth of factories fell squarely on the workers themselvs. This view sometimes manifested itself in a middle-class desire to see an improvement in working-class morals. The Brahmo social reformer Sasipada Banerjee was the most notable example of this trend.[139] More commonly however labourers

---

[136] Ibid.   [137] Ibid., p. 411.

[138] Prabhabati Mirza (née Das Gupta), 'Interview', pp. 11–12, 18–19.

[139] I have discussed his activities elsewhere: 'Sasipada Banerjee: A Study in the Nature of the First Contact of the Bengali Bhadralok with the Working Classes of Bengal', *Indian Historical Review*, Jan. 1976, pp. 339–64.

were seen simply as a social nuisance, an 'annoyance', as a police report of 1896 put it, to 'the quiet people' of the middle classes. The same report carried several references to bhadralok complaints regarding the 'unruly', 'noisy' and 'rowdy' character of the mill workers.[140] Towards the end of the century, as industries expanded and Bengali labourers were replaced by migrants from Bihar and the United Provinces, the moral view of the working class was further reinforced by the addition of the traditional contempt that the bhadralok had for the *merua*—a derisive Bengali term for any native speaker of Hindi. A poem written about the turn of the century by a Bengali Brahmin school-teacher—who lived in Bhatpara and saw that sleepy village change beyond recognition with the establishment of jute mills, municipal offices and the influx of migrant labourers—will illustrate this well. The poem is unremarkable for its literary qualities but captures in its bluntness the essence of bhadralok perception of an immigrant and indigent working class:

> Well done, Bhatpara Municipality!
> Gone are the old jungles and bamboo-grooves
> Of Kankinara and Jagaddal,
> Their places taken by palaces and bazars,
> Slums of meruas, factories and their sprouting chimneys.
> The bazars now bustle with the ghostly meruas
> Buying and selling in their strange Hindi.
> On holidays,
> They loaf about the town in groups,
> Drunk,
> Singing songs that sound like the howl of dogs.[141]

It would be tedious and unrewarding to list here the racial prejudices of the Bengali bhadralok; suffice it to say that the importation of socialist ideas, however vague, did much to change many of these consciously-held attitudes. There developed a new ideological interest in the working people in the 1920s and it became common practice to use words like 'worker' or 'labour' (or their Bengali or Hindi translations *sramajibi, sramik, mazdur*) in naming middle-class organizations and journals. The existence in the 1920s and later of parties like the Labour Swaraj Party (1925), the Workers' and Peasants' Party (1928), the Labour Party (1932), etc. testify to this new ideological development

---

[140] W.B.S.A., Judicial Dept Police Br., Jan. 1896 A6–11.
[141] Ramanuja Vidyarnava, 'Bhattapalli Gatha' in his *Kanthamala* (Bhatpara, n.d.[c. 1913?]).

in the bhadralok political scene.[142] By the late 1920s some of this spirit had even spilled over into the sacred world of Bengali literature. Tagore's irritated comment in 1928–9—'Do we enter a 'new era' in literature simply because so many writers [today] write about the coal-miner or the panwali?'—celebrates this new presence of the working class, if only negatively.[143]

To the Bengali bhadralok, the workers still presented a picture of moral degeneration, but in contrast to the nineteenth-century view this 'degeneration' was now assigned a cause (largely economic) outside of the worker's own morality and consciousness. The jute-mill worker, the *Amrita Bazar Patrika* said in 1928, was 'something less than a human being', but this condition was not of his own doing. This was a significant departure from the point of view of, say, Sasipada Banerjee. 'The modern industrial system' and the greed of the capitalist were now seen as the 'cause' of the worker's moral problems:

> Condemned to life in slums, . . . working long hours in closed and stuffy atmosphere and victims of all allurements held out by easily available grog and drug shops, and . . . deprived of the humanising influence of family life, he [the jute worker] is converted into something less than a human being . . . [This] condition of life . . . is incidental to the modern industrial system generally but . . . in very few industries the disproportion between profits and wages is so striking as in this [the jute industry].[144]

The same understanding informed K. C. Roy Chowdhury's play *Dharmaghat* (*The Strike*) which was staged in Calcutta in 1926. The 'moral degradation' of the worker and the 'stinking, unhealthy hovels around the jute mills at Naihati' are explained in this play in terms of capitalist neglect and exploitation. 'It is in the interests of the rich capitalist to treat the workers like beasts', says Shirish, who is by no means a radical character in the play.[145]

On this ideological ground was bred in the twenties and thirties a generation of bhadralok politicians whose commitment to their own ideological construct, the working class, was beyond question. Gopen

---

[142] The straightforward history of these parties and the journals (e.g. *Sramik, Sramajibi, Naya Mazdur*, etc.) they brought out is relatively well known and well documented. Two interesting analytical accounts of the period are Roger Stuart, 'The Formation of the Communist Party of India, 1927–1937: The Dilemma of the Indian Left' (A.N.U., Ph.D. thesis, 1978) and Tanika Sarkar, 'National Movement'.

[143] Tagore quoted in Sajanikanta Das, *Atmasmriti* (Calcutta, 1978), p. 197.

[144] *Amrita Bazar Patrika*, 31 Oct. 1928.

[145] Roy Chowdhury, *Dharmaghat*, p. 6.

Chakravarty, a Moscow-returned Communist, gave a dramatic demonstration of the commitment in 1926 when he joined a jute mill in Bhatpara 'as a machine-man in the steam room at Rs 14 a month'.

> Even this was not enough [he said in an interview]—so I rented a small cubicle in the jute line and lived with the workers . . . and told [them] . . . stories about [the] Russian revolution, Lenin and workers' raj, I also read out news from *Pratap* run by Ganesh Shankar Vidyarthi and also from our *Ganavani*.[146]

Gopen Chakravarty was not alone in showing such exemplary zeal for organizing the working class. Much of the political experience of the Bengali left in the '30s and afterwards can be written up—as indeed has been done sometimes—as stories of heroism and courage of men like Chakravarty. The impact of their commitment and activities is to be felt in the politics of West Bengal even today. 'The memory haunts', as a sensitive Bengali intellectual has recently written,

> the early dreams, oaths devoutly undertaken, careers forsaken, temptations thrust aside. For those who took to socialism, there was . . . a question of acute choice, one's convictions cut athwart one's class interests. They gladly made the transition. Forsaking homes and old loyalties, they fanned into the countryside to organize the poor peasants [and] pioneered the trade union movement in Greater Calcutta's belt . . .[147]

Yet I will insist that even these people, for all their sacrifice and commitment, remained imprisoned in the babu-coolie relationship insofar as the nature of their contact with the working class was concerned. Let me demonstrate this by analysing a document that was authored by the very same people as our hypothetical interlocutor referred to, the committed, self-sacrificing socialist-minded organizers of labour.

In January 1937 the manager of the Fort Gloster Jute Mill came upon a leaflet going around among his workers who were soon to vote in the coming provincial elections.[148] This was the first time that the Bengal Legislative Council would have its Labour Members elected and not nominated. The leaflet in question aimed at persuading the workers to vote for Sibnath Banerjee. Banerjee, a socialist, was then the President of the All India Trade Union Congress. His candidature was supported by the Communist Party and the Congress, and he actually won the elections.

[146] 'Interview' in Chattopadhyay, *Communism*, I, p. 135.
[147] Ashok Mitra, 'The Burnt-Out Cases' in his *Calcutta Diary* (London, 1976), p. 9.
[148] The leaflet is reproduced in W.B.S.A., Home Poll Confdl. no. 484/1937.

The document therefore was about representation. It asked the workers to elect *their* representative. A crucial task before the authors of the leaflet was to prove this identity of the representative with the class he would represent. Here of course there was an obvious problem. Banerjee was a member of the bhadralok community and therefore a babu. And so were the other contestants. How then could he represent the 'coolies', and why was his claim in this regard better than anybody else's?

Faced with these problems the leaflet began by introducing a real/spurious distinction between 'representatives' of labour.

> Friends, if we are to have [our] . . . grievances redressed, we must make, on the one hand, all the labour organizations more powerful, and on the other . . . see that the *real* labour representatives are sent to the Council . . . Friends, you will be glad to know that there are eight seats for the Labour constituency[ies]. For these eight seats, if we can send *real* representatives of labour . . . then their interests are safeguarded. [Emphasis added]

But how could a 'babu' become a 'real' representative of the 'coolie'? More importantly how would he make this 'reality' *visible* to the worker when all the usual signs of bhadralok existence set him apart from the working class? Our leaflet's answer was: by suffering himself, by making 'sacrifices' in the interests of the workers. 'Real' representatives are 'men who have *devoted* [emphasis added] their lives for the welfare of labourers'.

> To safeguard the interest of labourers, Comrade Banerjee has been to prison for many times. [*sic*] He was one of the accused in the Meerut Conspiracy case, and was in the lock-up for 2½ years, but [was] afterwards honorably acquitted. A few days back he was fined Rs 200/- by the . . . High Court for delivering speeches to the Calcutta Corporation workers. From the above facts it is evident that there is nobody like Comrade Banerjee for unholding [*sic*] the cause of labourers. If there is any man with *real* [emphasis added] sympathy for the labourers, then it is . . . Comrade Banerjee.

The point was also made in another such leaflet published on behalf of Sibnath Banerjee. This other leaflet too 'quoted and glorified the sentences of imprisonment and fines that had been passed on him', and then asked the labourers, ' "I have been prepared to suffer this for your sake, am I not the man for you?" '.[149]

So the display of 'sacrifice'—i.e. a demonstration of the willingness to share the poor man's suffering—was what made Banerjee better qualified to represent the workers. The claim to being a 'real'

---

[149] W.B.S.A., Home Poll Confdl. no. 72/1937.

representative of the working class was thus based in this argument on the respect traditionally due in Indian society to the figure of the renouncer. It was a moral claim that arose from an old feudal system of morality. There was in fact very little in common between this morality and the 'rationality' of the Leninist theory of representation. As is well known to any reader of *What Is To Be Done?* (1902), the Leninist 'representative' based his claim to represent the working class not on moral grounds but on his (supposed) access to superior, 'scientific' knowledge (i.e. theory) that was denied to the workers by their own conditions.

Besides, an appeal to the idea of sacrifice was really an appeal to the power that flowed from inequality. In order to be able to make sacrifices one needed to possess; he who did not possess could not sacrifice. The glory of the renouncer belonged to the 'possessor'. To talk of sacrifice was thus to talk of possessions, and hence of power. In the leaflet under discussion the authors needed to underscore, as it were, just 'how much' Banerjee had given up to become a 'real' representative of the workers. So they told the workers:

> Sibnath is an *educated man* and *has been to Europe*, and for the last ten years he has been serving the labourers, *leaving many high posts* formerly occupied by him. Friends, please vote for Sibnath without any hesitation. [Emphasis added]

But an 'educated man' who 'has been to Europe' and held 'many high posts' was not a coolie or a worker but a babu. And the logic of identification-through-sacrifice ends up making this clear. The discourse thus silently subverted from within its own claims about democratic representation, and the babu-coolie relationship reappeared in the very act meant to cause its disappearance. Gopen Chakravarty, the Moscow-returned Communist mentioned earlier, may have thought that the workers accepted him as 'one of them', but they still called him the 'Union *Babu*'.[150] So it is not surprising that in spite of his ideology and sacrifices—in fact it was precisely because of his sacrifices—that Sibnath Banerjee's union assumed no 'organizational form' for years and remained an 'out and out one man show', his 'zamindari'. Even a 'real' representative turned out to be a master.

VIII

Since we do not mean to suggest that the Bengali followers of Lenin were insincere people who made a rather cynical use of the concept of

150 Chakravarty, 'Interview', p. 135.

'sacrifice' only in order to manipulate the 'ignorant' workers, we need to ask another question: why was an idea steeped in feudal morality so central to a discourse that was self-consciously socialist?

There was clearly more at work here than historians have cared to admit or explore. The solution to the paradox of jute workers' organization is usually sought in economic (or 'structural') explanations or in arguments about political repression by the colonial state. Yet surely no amount of economic reasoning or evidence of state-repression will ever explain why even the socialist message of democratic representation was ultimately translated and assimilated into the undemocratic, hierarchical terms of the babu-coolie relationship; nor will they tell us why Banerjee's pamphlet addressed to the working class spoke so compulsively of his education, overseas trips and 'successful' career.

Perhaps a helpful distinction to make here would be between ideology, a body of conscious ideas (like Marxism), and culture, the 'signifying system through which necessarily a social order is communicated, reproduced, experienced and explored'.[151] Ideologically the Bengali left was committed to developing trade unions based on the democratic, contractual and voluntary procedures of organization that their theory of trade unionism entailed. In the culture of everyday life however they, as babus, related to the coolies through a hierarchy of status. Their education, their appearance, the language they spoke, the work they did, could all act as indicators of their authority and superiority over the coolies. The deployment of a system of *visible* status-markers that divided people into hierarchical categories of status and power had always been an important function of the culture to which they, the bhadralok, and the workers belonged. 'The working people', said Sasipada Banerjee in the nineteenth century, 'are in this country held as low, and as not important members of the society'.[152] Years later a young Sibnath Banerjee was to find the 'tattered clothes, bare feet, dirty appearance and the foul language' of the jute mill workers positively offensive to his bhadralok sensibilities.[153] The bhadralok clerks of the Burn Iron Works in

[151] Raymond Williams, *Culture* (Glasgow, 1981), p. 10. I may mention that I find Göran Therborn's attempt to do away with this distinction rather unhelpful. See Göran Therborn, *The Ideology of Power and the Power of Ideology* (London, 1980).

[152] Chakrabarty, 'Sasipada Banerjee', p. 346.

[153] S. Banerjee, interview transcript dated 19.7.75 (Centre for Studies in Social Sciences, Calcutta), p. 1.

Howrah staged a historic walk-out in September 1905 when the management asked them to record their attendance by the same 'new mechanical system' as the coolies were required to use.[154] An attempt in 1923 by the Scottish manager of the Anglo-India Jute Mill to hold a meeting of all of his employees to discuss a welfare scheme met with a very similar fate. 'The babus . . . refused to come to the same meeting as coolies, even if the latter sat on the floor'.[155]

It was these culturally-given relationships of power that entered the field of trade unionism as well. In terms of their theory the Bengali trade unionists no doubt aspired to build bourgeois-democratic organizations. In reality however they formed organizations based on 'loyalty' where authority did not flow through a grid of rules and procedures but derived directly from hierarchy and status. Indrajit Gupta, the C.P.I. trade unionist, was honest enough to suggest this in 1952. 'Ever since he can remember', said Gupta, 'the jute worker has understood by "union" nothing more than an office situated outside the mill and some union "*babus*" whose job is to write occasional petitions and hold gate, bustee or mass meetings'.[156]

By refusing to see these obvious signs of the feudal concerns of their own, everyday culture, and by seeing the cultural only as an instance of the economic, the Bengali left remained trapped, ironically enough, within the same culture they would have liked to see destroyed. Ideology in this case was not enough to erase the ties of power encoded in the culture. These ties derived from an older, feudal paradigm of power, and if we are to talk about a paradox in the history of jute workers' organization then this is where the paradox has to be located: at the intersection of ideology and culture.

---

154 Sarkar, *Swadeshi Movement*, pp. 200, 202.
155 W.B.S.A., Com. Dept Com. Br. April 1923 B77.
156 Gupta, *Capital and Labour*, p. 54.

Gandhi and the Critique of Civil Society

PARTHA CHATTERJEE

'My language is aphoristic, it lacks precision. It is therefore open to several interpretations.'

('Discussion with Dharmadev', *The Collected Works of Mahatma Gandhi*, Vol. 53, Appendix III, p. 485.)

I

Before presenting my own interpretation of the Gandhian ideology it will be useful to describe in brief the analytical framework in which I look at Gandhi's writings. Elsewhere I have discussed this framework in greater detail.[1] It is derived to a large extent from Antonio Gramsci's ideas on the relation between the fundamental classes and the 'people-nation', the achievement of hegemony by the creation of a 'national-popular' consensus, and the 'passive revolution'. The problem here is to identify the specific effectivity of the Gandhian ideology in the formation of the Indian state, not by reducing that ideology to a set of economic factors which could be said to constitute its historical context, but by granting to its domain a relative autonomy and its own rules of formation. More generally the problem is to undertake a concrete analysis of the relation of thought to the struggle between classes for domination as well as intellectual-moral leadership, the relation between intellectuals and the fundamental social classes, and most crucially, situations in which the fundamental social classes fail to achieve hegemony as well as the specific location of thought in such situations of incomplete domination and fragmented intellectual-moral leadership.

In his book *Orientalism*[2] Edward W. Said has shown how the

[1] Partha Chatterjee, *Nationalist Thought* (forthcomings), esp. Ch. 2.
[2] Edward W. Said, *Orientalism* (London, 1978).

post-enlightenment age in Europe produced an entire body of knowledge in which the Orient appeared as a 'system of representations framed by a whole set of forces that brought the Orient into Western learning, Western consciousness, and later, Western empire.' As a style of thought Orientalism is 'based upon an ontological and epistemological distinction made between "the Orient" and (most of the time) "the Occident".' On this basis an 'enormously systematic discipline' was created 'by which European culture was able to manage—and even produce—the Orient politically, sociologically, militarily, ideologically, scientifically, and imaginatively during the post-Englightenment period.' Orientalism *created* the Oriental; it was a body of knowledge in which the Oriental was '*contained* and *represented* by dominating frameworks', and Western power over the Orient was given the 'status of scientific truth'. Thus, Orientalism was 'a kind of Western projection onto and will to govern over the Orient.'

The central characteristics of this dominating framework of knowledge are described by Anouar Abdel-Malek[3] as follows, and this characterization has been adopted by Said. Abdel-Malek identified the *problematic* in Orientalism as one in which the Orient and Orientals were

> an 'object' of study, stamped with an otherness—as all that is different, whether it be 'subject' or 'object'—but of a constitutive otherness, of an essentialist character . . . . This 'object' of study will be, as is customary, passive, non-participating, endowed with a 'historical' subjectivity, above all, non-active, non-autonomous, non-sovereign with regard to itself: the only Orient or Oriental or 'subject' which could be admitted, at the extreme limit, is the alienated being, philosophically, that is, other than itself in relationship to itself, posed, understood, defined—and acted—by others.

At the level of the *thematic* on the other hand there was an

> essentialist conception of the countries, nations and peoples of the Orient under study, a conception which expresses itself through a characterized ethnist typology . . . .
>
> According to the traditional orientalists, an essence should exist—sometimes even clearly described in metaphysical terms—which constitutes the inalienable and common basis of all the beings considered; this essence is both 'historical', since it goes back to the dawn of history, and

---

[2] Edward W. Said, *Orientalism* (London, 1978).

[3] Anouar Abdel-Malek, 'Orientalism in Crisis', *Diogenes*, 44 (Winter 1963), pp. 102–40.

fundamentally a-historical, since it transfixes the being, 'the object' of study, within its inalienable and non-evolutive specificity, instead of defining it as all other beings, states, nations, peoples, and cultures—as a product, a resultant of the vection of the forces operating in the field of historical evolution.

Thus one ends with a typology—based on a real specificity, but detached from history, and, consequently, conceived as being intangible, essential—which makes of the studied 'object' another being with regard to whom the studying subject is transcendent; we will have a homo Sinicus, a homo Arabicus (and why not a homo Aegypticus, etc.), a homo Africanus, the man—the 'normal man', it is understood—being the European man of the historical period, that is, since Greek antiquity.

When one turns now from European knowledge of the Orient to nationalist thinking in the East in the nineteenth and twentieth centuries, what stares one in the face is the profound manner in which nationalist thought is itself shaped, indeed contained by the same dominating framework—the framework of Orientalism. Of course nationalism in colonial countries is premised on opposition to alein rule, in this case rule by a Western power. But it is vitally important to emphasize that this opposition occurs *within* a body of knowledge about the East (large parts of it purporting to be scientific) which has the same representational structure and shares the same theoretical framework as Orientalism.

We find in fact that the problematic in nationalist thought is exactly the reverse of that in Orientalism. That is to say, the 'object' in nationalist thought is still the Oriental who retains the essentialist character depicted in Orientalist discourse. Only he is not passive, non-participating. He is seen to possess a 'subjectivity' which he can himself 'make'. In other words while his relationship to himself and to others has been 'posed, understood and defined' by others, i.e. by an objective scientific consciousness, by Knowledge, by Reason, those relationships are not acted by others. His subjectivity he thinks is active, autonomous and sovereign.

At the level of the thematic on the other hand nationalist thought accepts and adopts the same essentialist conception based on the distinction between 'the East' and 'the West', the same typology created by a transcendent studying subject, and hence the same 'objectifying' procedures of knowledge constructed in the post-enlightenment age of Western science.

There is consequently an inherent contradictoriness in nationalist thinking because it reasons within a framework of knowledge whose representational structure corresponds to the very structure of power that nationalist thought seeks to repudiate. It is this contradictoriness in the domain of thought which creates the possibility of several divergent solutions being proposed for the nationalist problematic. Furthermore it is this contradictoriness which signifies in the domain of thought the theoretical insolubility of the national question in a colonial country, or for that matter of the extended problem of social transformation in a post-colonial country, within a strictly nationalist framework.

I have explored elsewhere[4] some of these contradictory aspects of élite-nationalist thought in the specific context of late nineteenth-century India. The purpose of the present essay is to examine how the Gandhian ideology, while fundamentally subverting this structure of élite-nationalist thought, provided at the same time the historical opportunity for the political appropriation of the popular classes within the evolving forms of the new Indian state.

II

Although Gandhi's *Collected Works* has run into more than eighty thick volumes, there exist few texts in which he can be seen attempting a systematic exposition of his ideas on state, society and nation. One of the first and perhaps the fullest is entitled *Hind Swaraj*, written in Gujarati in 1909 and published in an English translation in Johannesburg in 1910 after the original edition was proscribed by the Government of Bombay. It contains a statement of most of the fundamental elements of Gandhi's politics. Romain Rolland, one of his first sympathetic but critical commentators, saw in this book a reflection of the central features of Gandhi's thought: 'the negation of Progress and also of European science.'[5] A more recent commentator, Raghavan Iyer, sees it as 'a severe condemnation of modern civilization' and 'the *point d'appui* of Gandhi's moral and political thought.'[6] I prefer to read it as a text in which Gandhi's nationalism can be shown to rest on a fundamental critique of the idea of civil society.

On the surface it is indeed a critique of modern civilization, 'a civilization only in name'.[7] And the argument proceeds, as in many

---

[4] Chatterjee, *Nationalist Thought*, Ch. 3.

[5] Romain Rolland, *Mahatma Gandhi: A Study in Indian Nationalism*, tr. L. V. Ramaswami Aiyar (Madras, 1923), p. 30.

[6] Raghavan N. Iyer, *The Moral and Political Thought of Mahatma Gandhi* (New York, 1973), p. 24.

[7] *Hind Swaraj*, in *The Collected Works of Mahatma Gandhi* (hereafter *CW*), Vol. 10 (New Delhi, 1958), p. 18.

other nationalist writers, from a consideration of the question: Why is India a subject nation? To start with Gandhi's answer too seems to run along the same lines. He too is concerned more with locating the sources of Indian weakness than putting the blame on British avarice or deceit. But the emphasis is not so much on the elements of culture. Gandhi points much more forcefully to the moral failure.

> The English have not taken India; we have given it to them. They are not in India because of their strength, but because we keep them . . . . Recall the Company Bahadur. Who made it Bahadur? They had not the slightest intention at the time of establishing a kingdom. Who assisted the Company's officers? Who was tempted at the sight of their silver? Who bought their goods? History testifies that we did all this . . . . When our Princes fought among themselves, they sought the assistance of Company Bahadur. That corporation was versed alike in commerce and war. It was unhampered by questions of morality . . . . Is it not then useless to blame the English for what we did at the time? . . . it is truer to say that we gave India to the English than that India was lost.[8]

It was a moral failure on the part of Indians that led to the conquest of India. And in exploring the reasons behind this moral failue Gandhi's answer becomes diametrically opposed to that of most contemporary nationalists. It is not because Indian society lacked the necessary cultural attributes that it was unable to face up to the power of the English. It is not the backwardness or lack of modernity of India's culture that keeps it in continued subjection. And the task of achieving freedom would not be accomplished by creating a new modern culture for the nation. For Gandhi it is precisely because Indians were seduced by the glitter of modern civilization that they became a subject people. And what keeps them in subjection is the acceptance by leading sections of Indians of the supposed benefits of civilization. Indeed as long as Indians continue to harbour illusions about the 'progressive' qualities of modern civilization, they will remain a subject nation. Even if they succeed physically in driving out the English they will still have 'English rule without the Englishman', because it is not the physical presence of the English which makes India a subject nation: it is civilization which subjects.

Then follows an indictment of modern civilization as it has emerged in the West and as it has been imported into India. Fundamentally, Gandhi attacks the very notions of modernity and progress and subverts the central claim made on behalf of those notions, namely their correspondence with a new organization of society in which the

[8] *Hind Swaraj*, CW, Vol. 10, pp. 22–3.

productive capacities of human labour are multiplied several times, creating increased wealth and prosperity for all, and hence increased leisure, comfort, health and happiness. Gandhi argues that far from achieving these objectives, modern civilization makes man a prisoner of his craving for luxury and self-indulgence, releases the forces of unbridled competition and thereby brings upon society the evils of poverty, disease, war and suffering. It is precisely because modern civilization looks at man as a limitless consumer and thus sets out to open the floodgates of industrial production that it also becomes the source of inequality, oppression and violence on a scale hitherto unknown in human history.

Machinery for instance is intended to increase the productivity of labour and thus satisfy the never-ending urge for consumption. But it only whets the appetite, it does not satisfy it. What it does instead is bring exploitation and disease to industrial cities and unemployment and ruin to the countryside.

> When I read Mr Dutt's *Economic History of India*, I wept; and as I think of it again my heart sickens. It is machinery that has impoverished India. It is difficult to measure the harm that Manchester has done to us. It is due to Manchester that Indian handicraft has all but disappeared.[9]

The driving social urge behind industrial production is the craving for excessive consumption. It is in this context that Gandhi interprets the modern spirit of scientific inquiry and technological advance; a tendency to let the mind wander uncontrolled and chase the objects of our passions.

> We notice that the mind is a restless bird; the more it gets the more it wants, and still remains unsatisfied. The more we indulge our passions, the more unbridled they become. Our ancestors, therefore, set a limit to our indulgences. They saw that happiness was largely a mental condition . . . . Observing all this, our ancestors dissuaded us from luxuries and pleasures. We have managed with the same kind of plough as existed thousands of years ago. We have retained the same kind of cottages that we had in former times and our indigenous education remains the same as before. We have had no system of life-corroding competition . . . . It was not that we did not know how to invent machinery, but our forefathers knew that if we set our hearts after such things, we would become slaves and lose our moral fibres. They, therefore, after due deliberation decided that we should only do what we could with our hands and feet.[10]

Hence his solution to the social evils of industrialism is not just to remove its defects, because he thinks these so-called defects are

[9] Ibid., p. 57.   [10] Ibid., p. 37.

germane to the very fundamentals of the modern system of production. His solution is to give up industrialism altogether: 'instead of welcoming machinery as a boon, we should look upon it as an evil.'[11] It is only a complete change in moral values that will change our perception of our social needs and thus enable us once again to set deliberate limits to social consumption. Nothing short of this will succeed.

> A certain degree of physical harmony and comfort is necessary, but above a certain level it becomes a hindrance instead of help. Therefore the ideal of creating an unlimited number of wants and satisfying them seems to be a delusion and a snare. The satisfaction of one's physical needs, even the intellectual needs of one's narrow self, must meet at a certain point a dead stop, before it degenerates into physical and intellectual voluptuousness.[12]

Clearly then Gandhi's critique of British rule in India attempted to situate it at a much more fundamental level than most nationalist writers of his time. Where they were criticizing merely the excesses of Western notions of patriotism and national glory which inevitably pushed those countries towards the pursuit of colonial conquests and victories in war, Gandhi has no doubt at all that the source of modern imperialism lies specifically in the system of social production which the countries of the Western world have adopted. It is the limitless desire for ever-increased production and ever-greater consumption, and the spirit of ruthless competitiveness which keeps the entire system going, that impel these countries to seek colonial possessions which can be exploited for economic purposes. Gandhi stated this position quite emphatically as early as in *Hind Swaraj* and held on to it all his life. It was in fact in many ways the most crucial theoretical foundation of his entire strategy of winning *swaraj* for India.

> Napoleon is said to have described the English as a nation of shop-keepers. It is a fitting description. They hold whatever dominions they have for the sake of their commerce. Their army and their navy are intended to protect it. When the Transvaal offered no such attractions, the late Mr Gladstone discovered that it was not right for the English to hold it. When it became a paying proposition, resistance led to war. Mr Chamberlain soon discovered that England enjoyed a suzerainty over the Transvaal. It is related that someone asked the late President Kruger whether there was gold on the moon. He replied that it was highly unlikely because, if there were, the English would have annexed it. Many problems can be solved by remembering that money is their God . . . . If

[11] Ibid., p. 60.
[12] Discussion with Maurice Frydman, 25 August 1936, *CW*, Vol. 63, p. 241.

you accept the above statements, it is proved that the English entered India for the purposes of trade. They remain in it for the same purpose . . . . They wish to convert the whole world into a vast market for their goods. That they cannot do so is true, but the blame will not be theirs. They will leave no stone unturned to reach the goal.[13]

Thus in the case of modern imperialism, morality and politics are both subordinated to the primary consideration of economics, and this consideration is directly related to a specific organization of social production characterized not so much by the nature of owner-ship of the means of production but fundamentally by the *purposes* and the *processes* of production. That is to say whereas Gandhi is in this particular historical instance talking about the capitalist system of production in Britain, his characterization of the type of economy which leads to exploitation and colonial conquest is not necessarily restricted to capitalism alone, because as long as the purpose of social production is to continually expand it in order to satisfy an endless urge for consumption and as long as the process of production is based on ever-increased mechanization, those consequences would follow inevitably. And the purposes and processes of production take on this particular form whenever production is primarily directed not towards the creation of articles of immediate *use* but towards *exchange*—exchange between town and country and between metropolis and colony. Any kind of industrialization on a large scale would have to be based on certain determinate exchange relations between town and country, with the balance inevitably tipping against the latter whenever the pace of industrialization quickens. This would lead to unemployment and poverty in the villages or, which amounts to the same thing, to the exploitation of colonial possessions.

> Industrialization on a mass scale will necessarily lead to passive or active exploitation of the villagers as the problems of competition and marketing come in. Therefore we have to concentrate on the village being self-contained, manufacturing mainly for use.[14]

The mere socialization of industries would not alter this process in any way at all.

> Pandit Nehru wants industrialization because he thinks that, if it is socialized, it would be free from the evils of capitalism. My own view is that evils are inherent in industrialism, and no amount of socialization can eradicate them.[15]

13 *Hind Swaraj*, *CW*, Vol. 10, p. 23.
14 Discussion with Maurice Frydman, *CW*, Vol. 63, p. 241.
15 Interview to Francis G. Hickman, 17 September 1940, *CW*, Vol. 73, pp. 29–30.

In fact Gandhi's argument was that there is no feasible way in which *any* process of industrialization can avoid the creation of exploitative and inhumane relations of exchange between town and country. He states this quite clearly when he argues that *khādi* (homespun cotton textiles) is the only sound economic proposition for India:

> . . . 'Khadi is the only true economic proposition in terms of the millions of villagers until such time, if ever, when a better system of supplying work and adequate wages for every able-bodied person above the age of sixteen, male or female, is found for his field, cottage or even factory in every one of the villages of India; or till sufficient cities are built up to displace the villages so as to give the villagers the necessary comforts and amenities that a well-regulated life demands and is entitled to.' I have only to state the proposition thus fully to show that khadi must hold the field for any length of time that we can think of.[16]

It is true of course that in the midst of continuing controversy about the economic policies of the Congress, and especially the programme of khādi, Gandhi increasingly tended to emphasize the strict economic argument against heavy industrialization in a large agrarian economy with an abundance of under-employed labour. In the later years of his life he would often in fact prefer to suspend the debate about the larger moral issues of mechanization *per se* in order to win his point on the infeasibility of heavy industrialization in the particular context of India. 'I have no partiality', he would say, 'for return to the primitive methods of grinding and husking for the sake of them. I suggest the return, because there is no other way of giving employment to the millions of villagers who are living in idleness.'[17] At times he even conceded that mechanization might have an economic logic in situations of labour scarcity.

> Mechanization is good when the hands are too few for the work intended to be accomplished. It is an evil when there are more hands than required for the work, as is the case in India . . . . The problem with us is not how to find leisure for the teeming millions inhabiting our villages. The problem is how to utilize their idle hours, which are equal to the working days of six months in the year . . . . Spinning and weaving mills have deprived the villagers of a substantial means of livelihood. It is no answer in reply to say that they turn out cheaper, better cloth, if they do so at all. For, if they have displaced thousands of workers, the cheapest mill cloth is dearer than the dearest khadi woven in the villages.[18]

But this was only a debating point, an attempt to bring round to the cause of his economic programme those who did not share his

[16] 'Is Khadi Economically Sound?', *CW*, Vol. 63, pp. 77–8.
[17] 'Why Not Labour-saving Devices', *CW*, Vol. 59, pp. 413.
[18] 'Village Industries', *CW*, Vol. 59, p. 356.

fundamental philosophical premises. Because ever so often, even as he argued about the practical economic necessity of khādi, he would remind his readers where exactly he stood with regard to the fundamental moral issues.

> If I could do it, I would most assuredly destroy or radically change much that goes under the name of modern civilization. But that is an old story of life. The attempt is undoubtedly there. Its success depends upon God. But the attempt to revive and encourage the remunerative village industries is not part of such an attempt, except in so far as every one of my activities, including the propagation of non-violence, can be described as such an attempt.[19]

Even when it came to a question of the fundamental principles of organization of economic life Gandhi would unhesitatingly state his opposition to the concept of the *homo oeconomicus*, to the supposed benefits of the social division of labour, and to the current faith in the laws of the marketplace transforming private vices into public virtues.

> I am always reminded of one thing which the well-known British economist Adam Smith has said in his famous treatise *The Wealth of Nations*. In it he has described some economic laws as universal and absolute. Then he has described certain situations which may be an obstacle to the operation of these laws. These disturbing factors are the human nature, the human temperament or altruism inherent in it. Now, the economics of khadi is just the opposite of it. Benevolence which is inherent in human nature is the very foundation of the economics of khadi. What Adam Smith has described as pure economic activity based merely on the calculations of profit and loss is a selfish attitude and it is an obstacle to the development of khadi; and it is the function of a champion of khadi to counteract this tendency.[20]

And thus one comes back to Gandhi's condemnation of what he calls 'modern civilization', which in fact is a fundamental critique of the entire edifice of bourgeois society: its continually expanding and prosperous economic life based on individual property; the social division of labour and the impersonal laws of the market described with clinical precision and complete moral approbation by Mandeville and Smith; its political institutions based on a dual notion of sovereignty in which the people in theory rule themselves but are only allowed to do so through the medium of their representatives whose actions have to be ratified only once in so many years; its spirit of innovation, adventure and scientific progress; its rationalization of

[19] 'Its Meaning', *CW*, Vol. 60, pp. 54–5.
[20] 'New Life for Khadi', *CW*, Vol. 59, pp. 205–6.

philosophy and ethics and secularization of art and education. As early as in *Hind Swaraj* Gandhi launches a thoroughgoing critique against each of these constitutive features of civil society.

Parliament for instance he calls 'a sterile woman and a prostitute', the first because despite being a sovereign institution it cannot enact a law according to its own judgment but is constantly swayed by outside pressures, and the second because it continually shifts its allegiance from one set of ministers to another depending on which is more powerful. But basically Gandhi objects to an entire structure of politics and government in which each individual is assumed to have his own individual interest, individuals are expected to come together into parties and alliances in terms of those self-interests, these combinations of interests are then supposed to exert pressure on each other by mobilizing public opinion and manipulating the levers of the governmental machinery, and legislative enactments are then expected to emerge as choices made on behalf of the whole society.

> . . . it is generally acknowledged that the members [of Parliament] are hypocritical and selfish. Each thinks of his own little interest. It is fear that is the guiding motive . . . . Members vote for their party without a thought. Their so-called discipline binds them to it. If any member, by way of exception, gives an independent vote, he is considered a renegade . . . . The Prime Minister is more concerned about his power than about the welfare of Parliament. His energy is concentrated upon securing the success of his party. His care is not always that Parliament should do right . . . . If they are considered honest because they do not take what are generally known as bribes, let them be so considered, but they are open to subtler influences. In order to gain their ends, they certainly bribe people with honours. I do not hesitate to say that they have neither real honesty nor a living conscience.[21]

And the process by which support is mobilized on behalf of particular leaders or parties or interests is equally unworthy of moral approval.

> To the English voters their newspaper is their Bible. They take their cue from their newspapers which are often dishonest. The same fact is differently interpreted by different newspapers, according to the party in whose interests they are edited . . . [The] people change their views frequently. . . . These views swing like the pendulum of a clock and are never steadfast. The people would follow a powerful orator or a man who gives them parties, receptions, etc.[22]

Once again Gandhi's criticism is aimed against the abrogation of moral responsibility involved in the duality of sovereignty and the

---

[21] *Hind Swaraj*, CW, Vol. 10, pp. 17–8.   [22] Ibid., p. 18.

mediation of complex legal-political institutions which distance the rulers of society from those they are supposed to represent. He does not accept the argument that if effective combinations are formed among individuals and groups sharing a set of common self-interests, then the institutions of representative democracy will ensure that the government will act in ways which are, on the whole, in the common interest of the entire collectivity. His argument is in fact that the dissociation of political values based on self-interest, from social morality based on certain universal ethical values shared by the whole community, leads to a structure and process of politics in which the wealthy and the powerful enjoy disproportionate opportunities to manipulate the machinery of government to their own sectional interests. Besides, the legal fiction of equality before the law and the supposed neutrality of state institutions only have the effect of per-petuating the inequalities and divisions which already exist in society: politics has no role in removing those inequalities or cementing the divisions. In fact this very process of law and politics which thrives on conflict creates a vested interest among politicians, state officials and legal practitioners to perpetuate social divisions and indeed to create new ones.

> [The lawyers'] duty is to side with their clients and to find out ways and arguments in favour of their clients, to which they (the clients) are often strangers . . . . The lawyers, therefore, will, as a rule, advance quarrels instead of repressing them . . . . It is within my knowledge that they are glad when men have disputes. Petty pleaders actually manufacture them.[23]

Similarly the colonial state in India by projecting an image of neutrality with regard to social divisions within Indian society not only upholds the rigours of those divisions, such as the ones imposed by the caste system, but actually strengthens them.[24]

By contrast it is only when politics is *directly* subordinated to a communal morality that the minority of exploiters in society can be resisted by the people and inequalities and divisions removed. As a political ideal therefore Gandhi counterposes against the system of representative government an undivided concept of popular sovereignty where the community is self-regulating and political power is dissolved into the collective moral will.

> The power to control national life through national representatives is called political power. Representatives will become unnecessary if the

---

[23] Ibid., p. 33.
[24] Letter to David B. Hart, 21 September 1934, *CW*, Vol. 59, p. 45.

national life becomes so perfect as to be self-controlled. It will then be a
state of enlightened anarchy in which each person will become his own
ruler. He will conduct himself in such a way that his behaviour will not
hamper the well-being of his neighbours. In an ideal State there will be no
political institution and therefore no political power.[25]

In its form this political ideal is not meant to be a consensual
democracy with complete and continual participation by every
member of the polity. The utopia is *Rāmarājya*, a patriarchy in
which the ruler, by his moral quality and habitual adherence to truth,
always expresses the collective will.[26] It is also a utopia in which the
economic organization of production, arranged according to a perfect
four-fold *varṇa* scheme of specialization and a perfect system of
reciprocity in the exchange of commodities and services, always
ensures that there is no spirit of competition and no differences in
status between different kinds of labour.[27] The ideal conception of
Rāmarājya in fact encapsulates the critique of all that is morally repre-
hensible in the economic and political organization of civil society.

The argument is then extended to other aspects of civil society. The
secularization of education for instance has made a fetish of the
knowledge of letters and has thereby both exaggerated and rationalized
the inequalities in society. It ignores completely the ethical aspect of
education and the need to integrate the individual within the collectively shared moral values of the community, and instead cultivates
'the pretension of learning many sciences'. The result is a pervasive
feeling of dissatisfaction, of moral anarchy and a license to individual
self-seeking, to 'hypocrisy, tyranny, etc.'[28] It also rationalizes, by
ascribing an economic logic to it, one of the fundamental aspects of
the social division of labour in modern industrial society, namely the
distinction between mental and manual work. It denies that intellectual
labour is an aspect not of the creation of wealth but of human
self-fulfilment and must therefore be made available to every human
being, and this can only be done if all share equally in providing the
needs of the body.

> May not men earn their bread by intellectual labour? No . . . Mere mental,
> that is, intellectual labour is for the soul and is its own satisfaction. It
> should never demand payment.[29]

[25] 'Enlightened Anarchy: A Political Ideal', *CW*, Vol. 68, p. 265.
[26] For example, *CW*, Vol. 35, pp. 489–90; *CW*, Vol. 45, pp. 328–9.
[27] For example, *CW*, Vol. 59, pp. 61–7; *CW*, Vol. 50, pp. 226–7.
[28] *Hind Swaraj*, *CW*, Vol. 10, p. 36.
[29] 'Duty of Bread Labour', *CW*, Vol. 61, p. 212.

Bodily sustenance should come from body labour, and intellectual labour is necessary for the culture of the mind. Division of labour there will necessarily be, but it will be a division into various species of body labour and a division into intellectual labour to be confined to one class and body labour to be confined to another class.[30]

The spirit of scientific inquiry and technological innovation, too, is aimed more towards physical self-indulgence and luxury than towards the discovery of truth. The science of medicine, for instance, on whose behalf the tallest claims are made by the propagators of modernity, concerns itself more with enabling people to consume more than with the removal of disease.

I overeat, I have indigestion, I go to the doctor, he gives me medicine, I am cured. I overeat again, I take his pills again. Had I not taken the pills in the first instance, I would have suffered the punishment deserved by me and I would not have overeaten again. The doctor intervened and helped me to indulge myself.[31]

And this of course only perpetuates the disease, it does not cure it. The modern science of medicine is satisfied by treating illnesses merely at the surface level of physical causality. The scientific spirit, divorced as it is from considerations of morality, does not feel obliged to look deeper into the true causes of diseases which must lie in the very mode of social living.

III

What appears on the surface as a critique of Western civilization is therefore a total moral critique of the fundamental aspects of civil society. It is not at this level a critique of Western culture or religion,[32] nor is it an attempt to establish the superior spiritual claims of Hindu religion. In fact the moral charge against the West is not that its religion is inferior but that by wholeheartedly embracing the dubious virtues of modern civilization it has forgotten the true teachings of the Christian faith. At this level of his thought therefore Gandhi is not operating at all with the problematic of nationalism. His solution too is meant to be universal, applicable as much to the countries of the West as to nations such as India.

Not only that. What is even more striking but equally clear is that

---

[30] Discussion with Gujarat Vidyapith Teachers, *CW*, Vol. 58, p. 306.

[31] *Hind Swaraj*, *CW*, Vol. 10, p. 35.

[32] It is only a critique of the 'modern philosophy of life'; it is called 'Western' only because it originated in the West. *CW*, Vol. 57, p. 498.

Gandhi does not even think within the thematic of nationalism. He seldom writes or speaks in terms of the conceptual frameworks or the modes of reasoning and inference adopted by the nationalists of his day, and quite emphatically rejects their rationalism, scientism and historicism. As early as in *Hind Swaraj* Gandhi dismisses all historical objections to his project of freeing India, not by the strength of arms but by the force of the soul, by saying, 'To believe that what has not occurred in history will not occur at all is to argue disbelief in the dignity of man.'[33] He does not feel it necessary to even attempt a historical demonstration of the possibilities he is trying to point out. Indeed he objects that the historical mode of reasoning is quite unsuitable, indeed irrelevant, for his purpose. History he says is built upon the records not of the working of the force of the soul but of its exact opposite. It is a record of the interruptions of peace.

> Two brothers quarrel; one of them repents and re-awakens the love that was lying dormant in him; the two again begin to live in peace; nobody takes note of this. But if the two brothers, through the intervention of solicitors or some other reason take up arms or go to law—which is another form of the exhibition of brute force—their doings would be immediately noticed in the Press, they would be the talk of their neighbours and would probably go down in history. And what is true of families and communities is true of nations.[34]

History therefore does not record the Truth. Truth lies outside history; it is universal, unchanging. Truth has no history of its own.

Indeed it is instructive to compare the method Gandhi follows in his attempts to reinterpret the scriptures with those followed by practically every other nationalist reformer of this time. Not only does he not attempt a historical examination of the authenticity of scriptural texts or of the historicity of the great characters of sacred history, he quite explicitly states that such exercises are quite irrelevant to the determination of truth. In *Anāsaktiyoga*, his commentaries on the *Gītā*, Gandhi does not bother at all about the history of the text itself or about the historicity of Krishna, although he was quite aware of the debates surrounding these questions. Mahadev Desai, in his introductory note to the English translation of *Anāsaktiyoga*, mentions the debate about the 'original' text of the *Gītā* and says

> One may however say that, even when this original is discovered, it will not make much difference to souls like Gandhiji, every moment of whose

life is a conscious effort to live the message of the Gita. This does not mean that Gandhiji is indifferent to the efforts of scholars in this direction. The smallest questions of historical detail interest him intensely as I can say from personal knowledge . . . . But his attitude is that in the last analysis it is the message that abides, and he is sure that no textual discovery is going to affect by a jot the essence or universality of that message. The same thing may be said about questions of the historical Krishna and the genesis and history of the Krishna Vasudeva worship . . . .[35]

Further, Gandhi did not regard the *Gītā*, or even the *Mahābhārata* of which it appears as a part, as a historical narrative. The historical underpinnings were merely a literary device; the message had nothing to do with history

Even in 1888–89, when I first became acquainted with the Gita, I felt that it was not a historical work, but that, under the guise of physical warfare, it described the duel that perpetually went on in the hearts of mankind, and that physical warfare was brought in merely to make the description of the internal duel more alluring. This preliminary intuition became more confirmed on a closer study of religion and the Gita. A study of the Mahabharata gave it added confirmation. I do not regard the Mahabharata as a historical work in the accepted sense. The *Adiparva* contains powerful evidence in support of my opinion. By ascribing to the chief actors superhuman or subhuman origins, the great Vyasa made short work of the history of kings and their peoples. The persons therein described may be historical, but the author of the Mahabharata has used them merely to drive home his religious theme.[36]

Indeed whenever he was confronted with a historical argument about the great Indian epics, trying to point out for instance the reality of warfare and violence in human life and of the relevance of a text such as the *Gītā* as a practical consideration of the ethics of power politics, Gandhi would insist that the truth of the *Mahābhārata* or the *Rāmāyaṇa* was a 'poetic truth', not historical; the epics were allegories and not theoretical or historical treatises.

That they most probably deal with historical figures does not affect my proposition. Each epic describes the eternal duel that goes on between the forces of darkness and light.[37]

To discover this truth one would of course have to interpret the text to the best of one's knowledge and belief.

[35] Mahadev Desai, *The Gospel of Selfless Action or the Gita According to Gandhi* (Ahmedabad, 1946), p. 6.
[36] Ibid., pp. 123–4.
[37] 'Teaching of Hinduism', *CW*, Vol. 63, p. 339.

Who is the best interpreter? Not learned men surely. Learning there must be. But religion does not live by it. It lives in the experiences of its saints and seers, in their lives and sayings. When all the most learned commentators of the scriptures are utterly forgotten, the accumulated experience of the sages and saints will abide and be an inspiration for ages to come.[38]

There might of course be conflicting interpretations of the epics and the scriptures. But such a dispute could never be resolved theoretically. Only the living practice of one's faith could show whether or not one's interpretation was correct. Gandhi mentions for instance the difference between his interpretation of the *Gītā* and the one followed by those who believed in armed violence.

The grim fact is that the terrorists have in absolute honesty, earnestness and with cogency used the *Gita*, which some of them know by heart, in defence of their doctrine and policy. Only they have no answer to my interpretation of the *Gita*, except to say that mine is wrong and theirs is right. Time alone will show whose is right. The *Gita* is not a theoretical treatise. It is a living but silent guide whose directions one has to understand by patient striving.[39]

Gandhi's argument was exactly the same when dealing with questions such as scriptural sanctions for all those social practices which he thought were unjust and immoral. He would not admit that the mere existence of scriptural texts was proof that it must be a constituent or consistent part of true religion. Nor would he agree to submit his case to a historical examination of the origins or evolution of particular social institutions. On the caste system for instance his position was as follows:

Caste has nothing to do with religion. It is a custom whose origin I do not know and do not need to know for the satisfaction of my spiritual hunger. But I do know that it is harmful both to spiritual and national growth.[40]

When his critics argued that caste practices were quite explicitly sanctioned by the *śāstra*, his emphatic reply was: 'Nothing in the Shastras which is manifestly contrary to universal truths and morals can stand.'[41] So also on the question of the social status of women as described in the canonical *smṛti* texts:

---

[38] 'Dr Ambedkar's Indictment-II', *CW*, Vol. 63, p. 153.
[39] 'The Law of Our Being', *CW*, Vol. 63, pp. 319–20.
[40] 'Dr Ambedkar's Indictment-II', *CW*, Vol. 63, p. 153.
[41] 'Caste Has To Go', *CW*, Vol. 62, p. 121.

It is sad to think that the *Smritis* contain texts which can command no respect from men who cherish the liberty of woman as their own and who regard her as the mother of the race; . . . The question arises as to what to do with the *Smritis* that contain texts . . . that are repugnant to the moral sense. I have already suggested . . . that all that is printed in the name of scriptures need not be taken as the word of God or the inspired word.[42]

Gandhi's position then is that the true principles of religion or morality are universal and unchanging. There do exist religious traditions which represent the attempts by various people through the ages to discover and interpret these principles. But those traditions were the products of history; they could not be taken to represent a corpus of truths: 'The true dharma is unchanging, while tradition may change with time. If we were to follow some of the tenets of *Manusmriti*, there would be moral anarchy. We have quietly discarded them altogether.'[43] Not only did Gandhi not share the historicism of the nationalist writers, he did not share their confidence in rationality and the scientific mode of knowledge. He would repeatedly assert that the knowledge unearthed by the sciences was applicable only to very limited areas of human living. If one did not acknowledge this and pretended instead that rational inquiry and a scientific search for truth would provide the solution for every problem in life one would be either led to insanity or reduced to impotence.

Nowadays, I am relying solely on my intellect. But mere intellect makes one insane or unmanly. That is its function. In such a situation Rama is the strength of the weak. My innermost urge is for pure non-violence. My weakness is that I do not know how to make it work. I use my intellect to overcome that weakness. If this intellectual cleverness loses the support of truth, it will blur my vision of non-violence, for is not non-violence the same as truth? Mere practical sense is but a covering for truth. 'The face of truth is hidden by a golden lid.' The reasoning faculty will raise a thousand issues. Only one thing will save us from these and that is faith.[44]

[42] 'Woman in the Smritis', *CW*, Vol. 64, p. 85.

[43] Letter to Ranchhodlal Patwari, 9 September 1918, *CW*, Vol. 15, p. 45. Or, again, 'Khan Abdul Ghaffar Khan derives his belief in non-violence from the Koran, and the Bishop of London derives his belief in violence from the Bible. I derive my belief in non-violence from the *Gita*, whereas there are others who read violence in it. But if the worst came to the worst and if I came to the conclusion that the Koran teaches violence, I would still reject violence, but I would not therefore say that the Bible is superior to the Koran or that Mahomed is inferior to Jesus. It is not my function to judge Mahomed and Jesus. It is enough that my non-violence is independent of the sanction of scriptures.' Interview to Dr Crane, *CW*, Vol. 64, p. 399.

[44] Speech at Gandhi Seva Sangh Meeting, 28 March 1938, *CW*, Vol. 66, p. 445.

Perhaps the most celebrated public controversy over Gandhi's preference for instinctive faith over the claims of scientific reasoning was when he pronounced that the devastating earthquakes in Bihar in 1934 were a 'divine chastisement' for the sin of untouchability. Rabindranath Tagore reacted very strongly and criticized Gandhi not only for implying that God in inflicting punishment upon sinners was unable to distinguish between the guilty and the innocent—since an earthquake is indiscriminate in its destruction, but also for strengthening the forces of unreason which fostered the belief that cosmic phenomena had something to do with the fate of human beings on earth.[45] Gandhi stuck to his position with characteristic firmness, but there was a somewhat unusual touch of acerbity in his reply.[46] He refused to entertain questions about the rationality of divine action.

> I am not affected by posers such as 'why punishment for an age-old sin' or 'why punishment to Bihar and not to the South' or 'why an earthquake and not some other form of punishment'. My answer is: I am not God. Therefore I have but a limited knowledge of His purpose.[47]

He reiterated his belief 'that physical phenomena produce results both physical and spiritual. The converse I hold to be equally true.'[48] He admitted that his belief was 'instinctive' and that he could not prove it. 'But I would be untruthful and cowardly if, for fear of ridicule, when those that are nearest and dearest to me are suffering, I did not proclaim my belief from the house-top.'[49] In any case he felt there are very few things which we understand well enough to be able to prove by the use of reason. And 'where reason cannot function, it is faith that works.' Some physical phenomena are intricately related to our ways of living, and since we have only an 'infinitesimal' knowledge of the rational working of physical laws, the proper attitude is not to remain content with this partial knowledge but to take a unified moral view of those relations.

[45] For Tagore's statement, see Appendix I, *CW*, Vol. 57, pp. 503–4.

[46] To Vallabhbhai Patel he wrote: 'You must have read the Poet's attack. I am replying to it in *Harijan*. He of course made amends afterwards. He gets excited and writes, and then corrects himself. This is what he does every time.' Letter to Vallabhbhai Patel, 13 February 1934, *CW*, Vol. 57, p. 155.

[47] 'Bihar and Untouchability', *CW*, Vol. 57, p. 87.

[48] 'Superstition v. Faith', *CW*, Vol. 57, pp. 164–5.

[49] Ibid., p. 165.

Rain is a physical phenomenon; it is no doubt related to human happiness and unhappiness; if so, how could it fail to be related to his good and bad deeds? We know of no period in human history when countless people have not related events like earthquakes to sinful deeds of man. Even today, religious-minded people everywhere believe in such a relationship.[50]

Such faith was based on firm principles of morality. It was not therefore superstitious.

I beseech you not to laugh within yourself and think I want to appeal to your instinct of superstition. I don't. I am not given to making any appeal to the superstitious fears of people. I may be called superstitious, but I cannot help telling you what I feel deep down in me . . . . You are free to believe it or to reject it.[51]

But by believing it one could turn a human catastrophe into a social good. It did not matter what the correct scientific explanation was for such phenomena; by taking a firm moral attitude towards it one could strengthen one's resolution to fight all of those things which were evil in human life.

If my belief turns out to be ill-founded, it will still have done good to me and those who believe with me. For we shall have been spurred to more vigorous efforts towards self-purification, assuming, of course, that untouchability is a deadly sin.[52]

To Gandhi then truth did not lie in history, nor did science have any privileged access to it. Truth was moral: unified, unchanging and transcendental. It was not an object of rational inquiry or philosophical speculation. It could only be found in the experience of one's life, by the unflinching practice of moral living. It could never be correctly expressed within the terms of rational theoretical discourse; its only true expression was lyrical and poetic.[53] The universalist religiosity of this conception is utterly inconsistent with the dominant thematic of post-enlightenment thought.

IV

From this evidence it is tempting to characterize Gandhism as yet another example of that typical reaction of the intelligentsia in many

[50] 'Why Only Bihar?', *CW*, Vol. 57, p. 392.

[51] Speech at Reception by Merchants, Madura, 26 January 1934, *CW*, Vol. 57, p. 51.

[52] 'Superstition v. Faith', *CW*, Vol. 57, p. 165.

[53] 'Ramanama to me is all-sufficing . . . . In the spiritual literature of the world, the *Ramayana* of Tulsidas takes a foremost place. It has charms that I miss in the *Mahabharata* and even in Valmiki's *Ramayana*.' *CW*, Vol. 58, p. 291. Also, 'Power of "Ramanama" ', *CW*, Vol. 27, pp. 107–12.

parts of the world to the social and moral depredations of advancing capitalism: romanticism. For instance Gandhi's descriptions of the ideal moral order and the standpoint of his moral critique of civil society suggest strong similarities with that aspect of Russian *narodnichestvo* which Lenin called 'economic romanticism'.[54] In Gandhi too there seems to be the vision of a utopia—'a backward-looking petty-bourgeois utopia'—and an idealization of pre-capitalist economic and social relations. One could of course concede to Gandhi, as indeed Lenin did to the Populists, that despite the backwardness of his solution to the fundamental problems of a society in the throes of capitalist penetration, he nevertheless took 'a big step forward' by posing, comprehensively and in all its economic, political and moral aspects, the democratic demand of the small producers, chiefly the peasants. But in the *theoretical* sense Gandhian ideology would still be 'reactionary', since, as Lenin pointed out in the case of the Russian Populists, not only is there simply a romantic longing for a return to an idealized medieval world of security and contentment, there is also 'the attempt to measure the new society with the old patriarchal yardstick, the desire to find a model in the old order and traditions, which are totally unsuited to the changed economic institutions.'[55] In spite of conceding the 'democratic points' in Gandhi's thought therefore the Leninist would have to pronounce that it is based on a false, indeed reactionary theory of the world-historical process, or else that it refuses to acknowledge a theory of history at all. In either case it would be a variant of romanticism.

This characterization gains further weight when one considers the sources of literary influence, explicitly acknowledged by Gandhi himself, which went into the formation of his ideas on state and society. There was for instance Edward Carpenter's *Civilization: Its Cause and Cure* which greatly influenced Gandhi's ideas on the corrupting effects of science, especially modern medicine. On the social consequences of the processes of industrial production, perhaps the greatest influence was John Ruskin's *Unto This Last*, that intensely moralistic critique of 'the modern *soi-disant* science of political

---

[54] Thanks to the historical researches of Boris Pavlovich Koz'min and Andrzej Walicki, our present understanding of the complexities of Russian Populism has made us aware of many of the polemical excesses of Bolshevik criticism of the Narodniks. But this has sharpened, rather than obscured, the central theoretical opposition between Leninism and Populism.

[55] V. I. Lenin, *A Characterization of Economic Romanticism*, in *Collected Works*, Vol. 2 (Moscow, 1957), pp. 129–265, esp. p. 241.

economy'. On the fundamentally repressive nature of the powers of
the state and on the moral duty of peaceful resistance, a strong
formative influence came from the political works of Tolstoy. It is
true of course that Gandhi was highly eclectic in his borrowings, a
task made easier in his case by the fact that he was unhampered by the
formal theoretical requirements of scientific disciplines and philosophical schools. But there is little doubt that he was inherently
sympathetic to many of the strands of argument put forward by
nineteenth-century European romantics and critics of rationlism and
industrial progress.

A detailed examination of this question of influences would take us
a long way from the central argument of this paper. But the point
about Gandhi's selectiveness in picking ideas from his favourite
authors can be illustrated a little more in order to lead on to my next
proposition that the fundamental core of the Gandhian ideology does
not lie in a romantic problematic. For instance Gandhi liked Edward
Carpenter's argument about how the limitless increase of man's
powers of production brought on by the advent of modern science
and technology draws him away '(1) from Nature, (2) from his true
Self, (3) from his Fellows,' and how it works 'in every way to
disintegrate and corrupt man—literally to corrupt—to *break up* the
unity of his nature.'[56] But Carpenter's critique of modern-day civilization was also based on a somewhat idiosyncratic reading of the
anthropological theories in Lewis Morgan's *Ancient Society* and
Frederick Engel's *The Origin of the Family, Private Property and the
State*. This in fact was the main theoretical foundation on which
Carpenter built his argument about how civilization, by transforming
the nature of 'property', destroys man's unity with nature. Yet
Carpenter's theoretical efforts do not seem to have made any
impression on his more illustrious reader.

So also with Ruskin. Gandhi accepted Ruskin's criticism of that
'political economy founded on self-interest' which had made
'mammon service' the new religion of society. He particularly liked
the idea that although there had to be different professions, such as
those of the soldier, the physician, the pastor, the lawyer or the
merchant, their incomes must only be a payment to them from
society, a means of their livelihood and 'not the objects of their life'.
He approved of Ruskin's suggestion that 'that country is richest

[56] Edward Carpenter, *Civilization: Its Cause and Cure and Other Essays* (1889;
reprinted London, 1921), pp. 46–9.

which nourishes the greatest number of noble and happy human beings; that man is richest who, having perfected the functions of his own life to the utmost, has also the widest helpful influence, both personal, and by means of his possessions, over the lives of others.'[57] But Ruskin was also a historicist, influenced in important ways by German idealism and particularly by Hegel. Despite the contra- dictoriness which he shared with all the other critics of industrial civilization in Victorian England, Ruskin was in the fundamental elements of his thought a 'modernist'. Collingwood points out for instance that 'he cared intensely for science and progress, for political reform, for the advancement of knowledge and for new movements in art and letters.'[58] His critique of political economy was meant to show the painful contradictions between the dictates of a supposedly rational science and those of altruistic morality, and to suggest that there was something fundamentally wrong with that 'so-called science'. It was never meant to be a call for the abandonment of Reason. He was aware of the limits of the intellect but never supposed 'that "conscience" or "faith" may guide us where "intellect" breaks down.'[59]

All of these concerns were quite far removed from Gandhi's theoretical world. The critique of civil society which appears on the pages of *Hind Swaraj* does not emerge out of a consideration of the historical contradictions of civil society *as perceived from within it*. Quite unlike any of the European romantics Gandhi is not torn between the conflicting demands of Reason and Morality, Progress and Happiness, Historical Necessity and Human Will. His idealization of a peaceful, non-competitive, just and happy Indian society of the past could not have been 'a romantic longing for the lost harmony of the archaic world', because unlike romanticism Gandhi's problem is not conceived at all within the thematic bounds of post-enlightenment thought. He was not for instance seriously troubled by the problems of reconciling individuality with universalism, of being oneself and at the same time feeling at one with the infinite variety of the world. Nor was his solution one in which the individual, without merging into the world, would want to embrace the rich diversity of the world in himself. Indeed these were concerns which affected many Indian 'modernists' of Gandhi's time, perhaps the most illustrious of these being Rabindranath Tagore. Gandhi shared neither the spiritual

[57] John Ruskin, *Unto This Last* (1862; reprinted London, 1931), p. 83.
[58] R. G. Collingwood, *Ruskin's Philosophy* (1922; reprinted Chichester, 1971), p. 20.
[59] Ibid., p. 28.

anguish nor indeed the aestheticism of these literary romantics of his time. Instead his moral beliefs never seemed to lose that almost obdurate certitude which men like Tagore, or even Jawaharlal Nehru, found so exasperating.

The critique of civil society which forms such a central element of Gandhi's moral and political thinking is one which arises from an epistemic standpoint situated *outside* the thematic of post-enlightenment thought. As such it is a standpoint which could have been adopted by any member of the traditional intelligentsia in India, sharing the modes and categories of thought of a large pre-capitalist agrarian society and reacting to the *alien* economic, political and cultural institutions imposed on it by colonial rule. But if this is all there was to Gandhism it could hardly have acquired the tremendous power that it undoubtedly did in the history of nationalism in India and in the formation of the contemporary Indian state. It would be a gross error to regard Gandhi as merely another 'peasant intellectual'. Despite the inherently 'peasant-communal' character of its critique of civil society, the correct framework for understanding the Gandhian ideology as a whole is still that of the historical development of élite-nationalist thought in India. For Gandhism, like Russian Populism, was not a direct expression of peasant ideology. It was an ideology conceived as an intervention in the élite-nationalist discourse of the time and was formed and shaped by the experiences of a specifically national movement. It is only by looking at it in that historical context that it becomes possible to understand the unique achievement of Gandhism: its ability to open up the possibility for achieving perhaps the most important historical task for a successful national revolution in a country like India, namely the political appropriation of the subaltern classes by a bourgeoisie aspiring for hegemony in the new nation-state. In the Indian case the largest popular element of the nation was the peasantry. And it was the Gandhian ideology which opened up the historical possibility for its appropriation into the evolving political structures of the Indian state.

In its critique of civil society Gandhism adopted a standpoint that lay entirely outside the thematic of post-enlightenment thought, and hence of nationalist thought as well. In its formulation of the problem of town-country economic exchanges, of the cultural domination of the new urban educated classes, and above all of the legitimacy of resistance to an oppressive state apparatus, it was able to encapsulate perfectly the specific political demands as well as the modalities of thought of a peasant-communal consciousness. If one wishes to pursue the point about European influences on the formation of Gandhi's thought, it is in fact Tolstoy who emerges as the most interesting comparison. For unlike the Russian Populists, and particularly unlike N. K. Mikhaĭlovskiĭ against whom Lenin directed one of his first major polemical attacks,[60] Tolstoy was a consistent anarchist in his critique of the bourgeois political order, and this from a standpoint which, as Andrzej Walicki has pointed out, was 'genuinely archaic': unlike any of the Populists, Tolstoy was 'apparently more easily able to identify himself with the world outlook of the primitive, patriarchal villagers.'[61] Tolstoy like Gandhi believed that 'the cause of the miserable position of the workers' was not something specific to capitalism. 'The cause must lie in that which drives them from the villages.'[62] He too argued against the determinism inherent in the assumptions of economic science which was 'so sure that all the peasants have inevitably to become factory operatives in towns' that it continually affirmed 'that all the country people not only are not injured by the transition from the country to the town, but themselves desire it, and strive towards it.'[63] Even more significant was Tolstoy's characterization of the entire edifice of the state as the institutionalized expression of morally unjustifiable violence. His answer to state oppression was complete and implacable resistance. One must not, he said, 'neither willingly, nor under compulsion, take any part in Governmental activity . . . nor, in fact, hold any office connected with violence,' nor should one 'voluntarily pay taxes to Governments' or 'appeal to Governmental violence for the protection of his possessions . . .'.[64] This thoroughgoing anarchism in Tolstoy was not accompanied by any specific political programme. There was simply a belief that the exemplary action of a few individuals, resisting the state by the strength of their conscience, would sway the people towards a massive movement against the institutions of violence.

[60] V. I. Lenin, *What the 'Friends of the People' Are and How They Fight the Social-Democrats* in *Collected Works*, Vol. 1, pp. 129–332.

[61] Andrzej Walicki, *The Controversy over Capitalism: Studies in the Social Philosophy of the Russian Populists* (Oxford, 1969), p. 66. Also, Walicki, *The Slavophile Controversy: History of a Conservative Utopia in Nineteenth Century Russian Thought*, tr. Hilda Andrews-Rusiecka (Oxford, 1975), p. 280.

[62] Leo Tolstoy, *The Slavery of Our Times*, tr. Aylmer Maude (1900; reprinted London, 1972), p. 18.   [63] Ibid., p. 21.

[64] Ibid., p. 57.

Men who accept a new truth when it has reached a certain degree of dissemination always do so suddenly and in a mass . . . . The same is true of the bulk of humanity which suddenly, not one by one but always in a mass, passes from one arrangement of life to another under the influence of a new public opinion . . . . And therefore the transformation of human life . . . will not come about solely by all men consciously and separately assimilating a certain Christian conception of life, but will come when a Christian public opinion so definite and comprehensible as to reach everybody has arisen and subdued that whole inert mass which is not able to attain the truth by its own intuition and is therefore always swayed by public opinion.[65]

In one aspect of his thought Gandhi shared the same standpoint. But his thought ranged far beyond this specific *ideological* aspect. And it is here that the comparison with Tolstoy breaks down: because Gandhism also concerned itself with the practical organizational questions of a political *movement*. And this was a national political movement, required to operate within the institutional processes set up and directed by a colonial state. In its latter aspect therefore Gandhism had perforce to reckon with the practical realities of a bourgeois legal and political structure as indeed of the organizational issues affecting a bourgeois political movement. It was the unique achievement of Gandhian thought to have attempted to reconcile these contradictory aspects which were at one and the same time its integral parts: a nationalism which stood upon a critique of the very idea of civil society, a movement supported by the bourgeoisie which rejected the idea of progress, the ideology of a political organization fighting for the creation of a modern national state which accepted at the same time the ideal of an 'enlightened anarchy'. Clearly there are many ambiguities in Gandhism. And a proper understanding of its history must go into a detailed examination of how these ambiguities created the possibility for those two great movements that form part of the story of the formation of the new Indian state: on the one hand the transformation, in its own distinctive way in each region and among each strata, of the demands of the people into 'the message of the Mahatma',[66] and on the other the appropriation of this movement into the structural forms of a bourgeois organizational, and later constitutional, order. But that is

---

[65] Leo Tolstoy, 'The Kingdom of God is Within You' in *The Kingdom of God and Other Essays*, tr. Aylmer Maude (1893; reprinted London, 1936), pp. 301–2.

[66] For a remarkable study of this process, see Shahid Amin, 'Gandhi as Mahatma' in this volume.

the task of modern Indian historiography. For the present we can only indicate the elements in Gandhian thought which made possible the coexistence of these contradictory aspects within a single ideological unity. Here we must turn to the celebrated concepts of *ahiṃsā* and *satyāgraha* and their epistemic basis in a conception that can only be described, fully in accordance with Gandhian terminology, as 'experimental'.

V

'Truth', wrote Gandhi to Mirabehn in 1933, 'is what everyone for the moment feels it to be.'[67] It was a decidedly personal quest. But it did not for that reason imply a moral anarchy. A few days before in another letter he had explained to her:

> We know the fundamental truth we want to reach, we know also the way. The details we do not know, we shall never know them all, because we are but very humble instruments among millions of such, moving consciously or unconsciously towards the divine event. We shall reach the Absolute Truth, if we will faithfully and steadfastly work out the relative truth as each one of us knows it.[68]

More publicly, in the Introduction to the *Autobiography* in 1925, Gandhi had written:

> . . . for me, truth is the sovereign principle, which includes numerous other principles. This truth is not only truthfulness in word, but truthfulness in thought also, and not only the relative truth of our conception, but the Absolute Truth, the Eternal Principle, that is God. There are innumerable definitions of God, . . . But I worship God as Truth only. I have not yet found Him, but I am seeking after Him . . . . But as long as I have not realized this Absolute Truth, so long must I hold by the relative truth as I have conceived it. That relative truth must, meanwhile, be my beacon, my shield and buckler.[69]

There did exist an Absolute Truth, absolute and transcendental. To discover it was the purpose of our lives. But one could only proceed to find it in the experience of living, through an unswerving moral and truthful practice. At every stage one had to be firmly committed to the truth as one knew it. At the same time one had to be prepared to learn from experience, to put one's belief to the test, to accept the consequences and revise those beliefs if they were found wanting.

---

[67] Letter to Mirabehn, 20 April 1933, *CW*, Vol. 54, p. 456.
[68] Letter to Mirabehn, 11 April 1933, *CW*, Vol. 54, p. 372.
[69] *An Autobiography* in *CW*, Vol. 39, p. 4.

Only then would one have for one's moral practice an epistemic foundation that was both certain and flexible, determinate and yet adaptable, categorical as well as experiential.

So much has now been written about Gandhi's 'truths'—the Absolute Truth which must be sought for and the various relative truths of our conception—that it is difficult to talk about the subject without referring to various current interpretations of those concepts. But once again this will take us away from the central line of my argument. I must therefore accept the risk of inviting charges of distortion and oversimplification, and without explaining its relation to the vast body of Gandhian literature, simply proceed to state my own understanding of the conception of 'truth' in the overall structure and effectivity of the Gandhian ideology.

In *Hind Swaraj* the critique of modern civilization and the plea for a return to the simple self-sufficiency of 'traditional' village life were based on the idea that it was the very changelessness of Indian civilization, its timeless ahistoricity, which was proof of its truth. India was resistant to change because it was not necessary for it to change: its civilization had found the true principles of social organization.

> It is a charge against India that her people are so uncivilized, ignorant and stolid, that it is not possible to induce them to adopt any changes. It is a charge really against our merit. What we have tested and found true on the anvil of experience, we dare not change.[70]

All that was necessary now was to find a way of protecting that social organization from the destructive consequences of colonial rule and of eliminating the poverty that had been brought upon the people. The answer was a rejection of the entire institutional edifice of civil society, uncompromising resistance to its economic, cultural and political structures. There was no specific conception yet of a political process of struggle, of its organizational procedures, norms of practice, strategic and tactical principles. As Gandhi explained later in the *Autobiography*, 'In [*Hind Swaraj*] I took it as understood that anything that helped India to get rid of the grinding poverty of her masses would in the same process also establish swaraj.'[71] It was only in the context of the evolution of the political movement that the Gandhian ideology became something more than a utopian doctrine. It acquired a theory of the political process within which the movement

[70] *Hind Swaraj*, CW, Vol. 10, p. 36.
[71] *Autobiography*, CW, Vol. 39, p. 389.

was to function; it developed its own organizational principles of political practice. In course of the full working out of Gandhian thought, the sheer tactical malleability of the 'experimental' conception of truth became the principal means by which all the seemingly irreconcilable parts of that ideology were put together.

Consider satyāgraha, that celebrated Gandhian form of mass political action. In 1917 Gandhi explained that satyāgraha was not mere passive resistance. It meant 'intense activity'—political activity—by large masses of people. It was a legitimate, moral and truthful form of political action by the people against the injustices of the state, an active mass resistance to unjust rule. It was not aimed at the destruction of the state nor was it as yet conceived as part of a political process intended to replace the functionaries of the state.

> We can . . . free ourselves of the unjust rule of the Government by defying the unjust rule and accepting the punishments that go with it. We do not bear malice towards the Government. When we set its fears at rest, when we do not desire to make armed assaults on the administrators, nor to unseat them from power, but only to get rid of their injustice, they will at once be subdued to our will.[72]

Satyāgraha at this stage was intended to articulate only a negative consciousness. It is therefore easy to recognize why it could express so effectively the characteristic modes of peasant-communal resistance to oppressive state authority.[73] It was true of course that peasant resistance to injustice was not always restricted to non-violent forms: there was much historical evidence to this effect. But at this stage Gandhi was quite dismissive of these objections.

> It is said that it is a very difficult, if not an altogether impossible, task to educate ignorant peasants in satyagraha and that it is full of perils, for it is a very arduous business to transform unlettered ignorant people from one condition into another. Both the arguments are just silly. The people of India are perfectly fit to receive the training of satyagraha. India has knowledge of dharma, and where there is knowledge of dharma, satyagraha is a very simple matter . . . . Some have a fear that once people get involved in satyagraha, they may at a later stage take arms. This fear is illusory. From the path of satyagraha, a transition to the path of *a-satyagraha* is impossible. It is possible of course that some people who believe in armed activity may mislead the satyagrahis by infiltrating into their ranks and later making them take to arms. This is possible in all enterprises. But as

[72] 'Satyagraha—Not Passive Resistance', *CW*, Vol. 13, p. 523.
[73] For an explanation of the concept of negative consciousness, see Ranajit Guha, *Elementary Aspects of Peasant Insurgency in Colonial India* (New Delhi, 1983), Ch. 2.

compared to other activities, it is less likely to happen in satyagraha, for their motives soon get exposed and when the people are not ready to take up arms, it becomes almost impossible to lead them on to that terrible path.[74]

Nor were the questions of leadership and of the relations between leaders and the masses seen as being particularly problematical in the political sense.

People in general always follow in the footsteps of the noble. There is no doubt that it is difficult to produce a satyagrahi leader. Our experience is that a satyagrahi needs many more virtues like self-control, fearlessness, etc., than are requisite for one who believes in armed action . . . . The birth of such a man can bring about the salvation of India in no time. Not only India but the whole world awaits the advent of such a man. We may in the meantime prepare the ground as much as we can through satyagraha.[75]

It was this faith in the relatively spontaneous strength of popular resistance to injustice that lay behind the call to the nation to join in the agitations in 1919 against the Rowlatt Bill. There was little concern yet about the distinction between leader and satyāgrahī or the satyāgrahī and the masses, or about the precise degree of maturity before the masses could be asked to join a satyāgraha, or about the organizational and normative safeguards against the inherent unpredictability of a negative consciousness playing itself out in the political battleground. In March 1919 Gandhi was still able to say to the people:

. . . whether you are satyagrahis or not, so long as you disapprove of the Rowlatt legislation, all can join and I hope that there will be such a response throughout the length and breadth of India as would convince the Government that we are alive to what is going on in our midst.[76]

All this of course changed after the experience of the Rowlatt satyāgraha: 'a rapier run through my body could hardly have pained me more.'[77] He had made a massive error of judgment and there was he admitted some truth in the charge that he had ignored a few obvious lessons of political history.

I think that I at least should have foreseen some of the consequences, specially in view of the gravest warnings that were given to me by friends whose advice I have always sought and valued. But I confess that I am

[74] 'Satyagraha—Not Passive Resistance', *CW*, Vol. 13, p. 524.

[75] Ibid., pp. 524–5.

[76] Speech on Satyagraha Movement, Trichinopoly, 25 March 1919, *CW*, Vol. 15, p. 155.

[77] Speech at Mass Meeting, Ahmedabad, 14 April 1919, *CW*, Vol. 15, p. 221.

dense. I am not joking. So many friends have told me that I am incapable of profiting by other people's experiences and that in every case I want to go through the fire myself and learn only after bitter experience. There is exaggeration in this charge, but there is also a substance of truth in it. This denseness in me is at once a weakness and a strength. I could not have remained a satyagrahi had I not cultivated the quality of stubborn resistance and such resistance can only come from experience and not from inference.[78]

But the experience of his first political agitation on a national scale brought in Gandhi a 'new realization'. He now became aware of the fundamental incompatibility of political action informed solely by a negative consciousness with the procedural norms of a bourgeois legal order. The ethics of resistance, if it was to be relevant to a bourgeois political movement, would have to be reconciled with a theory of political obedience. 'Unfortunately', he said,

popular imagination has pictured satyagraha as purely and simply civil disobedience, if not in some cases even criminal disobedience . . . . As satyagraha is being brought into play on a large scale on the political field for the first time, it is in an experimental stage. I am therefore ever making new discoveries. And my error in trying to let civil disobedience take the people by storm appears to me to be Himalayan because of the discovery I have made, namely, that he only is able and attains the right to offer civil disobedience who has known how to offer voluntary and deliberate obedience to the laws of the State in which he is living.[79]

And from this fundamental discovery flowed a new organizational principle. As he later explained in the *Autobiography*:

. . . I wondered how I could have failed to perceive what was so obvious. I realized that before a people could be fit for offering civil disobedience, they should thoroughly understand its deeper implications. That being so, before restarting civil disobedience on a mass scale, it would be necessary to create a band of well-tried, pure-hearted volunteers who thoroughly understood the strict conditions of satyagraha.[80]

Thus was born the political concept of the satyāgrahī as leader. In the course of his evidence before the Hunter Committee appointed to inquire into the Rowlatt Bill agitations Gandhi was asked about his conception of the relation between leaders and followers.

C. H. Setalvad: I take it that your scheme, as you conceive it, involves the determination of what is the right path and the true path by people who are capable of high intellectual and moral equipment and a large

78 Letter to Swami Shraddhanand, 17 April 1919, *CW*, Vol. 15, pp. 238–9.
79 'The Duty of Satyagrahis', *CW*, Vol. 15, p. 436.
80 *Autobiography*, *CW*, Vol. 39, p. 374.

number of other people following them without themselves being able to arrive at similar conclusions by reason of their lower moral and intellectual equipment?

Gandhi: I cannot subscribe to that, because I have not said that. I do not say that they are not to exercise their judgment, but I simply say that, in order that they may exercise their judgment, the same mental and moral equipment is not necessary.

C. H. Setalvad: Because they are to accept the judgment of people who are capable of exercising better judgment and equipped with better moral and intellectual standard?

Gandhi: Naturally, but I think that is in human nature, but I exact nothing more than I would exact from an ordinary human being.[81]

While mass resistance to unjust laws was the final and only certain guarantee against state oppression, the people would have to depend on their leaders for guidance.

Jagat Narayan: My point is, having regard to the circumstances, a sort of sanctity attaches to the laws or the Government of the time being?

Gandhi: Not in my estimation . . . .

Jagat Narayan: That is not the best check on the masses?

Gandhi: Not a blind adherence to laws, no check whatsoever. It is because either they blindly adhere or they blindly commit violence. Either event is undesirable.

Jagat Narayan: So long as every individual is not fit to judge for himself, he would have to follow somebody?

Gandhi: Certainly, he would have to follow somebody. The masses will have to choose their leaders most decidedly.[82]

The point was further clarified when Gandhi was asked about his understanding of the reasons why the agitations had become violent. Soon after the events in Ahmedabad Gandhi had told a mass meeting: 'It seems that the deeds I have complained of have been done in an organized manner. There seems to be a definite design about them, and I am sure that there must be some educated and clever man or men behind them . . . . You have been misled into doing these deeds by such people.'[83] Elaborating on what he meant by 'organized manner', Gandhi said to the Hunter Committee:

In my opinion, the thing was organized, but there it stands. There was no question whether it was a deep-laid conspiracy through the length and breadth of India or a deep-rooted organization of which this was a part. The organization was hastily constructed; the organization was not in the

81 Evidence before the Disorders Inquiry Committee, *CW*, Vol. 16, p. 410.
82 Ibid., Vol. 16, p. 441.
83 Speech at Mass Meeting, Ahmedabad, 14 April 1919, *CW*, Vol. 15, pp. 221–2.

sense in which we understand the word organization . . . . If I confined that word to Ahmedabad alone, to masses of absolutely unlettered men, who would be able to make no fine distinctions—then you have got the idea of what that organization is . . . . There were these poor deluded labourers whose one business was to see me released and see Anasuyabai released. That it was a wicked rumour deliberately started by somebody I have not the slightest doubt. As soon as these things happened the people thought there should be something behind it. Then there were the half-educated raw youths. This is the work of these, I am grieved to have to say. These youths possessed themselves with false ideas gathered from shows, such as the cinematograph shows that they have seen, gathered from silly novels and from the political literature of Europe . . . . it was an organization of this character.[84]

The direct physical form in which the masses appeared in the political arena was always that of a mob. It had no mind of its own.[85] Its behaviour was determined entirely by the way it was led: '. . . nothing is so easy as to train mobs, for the simple reason that they have no mind, no premeditation. They act in a frenzy. They repent quickly.'[86] For this reason they were as susceptible to manipulation by mischief-makers as they were open to enlightened leadership. In order therefore to undertake mass political action it was necessary first of all to create a selfless, dedicated and enlightened group of political workers who would lead the masses and protect them from being misguided.

Before we can make real headway, we must train these masses of men who have a heart of gold, who feel for the country, who want to be taught and led. But a few intelligent, sincere, local workers are needed, and the whole nation can be organized to act intelligently, and democracy can be evolved out of mobocracy.[87]

This was the problematic which lay at the heart of what soon evolved into the other celebrated concept in the Gandhian ideology—the concept of ahiṃsā. In its application to politics, ahiṃsā

[84] Evidence, *CW*, Vol. 16, pp. 391–2.

[85] Alexander Herzen, often regarded as one of the progenitors of Russian Populism, wrote about the crowd: 'I looked with horror mixed with disgust at the continually moving, swarming crowd, foreseeing how it would rob me of half of my seat at the theatre and in the diligence, how it would dash like a wild beast into the railway carriages, how it would heat and pervade the air.' Quoted in Walicki, *The Controversy over Capitalism*, p. 11. Horror and disgust were the feelings which overwhelmed Gandhi too when he first encountered the Indian masses in a third-class railway carriage. See *Autobiography*, *CW*, Vol. 39, p. 305.

[86] 'Democracy v. Mobocracy', *CW*, Vol. 18, p. 242.

[87] 'Some Illustrations', *CW*, Vol. 18, p. 275.

too was about 'intense political activity' by large masses of people. But it was not so much about resistance as about the modalities of resistance, about organizational principles, rules of conduct, strategies and tactics. Ahiṃsā was the necessary complement to the concept of satyāgraha which both limited and, at the same time, made it something more than 'purely and simply civil disobedience'. Ahiṃsā was the rule for concretizing the 'truth' of satyāgraha. 'Truth is a positive value, while non-violence is a negative value. Truth affirms. Non-violence forbids something which is real enough.'[88] Ahiṃsā, indeed, was the concept—both ethical and epistemological because it was defined within a moral and epistemic practice that was wholly 'experimental'—which supplied Gandhism with a theory of politics, enabling it to become the ideology of a national political movement. It was the organizing principle for a 'science' of politics—a science wholly different from all current conceptions of politics which had only succeeded in producing the 'sciences of violence', but a science nevertheless—the 'science of non-violence', the 'science of love'. It was the moral framework for solving every practical problem of the organized political movement.

The 'science of non-violence' consequently dealt with questions such as the requirements for being a political satyāgrahī, his rules of conduct, his relations with the political leadership as well as with the masses, questions about the structure of decision-making, lines of command, political strategies and tactics, and about the practical issues of breaking as well as obeying the laws of the state. It was as much a 'science' of political struggle, indeed as much a military science as the 'sciences of violence', only it was superior because it was a science not of arms but of the moral force of the soul. At this level in fact it was not a utopian conception at all. There was no assumption, for instance, of collective consensus in the making of decisions, for that would be wishing away the existence of a practical political problem. Decisions were to be taken by 'a few true satyagrahis'. This would provide a far more economic and efficient method of political action than that proposed by the 'sciences of violence': '. . . we would require a smaller army of satyagrahis than that of soldiers trained in modern warfare, and the cost will be insignificant compared to the fabulous sums devoted by nations to armaments.'[89]

---

[88] 'Meaning of the "Gita" ', *CW*, Vol. 28, p. 317.
[89] 'What Are Basic Assumptions?', *CW*, Vol. 67, p. 436. It is quite remarkable how frequently Gandhi uses the military metaphor when talking about the 'science of non-violence'.

Second the practice of this 'experimental science' of mass political action was not conditional upon the masses themselves understanding all its principles or their full implications.

> A soldier of an army does not know the whole of the military science; so also does a satyagrahi not know the whole science of satyagraha. It is enough if he trusts his commander and honestly follows his instructions and is ready to suffer unto death without bearing malice against the so-called enemy . . . . [The satyagrahis] must render heart discipline to their commander. There should be no mental reservation.[90]

Third the political employment of ahiṃsā did not depend upon everyone accepting it as a creed. It was possible for it to be regarded as a valid political theory even without its religious core. This in fact was the only way it could become a general guide for solving the practical problems of an organized political movement.

> Ahimsa with me is a creed, the breath of life. But it is never as a creed that I placed it before India or, for that matter, before anyone except in casual or informal talks. I placed it before the Congress as a political weapon, to be employed for the solution of practical problems.[91]

And thus we come to an explicit recognition, within the overall unity of the Gandhian ideology as it took shape in the course of the evolution of the national movement, of a disjuncture between morality and politics, between private conscience and public responsibility, indeed between Noble Folly and *Realpolitik*. It was a disjuncture which the 'experimental' conception of ahiṃsā was meant to bridge. And yet it was a disjuncture the steadfast denial of whose very existence had been the foundation of the original conception of *Hind Swaraj*. Now however we see the spinning wheel, for instance, coming to acquire a dual significance, located on entirely different planes, and it is no longer considered politically necessary for the personal religion to be identified with a political programme.

> I have never tried to make anyone regard the spinning-wheel as his *kamadhenu* or universal provider; . . . When in 1908, . . . I declared my faith in the spinning-wheel in the pages of the *Hind Swaraj*, I stood absolutely alone . . . . I do regard the spinning-wheel as a gateway to *my* spiritual salvation, but I recommend it to others only as a powerful weapon for the attainment of swaraj and the amelioration of the economic condition of the country.[92]

[90] Ibid., pp. 436–7.
[91] Speech at A.I.C.C. Meeting, Wardha, 15 January 1942, *CW*, Vol. 75, p. 220.
[92] 'Cobwebs of Ignorance', *CW*, Vol. 30, pp. 450–1.

In 1930, on the eve of the Dandi March, we find Gandhi telling his colleagues that he did not know what form of democracy India should have. He was not particularly interested in the question: 'the method alone interests me, and by method I mean the agency through which the wishes of the people are reached. There are only two methods; one is that of fraud and force; the other is that of non-violence and truth.'[93] It did not matter even if the goal was beyond reach. The first responsibility of the political leader was to strictly adhere to his principles of morality.

> What I want to impress on everyone is that I do not want India to reach her goal through questionable means. Whether that is possible or not is another question. It is sufficient for my present purpose if the person who thinks out the plan and leads the people is absolutely above board and has non-violence and truth in him.[94]

And once there is a recognition of the disjuncture, the failure of politics to reach utopia could be attributed to the loftiness of the ideal, noble, truthful but inherently unreachable, or else equally credibly to the imperfections of the human agency. The vision of a non-violent India could be 'a mere day-dream, a childish folly'.[95] Or else one could argue with equal validity that the problem lay not with the ideal but with one's own deficiencies.

> I do not think it is right to say that the principles propounded in *Hind Swaraj* are not workable just because I cannot practise them perfectly .... not only do I refuse to excuse myself, but positively confess my shortcoming.[96]

The result of course was that under the moral umbrella of the quest for utopia the experimental conception of politics could accommodate a potentially limitless range of imperfections, adjustments, compromises and failures. For the authority of the political leader derived not from the inherent reasonableness of his programme or the feasibility of his project, not even from the accordance of that programme or project with a collective perception of common interests or goals. It derived entirely from a moral claim—of personal courage and sacrifice and a patent adherence to truth. So much so that the supreme test of political leadership was death itself. That was the final proof of the leader's claim to the allegiance of his people. At Anand, in the middle of the Dandi March, Gandhi said—

[93] 'Answers to Questions', *CW*, Vol. 43, p. 41.   [94] Ibid.
[95] 'A Complex Problem', *CW*, Vol. 40, p. 364.
[96] Letter to Labhshankar Mehta, 14 April 1926, *CW*, Vol. 30, p. 283.

This band of satyagrahis which has set out is not staging a play; its effect will not be merely temporary; even through death, it will prove true to its pledge—if death becomes necessary . . . . Nothing will be better than if this band of satyagrahis perishes. If the satyagrahis meet with death, it will put a seal upon their claim.[97]

And when Jairamdas Doulatram was injured in a police firing in Karachi during the Civil Disobedience movement, Gandhi sent a telegram to the Congress office saying:

CONSIDER JAIRAMDAS MOST FORTUNATE. BULLET WOUND THIGH BETTER THAN PRISON. WOUND HEART BETTER STILL. BAPU.[98]

Gandhism finally reconciled the contradictions between the utopian and the practical aspects of its political ideology by surrendering to the absolute truthfulness and supreme self-sacrifice of the satyāgrahī. It had gained its strength from an intensely powerful moral critique of the existing state of politics. In the end it saved its Truth by escaping from politics.

VI

And yet as Gandhi himself put it, 'politics encircle us today like the coil of a snake.'[99] The historical impact of the Gandhian ideology on the evolution of Indian politics was of monumental significance.

The 'science of non-violence' was the form in which Gandhism addressed itself to the problematic of nationalism. That was the 'science' which was to provide answers to the problems of national politics, of concretizing the nation as an active historical subject rejecting the domination of a foreign power, of devising its political organization and the strategic and tactical principles of its struggle. In its specific historical effectivity, Gandhism provided for the first time in Indian politics an ideological basis for including the whole people within the political nation. In order to do this it quite consciously sought to bridge even the most sanctified cultural barriers that divided the people in an immensely complex agrarian society. Thus it was not simply a matter of bringing the peasantry into the national movement, but of consciously seeking the ideological means for bringing it in as a whole. This for instance is how one can read the strenuous efforts by Gandhi to obliterate the 'sin' of the existing *jāti* divisions in Indian

---

[97] Speech at Anand, 17 March 1930, *CW*, Vol. 43, p. 93.
[98] Telegram to N. R. Malkani, 18 April 1930, *CW*, Vol. 43, p. 282.
[99] 'Neither a Saint nor a Politician', *CW*, Vol. 17, p. 406.

society, and the 'deadly sin' of untouchability in particular, and to replace it by an idealized scheme based on the varṇa classification. 'Do you not think', Gandhi was asked, 'that the improvement of the condition of starving peasants is more important than the service of Harijans? Will you not therefore form peasant organizations which will naturally include Harijans in so far as their economic condition is concerned?' 'Unfortunately', Gandhi replied,

> the betterment of the economic condition of peasants will not necessarily include the betterment of that of the Harijans. The peasant who is not a Harijan can rise as high as he likes and opportunity permits him, but not so the poor suppressed Harijan. The latter cannot own and use land as freely as the *savarna* peasant . . . therefore, a special organization for the service of Harijans is a peremptory want in order to deal with the special and peculiar disabilities of Harijans. Substantial improvement of these, the lowest strata of society, must include the whole of society.[100]

Whether this idiom of solidarity necessarily referred to a cultural code that could be shown to be 'essentially Hindu', and whether that in turn alienated rather than united those sections of the people who were not 'Hindu', are of course important questions, but not strictly relevant in establishing the ideological intent behind Gandhi's efforts.

Thus while the search was for an ideological means to unite the whole people, there was also a determinate political structure and process, specific and historically given, within which the task had to be accomplished. And here it was the 'experimental' conception of truth, combining the absolute moral legitimacy of satyāgraha with the tactical considerations of ahiṃsā which made the Gandhian ideology into a powerful instrument in the historical task of constructing the new Indian state.

For now one could talk within the overall unity of that ideology of the constructive relation of the national movement to the evolving institutional structure of state power. Gandhi could say on the one hand, 'I shall retain my disbelief in legislatures as an instrument for obtaining *swaraj* in terms of masses', and in the same breath go on to argue

> But I see that I have failed to wean some of the Congressmen from their faith in council-entry. The question therefore is whether they should or should not enforce their desire to enter legislature as Congress representatives. I have no doubt that they must have the recognition they want. Not to give it will be to refuse to make use of the talents we possess.[101]

100 'Harijan v. Non-Harijan', *CW*, Vol. 58, pp. 80–1.
101 Speech at A.I.C.C. Meeting, Patna, 19 May 1934, *CW*, Vol. 58, pp. 9–10.

Indeed the truth of the moral conception of utopia was forever safe, no matter what compromises one had to make in the world of practical politics.

> The parliamentary work must be left to those who are so inclined. I hope that the majority will always remain untouched by the glamour of council work. In its own place, it will be useful. But . . . Swaraj can only come through an all-round consciousness of the masses.[102]

Similarly the acceptance of ministerial office by Congressmen in 1937, an act apparently in complete contradiction with the spirit of non-co-operation enshrined in the Congress movement in 1920, now became 'not a repudiation but a fulfilment of the original, so long as the mentality behind all of them remains the same as in 1920'.[103] And if the disharmony between the act and the mentality became much too gross, the final moral act that would save the truth of the ideal was withdrawal. When the evidence became overwhelming that Congressmen as officers of the state were not exhibiting the selflessness, ability and incorruptibility that was the justification for their being in office, Gandhi's plea to Congressmen was to make a choice:

> . . . either to apply the purge I have suggested, or, if that is not possible because of the Congress being already overmanned by those who have lost faith in its creed and its constructive programme on which depends its real strength, to secede from it for its own sake and proving his living faith in the creed and programme by practising the former and prosecuting the latter as if he had never seceded from the Congress of his ideal.[104]

Then again the ideal of property as trust was 'true in theory only'. Like all other ideals it would

> remain an unattainable ideal, so long as we are alive, but towards which we must ceaselessly strive. Those who own money now are asked to behave like trustees holding their riches on behalf of the poor. You may say that trusteeship is a legal fiction . . . Absolute trusteeship is an abstraction like Euclid's definition of a point, and is equally unattainable. But if we strive for it, we shall be able to go further in realizing a state of equality on earth than by any other method.
>
> Q. But if you say that private possession is incompatible with non-violence, why do you put up with it?
>
> A. That is a concession one has to make to those who earn money but who would not voluntarily use their earnings for the benefit of mankind.[105]

---

[102] Ibid., p. 11.
[103] 'My Meaning of Office-Acceptance', *CW*, Vol. 66, p. 104.
[104] 'Choice Before Congressmen', *CW*, Vol. 67, p. 306.
[105] Interview to Nirmal Kumar Bose, 9 November 1934, *CW*, Vol. 59, p. 318.

Sometimes the justification for this concession was crassly empirical:
'. . . I am quite clear that if a strictly honest and unchallengeable
referendum of our millions were to be taken, they would not vote for
wholesale expropriation of the propertied classes'.[106] At other times
it would seem to rest on a fairly sophisticated reading of the lessons of
political history:

> [The zamindars] must regard themselves, even as the Japanese nobles did,
> as trustees holding their wealth for the good of their wards, the ryots . . . I
> am convinced that the capitalist, if he follows the Samurai of Japan, has
> nothing really to lose and everything to gain. There is no other choice than
> between voluntary surrender on the part of the capitalist of superfluities
> and consequent acquisition of the real happiness of all on the one hand,
> and on the other the impending chaos into which, if the capitalist does not
> wake up betimes, awakened but ignorant, famishing millions will plunge
> the country and which not even the armed force that a powerful Govern-
> ment can bring into play can avert.[107]

But in considering questions of this sort, having to do with the
practical organizational issues of a bourgeois political movement,
Gandhism would inevitably slip into the familiar thematic of nationalist
thought. It would argue in terms of categories such as capitalism,
socialism, law, citizenship, private property, individual rights, and
struggle to fit its formless utopia into the conceptual grid of post-
enlightenment social-scientific thought.

> Let us not be obsessed with catchwords and seductive slogans imported
> from the West. Have we not our own distinct Eastern traditions? Are we
> not capable of finding our own solution to the question of capital and
> labour? . . . Let us study our Eastern institutions in that spirit of scientific
> inquiry and we shall evolve a truer socialism and a truer communism than
> the world has yet dreamed of. It is surely wrong to presume that Western
> socialism or communism is the last word on the question of mass poverty.[108]

> Class war is foreign to the essential genius of India which is capable of
> evolving a form of communism broad-based on the fundamental rights of
> all and equal justice to all.[109]

Sometimes in trying to defend his political strategy of nationalist
struggle Gandhi would even feel forced to resort to some of the most
naive cultural essentialisms of Orientalist thought:

[106] 'Answers to Zamindars', *CW*, Vol. 58, p. 247.
[107] 'Zamindars and Talukdars', *CW*, Vol. 42, pp. 239–40.
[108] 'Discussion with Students', *CW*, Vol. 58, p. 219.
[109] 'Answers to Zamindars', *CW*, Vol. 58, p. 248.

By her very nature, India is a lover of peace . . . On the other hand Mustafa Pasha succeeded with the sword because there is strength in every nerve of a Turk. The Turks have been fighters for centuries. The people of India have followed the path of peace for thousands of years . . . There is at the present time not a single country on the face of the earth which is weaker than India in point of physical strength. Even tiny Afghanistan can growl at her.[110]

Beginning its journey from the utopianism of *Hind Swaraj* and yet picking up on the way the ideological baggage of nationalist politics, Gandhism succeeded in opening up the historical possibility by which the largest popular element of the nation, namely the peasantry, could be appropriated within the evolving political forms of the new Indian state. While it was doubtless the close correspondence of the moral conception of Gandhi's *Rāmarājaya* with the demands and forms of political justice in the contemporary peasant-communal consciousness which was one of the ideological conditions that made it possible for those demands to be transformed into 'the message of the Mahatma', the historical consequence of the Gandhian politics of non-violence was in fact to give to this process of appropriation its moral justification and its own distinctive ideological form. While it was the Gandhian intervention in élite-nationalist politics in India which established for the first time that an authentic national movement could only be built upon the organized support of the whole of the peasantry, the working out of the politics of non-violence also made it abundantly clear that the object of the political mobilization of the peasantry was not at all what Gandhi claimed on its behalf, 'to train the masses in self-consciousness and attainment of power'. Rather the peasantry was meant to become a willing participant in a struggle wholly conceived and directed by others. Champaran, Kheda, Bardoli, Borsad—those were the model peasant movements, specific, local, conducted on issues that were well within 'their own personal and felt grievances'. This for instance was the specific ground on which Bardoli was commended as a model movement:

The people of Bardoli could not secure justice so long as they were afraid of being punished by the Government . . . They freed themselves from its fear by surrendering their hearts to their Sardar. From this we find that the people require neither physical nor intellectual strength to secure their own freedom; moral courage is all that is needed. This latter is dependent on faith. In this case, they were required to have faith in their Sardar, and such faith cannot be artificially generated. They found in the Sardar

[110] 'Divine Warning', *CW*, Vol. 22, pp. 426–7.

a worthy object of such faith and like a magnet he drew the hearts of the people to himself . . . This is not to say that the people had accepted non-violence as a principle or that they did not harbour anger even in their minds. But they understood the practical advantage of non-violence, understood their own interest, controlled their anger and, instead of retaliating in a violent manner, suffered the hardships inflicted on them.[111]

While the national organization of the dominant classes could proceed to consolidate itself within the institutional structures of the new Indian state, '*kisans* and labour' were never to be organized 'on an all-India basis'.[112]

And so we get within the ideological unity of Gandhism as a whole the conception of a national framework of politics in which the peasants are mobilized but do not participate, of a nation of which they are a part but a national state from which they are forever distanced. It still remains a principal task of modern Indian historiography to explain the specific historical process by which these political possibilities that were inherent in the Gandhian ideology became the ideological weapons in the hands of the Indian bourgeoisie in its attempt to create a viable state structure within a process of class struggle in which its dominance was constantly under challenge and its moral leadership forever fragmented.[113]

But the logic of utopia is inherently ambiguous. Thomas More has been read as the author of a text that laid the moral foundations for the political demands of a rising but still far from victorious bourgeoisie. He has also been regarded as the progenitor of utopian socialism, that inchoate articulation of the spirit of resistance of the early proletariat in Europe.[114] It is not surprising therefore that in the unresolved class struggles within the social formation of contemporary

---

[111] 'Government's Power v. People's Power', *CW*, Vol. 37, pp. 190–1.

[112] 'Constructive Programme: Its Meaning and Place', *CW*, Vol. 75, pp. 159–60.

[113] For a discussion of how the ideological unity of Gandhism was broken up once again by the rationalist analytic of a mature bourgeois ideology, and how its political consequences were appropriated within the thought of an emergent nationalist state leadership, see Chatterjee, *Nationalist Thought*, Ch. 5.

[114] Martin Fleisher, *Radical Reform and Political Persuasion in the Life and Writings of Thomas More* (Geneva, 1973); Karl Kautsky, *Thomas More and His Utopia*, tr. H. J. Stenning (London, 1979).

India, oppositional movements can still claim their moral legitimacy from the message of the Mahatma.*

* This paper was written during my year's stay in 1981–82 at St Antony's College, Oxford. I am grateful to the Nuffield Foundation, London for a travelling fellowship. I am also grateful to Shahid Amin, David Arnold, Dipesh Chakrabarty, Bernard Cohn, Ranajit Guha, David Hardiman, Gyan Pandey, Sumit Sarkar, Abhijit Sen, and my colleagues at the Centre for Studies in Social Sciences, Calcutta, for their comments on an earlier draft of this paper, and to Anthony Low and the other participants at the Subaltern Studies Conference in Canberra in November 1982.

Adivasi Assertion in South Gujarat: the Devi Movement of 1922–3

DAVID HARDIMAN

I

In early November 1922 large numbers of adivasi—or tribal—peasants began to gather together in south Gujarat to listen to the teachings of a goddess (*mata* or *devi*) known as Salahbai. The Devi, who was not generally represented by any image, was supposed to have come out of the mountains to the east and expressed her demands through spirit mediums. The adivasis of several villages met together at a central place and listened while a number of them went into a state of trance. These men would shake their heads violently and begin to utter what were believed to be the Devi's commands. The principal commands were to abstain from eating flesh or drinking liquor or toddy, to take a bath daily, to use water rather than a leaf to clean up after defecation, to keep houses clean, to release or sell goats and chickens (which were kept for eating or sacrifice), and to boycott Parsi liquor dealers and landlords. It was believed that those who failed to obey these divine orders would suffer misfortune at the very least, and perhaps even go mad or die. The meetings normally went on for several days, after which the Devi moved on to another group of villages where the process was repeated.

This wave of possession by the Devi spread rapidly. Starting in the Baroda sub-divisions of Songadh and Vyara, it had by mid-November 1922 affected the whole of the British sub-division of Valod.[1] No adivasi village in this extensive tract was left untouched. By late November it had spread to Bardoli and Mandvi talukas; by 2 December it had reached Jalalpor taluka and by 14 December Surat city and the coastal areas. In December some new commands of the Devi began to

[1] To locate these sub-divisions see the map provided with this essay.

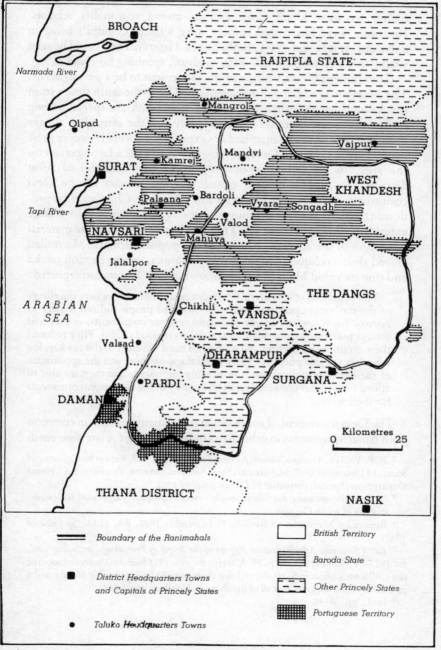

BROACH

Narmada River

RAJPIPLA STATE

Olpad

Mangrol

Vajpur

SURAT

Kamrej

Mandvi

WEST
KHANDESH

Tapi River

Palsana

Bardoli

Vyara

Songadh

NAVSARI

Valod

Mahuva

Jalalpor

ARABIAN
SEA

Chikhli

THE DANGS

VANSDA

Valsad

DHARAMPUR

PARDI

SURGANA

DAMAN

Kilometres

0   25

THANA DISTRICT

NASIK

—— Boundary of the Ranimahals

☐ British Territory

▬ Baroda State

■ District Headquarters Towns
    and Capitals of Princely States

▭ Other Princely States

● Taluka Headquarters Towns

▨ Portuguese Territory

Ranimahals of South Gujarat

be heard. Salahbai was telling the adivasis to take vows in Gandhi's name, to wear khadi cloth and to attend nationalist schools. Rumours were heard that spiders were writing Gandhi's name in cobwebs. It was said that Gandhi had fled from jail and could be seen sitting in a well side-by-side with Salahbai, spinning his *charkha*.[2]

Government officials expected the movement to be a passing affair. The Mamlatdar of Bardoli commented: 'This is the tenth time within my knowledge that such rumours to stop drink are spread among Kaliparaj.[3] Such rumours spread rapidly but the effect has always been temporary.'[4] The mamlatdar's expectations were however to be proved wrong, for the Devi movement was to have a lasting effect on the area. In his annual report for 1922–3 the Collector of Surat district, A. M. Macmillan, noted that the impact of the Devi continued—particularly in the area in which the Chodhri tribe predominated. In this area liquor and toddy drinking had to a large extent stopped, and there was a marked improvement in the material condition of the adivasis. In response to popular demand Macmillan closed thirteen liquor shops in Mandvi taluka, one in Bardoli taluka and one in Valod Mahal.[5] In the following year Macmillan reported:

> The beneficial effects in the Chowdra areas of Mandvi where the effects of the movement persisted were obvious. The people did not require to borrow from sawkars to pay their land revenue instalments, as they had always previously done whether seasons were good or bad. They reduced their ceremonial expenses and so did not need to resort to the sawkars for advances for this purpose. Their general appearance, and the appearance of their houses and villages is noticeably improved, and they are able to afford to use brass cooking vessels and to buy better clothes and ornaments for their wives.[6]

The Devi movement of south Gujarat had many features in common with tribal movements in other parts of India during the late nineteenth

[2] B. P. Vaidya, *Rentima Vahan* (Ahmedabad, 1977), p. 177. Report by Collector of Surat, 14 December 1922, Maharashtra State Archives, Bombay (hereafter BA), Home Department (Special) (hereafter H.D. (Sp.)) 637 of 1922.

[3] 'Kaliparaj'—meaning the 'black people'—was a derogatory term used to describe the adivasis of south Gujarat.

[4] Report by Mamlatdar of Bardoli, 15 November 1922, BA, H.D. (Sp.) 637 of 1922.

[5] *Land Revenue Administration Report of the Bombay Presidency, including Sind, for 1923–24* (Bombay, 1925), p. 39. A list for the year 1914 found in the record room of the Collector's office in Surat showed that there were 13 liquor shops in Mandvi and 8 in Valod, which suggests that all of the shops in Mandvi were closed.

[6] Ibid., pp. 39–40.

and early twentieth centuries. These movements have not on the whole received much attention from scholars. The chief exception to this is the Tana Bhagat movement of 1914 among the Oraons of Chhota-nagpur in Bihar, which shows many striking similarities to the Devi movement.[7] Other such movements have been reported in a summary form from tribal regions all over India. There are cases of such movements among the Bhils of east and north-east Gujarat,[8] among the Bhils of north-west Maharashtra,[9] among the Gonds of Madhya Pradesh and UP,[10] among the Oraons, Santals and Bhumij of Bihar,[11] and among the Khonds of Orissa.[12] In these areas movements with similar programmes swept through the tribal villages with surprising speed and force. They were relatively peaceful and often had a lasting effect. There were in addition many more violent movements involving adivasis, such as that of Birsa Munda,[13] which incorporated pro-grammes of social reform.

In this essay I shall discuss the Devi movement in some detail in an attempt to gain a greater understanding of such movements in general. The themes which will be taken up concern the social, economic and political background, the actual history of the movement, and the meaning and significance of the reform programme adopted by the adivasis.

II

The adivasis who form the subject of this paper lived for the most part in a region known as the Ranimahals, or forest tract, of south Gujarat. This region is demarcated on the map. The Ranimahals are relatively flat; the precipitous mountains of the Sahyadri ranges appear only on their eastern borders. In the early nineteenth century

[7] The classic study of the Tana Bhagats is by S. C. Roy, *Oraon Religion and Customs* (1928; reprinted Calcutta, 1972), pp. 246–97.

[8] Stephen Fuchs, *Rebellious Prophets* (Bombay, 1965), p. 240. T. B. Naik, *The Bhils* (Delhi, 1956), p. 324.

[9] BA, H.D. (Sp.) 982 of 1938–42.

[10] Fuchs, p. 79. L. K. Mahapatra and C. Tripathy, 'Raj Mohini Devi: A Social Reformer among Tribals of North Central India', *Vanyajati*, 4:4 (October 1956).

[11] Fuchs, pp. 57 and 68; Surajit Sinha, 'Bhumij-Kshatriya Social Movement in South Manbhum', *Bulletin of the Department of Anthropology*, 8:2 (July 1959), pp. 16–19.

[12] *Report of the Excise Committee Appointed by the Government of Bombay, 1922–23*, Vol. I (Bombay, 1924), pp. 32–3.

[13] Suresh Singh, *The Dust-Storm and the Hanging Mist: A Study of Birsa Munda and his Movement in Chhotanagpur (1874–1901)* (Calcutta, 1966).

the Ranimahals were covered largely by forest; during the course of the century the area was cleared of trees and fields were carved out. By 1920 the only extensive forests left were those in the northern and north-eastern portions. The soil of the Ranimahals was fertile and the rainfall plentiful, so that once the land was brought under the plough good harvests could be obtained from year to year from the same plot of land.

The chief tribes known as the Kaliparaj were the Chodhris, Gamits, Dhodiyas and Konkanis. There were also some smaller tribes such as the Naikas, Kotvaliyas and Kathodiyas. The parts of the Ranimahals inhabited by the four main tribes were adjacent to each other with borders overlapping to a large extent. The Chodhris were found chiefly in the talukas of Mandvi, Valod, Vyara and Mahuva. The Gamits were concentrated in Vyara and Songadh talukas and in west Khandesh. The Dhodiyas were to the south, in Mahuva, western Vansda, Chikhli, eastern Valsad, western Dharampur and Pardi. The Konkanis spread beyond the Ranimahals and into the Sahyadris, being found in Vansda, Dharampur, the Dangs, Surgana and Nasik district. The Bhils, the largest of the western Indian tribes, were not found in the Ranimahals to any large extent; their area started in Vajpur and Rajpipla state. An exception was in the Dangs where the ruling chiefs were Bhils, the mass of the peasants being Konkanis. The tribes of south Gujarat were culturally quite distinct from the Bhils; they were not a mere offshoot of this major tribe.

The adivasis of the Ranimahals were for the most part settled peasant farmers who lived in small hamlets (*faliyas*). Several faliyas normally made up one revenue village. The villages lacked any nucleus for they were without artisans and other specialist castes. In this the adivasi village provided a marked contrast to many of the so-called 'traditional' Indian villages with their hierarchies of Brahman priests, dominant castes, subordinate labouring castes, Vaniya shopkeepers, artisan castes and untouchables. In most adivasi faliyas the members were exclusively of one tribe. They either owned or rented land and they normally possessed their own agricultural implements and draught bullocks.

As an example of an adivasi village we can take Sathvav in Mandvi taluka, which was surveyed in great detail in the early 1930s by the sociologist B. H. Mehta.[14] Sathvav had at that time a population of

---

[14] B. H. Mehta, 'Social and Economic Conditions of the Chodhras, an Aboriginal Tribe of Gujarat' (M.A. thesis, University of Bombay, 1933). The landholding figures have been compiled from the appendix volume of family schedules.

588, divided into 114 families of which 106 were of the Chodhri tribe, 4 were Bhils, 2 Dhed untouchables and 2 Parsis. Mehta collected figures for the amount of land owned and/or rented by each family which enable us to compile the following table:

Land held (in acres)	Families No.	%
Nil	21	18
Under 5	21	18
5 – 10	14	12
10 – 20	34	30
20 – 30	12	11
30 – 40	5	4
40 – 50	3	3
Over 50	4	4
Total	114	100

The largest landholder was a Parsi who had 108 acres, while three Chodhris held 64, 60 and 52 acres respectively. According to Mehta at least twenty acres were required to provide an adequate livelihood for a family.[15] 88 (77 per cent) of the families were either landless or held farms below this acreage. It is likely therefore that the large majority of the adivasis of Sathvav were living in conditions of considerable poverty. We can conclude that not only were they poor, but also that by the 1930s there was a fair degree of differentiation in the villages. However the differentiation was a good deal less extreme than in the non-tribal villages of south Gujarat in which there were many bonded labourers working for high caste landowners.

Despite these inequalities there was little exploitation of one adivasi by another. The worst exploitation was carried out by high caste moneylenders and Parsi liquor dealers. The colonial bureaucracy also took its share of the fruits of the adivasi's labour, either through taxation or through forced labour and illegal levies. Policemen, revenue, excise and forest officers all took their cut. The moneylenders were mostly Vaniyas, Parsis and Brahmans. Vaniyas and Brahmans lived in the taluka headquarter towns. They lent their money either from their houses in the towns or from the weekly markets (*haats*) held at convenient centres throughout the adivasi tracts. Parsis, who

[15] Ibid., p. 470. There were no irrigation facilities in Sathvav, so that the area needed for subsistence was greater than in many other regions.

tended to combine moneylending with liquor dealing, normally lived in the larger tribal villages. In these villages they had an exclusive right to sell liquor. We can get some idea about the numbers of the rural Parsis and their influence by noticing that there were 13 liquor shops in the 135 villages of Mandvi taluka, or an average of about one shop for ten villages. They quite commonly owned land in more than one village. By the early twentieth century some had accumulated huge estates and had retired to the towns, leaving their land to be managed by local agents. But many of the smaller Parsi landlords continued to live in the tribal villages. Their houses were double-storied and made of brick and tiles in contrast to the mud and thatch dwellings of the adivasis. They advanced liquor and toddy throughout the year, being repaid at greatly inflated rates in grain at harvest time. Landless adivasis paid back their debts by labouring in the fields of the Parsis.[16] There are numerous accounts of the heavy-handed methods used by the latter to control the adivasis.[17] Besides taking labour they took sexual advantage of adivasi women.[18] The tribal poor lived in constant fear. Any protest was met with a swift beating by the Parsi or his resident strongmen. Local officials and the police invariably took the side of the Parsis.

The position of the Parsis was strengthened considerably by the colonial liquor laws. Chief of these was the Bombay Abkari Act of 1878. Prior to this date the right to distil and sell liquor had been farmed out and the tax on liquor had been low. Liquor (known in Gujarat as *daru*) had been distilled in the villages, using as a base the sugary flower of the mhowra tree. Toddy, which was fermented palm juice similar in strength to beer, was taxed through a small levy on toddy-bearing palm trees. The British disliked this system as it allowed considerable evasion of revenue on daru and toddy. The Act of 1878 banned all local manufacture of liquor, permitting only the operation of a central distillery at the headquarter town of a district. Central distilleries were run by district monopolists who had to pay a large annual sum to the government. This centrally-taxed liquor was sold in the villages by men who paid an annual license fee to the government. As it was felt that toddy might undercut the new more

---

[16] *Gazetteer of the Bombay Presidency, Volume II, Surat and Broach* (Bombay, 1877), p. 190.

[17] See, for instance, Sumant Mehta, *Samaj Darpan* (Ahmedabad, 1964), p. 340.

[18] Dr U. L. Desai of Vyara to A.D.C. to Gaikwad of Baroda, 5 December 1923, Baroda Records Office (hereafter BRO), Confidential Department, File 301.

highly-priced liquor, the tax on toddy trees was greatly enhanced and a more rigorous listing of the trees undertaken.[19]

Under this new system the excise revenue rose enormously, as the following table shows. The figures in the left-hand column are for percentages of the total revenue of Bombay Presidency and may be studied in comparison with the corresponding percentages in terms of the land revenue—the chief revenue earner—for the same years.[20]

Years	Akbari (excise)	Land revenue
1865–6	4.4	40.3
1875–6	4.2	38.8
1885–6	8.2	38.7
1895–6	7.7	34.7
1905–6	8.9	24.2
1915–16	13.7	31.4
1925–6	29.3	38.1

How the excise on country liquor and toddy rose over the years for one single district, namely Surat, can be seen from the amounts shown below in rupees.[21]

Revenue Year	Revenue (rupees)
1877–8	3,70,423
1885–6	7,94,221
1895–6	11,64,585
1905–6	11,67,718
1915–16	17,44,867
1925–6	34,36,291

The burden of this increase in Surat district fell on the lower castes and particularly on the adivasis. The liquor sellers did very well out of the new system. Although they had lost the right to distil liquor, they still had a monopoly of the sale of factory-made alcohol in extensive clusters of villages. Because they lived in the villages the

[19] *Report of the Excise Committee Appointed by the Government of Bombay, 1922–23*, Vol. I, p. 43; Vol. II, p. 301.

[20] Figures from annual *Reports on the Administration of the Bombay Presidency*.

[21] Figures from annual *Reports on the Administration of the Abkari Department in the Bombay Presidency, Sind, and Aden*.

liquor vendors were able to prevent most illicit distillation. Profits were made on the high-priced factory product by giving short measures, by watering it down, or by advancing amounts of it on credit against usurious rates of interest. While the shopkeepers lined their pockets thus by fraud and extortion, the excise officials could be bribed to look the other way.[22] According to Haribhai Desai of Surat, who testified before the Bombay Excise Committee in 1923, the excise officers always gave plenty of advance warning before visiting a liquor shop. Often the shopkeepers lent money to the officers and obliged them in other ways so as to keep them in their power. Desai continued:

> In fact, a liquor shopkeeper is, under the present system, a master in the village, whereas he was a pariah in the old regimes . . . To speak honestly and candidly, I have known the Abkari shopkeepers to be the only men of means in many of the villages. Their connection with the officials, coupled with this, makes them really dangerous as far as the internal affairs of a village are concerned. It is they who make and unmake quarrels, and under the warmth of official favour and countenance, they do not hesitate to ruin the reputation of many a respectable person. The less said about these shopkeepers the better.[23]

The profits made from moneylending and liquor selling were invested to a large extent in land. Before the land revenue settlements of the 1860s the adivasis had used land in the customary manner of shifting the area of cultivation from year to year. They did not think of themselves as owners of individual plots of land. During the 1860s however the tribal peasantry of south Gujarat was given ownership rights on the land which it happened to be cultivating at the time, and for the first time land became a marketable commodity. Because they lacked political weight and were relatively docile (for they had never before been forced to defend their land), the adivasis were soon being deprived of their new proprietary rights by moneylenders and liquor dealers, and turned into tenants who, meek as they were, could be exploited with distressing ease.

This new system of exploitation rested therefore on the formation of property rights in land and on the liquor laws. Baroda and other adjoining princely states adopted similar measures in the late nineteenth century, so that the situation was much the same there. The colonial authorities soon noticed the dire effects their rule was having

---

[22] *Report of the Excise Committee Appointed by the Government of Bombay, 1922–23*, Vol. I, p. 49. [23] Ibid., Vol. II, p. 526.

on the adivasis, but rather than question the system itself they laid the responsibility on the supposed moral depravity of the tribal peasants. In particular they blamed their 'addiction to drink'. In the words of a Deputy Collector of Surat district, writing about the Chodhris of Mandvi taluka in 1881:

> These Kaliparaj people are addicted to much drinking; in fact the whole Abkari revenue amounting to upwards of Rs 25,000 [for Mandvi taluka] is mostly derived from these people. If half the amount spent in drinking were used by them in improving their land and in supporting themselves with better means of cultivation, their condition will be gradually improved, whereas at present they give the superior produce of their fields such as rice, toover etc. to their Sowcars towards the liquidation of their debt, reserving only kodra, naglee and other coarse grain for their subsistence.[24]

The answer it appeared was to educate the adivasis so that they would learn to appreciate the advantages of temperance and moderation. According to one Assistant Collector of Surat, 'Until they are sufficiently educated and are so much more advanced as to appreciate the rules of moderation, any attempt to emancipate them from their fancied thraldom must prove simply waste of labour.'[25] This sentiment was endorsed by another Assistant Collector writing seven years later:

> It is no exaggeration to say that the average Chodhra *cannot count above ten*, and he certainly abhors a school as a device of Brahmanism, but the inference that no perseverance would teach him anything is negatived by the example of Walod, which has been less neglected than Mandvi. That Mahal boasts 2 or three purely Chodhra schools and actually two or three Chodhra schoolmasters, and I have observed that in those villages where there are schools—and in these only—there are Chodhras who live in brick houses, who feed on something better than *Kodra* and *Nagli*, who store up fodder against the hot weather, and who know that plough oxen cannot legally be carried off in payment of a debt.[26]

The colonial panacea for the pauperization of the adivasis was thus education.

Primary schools were opened in the adivasi villages. The experiment was not much of a success. High caste teachers were unwilling to serve in remote tribal tracts and there were few adivasis either qualified

[24] District Deputy Collector's report, 1880–1, BA Revenue Department (hereafter R.D.) 1881, Vol. 22, Comp. 1435.

[25] Assistant Collector's report, 1886–7, BA, R.D. 1887, Vol. 26, Comp. 1548.

[26] Assistant Collector's report, 1893–4, BA, R.D. 1894, Vol. 36, Comp. 1305.

to teach or indeed interested in promoting any education at all. Many believed that boys who went to school died young.[27] The schools were poorly attended and several had to be closed. The picture was not however entirely bleak, for Baroda state had had a small but important success in adivasi education. In 1885 after a tour of the Ranimahals Sayajirao Gaikwad ordered that a hostel for adivasi boys be opened at Songadh so that they could study full-time at the primary school in the town. Initially it proved hard to attract boarders. But the first superintendent, Fatehkhan Pathan, was determined to succeed and he went out to the villages to recruit pupils. The adivasis merely fled into the forest at his sight. The breakthrough came when he managed to persuade a prominent figure in the Gamit community to send two of his sons to the hostel. One of them, Amarsinh Gamit, was later to become a leading social reformer.[28] By 1900 the hostel was well attended and producing an annual quota of adivasis who had passed their seventh-standard Gujarati examination, which was the qualification required for a teacher. In 1904 the British decided to open a similar hostel of their own in Mandvi taluka. This institution—the Godsamba Boarding House—attracted boys from all over Surat district. Many of those who passed through the hostel were to become leading social reformers amongst the adivasis of the Ranimahals.

The most prominent of these social reformers was the ex-pupil of Songadh, Amarsinh Gamit (1873–1941). In 1905 he and Fatehkhan Pathan organized a conference for adivasis at his village in Vyara taluka. Resolutions were passed urging them to give up liquor, to acquire education, to abandon various superstitious practices and to free themselves from debts to moneylenders.[29] During the following years Amarsinh Gamit travelled from village to village encouraging the adivasis to reform their way of life. He tried to persuade them to take a daily bath, to keep their houses clean and to use modern medicine when they were ill rather than go to a shaman-healer.[30] He also campaigned against a big Parsi landlord, Ratanji Daboo, who was exploiting the tribals in a particularly blatant manner. The going was however hard and the success limited.

In the British areas, and in particular Mandvi taluka, young Chodhris educated at the Godsamba Boarding House began to form song-groups, known as *bhajan mandalis*, for the propagation of social

[27] I. I. Desai, *Raniparajma Jagrati* (Surat, 1971), p. 9.　　　[28] Loc. cit.
[29] Ibid., p. 10.　　　[30] Ibid., p. 11.

reform ideas. A leading figure was Marvadi Master, a Chodhri who passed his Gujarati final examination from Godsamba in 1909. His father, who was from a village of Mandvi taluka, was a cultivator with about forty acres of land, so that Marvadi may be said to have come from a more prosperous Chodhri family. He became a school-master and taught in various villages of Mandvi taluka. He and some other ex-students of Godsamba organized a song-group to tour the villages on their days off, singing songs in praise of temperance, self-sufficiency and the need to stand up against alien moneylenders and Parsis. One such song went:

Oh friends! Do not drink daru and toddy.
Oh friends! If you drink the Parsi will plunder your property.
If you go to the Parsi your wealth will be plundered.
Oh friends! Do not drink daru.
If you go to drink the Vaniyas and Ghanchis will plunder your property.[31]

Once a crowd had been attracted by the singing the reformers gave lectures on these subjects in the Chodhri dialect.

Thus during the first two decades of the twentieth century young adivasis began to appear in the role of social reformers within their communities. Such men often came from the more prosperous adivasi families—the ones which could afford to release a son or two from fieldwork to attend school. From such families emerged a leadership capable of standing up against outside exploiters. Being educated these social reformers enjoyed considerable prestige among their people, and some of them initiated movements which anticipated the Devi movement. In 1905 for instance the Assistant Collector of Surat district reported:

The last two months of the year were marked by a remarkable total abstinence movement among the Kaliparaj. The origin was in Baroda territory, where a schoolmaster said he had received from a god an authoritative prohibition of drinking any intoxicating liquor. The news went first to Bulsar, and prohibiting circulars were widely disseminated there. Some Anavla Patels energetically encouraged the movement. Mysterious letters from the god were alleged to be found in many villages. The Kaliparaj began to hold large meetings at which they decided after indulging in a big final debauch to abstain totally. Up to the present they

[31] The song was recited to me by a former member of Marvadi Master's song group, Dalubhai Chodhri of Salaiya (Mandvi taluka). The song, which I have translated from the Chodhri dialect with assistance from Professor I. P. Desai of Surat, uses the terms *Parha* for 'Parsis' and *Vange* for 'Vaniyas'. Professor Desai says that these terms would have been regarded by Parsis and Vaniyas as being highly insulting.

have rigidly kept their pledge . . . . In adjoining native territory the abstainers have been severely threatened by the state, who feared the loss of Abkari revenue. But the people have replied that the god's command is greater than the state's and have continued to abstain. The movement is, I think, in no sense a strike against the high price of liquor, but is entirely a moral and religious one.[32]

In the following year the movement was reported to have died out. However a number of other movements of this type also occurred during this period, so that by 1922 they had become something of a tradition in the area.

III

The ground had thus been prepared for the coming of the Devi. This movement did not however start in the Ranimahals of south Gujarat, but in the coastal villages of Bassein, just to the north of Bombay city. The origins of the movement are undocumented and obscure, and my information comes entirely from interviews with old fishermen of the area.[33] It appears that early in the year 1922 the Mangela Koli fisherfolk were hit by an epidemic of smallpox. They believed this epidemic to have been caused by a goddess who had therefore to be propitiated. Ceremonies were held at which Mangela Koli women became possessed by the deity. Through these mediums she made it known to the community that she would be satisfied only if they gave up meat, fish, liquor and toddy for a limited period. The Mangela Kolis followed this advice. The women who were possessed were known as 'salahbai', meaning 'woman (*bai*) who gave advice (*salah*)'. This propitiatory movement spread fast up the coast northwards to other fishing villages in Thana district, Daman and then Surat district. From the coastal villages of Daman, Pardi and Valsad talukas it spread to the Dhodiya adivasi villages of the interior. By this time the goddess herself had come to be known as 'Salahbai' and, as was the custom with adivasis, both men and women were becoming possessed. During this stage the cult spread comparatively slowly, as the ceremonies of possession took place in people's houses and the attendance was small. As yet it had not come to the attention of the authorities. From Valsad and Pardi the movement spread east into Dharampur

---

[32] Assistant Collector's report, 1904–5, BA, R.D. 1906, Vol. II, Comp. 511, Pt. VI.

[33] I am grateful for the help given me in this respect by Sudha Mokashi of the S.N.D.T. University, Bombay, who introduced me to the fishing villages of Bassein and Palghat talukas of Thana district.

state where it took hold amongst the Konkani tribe. It then spread up the ghat into Surgana state and Nasik district and, at the same time, north-east into the Dangs. It reached this latter area around August 1922.[34]

In the Dangs the movement underwent an important change. Until then it had been conducted in a low key and there had been nothing in it which could be perceived as a challenge to the local status quo. In the Dangs groups of villages began to attend the meetings *en masse*, so that forest officials began to find it hard to obtain labour for the felling and transport of timber. The movement became better organized, with Dangi shamans, known as *gaulas*, carrying it from one group of villages to another. Many Dangi adivasis stopped drinking liquor so that the local Parsis were soon complaining to the authorities about a serious fall in sales and profits. From the Dangs the gaulas themselves carried the movement into Khandesh in the north-east and into Songadh taluka in the north-west. The first Devi meetings in these areas were organized by Dangi gaulas.[35] But after going a certain distance they turned back, leaving the movement to spread of its own accord. In Khandesh it did not go beyond the area covered by the gaulas, but in the Ranimahals of south Gujarat it gathered momentum enough to spread westwards right up to the Arabian Sea.

In this area the movement was relayed from village to village either by those who had already been possessed by the Devi or by those who wanted to bring the Devi to their neighbourhoods. The local adivasis were already anticipating the coming of the goddess as a result of rumours which had been circulating for some time. When a meeting was convened—normally by the leading men of a village—large numbers would gather there from the surrounding hamlets. Once assembled, any man or woman could become possessed and speak the commands of the Devi. Many of those who were possessed were ordinary peasants with no personal history of possession and were never to be possessed in a similar manner again. The meetings usually continued for several days, with the participants either staying

---

[34] Tracing the route of the movement proved to be a laborious—though fascinating—task, as the contemporary documents are very vague on the subject. It was necessary to start from Khandesh and work backwards village by village. Dates are difficult to establish by such a method, but according to the Collector of Surat at the time, the Devi was in the Dangs in August and September of 1922. *Land Revenue Administration Report of the Bombay Presidency for 1922–23*, p. 43.

[35] For a description of such a meeting, see *Raniparajma Jagrati*, pp. 138–41.

on at the meeting-ground or reassembling each morning. They freed or sold off their chickens and goats so as not to be tempted to eat them. They started to take daily baths. They were careful not to touch a drop of daru or toddy. Numerous cases were cited of unreformed individuals secretly persisting in 'impure' habits and then being detected miraculously by the Devi mediums and forced to make a public confession of their guilt. The meetings closed with a mass feast and a final ceremony of worship for the goddess.

This was a highly democratic movement in which any adivasi could, through possession, become for a time a respected leader with great authority. In its structure the Devi movement was not therefore what is known as 'messianic'.[36] Its central feature at this stage was that of possession by the deity. Throughout the world the poor and lowly have often chosen this method to voice their collective grievances and desires. I. M. Lewis has shown in his study of possession cults that tribes which have experienced the worst hardships over the past century have been particularly prone to outbursts of spirit possession.[37] In these they find the strength to protest against their oppressors. Writing about India Richard Lannoy has argued that 'possession is not a mere chaotic hysteria but a structured, and in some cases a highly formalized phenomenon, which can be culture-creating and enrich the consciousness of the individual and the

[36] Michael Adas has argued that the single most important feature of the messianic movement is the presence of a messianic or prophetic leader. See M. Adas, *Prophets of Rebellion: Millennarium Protest Movements against the European Colonial Order* (Chapel Hill, 1979), pp. 92–3 and 115. Adas relies here on an article by Norman Cohn, 'Medieval Millennarianism', in S. L. Thrupp (ed.), *Millennial Dreams in Action* (New York, 1970), pp. 32–43. Several tribal movements in India have had messianic-style leaders, most notably that of Birsa Munda. But the fact that many—such as the Devi—did not, suggests that we need to question this concept as an explanation for such movements. In this context, we may also take note of the writings of Stephen Fuchs. In *Rebellious Prophets* he describes several reformist movements amongst Indian tribals (though not the Devi) and labels them as 'messianic'. In his opening chapter he lists fourteen features of the 'messianic movement', which he says can be found either together or in part in such movements. The list is very comprehensive, and it is unlikely that all of these features would be found in one movement. Fuchs has not therefore provided us with a theory to explain such movements, for the essence of a theory is that the parts should fit together. The concept is thus a poor one which, beyond describing the nature of the leadership of certain tribal movements, does not advance our understanding very far.

[37] The Shona of Zimbabwe provide an example: see I. M. Lewis, *Ecstatic Religion: An Anthropological Study of Spirit Possession and Shamanism* (Harmondsworth, 1978), pp. 141–3.

group.'[38] The Salahbai phenomenon of 1922–3 needs to be understood in such terms. The wave of possession helped to articulate the deep-seated sense of wrong and the aspirations shared by the mass of the adivasis of south Gujarat.

IV

As could be expected in a movement in which authority was so dispersed, the commands of the Devi, as voiced by the spirit mediums, differed considerably from gathering to gathering. Some of these were clearly specific to local circumstances. For instance in Vyara taluka the Devi commanded the adivasis not to become Christians.[39] Vyara was a centre for missionary activities. However, in the midst of all the variety, it is possible to identify a core of commands and classify the material under the following heads:

1. *Alcohol*	(a) Do not drink liquor or toddy.
	(b) Do not serve in liquor or toddy shops.
	(c) Do not tap toddy trees.
2. *Flesh*	(a) Do not eat meat or fish.
	(b) Dispose of all live fowls, goats and sheep (kept for eating or sacrifice).
	(c) Destroy all cooking vessels used for cooking meat.
	(d) Remove and burn roofs of houses (normally of thatch in adivasi villages) as smoke from fires used to cook meat has passed through them.
3. *Cleanliness*	(a) Take a bath daily (in some cases twice or thrice a day).
	(b) Use water to clean up after defecation.
	(c) Keep houses and compounds scrupulously clean.
4. *Dominant classes*	(a) Boycott Parsis.
	(b) Boycott Muslims.
	(c) Do not work for anyone connected with the liquor trade.
	(d) Demand higher wages.
	(e) Take a bath when crossed by the shadow of a Parsi.

[38] Richard Lannoy, *The Speaking Tree: A Study of Indian Culture and Society* (New York, 1975), pp. 198–9.

[39] Police Report of 28 November 1922, BRO, Confidential Dept. 327.

The commands demanded a profound change in the style of life of the adivasis. The drinking of daru and toddy was very much a part of their culture. Not only did these beverages provide a valuable food—important particularly during the hot season when foodstocks were low—but they were also used in religious and social functions, being consumed freely during many religious festivals and at marriages and funerals.[40] Likewise the sacrifice of live animals played an important part in adivasi rituals, the flesh of the animal being eaten afterwards. Daily bathing was not at that time a common practice for water supplies in the tribal villages were often very inadequate even for purposes of drinking. Not all the commands of the Devi were thus meant to make life easy for her followers and we need to examine more closely their underlying rationale.

Several observers at the time saw this as a movement for the 'purification' of the adivasis. The Gandhian leader Sumant Mehta, for instance, described it as *atmashuddhi*, or self-purification, by the adivasis.[41] This perception may be seen to underlie the concept of 'Sankritization' put forward by M. N. Srinivas in the following manner:

> Sanskritization is the process by which a 'low' Hindu caste, or tribal or other group, changes its customs, ritual, ideology, and way of life in the direction of a high, and frequently, 'twice-born' caste. Generally such changes are followed by a claim to a higher position in the caste hierarchy than that traditionally conceded to the claimant caste by the local community. The claim is usually made over a period of time, in fact, a generation or two, before the 'arrival' is conceded.[42]

In terms of this concept Indian society is depicted as something like a very sluggish game of snakes and ladders. The game is entered in a state of impurity and a gradual advance is made over the generations

---

[40] *Papers Relating to the Revision Survey Settlement of the Mandvi Taluka of the Surat Collectorate. Selections from the Records of the Bombay Government*, No. CCCCXXVI — New Series (Bombay 1904), p. 41. F. S. P. Lely to J. G. Moore, 22 May 1886, BA, R.D. 1887, Vol. 7, Comp. 264. Assistant Collector's report 1885–6, BA, R.D. 1886, Vol. 32, Comp. 1548.

[41] S. Mehta, 'Kaliparaj', *Yugdharma*, 2:3 (1923), p. 220.

[42] M. N. Srinivas, *Social Change in Modern India* (Bombay, 1972), p. 6. This represents Srinivas's modified definition of sanskritization which takes account of various criticisms made of his original statement in 'A Note on Sanskritization and Westernization' in *Caste in Modern India* (Bombay, 1962). For a critical discussion of Srinivas's theory and his changes in position see Yogendra Singh, *Modernization of Indian Tradition: A Systematic Study of Social Change* (Delhi, 1973), pp. 7–12.

towards the goal of Brahmanical purity. Many pitfalls lie along the way and most communities never make it to the top. There is no doubt however what the goal is: 'The Brahmanical, and on the whole, puritanical, model of Sanskritization has enjoyed an over-all dominance, and even meat-eating and liquor-consuming Kshatriyas and other groups have implicitly conceded the superiority of this model to the others.'[43]

Srinivas continues: 'Sanskritization is not confined to Hindu castes but also occurs among tribal and semitribal groups such as the Bhils of Western India, the Gonds and Oraons of Central India, and the Pahadis of the Himalayas. This usually results in the tribe undergoing Sanskritization claiming to be a caste, and therefore, Hindu'.[44] In the case of the Devi movement it could be argued that in observing new rules of purity such as temperance, vegetarianism and cleanliness the adivasis of south Gujarat were advancing a claim to be accepted as clean castes within the Hindu hierarchy. It can therefore be seen as a dramatic example of the process of tribal sanskritization.

There are however some difficulties in the use of this concept. In the statement quoted above Srinivas refers to the Oraons. A reading of S. C. Roy's classic work on reform movements among the Oraons reveals that Roy himself did not accept such an interpretation. He wrote that Hindu reformist groups, most notably the Arya Samaj, had attempted to win the Oraons to the Hindu fold by means of such things as *shuddhi* (purification) ceremonies, but had no success. For according to Roy, 'enlightened leaders among the Oraons naturally fight shy of such propagandists under the reasonable apprehension that orthodox official Hinduism with the religious and social exclusiveness of the twice-born castes, would relegate aboriginal converts to a very low, if not the lowest, stratum in the hierarchy of Hindu castes'.[45] Evidence from elsewhere also suggests that on the whole adivasis do not claim a rank in the caste hierarchy. It is true that in some cases they have demanded to be regarded as Kshatriyas.[46] This in itself is significant for Kshatriyas enjoy high status while continuing to practice 'impure' customs such as meat-eating and liquor-drinking.

---

[43] Srinivas, *Social Change*, p. 26. [44] Ibid., p. 7.

[45] Roy, p. 293. Suresh Singh makes the same point for the Birsa Munda movement, pp. 198–9.

[46] Fuchs gives brief histories of many adivasi movements in *Rebellious Prophets*. Only in two cases (cited on p. 67 and p. 69) did adivasis advance a claim to caste status, and in both it was for Kshatriya status.

In other words adivasis who claim Kshatriya status are asking that they be accorded greater respect despite their 'impure' habits. But in modern times this has been the exception[47] and movements for purification such as that of the Devi clearly have adopted very different tactics. In such movements adivasis have adopted certain Hindu values without making an accompanying claim to caste status. There is no reason therefore why we should consider these as examples of acceptance of the caste system on the part of adivasis; we may just as well say that by adopting a way of life akin to that of a high caste the adivasis are claiming equality of status with high caste Hindus.

A further drawback in the theory of sanskritization is that it underestimates the amount of conflict involved in making good such claims and demands. Louis Dumont, in a discussion of Srinivas's theory, has pointed out that low castes or tribes which reform their way of life can hardly hope to enhance their status through such means alone. Higher castes have to be forced through political action to concede such a status. As a result there tends to be a correlation between the political power held by a community and its position in the caste hierarchy.[48] It would therefore be futile for adivasis to demand higher status or a position of equality without at the same time mounting a political challenge to the dominance of the higher communities. If we look at the commands of the Devi we find that this was indeed the case; the adivasi's programme combined adoption of certain high caste values with a boycott of the dominant Parsi landlords and liquor dealers. The theory of sanskritization in emphasizing only the aspect of 'purification' fails to take account of the sharp challenge to the existing social structure which forms a necessary part of such movements.

In addition the theory lacks any convincing historical dimension. Throughout time the goal towards which everyone is supposed to strive is that of Brahmanical purity. In Srinivas's words: '. . . the mobility associated with Sanskritization results only in *positional changes* in the system and does not lead to any *structural change*. That is, a caste moves up above its neighbours and another comes down, but all this takes place in an essentially stable hierarchical

[47] During the medieval period there was probably a considerable amount of what Surajit Sinha calls 'Rajputization' of tribes—i.e. claims for Rajput or Kshatriya status ('Bhumij-Kshatriya Social Movement in South Manbhum'). With the failure of Rajput power over the centuries this model appears to have become increasingly less popular.

[48] Louis Dumont, *Homo Hierarchicus* (London, 1972), p. 244 and p. 283.

order. The system itself does not change.'[49] The theory thus represents a structural functionalist attempt to explain change in a society which it is believed does not itself change in its essentials.[50] To use our earlier analogy the game of snakes and ladders goes on but the board itself never alters. An alternative historical and dialectical approach would be to argue that any given social system is a synthesis arising out of pre-existing social systems. The interaction between tribal and Hindu society produces over the years a fresh synthesis which is neither purely tribal nor purely Brahmanical. Movements such as that of the Devi can thus be regarded as being specific to particular historical periods when the contradiction between tribal and non-tribal elements became particularly intense, leading to a strong thrust towards synthesis.

The evidence suggests that adivasi movements of this type started on a large scale in the late nineteenth century. They have continued to this day. In the past the adivasis had managed to isolate themselves to a large extent from the mainstream of Indian life; they were not expected to assimilate the values of the non-tribal élites and they did not feel compelled by their material circumstances to do so. Assimilation, where it did occur, was either extremely partial or affected only a small élite among the adivasis who then distanced themselves from their community by assuming prestigious designations, such as that of 'Rajput'. The change came with the conquest and subjugation of the tribal areas by the British, a process which had been largely completed by the middle of the nineteenth century. Rights in property were established, colonial laws were imposed and the tribal territories were opened up to economic exploitation. The historical context from which these movements issued was thus that of the process of the formation of the modern Indian state. Out of this emerged the adivasi reformers intent on forging that cultural synthesis which they believed would afford to their communities a respected position in the new society.

Another concept which has been used in connection with such movements is that of revitalization. This does not suffer from being undialectical. The idea, advanced originally by Anthony Wallace,[51] has been applied by Edward Jay to India in an article written originally

[49] *Social Change*, p. 7.

[50] Ramakrishna Mukherjee, *Sociology of Indian Sociology* (New Delhi, 1979), p. 51.

[51] A. Wallace, 'Revitalization Movements', *American Anthropologist*, 58 (1956), pp. 264–81.

in 1959.[52] Jay listed four main characteristics of the revitalization movement in the Indian context:

1. They are expressions of group solidarity and social cohesion and have acted as unifying forces for groups under conditions of social disorganization.
2. They represent attempts to establish a new moral order where the old one has been destroyed.
3. They have acted as mediators between the Great and Little Traditions of India, or, more broadly speaking, as catalysts of acculturation.
4. They have aided in the structuring of a new social system of which both Hindu and tribal societies are a part.[53]

Jay makes an important modification to Wallace's original statement. Wallace laid considerable stress on individual psychological disorientation leading to personal revitalization. Jay emphasizes the social disruptions which disorientate entire communities, leading to the revitalization of the group as a whole.[54] He does not find it fruitful to approach these movements in terms of the mental problems of individuals.

Although there is much that is good in Jay's approach, some reservations have to be made. Jay argues that there have been two basic types of revitalization in India, the resistive and the emulative. In the former the synthesis between the dominant and subordinate cultures is poorly worked out, there are serious barriers against integration, and the movements tend to develop into a state of violent resistance. In the latter the synthesis is better worked out, the barriers to integration are weak or non-existent, and the movements are peaceful.[55] On the surface this distinction may seem to explain the difference between violent movements such as that of Birsa Munda, and non-violent ones such as that of the Tana Bhagats or the Devi. In fact the distinction is of questionable value. All attempts at synthesis will encounter opposition from those who wish to maintain the status quo. Opposition will come from outsiders and from conservative members of the community itself. In this conflict there is always some potential for violence. Whether or not violence actually occurs depends on specific local conditions such as the relative strengths of the opposing groups, the political situation of the day,

---

[52] The version of the article referred to here is a revised and modified one of 1961. Edward Jay, 'Revitalization Movements in Tribal India', in L. P. Vidyarthi (ed.), *Aspects of Religion in Indian Society* (Meerut, 1961), pp. 282–315.

[53] Ibid., p. 282.   [54] Ibid., p. 302.

[55] Ibid., p. 304.

and community traditions of resistance to the upper classes (some tribes have a more militant tradition than others).[56]

A more serious drawback is that Jay fails to place the revitalization movement in a particular historical context. The examples which he cites all relate to the period 1850–1940. He does not however argue that the revitalization movement is specific to this period; the assumption is that such movements have been going on throughout Indian history. Jay's concept like that of Srinivas thus suffers from being ahistorical. The idea of a synthesis between the Great and Little Traditions is also problematic. Jay fails to spell out what is meant by the Great and Little Traditions in the Indian context, so that the statement remains vague. But even when set out more rigorously the idea does not take us very far, for although it explains how change occurs it fails to specify the direction of this change and why particular values are preferred to others.[57] In this respect Srinivas's concept of sanskritization is more precise about preferred values. However the flaw in this approach lies in the assumption that there are values— such as those of Brahmanism—which do not change in their essentials over time, as in practice all value systems are in a constant state of flux and any attempt to define their essence invariably runs into difficulty. How do we overcome this problem?

The best approach appears to be to relate values to power. The values which the adivasis endorsed were those of the classes which possessed political power. In acting as they did the adivasis revealed their understanding of the relationship between values and power, for values possess that element of power which permits dominant classes to subjugate subordinate classes with a minimum use of physical force. To take an obvious example, the Brahmanical notion of 'purity' has provided a most potent means for the control of the supposedly 'impure' subordinate classes of India. By appropriating and thus democratizing such values the adivasis sought to deprive them of their power of domination.

[56] In this context it is interesting to note that in February 1898 Birsa Munda told his followers that they could adopt two tactics to fight for the Munda kingdom: either the 'religious' or the 'forcible' method. As there was a strong religious content to the 'forcible' method, what he meant was that they could choose to challenge the status quo either violently or non-violently. The violent method was chosen, leading to a disastrous defeat. After the outbreak was over the Mundas returned to non-violent methods. In the Munda movement we see a constant interchange, therefore, between violent and non-violent methods. Suresh Singh, pp. 82–3.

[57] For a full discussion of this point see Yogendra Singh, pp. 13–16.

We are not therefore dealing with value systems as such but with relationships of power. Once this central fact is grasped it becomes easier to understand the rationale underlying the various programmes adopted by adivasis in different areas. In many cases adivasis have adopted the values of the locally dominant classes among the indigenous population. In north-eastern India on the other hand adivasis converted to Christianity in large numbers because they associated the value system of the Christian missionaries with the power of the British. In south Gujarat they rejected the values of their direct exploiters, the Parsis, but endorsed the dominant regional culture of the Brahmans and Vaniyas. The values which were appropriated could therefore be those of the colonial ruling class, or of a regionally dominant indigenous class, or of the actual local exploiters of the adivasis. The values endorsed differed profoundly. What they had in common was their association with the exercise of power.

One great strength to such programmes of assimilation of dominant values—as opposed to programmes of outright rejection of such values—was that they provided a meeting point between the adivasis and certain progressive members of the dominant classes. Amongst this latter group were the men of advanced liberal views: those who believed in national integration and the forging of a democratic Indian nation state. There were also the politicians who viewed the adivasis as a potential power base. Such men could play a vital role in convincing the colonial rulers and other members of their own class that the claims of the tribal peoples were reasonable and just. Adivasi movements of this type therefore took advantage of divisions amongst the élites.

Going back to the commands of the Devi therefore we can argue that they made up a mutually reinforcing package. On the one hand they sought to appropriate (and thus democratize and implicitly change) the values associated with the regionally dominant high caste Hindus. In this respect it was significant that the commands never included any boycott of Vaniya and Brahman merchants and usurers, even though they exploited the adivasis. The boycott was imposed only on Parsis and in a few cases Muslims. The logic of this was that the Vaniyas and Brahmans lived the 'pure' way of life which the adivasis sought to assimilate whereas Parsis and Muslims were 'impure'. On the other hand the commands of the Devi represented an act of assertion against the most rapacious of the local exploiters, the Parsis. By refusing to drink liquor and by refusing to work for anyone connected with the liquor trade the adivasis were cutting the economic cords which bound them to the Parsis. Renouncing liquor was in this respect a far more effective act of assertion than resorting to subterfuge, such as illicit distillation, for the act of giving up had behind it a great moral force.

The commands of the Devi thus represented in this specific locality a powerful programme for adivasi assertion. The movement had unsettling implications for all those who wished to maintain the status quo in the Ranimahals, and in particular it sounded a challenge to the Parsi liquor dealers-cum-landlords. It is to the reaction of the non-adivasis to the movement that we shall now turn.

V

In the majority of cases possession cults do not pose any urgent threat to the status quo. I. M. Lewis has pointed out that they are often tolerated in an uneasy manner by the dominant classes. Possession is regarded as a safety valve through which the potentially subversive emotions of the lower classes can be worked off with least disruption to society.[58] The dividing line between purely ritual and more positive resistance can however be easily crossed. This is why the dominant classes keep a wary eye on such cults so that they can be quick to take action if things go 'too far'. In the case of the Devi movement the dominant groups sat up and took notice as soon as large groups of adivasis began to gather, for in such mass meetings lay the seeds of more active protest and subversion.

For the Parsis it soon became clear that the Devi movement was a disaster. Their trade in liquor dwindled to nothing, adivasis refused to tap their toddy trees, nobody would work in their fields or carry out domestic labour in their houses, and they were subjected to social boycott. To insult them even further adivasis who were crossed by the shadow of a Parsi took a bath to 'purify' themselves; some even told the Parsis that it would be better if they went back to Persia. The manner in which the latter reacted to the movement revealed how seriously they took the threat to their position. Their strongmen, assisted on occasions by excise officials, would seize an adivasi, hold him down and pour liquor down his throat, thus breaking his vow and making him ritually impure once again. Those who resisted were abused and beaten and even arrested on trumped-up charges.[59]

[58] I. M. Lewis, p. 128.
[59] S. Mehta, *Samaj Darpan*, pp. 341–2.

In some cases Parsis poured toddy into village wells so that the tribals would be forced to take alcohol with their drinking water. So as to mock the new 'purity' they urinated and defecated in the adivasi's shrines and holy places.[60]

The Devi movement was not popular with many local officials either. They had always regarded the adivasis as a debased and docile people whom they could exploit with little trouble and no qualms. Now with the new spirit of assertion they found that the supply of free goods, services and labour was not forthcoming as before. Their income from bribes dried up. They therefore did their best to undermine the movement, often aiding the Parsis in their efforts to break the spirit of the adivasis. In the British areas the local officials did not get any support from the higher authorities in this, whereas in the Baroda state areas they did. In the following pages we shall examine the differing reactions of the authorities to the movement in the Baroda state and British areas.

The first reaction by the Baroda officials of Vyara taluka was to instruct the police 'to bind down those people who come from the foreign limits and start this sort of gossip.'[61] Attempts were made to induce adivasis who had given up liquor to drink once more. When the Reverend Blunt of the Vyara Mission, a believer in temperance, heard about this he protested to C. N. Seddon, one of the leading ministers of the Gaikwad of Baroda. Seddon issued orders that officials were not to interfere with the Devi movement and that they were to allow it to spread from village to village.[62] In December 1922 a deputation of about twenty-five Parsis went to Navsari to request the district authorities to put a stop to the movement. Neither the police chief nor the Suba (equivalent of District Collector) were prepared to oblige.[63]

Soon after this the Dewan of Baroda, Sir Manubhai Mehta, came to a decision that the movement must be stopped. He later gave his reasons in a letter to the Gaikwad who was then on a tour of Europe.[64] He argued that political agitators and non-co-operators had taken advantage of the movement; Parsis were being intimidated

[60] S. Mehta, 'Kaliparaj', p. 222.

[61] Report by Police Naib Suba, Navsari, 13 November 1922, BRO, Confidential Dept. 327.

[62] Manubhai Mehta to Gaikwad, 7 June 1923, BRO, Confidential Dept. 273.

[63] Report by Police Commissioner, Baroda, 16 December 1922, BRO, Confidential Dept. 327.

[64] Manubhai Mehta to Gaikwad, 7 June 1923, BRO, Confidential Dept. 273.

and a racial feud had developed; the agitators were threatening to cut down a large number of toddy trees and this would damage the state excise revenue; many schoolmasters were supporting the campaign and were criticizing the excise policy of the state in speeches at public meetings; the British authorities had started to take action against people involved in the movement; the operations of the forest department were being hampered; the adivasis were ruining themselves economically by not cultivating their land and by refusing to work for Parsis, thereby losing wages. Manubhai Mehta thus revealed a marked lack of sympathy for the aims of the movement. He showed a bureaucratic desire to maintain the excise revenue at any cost, a strong partiality towards the Parsi point of view (who was intimidating whom?), considerable ignorance of the movement (the adivasis never refused to work their own lands), and a fear that the nationalists of the state might use the movement to gain for themselves a firm base among the adivasis of Navsari district.

Orders were issued forbidding the holding of meetings in the Ranimahals. Government servants and schoolmasters were directed not to take part in Devi-linked activities. Cutting of toddy trees was forbidden throughout Navsari district.[65] Extra police were dispatched to Mahuva taluka, the area in which the conflict between Parsis and adivasis was most intense.[66]

The nationalists of Baroda state were not prepared to take this lying down. In Navsari town there had been strong support for the Gandhian movement for the past three years.[67] In early 1923 the leading nationalists of the town started a body called the Kaliparaj Sankat Nivaran Mandal (Kaliparaj Grievances Relief Association). The Baroda city leader Sumant Mehta agreed to be its president. Members of the committee began to go out to the villages in order to protect the adivasis from harassment by the authorities. In March 1923 Sumant Mehta came to Navsari to investigate for himself the repression being carried on by the state against the reformed adivasis. After his return to Baroda he saw the Dewan who was a relative and demanded that prohibition be brought into Navsari district. Manubhai Mehta rejected this plea on the grounds that prohibition had failed in the United States of America but he did agree to order the closure of a few liquor shops in the area in which the movement was strongest.[68]

---

[65] Loc. cit.

[66] S. Mehta, 'Kaliparaj ke Raniparaj', *Yugdharma*, 3 (1924), p. 444.

[67] *Bombay Chronicle*, 27 April 1922.

[68] Manubhai Mehta to Gaikwad, 7 June 1923, BRO, Confidential Dept. 273.

In July 1923 the Baroda government prosecuted five of the leading members of the Kaliparaj Sankat Nivaran Mandal for holding meetings in the Ranimahals. The case was heard in early August, the leaders being defended by a prominent Vyara lawyer, Gopalji Desai. He managed to prove that the Navsari leaders had only had informal talks with some adivasis and had not held any meetings as such, and they were as a result acquitted.[69] Having failed to stop the urban leaders the Suba of Navsari then took out a case against some prominent adivasis. They were accused of forcibly preventing members of their community from working on the farms of Parsis and other non-adivasis. They were bound over to maintain the peace for varying periods.[70] Despite this repression the temperance movement and boycott of Parsis continued strong in the Baroda Ranimahals, particularly Mahuva taluka.[71] If anything this demonstrated how marginal to the movement were the efforts of the outside nationalist leaders. Finally in frustration Manubhai Mehta issued an order on 1 November 1923 which continued the ban on meetings in the Ranimahals for a further six months and also prohibited all gatherings under the influence of Devis.[72] So finally the Baroda raj came to ban the Devi! Some of the sentiments expressed in Mehta's decree (issued under the name of the Suba of Navsari) throw an interesting light on the Baroda government's perception of the movement. There was an implication that the Devi had been manufactured by urban troublemakers:

> . . . certain intriguing people not knowing the true nature of the welfare of the ruler and the ruled, misrepresented matters to the Kaliparaj people, intimidated them and enticed them to hold large meetings. . . . these persons attempt to instigate the Kaliparaj against the officers of the state, thereby reducing the established authority of the Government, to undermine the faith of the Kaliparaj in the justice administered by the Government and to impress upon them that this Government is careless of the true welfare of their community.[73]

Rather inconsistently the decree also tried to make out that the Devi was an evil spirit misleading the people and that the 'wicked actions' of this goddess could not be tolerated. These statements were not only contradictory but revealed in a most transparent manner that this supposedly 'progressive' princely state had no time for movements

[69] *Times of India*, 4 August 1923. *Servant of India*, 30 August 1923, p. 363.
[70] *Times of India*, 18 September 1923.
[71] Manubhai Mehta to Gaikwad, 5 October 1923, BRO, Confidential Dept. 273.
[72] *Bombay Chronicle*, 30 November 1923.
[73] Loc. cit.

of adivasi self-assertion. The state which had pioneered adivasi education in the late nineteenth century was not prepared to accept the consequences of this policy a generation later.

The Gaikwad himself proved to be rather more benevolent than his dewan. On 23 November 1923 he arrived back in India after a long sojourn in the health resorts of Europe. In December a deputation of over two hundred adivasis of Mahuva, Vyara and Songadh talukas came to Baroda to lay their grievances before the Maharaja.[74] Soon after this the suba of Navsari was relieved of his post and an order was issued permitting meetings in the Ranimahals for purposes of temperance and prohibition work. Local officials were ordered to co-operate with such activities.[75] In response to this new mood Sumant Mehta led a delegation on a tour of the Ranimahals in January 1924 during which he addressed large groups of adivasis. Conforming to the recent order these meetings were concerned purely with temperance. But this hardly mattered; what was important for the adivasis was that they were allowed to gather together once more to emphasize their solidarity in the struggle with the landlords and liquor sellers. Sumant Mehta found that the repression of the past year had failed to break the movement. The adivasis demonstrated to him an earnest desire for self-improvement and social reform. It was during this tour that Sumant Mehta became the first of the non-adivasis to question the use of the term 'Kaliparaj'. He remembered the bitter torment he had suffered in Britain when people had called him 'nigger' or 'blackie', and he decided to use henceforth the term 'Raniparaj' (people of the forest) to refer to the adivasis of the Ranimahals.[76] The term was soon accepted by nationalists throughout Gujarat. It provided a significant indicator of the increasing respect which the adivasis had earned, thanks to their self-assertion, from the more progressive members of the middle class of south Gujarat.

The British reaction to the Devi movement was of a different quality from that of Baroda state. In the past they had often adopted a tough policy towards popular anti-liquor movements. For instance when in 1886 large numbers of peasants of Thana and Kolaba districts resolved not to take liquor the local authorities promptly imprisoned the leaders of that campaign. The Abkari Commissioner for Bombay Presidency had justified this action in the following words:

[74] *Bombay Chronicle*, 11 December 1923.
[75] *Bombay Chronicle*, 28 January 1924.
[76] S. Mehta, 'Kaliparaj ke Raniparaj', p. 446.

The question for decision is, shall we sit quiet and allow the movement to continue and to spread and thereby forfeit a large amount of revenue, or are measures to be adopted which will bring the people to their senses?[77]

By 1922–3 such a reaction was not to be expected. Under the Montagu-Chelmsford reforms excise had been made a transferred subject. The first popular minister was Sir Chunilal Mehta who had expressed his determination to 'combat the drink evil' at the very first meeting of the reformed council.[78] He had introduced a policy of gradual prohibition through increasingly rigorous rationing of supplies to liquor shops. He had also appointed a committee to consider the question of total prohibition in Bombay Presidency. The Collector of Surat, A. M. Macmillan, therefore had little choice but to show a benevolent attitude towards the temperance programme of the Devi.

Being foreigners the British were less concerned about the upset to the local hierarchy than with what looked like an emerging alliance between the adivasis and the Gandhian nationalists of Gujarat. Initially the movement was classified as 'religious' and not 'political', and therefore to be tolerated. But it was to be watched carefully lest it showed any tendency to 'drift into politics'.[79] Macmillan paid a visit to the Ranimahals as soon as he could to discover whether the nationalists of Bardoli had instigated the movement. He concluded after his tour that the movement was in fact 'spontaneous' and that it was 'doing the people no particular harm'.[80] However towards the end of December reports came that the Devi had started to advocate the burning of foreign cloth and boycott of government schools—both key features of the non-co-operation programme. So by January 1923 Macmillan began to have second thoughts on the subject:

> I am considering whether it is not time to get people of influence to put a brake on the Mata movement, as it is beginning to take objectionable forms, both through the interference of interested people and through the natural tendency of such a movement so long as it is entirely immune from the restraining influence of outside criticism and the exercise of ordinary common sense to assume crudely absurd exaggerated forms.[81]

In Jalalpor taluka a Devi medium was prosecuted for forcing a Parsi toddy-shop owner to pay a fine of Rs 120 to a local nationalist

---

[77] *Report of the Excise Committee Appointed by the Government of Bombay 1922–23*, Vol. I, p. 45.   [78] Ibid., p. 50.
[79] M. S. Jayakar to Macmillan, 16 November 1922, BA, H.D. (Sp.) 637 of 1922,
[80] Macmillan to Crerar, 1 December 1922, ibid.
[81] Report by Macmillan, 19 January 1923, ibid.

school.[82] He was judged guilty of extortion and sentenced to fifteen days imprisonment and a fine of Rs 300.[83] In Jalalpor taluka the Devi movement was weak (it was not an adivasi area) and by early February 1923 the local police chief was able to report that the movement had died down as a result of the prosecution.[84]

In the Ranimahals the movement could not be crushed with such ease. Here Macmillan felt that it was best not to interfere. He felt rather that it was better to go along with the tribal people so that they would not be driven into the arms of the nationalists. In pursuit of this policy he persuaded the Excise Commissioner to allow sixteen liquor shops in the Ranimahals to be closed. Macmillan later argued in his annual report that his policy had been a success: 'Attempts were made by the local non-co-operation leaders to capture the movement for political purposes. Where it was superficial as in Jalalpor, they were fairly successful while it lasted but in Mandvi where it was deep and genuine, their efforts were more or less ignored.'[85] Can this verdict be accepted? Only partially, for the Gandhians linked up with the Devi movement with considerable skill. They did this by emphasizing those aspects of the programme which agreed with their own schemes and downgrading those which did not.

The Gandhians had been working among the adivasis of Bardoli taluka and Valod Mahal since late 1921. During that year Gandhi had insisted that before a campaign of civil disobedience be launched in these two sub-divisions, the adivasis must be brought into the nationalist movement. Until then the latter had shown no interest in the cause. As a result of a remarkable campaign in the tribal villages by the Congress leader Kunvarji Mehta, the adivasis not only became familiar with the name of Gandhi, but far more sympathetic to the movement.[86] It was not therefore surprising that in the following year the Devi mediums soon linked the name of Gandhi to that of the Devi. For many Gandhians the Devi movement appeared as an act of divine providence, for it seemed that at a stroke the adivasis had purified their way of life in accord with Gandhi's teachings. Soon

---

[82] Reports of 12 and 13 January 1923, ibid.

[83] Report by Macmillan, 20 January 1923, ibid.

[84] Report of 10 February 1923, ibid.

[85] *Land Revenue Administration Report of the Bombay Presidency for 1922–23*, p. 43.

[86] For details, see the biography of Kunvarji Mehta by B. P. Vaidya, *Rentima Vahan*, pp. 165–77.

after it began some of the Gandhian leaders of Bardoli taluka visited the adivasi areas and attended some Devi meetings. They suggested to some of the mediums that the usual list of the Devi's commands could be reinforced by such prescriptions as the need to wear khadi. Many of the mediums followed these suggestions.[87]

The Bardoli Congressmen decided to organize a Kaliparaj Conference at which Vallabhbhai Patel was to preside. They informed the adivasis that Gandhi himself was now in jail, but that his *gadi* (throne) was being occupied in his absence by Vallabhbhai Patel, and they invited them to come to the conference to hear Vallabhbhai and Gandhi's wife Kasturba. Large numbers promised to come. The First Kaliparaj Conference was thus held at Shekhpur in Mahuva taluka of Baroda state on 21 January 1923. About 20,000 adivasis attended—a large number if it is considered that their population was scattered and not very great (the total Chodhri population of Valod was for example only 8,000). The conference was very significantly divided into two separate sections. One of these was devoted to formal proceedings with speeches by Gandhian leaders addressed to a disciplined audience. The nationalists promised to give full support for a vigorous campaign to improve the condition of the adivasis and resolutions were passed advocating the cutting of toddy trees, the closure of liquor shops and propagation of khadi.[88] In the other section of the conference a large number of Devi mediums were brought together. They had been kept apart as it was feared that they might disturb the work of the formal conference. After the formal conference was over Vallabhbhai and Kasturba came to address the Devi mediums. As soon as they entered the mediums went into a state of mass possession, nodding their heads violently and waving red clothes in their hands. After ten minutes they quietened somewhat and Vallabhbhai began to speak, but as soon as they heard him they became once more possessed, shouting '*garam, garam, garam!*' (hot, hot, hot!). The meeting was considered a great success by all concerned.[89]

The First Kaliparaj Conference symbolized in a most striking manner the transition from the old style of politics to the new. Henceforth mass meetings of the adivasis of the Ranimahals were to

[87] Ibid., p. 170.

[88] *Bombay Chronicle*, 7 February 1923. Report by Baroda Police Commissioner, 25 January 1923, BRO, Confidential Dept. 327.

[89] *Rentima Vahan*, p. 171. *Raniparajma Jagrati*, pp. 25–6.

become increasingly secular in tone. Less and less did authority flow from divine possession, more and more from resolutions put to a mass vote. In addition we see at this juncture the emergence of a new leadership among the adivasis. In the past bitter experience had made them wary of outside leadership. Too often they had been betrayed. From this time on however they began to place considerable trust in the Gandhian leaders and give them pride of place at their meetings.

Once accepted by the adivasis the Gandhians tried to modify the Devi movement still further. They believed that the chief value of the movement lay in the atmashuddhi, or self-purification, of the adivasis. By turning over a new leaf in this manner the adivasis would become worthy citizens of independent India. The Gandhians may be said to have anticipated the sanskritization theorists in so far as they assumed that such purification would *in itself* bring about the uplift of the lower orders. They therefore poured cold water on that aspect of the movement which they not only felt to be less important but also socially divisive—and hence unhelpful for national integration— namely the adivasi's challenge to the dominance of the Parsis. When some Parsis came to complain about being boycotted the Gandhians responded by telling the adivasis that while they were right to refuse to carry out impure work for the Parsis, such as serving in liquor shops and tapping toddy trees, they were wrong to refuse to labour in their fields. When a second Kaliparaj Conference was held at Dosvada in Songadh taluka on 25 February 1923 Vallabhbhai Patel sent a message to be read out as follows:

> Everyone is surprised to see the awakening in your community. But you should be very careful. If you try to run too fast, you are likely to fall. Your decision not to work as labourers for Parsis and Muslims is very serious. Whatever steps you take should be well thought out.[90]

Kasturba Gandhi who was presiding over the conference was more blunt: she told the adivasis that they should go back to work for the Parsis.[91] The adivasis did not accept this advice. They argued in reply that the Parsis were extremely cunning and that they had been tricked many times in the past when they had tried to give up liquor. They feared that once they put themselves in the Parsi's power by labouring for them they would be forced to drink. The Parsis were prepared even to hand out free drinks so as to entice them. No longer were they prepared to be lenient to the Parsis. The complete boycott continued.[92]

---

[90] *Raniparajma Jagrati*, p. 70.   [91] Loc. cit.   [92] Ibid., p. 28.

It was perhaps this sort of disagreement between the Gandhians and the adivasis which Collector Macmillan had in mind when he reported that the adivasis had not accepted the leadership of the Gandhians. In other respects however a significant number of adivasis continued to show enthusiasm for the Gandhians and the Gandhian programme. They demonstrated most interest in khadi. Khadi production had not only economic attractions, but a somewhat magical significance for the adivasis. It may be remembered that when they had visions of Gandhi in the well he was seen spinning his charkha. It came to be believed by the adivasis that spinning of cotton on the wheel was a kind of ritual which would hasten both national independence and their own liberation.

Because of this interest in the charkha the adivasis asked for instructors to teach them how to spin and how to maintain the wheels. In 1924 a full-time khadi worker was sent to the Ranimahals. The man chosen was Chunilal Mehta, a Brahman from a village near Ahmedabad city. He went to live with an enthusiastic Chodhri social reformer of Vedchhi village in Valod taluka called Jivan Chodhri.[93] He started a training class in Vedchhi and toured the surrounding villages propagating khadi.[94] In January 1925 the Third Raniparaj Conference was held at Vedchhi (the Gandhians of the British areas had by now adopted Sumant Mehta's term for the adivasis). Gandhi, now out of jail, was president. He was particularly pleased to see large numbers of adivasis spinning khadi yarn.[95] Jivan Chodhri was chairman of the reception committee and in his speech he summed up what his community felt about Gandhi:

> We are satisfied and happy to have with us Jagatguru Bhagwan Mahatma Gandhi. We should worship the perfect god. From now on no other god can give us as much wisdom as this one can.[96]

Over the next two decades in 1928, 1930–1 and 1942 many Chodhris were to live up to this commitment by giving firm support to the Gandhian movement and the Indian national struggle against British rule. Macmillan was therefore wrong when he said that the adivasis had more or less ignored the Gandhians. The alliance between these two groups was fraught with difficulties but it was, still, a very real one.

---

[93] Jugatram Dave, *Khadibhakta Chunibhai* (Ahmedabad, 1966), pp. 13–20.

[94] *Raniparajma Jagrati*, pp. 52–3.

[95] Ibid., pp. 53–4. By this time Chunilal Mehta had sold 520 *charkhas* to the adivasis of the area. Ibid., p. 72.

[96] Ibid., p. 71.

VI

After a year many adivasis began to abandon their vows of temperance and vegetarianism. By mid-1924 Collector Macmillan was reporting an increase in the demand for liquor in the Ranimahals. He re-opened four liquor shops in Mandvi taluka, one in Valod and one in Bardoli.[97] The temperance movement had been undermined not only by the Parsis and officials but also by people within the adivasi community. Opposition came from the many backsliders who failed to keep their vows and also from the adivasi shamans whose honoured position in the old society was threatened by the urge for reform. Many were still suspicious of placing their trust in non-tribal ways of life and leadership. Within a couple of years the conflict within the community had become acute. A divide emerged between the 'Varjelas' or those who followed the new way of life laid down by the Devi, and the 'Sarjelas' or those who had relapsed. The Varjelas tended to be firm supporters of the Gandhian Congress. In some cases they became an isolated minority shunned by other villagers, while in other cases, as in Vedchhi, they were in the majority. On the whole the Varjelas were in a minority. At times the conflict between the two groups became acute. In December 1929 for instance there was a pitched battle between Sarjelas and Varjelas at Pipalvada in Mandvi taluka when some Sarjela Chodhris tried to carry out an animal sacrifice to the Chodhri god Ahin.[98] Some of the commands of the Devi concerning purification continued to be held, however, by the mass of the adivasis. The habits of taking a daily bath, of using water to clean up after defecating and greater cleanliness in the home became general amongst adivasis of the area.

Although the movement for cultural reform thus had its limitations, as a movement for assertion against landlords, moneylenders and liquor dealers it can be judged to have had a considerable success. After the Devi things were never the same again for the Parsis, for just as the nationalist movement had undermined people's awe for the British so had the Devi undermined the adivasi's fear of the Parsi. The struggle was by no means over and during the following decades the

---

[97] *Land Revenue Administration Report of the Bombay Presidency for 1923–24*, pp. 39–40.

[98] B. H. Mehta, 'Social and Economic conditions of the Chodhris', p. 178. Divides such as these have often developed amongst adivasis as a result of reform movements. In some cases the reformed group has become a separate sub-caste. For an example see Roy, pp. 286–90.

Parsis attempted to make a come-back. But the nationalists proved good allies to the adivasis, and Indian independence brought land reforms which, in Gujarat, had greater force than in many other parts of India. For the most part the Parsis and high caste Hindu landlords lost their estates to the tribal peasantry of the Ranimahals.[99] The misfortune of the Parsis was compounded by the imposition of prohibition in Bardoli and Valod talukas in 1938 and in the rest of south Gujarat in 1950. This destroyed their liquor and toddy businesses. Since then the adivasis have enjoyed cheap daru distilled illicitly in their homes. However dubious this beverage may be, one thing is sure—liquor has ceased to be a major fulcrum of exploitation.

The Devi movement can thus be seen as a landmark in the struggle between the adivasis of south Gujarat and their exploiters. However, at the same time, it represented a stage in the growth of a class of richer peasants within the adivasi community. This process had already begun before the Devi movement but it was given a boost by the movement itself, for it helped the more substantial adivasis to achieve both economic independence and respectability within Gujarat society. Since then as the Parsis have declined, so have the richer adivasi peasants become one of the leading exploitative groups within the Ranimahals. There is no need therefore to romanticize this movement. One should rather recognize it for what it was—on the one hand a great liberation but on the other a movement which laid the foundations for new forms of exploitation.

[99] The land was not necessarily distributed equitably; the bigger adivasi landowners benefited most, leading to a growing polarization between rich and poor adivasis in the years since independence. Ghanshyam Shah, 'Tribal Identity and Class Differentiations: A Case Study of the Chaudhri Tribe', in *Economic and Political Weekly*, Annual Number, February 1979, pp. 459–64.

'Encounters and Calamities': The History of a North Indian *Qasba* in the Nineteenth Century.[1]

GYANENDRA PANDEY

The Sources

The history of colonial India has generally been written on the basis of British official records for the simple reason that non-official sources are neither quite so abundant nor as easily accessible. This is especially true for the period up to the end of the nineteenth century, i.e. before organizations like the Indian National Congress had emerged and the memoirs of leaders, as well as newspapers and journals in Indian languages and in English, became available in some number. This paper seeks to re-examine a small part of this earlier colonial history in the light of a local historical account, or more precisely a chronicle of events entitled *Wāqeāt-ō-Hādesāt: Qasba Mubarakpur*, written in the 1880s and preserved in an Urdu manuscript in the qasba of Mubarakpur in the district of Azamgarh,

[1] I am deeply indebted to Qazi Atahar of Muhalla Haidarabad, Mubarakpur, who allowed me to use Sheikh Mohammad Ali Hasan's manuscript history, *Wāqeāt-ō-Hādesāt: Qasba Mubarakpur* (which is maintained in Qazi Atahar's personal library), spent several days translating this and two other valuable documents (referred to in notes 47 and 58 below) that he had traced in the course of his own researches, and helped in many other ways with his intimate knowledge of the area. I owe thanks also to Maulvi Kamruzzaman, Babu Saroj Agrawal and others in Mubarakpur who were unstinting with their time in answering my questions and showing me around.

'*Wāqeāt-ō-Hādesāt*': according to Platts' *Classical Urdu Dictionary*, *Wāqeāt* = 'events, occurrences; accidents; grievous calamities, battles; conflicts; casualties; deaths'; *Hādesāt* = 'new things; accidents; incidents; events; occurrences; adventures; casualties; mishaps; misfortunes; disasters; calamities; afflictions'. 'Events' and 'occurrences' would cover both these terms but I have translated them as 'Encounters and Calamities' in the title of this paper as this seems to me to convey somewhat better the rhetoric and the sense of Ali Hasan's title.

eastern UP. I hope through this re-examination to say something about the way in which the people of Mubarakpur perceived the formidable developments of the period, something of how *they* read their history.

In the past it has generally been the anthropologist rather than the historian who has undertaken this kind of task,[2] and several distinguished anthropologists have written about the experience of small towns and cities under colonialism. As we shall see, some of their observations and conclusions are not entirely inappropriate to the history which is the subject of this paper. Mubarakpur was a major textile centre in the eighteenth and early nineteenth centuries specializing in the production of silk and mixed silk-and-cotton fabrics known as *sangi* and *ghalta*, and dependent to a large extent on the patronage of the courts and the nobility of Awadh, Nepal and other places. The establishment and consolidation of a centralized colonial power, the representative of a powerful manufacturing nation, entailed considerable dislocation in Mubarakpur and its environs. The cloth trade was seriously affected, though it survived better here than in many other textile centres of the region. The rules under which land was held were altered and—with their rent-free lands being reduced, other lands fragmented and sub-divided or sold under the pressure of heavy taxation and increased dependance on cash, credit and markets—many like the Sheikh Muslim zamindars of Mubarakpur and neighbouring areas came under severe pressure. Professional moneylenders and traders apparently entered a period of increased prosperity at the turn of the nineteenth century but did not make such headway as to overthrow the existing relations of power in the qasba of Mubarakpur or the countryside around. In Mubarakpur there were other colonial innovations, among them the establishment of a police outpost, an Imperial Post Office and Middle School. Nevertheless, while the power of the panchayat and the zamindars was much reduced, these remained the major court of appeal for most local disputes; and most of those who studied still obtained a traditional religious education.

[2] This paper was completed before I was able to see C. A. Bayly's 'The Small Town and Islamic Gentry in North India: The Case of Kara' in K. Ballhatchet and J. Harrison (eds.), *The City in South Asia* (London, 1980) or the same author's *Rulers, Townsmen and Bazaars: North Indian Society in the Age of British Expansion 1770–1870* (Cambridge, 1983). Bayly's excellent account of the small town 'gentry' under pressure, based on local non-official as well as official sources, is not however directly concerned with consciousness and the perceptions of change that are central to this essay.

The 'advance towards vagueness' that Geertz writes about for Modjokuto in east central Java[3] might be a suggestive description of the nineteenth-century history of Mubarakpur too. The 'uncertainty', the 'sense of disequilibrium and disorientation' that he and others find among the population of such towns by the end of the colonial period[4] is however scarcely a satisfactory indication of the local people's perceptions and responses, or of their will to live with dignity, to carve out and preserve for themselves areas of independence and honour.

The problem remains one of finding sources adequate to our purpose. In the case of Mubarakpur, while the official colonial records provide us with a particular élite perception (necessarily biased in a certain way), what the *Wāqeāt-ō-Hādesāt* provides is an alternative élite perception, closer to the ground to be sure but not the less one-sided for that. Sheikh Mohammad Ali Hasan, its author, was a member of a local Muslim zamindari family. He wrote the chronicle at an advanced age, within a few years of his death in 1888. And the *Wāqeāt*, without ever referring to the wider politics of the emerging public associations (Muslim or other), mirrors several of the contemporary concerns and attitudes of élite Muslim groups in many different parts of northern India—of men who were in many cases from a zamindari background similar to Ali Hasan's who felt their position in political and economic affairs, as well as important areas of their erstwhile cultural domination, threatened.

We have nothing comparable to the *Wāqeāt* that emanates from the lower classes of Mubarakpur. Yet we are allowed glimpses of how the ordinary labouring people of the qasba spoke and acted—both in the official record relating to a succession of violent outbreaks in the nineteenth century and in Ali Hasan's detailed narration of these and other events. I have been fortunate enough also to gain access to two sketchy but valuable documents that come from the weavers of Mubarakpur: one a petition drawn up by the leaders of the weaving community to try and clear themselves from blame for the violent outbreak of 1813; the other the occasional 'notes' (or diary) of a weaver that dates from the end of our period.

In what follows I first summarize some of the basic information

---

[3] C. Geertz, *The Social History of an Indonesian Town* (Cambridge, Massachusetts, 1965), p. 5.

[4] R. G. Fox, *Urban Anthropology: Cities in their Cultural Settings* (New Jersey, 1977), p. 139.

regarding numbers, occupations and class differences among the people of Mubarakpur in the nineteenth century, and then set out side by side the alternative versions of the history of the qasba as it appears in the official accounts and Ali Hasan's chronicle. I then use the evidence that can be drawn out of these histories and the weavers' own isolated statements to make a few comments regarding subaltern consciousness in nineteenth-century Mubarakpur.

The Qasba

The most important elements in the population of Mubarakpur were the zamindars, the weavers and the trader-moneylenders. There was also a sizeable body of cultivating tenants and labourers as well as men and women belonging to various other service groups. In 1813 the population was estimated at between 10,000 and 12,000. Of these 3,000 were supposed to be 'weavers of the Mussulman cast [sic]', i.e. Julahas, while some were wealthy Hindu traders.[5] In 1881, according to the census of that year, the population was 13,157 (9,066 Muslims and 4,091 Hindus). Among 'actual workers' the principal groups were 143 'landholders'; 560 'cultivators and tenants'; 1,877 weavers; 43 *halwais* (makers and sellers of Indian sweets); 49 *pansaris* (condiment sellers); 254 'general labourers' and 44 'beggars'.[6] By 1901 the population had risen to 15,433 inhabitants—11,442 of them Muslims and the remaining 3,991 Hindus.

The zamindars were the 'leaders' of the qasba in historical memory—since their ancestors had re-established the place in the eighteenth century and presumably induced weavers, traders and other groups to come and settle there[7]—and by virtue of their

[5] UP Regional Archives, Allahabad (hereafter UPRAA): MG4, Judl. Series I, Acc. 169, Vol. 168, R. Martin, Magistrate Goruckpore to G. Dowdeswell, Camp Mobarruckpore, 25 April 1813.

[6] F. H. Fisher, *Statistical, Descriptive and Historical Account of the North Western Provinces, Vol. XIII, Pt I: Azamgarh* (Allahabad, 1883), p. 171.

[7] D. L. Drake-Brockman, *Azamgarh: A Gazetteer, being Vol. XXXIII of the District Gazetteers of the United Provinces of Agra and Oudh* (Allahabad, 1911), notes that little is known of the early history of Mubarakpur. It was said to have been called Qasimabad earlier and to have fallen into decay before it was resettled under the name of Mubarakpur in the eighteenth century (pp. 260–1). For the way in which Maunath Bhanjan and Kopaganj, the other major weaving towns of Azamgarh district, were established and fostered, see my 'Economic Dislocation in Nineteenth-Century Eastern U.P.: Some Implications of the Decline of Artisanal Industry in Colonial India' (Centre for Studies in Social Sciences, Calcutta. 'Occasional Paper' No. 37, May 1981), pp. 15 & 34.

recognition as revenue-payers and local 'representatives' by the colonial authorities. They received a small *kargahi* for every working loom (*kargah*) in the qasba, said to be no more than a few annas in the 1830s but 'highly prized by the Zemindars and cheerfully paid by the weavers'.[8] They also collected certain feudal dues from the local traders and merchants of various castes as well as other dues and services from the weavers and members of other artisanal and service castes.[9] For 'agriculturists' what the Settlement Officer, J. R. Reid, wrote for the district as a whole in 1877 applied to Mubarakpur as well. High-caste tenants, both resident and non-resident—and of these there were few in Mubarakpur—paid a fixed rent in cash or grain; and non-resident low-caste tenants did the same. But resident low-castes called *parjas* (*praja* = subjects) rendered to the landlord 'a number of petty dues and services besides rent, and . . . look[ed] upon him as a feudal superior'. In villages, or qasbas such as Mubarakpur with several proprietors, the parjas were generally distributed among them, but the distribution was not necessarily proportionate to the land held. 'A *parja* allotted to a sharer remains solely his, though the man cultivate[s] land under another sharer, and even though he cease[s] to cultivate land under his superior. The sale and mortgage of *parjas*—that is, of the dues and services they render—is not unknown'.[10]

By this time however the Sheikh zamindars of Mubarakpur held 'only a few villages' and were said to be 'in difficulties'.[11] That there were as many as 143 'landholders' listed among the inhabitants of Mubarakpur, and others living in neighbouring Sikhthi and Amlo also held parts of the qasba, indicates the extent of the sub-division of zamindaris. There is evidence too from early in the century of the impoverished state of several of these zamindars. Thus Rikhai Sahu, 'a Mahajan of considerable wealth' who was killed in the course of a major clash between Hindus and Muslims in April 1813, was reckoned to be 'the chief person' residing in the qasba; and we know that at least two of the zamindars of Mubarakpur were in debt to him. Also

---

[8] J. Thomason, *Report on the Settlement of Chuklah Azimgurh* (Agra, 1837), pp. 130–1.

[9] Azamgarh Collectorate Record Room: Zila Bandobast, Mauza Mubarakpur, Tappa Bihrozpur, Pargana Muhammadabad (1280 F., i.e. AD 1873), *Wajib-ul-arz*, for 'Mubarakpur-Chak Sikhthi', 'Sikhthi-Shah Mahammadpur', 'Mubarakpur Rasulpur', .esp. section 6.

[10] J. R. Reid, *Report on the Settlement of the Temporarily Settled Parganas of Azamgarh District, 1877* (Allahabad, 1881), pp. 86–7.   [11] Ibid., p. 70.

prominent in the events of April 1813 (apparently instrumental in drawing into the fight Hindu zamindars and their men from a wide area around) was Devi Dube of Amlo—'second to (Rikhai Sahu) in point of wealth and influence and more intimately connected with the surrounding zamindars for his having the management of landed property to a considerable extent in the neighbourhood'.[12]

It was the traders and moneylenders who profited most in this period from the cloth trade that was the very life blood of Mubarakpur. Eight or ten years before the outbreak of 1813, Rikhai Sahu had built a grand *thakurduara* outside the south-eastern limits of the qasba which the Gorakhpur magistrate described after personal inspection as 'a beautiful building ornamented with marble images, adorned with gold and silver ornaments'. 'Such a magnificent building was not to be found anywhere else in Azamgarh', Ali Hasan records in his chronicle of events in qasba Mubarakpur.[13] Family tradition has it that under the headship of Babu Ramdas, and therefore probably not long after the events of 1813, the family had a grand *rangmahal* constructed at Ayodhya for use by any relatives who went there on pilgrimage.[14] Again, Bicchuk Kalwar, who was one of the principal targets of attack in another major outbreak of violence in 1842, had 'by great care, pecuniousness, and usury raised himself to be a dabbler in Mahajunee' and built for himself a 'fine, delicate' two-storied house not long before that event. According to the officials who undertook a detailed enquiry in the qasba following this outbreak, Bicchuk was 'a hard unrelenting creditor' who had 'several of the reckless and profligate Mussulman weavers of Mubarakpur' in his debt.[15]

That 'recklessness' and 'profligacy' alone were not responsible for this state of affairs is however made abundantly clear by other evidence. In 1881–2 there were 65 *karkhanas* (or firms) employing a total of 315 artisans for the manufacture of silk and satinette in Mubarakpur and the neighbouring (and far smaller) weaving centre of Khairabad. Together with another 2,168 artisans who worked 'independently', these weavers produced sangi and ghalta valued at approximately Rs 3.5 lakhs per annum.[16]

---

[12] UPRAA: MG4, Judl. Series I, Acc. 169, Vol. 168, Magistrate Gorakhpur's letter of 17 Dec. 1813, para 3.

[13] Ibid., para 4; Ali Hasan, *Wāqeāt-ō-Hādesāt*, pp. 9–10.

[14] Interview with Babu Saroj Agrawal of Mubarakpur.

[15] UPRAA: COG, Judl. Azamgarh, Vol. 68, File 47, Craigee-Morrieson, 25 March 1842.

[16] *Report on the Railway-borne Traffic of the North-Western Provinces and Oudh during the year ending 31 March 1882* (Allahabad, 1883), p. 37.

Yet, as was reported for the most important silk-weaving centre of this area, Banaras, the weavers were bound down by 'hopeless indebtedness to the firms who employ them, and their remuneration depends as little on the demand which may exist for their goods as if their condition was one of actual slavery'. 'Even those [who are] styled independent for want of a better word are in reality in the hands of mahajans, who advance them what is necessary for the support of life and absorb all the profits of their labour'.[17] In Banaras a man who produced in one month a brocade worth Rs 200 was paid a pittance of 2 annas (1/8 of a rupee per day). In Mubarakpur and Khairabad, we are told, 'the *julahas* . . . are miserably poor, but the master weavers are some of them very well off. Three of them are landholders and own indigo factories'.[18]

Such are some of the bare facts of 'economic' relations as they existed among the principal groups of inhabitants in nineteenth-century Mubarakpur. It remains to say a word about the relations of the qasba with the towns and countryside around. There is evidence of prolonged zamindari quarrels for control of land and power in this region during the eighteenth century.[19] This contest appears to have been accentuated by the uncertain conditions produced by the end of nawabi rule, and the nineteenth century is replete with instances of tension and conflict between the zamindars of Mubarakpur and those of neighbouring villages and estates.[20]

At the same time, in more everyday terms, Mubarakpur was like other qasbas something of a nodal point for the economy of the surrounding countryside. Milk and vegetable sellers brought their goods to sell here; a number of weavers came in to work from their homes in nearby villages; and of course the landholders, tenants and

[17] Loc. cit., and ibid., for year ending 31 March 1883, p. 37.

[18] Loc. cit.

[19] In the course of these struggles several of the local notables linked up with some of the greater powers beyond the district such as the Nawab of Awadh, the Raja of Banaras, and the Bangash Pathans who had at one stage extended their influence as far as Jaunpur. In an attempt to resolve the intrigues of men at a higher level the Nawab of Awadh settled the revenue of Azamgarh in 1764 with 'local farmers', among them Mir Fazl Ali of Muhammadabad. But following the Battle of Buxar, Azam Khan, the Raja of Azamgarh, appears to have regained favour at the court and his authority over the district. On his death in 1771 the district was put under a *chakladar* under whom it remained until 1801. See Drake-Brockman, *Azamgarh Gazetteer*, pp. 172–3; A. L. Srivastava, *The First Two Nawabs of Oudh* (Lucknow, 1933).

[20] Several examples will be found in the discussion below. See also Thomason, *Settlement of Chuklah Azimgurh* (1837), pp. 130–1; Reid, *Settlement of Azamgarh District 1877*, pp. 70–1.

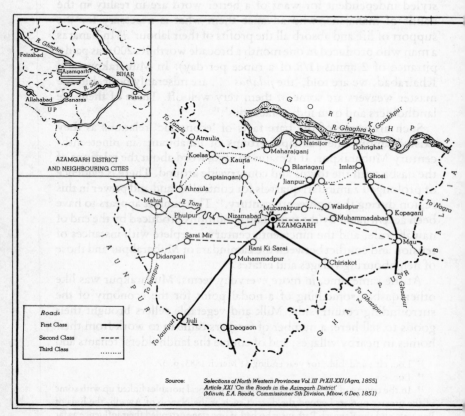

AZAMGARH DISTRICT
AND NEIGHBOURING CITIES

Roads
First Class
Second Class
Third Class

Source: *Selections of North Western Provinces Vol. III Pt XII-XXI (Agra, 1855),*
Article XXI 'On the Roads in the Azimgarh District'
(Minute, E.A. Reade, Commissioner 5th Division, Mhow, 6 Dec. 1851)

Mubarakpur and Azamgarh Road Links, *circa* 1850

cultivators of the place held and worked a certain amount of land outside Mubarakpur. But in the vicinity there were other centres that vied for this position of leadership as meeting-place and reference-point.

Six miles south-east of Mubarakpur stood the substantial qasba of Muhammadabad Gohna (or simply Muhammadabad), residence of pargana officers and a *qazi* under nawabi rule and headquarters of the pargana and tahsil of Muhammadabad under British administration (see map). Eight miles west of it was Azamgarh town, founded and nurtured by the important family of the rajas of Azamgarh since the seventeenth century, enjoying fairly good road communications at least from that time and further favoured when it was adopted as the headquarters of a British district from 1832.

Consequently Mubarakpur seems never to have been very important as a commercial or administrative centre. Whereas a bazaar or retail market for the sale of sundry commodities was held here twice a week in the later nineteenth century, Muhammadabad had a similar bazaar four times a week. Significantly too the list of 'principal occupations' for Muhammadabad at the beginning of the 1880s included 'petty bankers and traders' and 'shopkeepers' as well as 'landowners', 'agriculturists', weavers and other artisans. Recall that the first two groups were not numerous enough to be mentioned in the corresponding list of 'principal occupations' for Mubarakpur.[21]

It is interesting to compare the above information with that regarding Maunath Bhanjan (or Mau), the other major cloth-producing centre of Azamgarh district in the nineteenth century. Mau, with a population that was only slightly larger than that of Mubarakpur in 1881 (14,945 against Mubarakpur's 13,157), appears to have combined in itself the roles of Mubarakpur and Muhammadabad, and added a little more besides, since it was that much further from the district headquarters (see map). A bazaar was held here daily and the 'principal occupations' included: employment under the government or municipality; 'ministers of the Hindu religion'; domestic servants; hackney-carriage keepers and drivers; palanquin keepers and bearers; 'messengers'; landholders; cultivators and tenants; agricultural

---

[21] Fisher, *Statistical, Descriptive and Historical Account of . . . . Azamgarh*, pp. 171, 176. I have some doubts about the accuracy of occupational details for Mubarakpur as found in this report but have unfortunately not managed to obtain the district census data for either 1881 or 1891. Nevertheless the general point made here remains valid, I think.

labourers; carpenters; weavers; cloth merchants (*bazzaz*); tailors; shoe-makers and sellers; washermen; corn and flour dealers; general labourers; and beggars.[22]

The accompanying map of road links in the mid-nineteenth century shows, too, the poor state of the long distance communications of Mubarakpur. This is one reason why Maharajganj on the Choti Sarju river, which lay some fifteen miles north-west of Azamgarh town and not far from the border of Awadh, had become the chief mart for cloths from Mubarakpur (as well as from Mau, Kopaganj and other places).

The nineteenth century brought important changes in communications, the direction of trade and Mubarakpur's general outlook on the world. The movement of traffic to and from Azamgarh seems always to have been northward towards the Ghaghra and southward towards the Ganga, not eastward and westward. This remained the case throughout the nineteenth century both for Azamgarh district as a whole and for the qasba of Mubarakpur. But soon after the uprising of 1857–9 the old road from Allahabad and Jaunpur through Azamgarh town and Jianpur to Dohrighat and (across the Ghaghra) to Gorakhpur was metalled. So was the road linking Dohrighat with Mau and Ghazipur. Within the next couple of decades metalled roads were also developed to connect Azamgarh town directly with Ghazipur and Banaras, and (through Muhammadabad) with Mau on the east. By the end of the century a branch railway line had also been laid to connect Azamgarh and Muhammadabad with Mau, from where a section of the Bengal and North-Western Railway ran to Banaras.

The opening up of the interior and the growing influx of mill-cloth from Britain led also to a reversal in the direction of the cloth trade. In the later nineteenth century the East Indian and Oudh and Rohilkhand railways, fed by the improved roads, became the main passages out of Azamgarh district for sugar exports to the south and west and indigo exports to the east, and into it for imports of not only raw cotton and grain but cloth, metal and 'other manufactured wares'.[23] After the artificial 'boom' in exports created by the East India Company's 'investments' at the beginning of the nineteenth century, the balance of trade in quality cloth had soon turned against the district. The weaving industry of Mubarakpur survived rather better than that of the other neighbouring textile centres: 'In silk fabrics, especially of

22 Ibid., p. 169.
23 Reid, *Settlement 1877*, p. 23.

the mixed kind manufactures in this district', one official observed, 'there is a peculiar adaptation to local conditions and prejudices, which enables the industry to hold its own, or at least to *decline less slowly than it would otherwise have done*'.[24] Thus the exports of sangi and ghalta (along with some cottons from Mau and Kopaganj) continued.[25] But the scale was much reduced, the increasing competition for raw material and its cost tended to increase dependence on moneylenders and other intermediaries; and the trade depression of the 1870s to 1890s dealt yet another crippling blow to the local industry, compelling many of the weavers of Mubarakpur to shift to the weaving of cotton handkerchiefs and turbans which were now 'more in demand than satins'.[26]

By the end of the century the chief exports of Azamgarh were refined sugar and oilseeds (and, one might add, labour in the form of migrants to the industrial belt of eastern India and colonial plantations overseas): 'with the money obtained therefrom, and from their relatives abroad, the inhabitants meet their revenue and the cost of their litigation, and pay for the cloth, metal goods and foodgrains they have to import'.[27] The situation of Mubarakpur was in essentials the same. By this time, it would be fair to say, Mubarakpur faced not, as it had done at the start of our period, north and west to Maharajganj, Nepal and the kingdom of Awadh, but south—to the road and the railway that linked the qasba with the district headquarters and with Ghazipur, Banaras and faraway Calcutta. What bearing all this had on power relations within the qasba and the consciousness of its people is a theme that should emerge out of the 'histories' that have been handed down to us.

Two 'Histories'

If one draws up a chronology of events in nineteenth-century Mubarakpur from the official records and from Ali Hasan's *Wāqeāt*,

[24] A. Yusuf Ali, *A Monograph on Silk Fabrics Produced in the North-Western Provinces and Oudh* (Allahabad, 1900), p. 103. Emphasis added.

[25] Ibid., 170; Fisher, *Statistical, Descriptive and Historical Account of Azamgarh*, p. 124.

[26] Drake-Brockman, *Azamgarh Gazetteer*, p. 262. See also Gorakhpur Commissioner's Record Room, Dept. XIII, File 40/1905–9, 'Rules for the relief of distressed weavers' that became necessary (as the Chief Secretary to the Government put it in a circular to District Officers on 28 Jan. 1908) 'owing to scarcity and high prices having rendered it difficult, and in some cases impossible for them [the weavers] to find a market for their manufactured goods'.

[27] C. E. Crawford, *Final Report on the Seventh Settlement of the Azamgarh District of the United Provinces, 1908 A. D.* (Allahabad, 1908), p. 9.

one obtains very different results. I set out these chronologies in the table below, placing Ali Hasan's more detailed list of events on the left (see Table 1).

I have omitted from the right-hand column some purely administrative 'Events' such as the establishment of a Police Station in 1813 or its reduction to a smaller police outpost later on, and included in both columns certain '*Non*-Events' or '*Near* Events' (N) that were recorded by the respective sources as being of significance for one reason or another. It is plain that what makes an Event in the official reckoning is a marked positive or negative correlation with the question of 'law and order'. Everything in this account is dated from the 'accession' of 1801, which allegedly divides darkness from light, the days of 'order' and 'improvement' from the previous regime of 'anarchy' and 'misrule'. 1857 is a notable Non-Event, for in this dangerous moment when 'order', 'progress' and 'civilization' were threatened all over northern India, Mubarakpur remained peaceful. Horne, the Magistrate of Azamgarh, reported in September 1857 that the Muhammadabad tahsil was the 'best' in the district, with 'crime' low and roads safe. It was a matter for self-congratulation as 'there is great distress at present in Mubarakpur and Mhow, in each of which places there are about 5,000 Julahas, who have lost all their capital by the robbery of their stocks of manufactured goods, which had been sent out for sale at the time of the outbreak'. Moreover 'these people are generally very turbulent'. On this occasion however they had been 'excellently kept in order by the tehseeldar Mahomed Tukee, who deserves great credit every way'.[28]

Almost all the other entries in the official chronology relate to outbreaks or threatened outbreaks of violence over the desecration of religious symbols—proof in this view of the essential irrationality and fanaticism of the local people, ingredients that would ensure a return to anarchy if ever the controlling hand of the colonial power were to be withdrawn. Often there is a harking back to 1813, the year of 'the great disturbances' in Mubarakpur when 'disorder reigned for several days unchecked'.[29] Or as the Azamgarh District Gazetteer of 1911 put it in a classic summary of the history of Mubarakpur since 'accession':

[28] *Parliamentary Papers. House of Commons. Accounts and Papers. Vol. 44, Pt 3. 1857–58*, Memorandum on Azamgarh, 11 Sept. 1857 (p. 571).

[29] UPRAA: COG, Judl. Azamgarh, Vol. 68, File 47, Thomason-Currie, 23 May 1835; ibid., Letter no. 96, Sessions Judge Azamgarh to Commissioner 5th Division, 29 May 1844.

TABLE 1: *Chronology of Events in Mubarakpur in the Nineteenth Century*[30]

	According to the Wāqeāt-ō-Hadesāt			According to the Official Records			
Event	Date	Nature of Occurrence	Supposed Implications	Event	Date	Nature of Occurrence	Supposed Implications
I	Late 1790s	Shia-Sunni riot. One killed.	Pro-Shia stance of local Nawabi officials.	1	1801	'Accession'. Establishment of direct British administration in Azamgarh and eastern UP.	Establishment of law and order.
II	1810 (1226 Hijri)	'Nakku Shahi'. Shia-Sunni quarrel; Nakku seriously wounded.					
III	1813	'Rikhai Shahi'. Great Hindu-Muslim clash. Arson and looting for nine days. Rikhai Sahu and numerous others killed.	Growing insolence of Hindu money-lenders. the bravery of the Mubarakpur Muslims.	2	1813	Great 'disturbance', sanguinary battle and plunder for days until British magistrate and troops arrived.	Religious fanaticism. Breakdown of law and order.
IV	n.d.	Suicide of a Brahman.					
N1	n.d.	Cow killed, head placed on platform. Riot averted by local officials.	Greatness of British rule.				

[30] In this Table the words 'Supposed Implications' refer to inferences which are neither explicitly drawn or implied in the relevant records; 'N' stands for an occurrence or incident that is mentioned in the records but does not rank as a major 'Event'.

(Table 1 *continued*)

		According to the *Waqāeʾ-ō-Hādesāt*				According to the Official Records	
Event	Date	Nature of Occurrence	Supposed Implications	Event	Date	Nature of Occurrence	Supposed Implications
V	n.d.	'Katuaru Shahi'. Katuaru, a tailor, apprehended and killed during a burglary.					
VI	n.d.	'Ali Shahi'. Quarrel between two teams of wrestlers. One killed.					
VII	1832 (1247 H.)	'Daka Zani'. Several dacoits apprehended and killed while attacking a money-lender's house.	Bravery of the townsfolk.				
VIII	1834	'Sukhlal Shahi'. Piglet killed and placed on Panj-i-Sharif. Sukhlal Singh, Hindu *barkandaz* wounded, succumbed to injuries.		3	1834	Dead pig on Panj-i-Sharif. Hindu *barkandaz* who went to investigate received several sword-cuts.	Near breakdown of law and order.
N2	1834–41	Successful tenure of Mirza Wali Beg as thanadar or Mubarakpur.		N1	1835	Dead pig on a *chauk*. *Thanadar* had it quickly removed.	Near breakdown of law and order.

IX	1842	'Bicchuk Shahi'. Clash between Muslims and Hindu moneylenders. Several of the latter killed.	4 1842	Serious riot. Several killed.	Religious fanaticism. Breakdown of law and order.
X	1849 (1265 H.)	'Doma Shahi'. Quarrel between two teams of wrestlers. One killed.			
XI	n.d.	'Karima-Shahi'. Murder of a girl and theft of her jewellery.			
XII	1850 (1266 H.)	'Daka Zani'. Dacoits attacked a money-lender's house. Chased away by townsfolk.	Solidarity and bravery of the townsfolk.		
XIII	n.d.	'Tilanga Shahi'. Suicide of a sepoy carried away by his grief while participating in the lamentations at Muharram.			

(Table 1 *continued*)

| | | According to the *Wāqeāt-ō-Hādesāt* | | | | According to the Official Records | |
Event	Date	Nature of Occurrence	Supposed Implications	Event	Date	Nature of Occurrence	Supposed Implications
XIV	1851 (1267 H.)	'Baqridu Shahi'. Baqridu killed in a game of *kabaddi*.					
XV	n.d.	'Amanullah Shahi'. Amanullah, *hajjam*, apprehended and killed during burglary.					
XVI	n.d.	'Faqruddin Shahi'. Faqruddin killed a pig and placed its carcass on the Jama Masjid, nearly causing a riot.					
XVII	1857	Mubarakpur threatened repeatedly by the rebels, but preparations and warnings staved off any attack.	Renowned bravery of townsfolk. Courageous leadership of the zamindars and *sardars* of the qasba.	N2	1857	No disturbance, though great distress among the weavers.	Near breakdown of law and order. Yeoman service by local officials.

The Jublahganj of Mubarakpur constitutes the major part of the... and commercial... feature of religious antipathy between the... able Muslim town and neighbourhood is always such... Serious... occurred between the two from time to... between... and 1904. The features of all these disturbances... similar... the question of what took place on the first occasion will suffice to indicate their character. In 1813 a party was... including, within the grounds of a Hindu temple or a building... next Muharram, made a platform was as follow: first by the... the statue of a cow by the Muhammadans, and then by the... platform and of a neighbouring assembly with pig's blood... The Muslim trader was killed by cruelly murdering a rich... merchant called... by name Rikhi Sahu, by plundering his... house and by destroying a handsome temple which he had erected. Thereupon the whole Hindu population of the vicinity rose and a sanguinary battle ensued in which the Muhammadans were overpowered after many had been killed and wounded on both sides. The Muslim party of the town fled... and the place was given up to plunder for some days till a magistrate... arrived with troops from Gorakhpur and restored order. Similar disturbances occurred in 1893–94 and punitive police were quartered on the town for several months.

The power of auto-suggestion displayed here is truly remarkable. Consider the writer's statement on the 'disturbances of 1893–94'. 1893 was a year of widespread strife between groups of Hindus and Muslims, when the agitation for cow protection led to violent demonstrations and clashes in many places in Azamgarh and other districts of this region. Now both the detail... the official records relating to these events, however... consistent... the newspaper is reported that Mubarakpur was involved in these outbreaks. Nor is the qasba included in the list of places... upon which a punitive police force was... that... disturbances had occurred at numerous... places... Ghazipur, Shahabad and Ballia, not to mention Mau, Azamgarh... and most of other places close to Mubarakpur... in the compiler... of the District Gazetteer... that serious communal animosity between Muslims and Hindus was always smouldering. There were serious conflicts between them in 1813, 1842 and 1904, or 'from time to time' in his phrase. So the utterances of 1893–94 which were not mentioned at the beginning of the paragraph on the history of...

... Gazetteer, op. cit. 96–7.
?? For an account of these, see the Railway Board etc. Commission studies in the... District Report, e.1885–191..., tabulated in...

XVIII	1877	'Manohar Shahi'. Prolonged dispute over Manohar Das Agrawal's building of a temple inside the qasba.	Qasba tradition defended.
N3	1860–80s	Repair and extension of Jama Masjid, Imambarah, etc. through contributions of all castes and communities.	Qasba tradition honoured.
5	1860	Introduction of local administration under Act XX of 1856. Local revenue to pay for police and 'improvement'.	Extension of local self-government and works of 'improvement'.
6	1893–4	'Religious disturbances'.	Religious fanaticism. Breakdown of law and order.
7	1904	Riot.	Religious fanaticism. Breakdown of law and order.

The Muhammadans [of Mubarakpur] consist for the most part of fanatical and clannish Julahas, and the fire of religious animosity between them and the Hindus of the town and neighbourhood is always smouldering. Serious conflicts have occurred between the two from time to time, notably in 1813, 1842 and 1904. The features of all these disturbances are similar, so that a description of what took place on the first occasion will suffice to indicate their character. In 1813 a petty dispute about the inclosing within the grounds of a Hindu temple of a little piece of land near a Muhammadan *takia* platform was followed first by the slaughter on the spot of a cow by the Muhammadans and then by the defiling of the platform and of a neighbouring *imambara* with pig's blood by the Hindus. The Muhammadans retaliated by cruelly murdering a wealthy Hindu merchant of the place name Rikhai Sahu, by plundering and burning his house and by defacing a handsome temple which he had erected. Hereupon the whole Hindu population of the vicinity rose and a sanguinary battle ensumed in which the Muhammadans were overpowered after many had been killed and wounded on both sides. The inhabitants of the town fled and the place was given up to plunder for some days till a magistrate arrived with troops from Gorakhpur and restored order. Similar disturbances occurred in 1893–94 and punitive police were quartered on the town for several months.[31]

The power of auto-suggestion displayed here is truly remarkable. Consider the writer's statements on the 'disturbances of 1893–94'. 1893 was a year of widespread strife between groups of Hindus and Muslims, when the agitation for cow protection led to violent demonstrations and clashes in many places in Azamgarh and other districts of this region.[32] Nowhere in the detailed official records relating to these events, however, or in contemporary newspapers is it reported that Mubarakpur was involved in these outbreaks. Nor is the qasba included in the list of villages and towns upon which a punitive police force was imposed in their wake. But riots *had* occurred at numerous spots in Banaras and Ghazipur, Shahabad and Ballia, not to mention Mau and Kopa, Azmatgarh and a host of other places close to Mubarakpur. And in Mubarakpur itself, as the compiler of the District Gazetteer saw it, 'the fire of religious animosity' between Muslims and Hindus was 'always smouldering'. There were serious conflicts between them in 1813, 1842 and 1904: or 'from time to time' in his phrase. So the 'disturbances of 1893–94' which were not mentioned at the beginning of this paragraph on the history of

[31] Drake-Brockman, *Azamgarh Gazetteer*, pp. 260–1.
[32] For an account of these, see my 'Rallying Round the Cow: Sectarian Strife in the Bhojpuri Region, *c.* 1888–1917', in R. Guha (ed.), *Subaltern Studies II* (Delhi, 1983).

Mubarakpur had become a major Event by the end of it, 'and
punitive police were quartered on the town for several months'.[33]

Ali Hasan's *Wāqeāt-ō-Hādesāt* gives us a very different 'history'.
First, it contains no reference to the 'accession' of 1801, that favourite
date of colonial administrators of the region. There is a statement, in
the discussion on Event II, that the British power was already installed.
But in this narrative the Great Event, the turning-point, is Event
III—the 'Rikhai Shahi' of 1813. 'British rule' it would seem was
established only when an English magistrate and troops first arrived
in Mubarakpur after the outbreak of violence in April that year. It
was in 1813 we are told, after the 'riot', that a *thana* was established in
Mubarakpur and courts in Azamgarh[34]—though the latter suggestion
is clearly incorrect for it was only in 1820 that a Deputy Magistracy
under the Jaunpur collectorate was established at Azamgarh, and
Muhammadabad pargana (which contained Mubarakpur) was then
part of Ghazipur district.

This difference in perspective is not attributable simply to the
inevitable distance that separates a local from a wider—regional,
national or colonial—view. If 1801 was the beginning of a new era in
colonialist reckoning for obvious reasons, 1813 was for equally good
reasons a watershed in the eyes of the people of Mubarakpur which
became a point of reference for a long time afterwards. This was not
however—as officials would have it—because of the 'delightful license'
to plunder that 1813 had provided.[35] (Otherwise 1857 would have
been welcomed as another great opportunity for this pastime: on the
contrary, the people of Mubarakpur prepared for battle to defend the
qasba's moneylenders when these were threatened by rebels in the
vicinity[36]). What 1813 stood for locally was a dreadful calamity—
such a blood-bath, writes Ali Hasan, that 'God save every Musalman
from such a fate' (*Wāqeāt-ō-Hādesāt*, p. 18)—and what people
feared was the repetition of such a massacre. So in N1 (see Table 1)
the thanadar Mirza Karam Ali Beg promised that what had happened
in the 'Rikhai Shahi' would not happen again (*Wāqeāt*, p. 22). Or
more strikingly in Event VII, the armed dacoity of 1832, Muslim

---

[33] Yet the District Gazetteers compiled by the British are relied upon heavily by
most writers on the political history of colonial India. And the argument is still readily
put forward that 'the interpretation may be biased, but the facts are correct'.

[34] *Wāqeāt-ō-Hādesāt*, p. 20.

[35] COG, Judl. Azamgarh, Vol. 68, File 47, Sessions Judge Azamgarh to Commissioner 5th Division, 29 May 1844.

[36] Ali Hasan, *Wāqeāt-ō-Hādesāt*, pp. 60–73.

youth like Fateh and his comrades moved to the defence of Babu Ramdas, mahajan, with some slight hesitation because the dacoits were Hindus (mainly Rajputs) and the youths did not want to arouse Hindu fears of another 'Muslim' attack upon Hindus (*Wāqeāt*, p. 30). It is noteworthy too that Ali Hasan undertook to write this history, as he tells us in a prefatory statement, one day in the early 1880s when conversation turned to the bloodshed of 1813 and someone remarked that such a holocaust had never occurred before or since (*Wāqeāt*, p. 1).

The difference between the colonialist outlook and that of the *Wāqeāt* is revealed very clearly indeed in the criterion employed for the selection of Events. If it is the question of 'law and order', its consolidation, its breakdown or its being endangered, that made an Event in the colonialist reckoning, it seems to have been 'unnatural death' that did so in Ali Hasan's. Thirteen of the eighteen Events recorded in the *Wāqeāt*—all except II, XII, XVI, XVII and XVIII (see Table 1)—involved the violent death of one or more persons killed in the course of quarrels, riots, dacoities and, in two cases (IV and XIII), through suicide. Of the remaining five Events too, two involved casualties. In the 'Nakku Shahi', Event II, Nakku was badly beaten up and left for dead, though Ali Hasan tells us that he died a natural death shortly after the termination of the court case that arose out of this incident. (*Wāqeāt*, pp. 6–7). In Event XVII (1857) of course there was a considerable amount of violence and deaths all around; and the author takes care to note what he calls 'the only death of the Mutiny period' in Mubarakpur—that of a young lad called Magrooh, attacked one night as he was returning from the Katra bazaar by some constables from the local police outpost, possibly on account of a personal grudge (*Wāqeāt*, p. 73). The very title of Ali Hasan's chronicle, *Wāqeāt-ō-Hādesāt*, with its suggestion of disasters and calamities, perhaps reflects this concern with violent, 'unnatural' occurrences and incidents, interruptions in the normal progress of the life of the qasba.

To put it differently and perhaps more fairly, what makes an Event in the eyes of the author of the *Wāqeāt* is its 'public' character—the fact that the qasba community as a whole was interested, involved in or affected by a particular happening. It is possible to say a little more about this collective, the 'public', for with all the attention to violence and death there are certain other principles of selection at work in the compilation of this 'history'. The *Wāqeāt* is very clearly a *Muslim* account. This perhaps is one reason why N1 in the Table above, an incident in which a cow was killed and its head placed on a *chauk*, and an explosive situation developed, is mentioned but not given the status of an independent Event, whereas No. XVI which is very similar—a piglet being killed and placed on the Jama Masjid, and tension mounting—is discussed as a major Event, the 'Faqruddin Shahi'. The nature of the discussion on this Event is even more revealing. Ali Hasan begins by saying that now he has to write about a great outrage, an insult to Muslims, perpetrated by a Muslim (Faqruddin): 'but since the *wāqeāt* [occurrences, misfortunes] of the qasba are being related, it is necessary to include this incident too' (*Wāqeāt*, p. 56). 'Faqruddin' means 'the pride of religion', but this man should have been called 'Faqrushsheyatin'—'the pride of the *shaitans* (devils)', for he betrayed his religion by this base deed in the hope of profiting from the plunder that might follow. Fortunately such a calamity was averted. Faqruddin was discovered to have been the rogue responsible for the act, arrested and sentenced to three years rigorous imprisonment. On his return he was not accepted back into the community, for he was '*zalil-o-khar*' (base and dis-agreeable).[37] He was still alive when Ali Hasan wrote, had become a faqir, wandered from village to village and was known as Pakhurdia *badmaash*. (*Wāqeāt*, p.60).

Equally significant is the choice of other Non-Events (N2 and N3) that are included in the record, and of the remaining Event that was unaccompanied by unnatural death or grievous injury—the 'Manohar Shahi' of 1877 (Event XVIII). N2 refers to Mirza Wali Beg's 'memorable' tenure as thanadar of Mubarakpur. What made it memorable, we learn from the brief entry, was that Wali Beg, a Shia, called excellent *marsia* readers to participate in the Muharram cele-brations in the qasba: this was something that people still remarked upon forty years later when Ali Hasan wrote (*Wāqeāt*, p. 35).[38] N3 relates to the repair of the *mazār* of Raja Mubarak Shah, a Sufi saint of the eighteenth century after whom Mubarakpur was named, and the

[37] According to Ali Hasan a similar punishment was meted out to those Muslims who gave evidence against Muslims involved in the attack on Hindu moneylenders and the temple in 1842. They were thrown out of the community and not re-accepted even after two of them had performed the *haj* to Mecca: '*lekin yah daag hamesha ke liye raha aur tamam Musalmanon men hamesha zalil-o-khar rahe*': *Wāqeāt-ō-Hādesāt*, pp. 45.
[38] For the central place of the Muharram celebrations in the life of other such habitations, see Rahi Masoom Raza, *Aadha Gaon* (Delhi, 1966), *passim*.

repair and extension of the Jama Masjid and Imambarah that were built adjacent to it, tasks that had gone on for twenty years and more from 1866–7 until the last pages of the *Wāqeāt* came to be written. And Event XVIII (which does not find place in the colonial 'history') was a long drawn out dispute that arose when Manohar Das, mahajan, challenged a long established custom by building a *shivalaya* (temple) within the limits of the qasba.

The last two entries lead us on to a rather different perspective. The *Wāqeāt* is the work of a Muslim who is steeped in and deeply concerned about the traditions of an isolated qasba, settled in the eighteenth century by Sheikh Muslim zamindars and made prosperous by the patronage of the nawabs of Awadh and other contemporary rulers. 'Mubarakpur', rather than 'British rule' or even the 'Muslim community', emerges as the real hero of this story. There is striking testimony to this in Ali Hasan's discussion of the defence of the qasba's Hindu moneylenders on different occasions when they were attacked by dacoits (Events VII and XII and again in 1857, Event XVII).

When the 'Daka Zani' of 1832 (Event VII) occurred a large number of townsfolk turned out as the cry went up for help from the house of Babu Ramdas, mahajan: such a crowd congregated that 'it was difficult to find standing space' inside or around the house. The dacoit gang was surrounded, engaged in battle and a number of its members killed. Later on, Ali Hasan tells us, a wounded dacoit who was arrested told the magistrate of the district that the gang included such renowned and dreaded dacoits as Bagi Singh and Chatar Singh, that they had attacked and looted all sorts of places before, including the government treasury, but no one had stood up to them until they encountered the 'warlike' (*jangi*) men of Mubarakpur (*Wāqeāt*, pp. 30–2).

In 1857 Rajab Ali, the rebel landowner of village Bamhur a couple of miles south-west of Mubarakpur, announced his intention of plundering the mahajans of the qasba in a letter addressed to Sheikh Gada Husain, zamindar, and Baksh Mehtar, '*sardar nurbaf*', the head of the weavers. 'Everyone' in Mubarakpur was enraged, writes Ali Hasan, and after consultations Gada Husain threw back the challenge to Rajab Ali with the warning that if the rebels tried to enter Mubarakpur to loot the mahajans they would have to bear all the consequences. 'Do you think that the inhabitants of Mubarakpur are dead that you have made this decision [to loot the mahajans]? If ever again such a threat [*kalma*, literally 'word'] escapes from your mouth, then you should prepare to defend your own village. Let us see who has the greater abilities in war' (*Wāqeāt*, p.63). And regarding a further message (possibly, a ruse) in which Rajab Ali expressed his desire to make offerings at the Panj-i-Sharif and Raja Sahib's *mazār* in Mubarakpur, the 'Mubarakpur people together' wrote in reply that four or five persons could come unarmed and fulfil this wish for prayer. But if a larger number came or any were armed, then '*tum apnon ko misl shirini-niaz ke tassawur karna* (you can think of yourselves as sweets which will be distributed and eaten). We have 1,700 guns and 9 maunds of powder and shot ready for you' (*Wāqeāt*, p. 64).

It is noteworthy too that Ali Hasan emphasizes that all castes and communities, Hindu as well as Muslim, contributed to the repair of Raja Mubarak Shah's *mazār* and certain extensions of the Jama Masjid. We are told that the Hindu mahajans of Mubarakpur revered the memory of Raja Sahib and lit lamps and made offerings of sweets at his *mazār* every Thursday. But the poor state of the walls of the Jama Masjid, which lay in the same compound as the *mazār*, meant that 'dogs and cats' got to these offerings and put out the lamps. Sometime in 1866–7 (1281 H.) therefore Sheikh Gada Husain, a widely respected and influential zamindar, appealed to the mahajans to help in the repair of these walls. Ali Hasan records that the latter responded very generously indeed at that time and later on, so that 'the entire wall along the length of the *mazār* was built through the donations of the Hindus', and work estimated to take all of six months for repairing the walls and the floors, as well as for the construction of a washroom and excavation of a well adjacent to the mosque, was completed in four (*Wāqeāt*, pp. 86, 88).[39]

Ali Hasan's description of the defence of the traditions of the qasba in the 'Manohar Shahi' of 1877—occurring as it did while the joint endeavours described above were still in progress—is again instructive. When it was discovered that Manohar Das had built a small shivalaya inside the compound of his house, anger flared up among the Muslims of Mubarakpur. It should be mentioned that there was already a history of such moneylender encroachment on the rights of the Muslims as embodied in the traditions of the place: in 1813, Angnu

---

[39] For a similar corporate identity and pride in other Muslim qasbas in the region, and the role of the Sufis in their establishment, see Bayly, *Rulers, Townsmen and Bazaars*, Ch. 9, esp. pp. 366–7.

(Aknu?) Kalwar had built a shivalaya inside the qasba and an attempted
extension of its boundary was the immediate cause of the outbreak of
violence on that occasion; in the years before the 1842 outbreak too
there had been continuous friction between the mahajans and the
Muslims after Bicchuk Kalwar and Babu Ramdas Agrawal had
extended a wall onto the road and thus created an obstruction in the
path of the *tazias* taken out in procession during the Muharram.[40]
Now in 1877 Sheikh Gada Husain and other Muslim leaders questioned
Manohar Das over this new development and, receiving no satisfactory
reply, reported the matter at the police station in Muhammadabad
and to the Collector in Azamgarh. The latter came to Mubarakpur to
make an on-the-spot enquiry along with another English official who
was, by chance, already there and some of the exchanges that Ali
Hasan reports as having taken place before them are of the utmost
interest.

Manohar Das argued that he had built the temple within the
compound of his own house and the zamindars had nothing to do
with that area. He pointed out too that the Muslims of Mubarakpur
built mosques and other places of worship wherever they liked
without objection from any source; that no more than five or seven
months ago Faqir Kunjra erected a *masjid* close to a place that was
sacred to the Hindus and 'we did not object'. Yet the Muslims wished
to destroy the small shivalaya that he had built inside his own house:
this was nothing but 'a show of power and tyranny'. To this Muslim
leaders replied that Faqir Kunjra had built his masjid with the permission of 'us zamindars': all the zamindars of Mubarakpur were
Muslims, none Hindu—so 'what right had the Hindus to object or
allow?' (*Wāqeāt*, pp. 77–8, 81–2).

Gada Husain put the rest of the case against Manohar Das's new
shivalaya as follows: Raja Mubarak was 'the guiding light of his age'
and the founder of Mubarakpur. It was Raja Sahib's 'blessing' that
had maintained the prosperity of Mubarakpur, and it was his *farman*
(injunction) that 'when any person shall try to rise higher than me in
this habitation [i.e. erect a building that rises higher than the height of
Raja Sahib's mazār], he and his line will be no more'. The qasba had
many great and very wealthy mahajans and many rich Muslims as
well, Gada Husain said. But because of Raja Sahib's farman, 'no one
has a two-storied house'. Only once was this injunction defied, when

[40] See Pandey, 'Rallying Round the Cow' for an analysis of the circumstances
leading to these outbreaks.

Angnu Sahu had a shivalaya built inside the town. He spent a great sum of money and all the Hindus of the town worshipped there. But, Gada Husain went on, the shivalaya lasted less than ten years. In the plunder, arson and bloodshed of 1813 which raged for nine days and nights, the building was destroyed and Angnu killed while his son 'so lost his mind that he began to eat the food of the Musalmans, and perished in his madness. Now no one survives from that family'. (*Wāqeāt*, pp. 81–2). Ultimately the shivalaya was dismantled, but that is not the point of this digression.

What emerges from the evidence is a certain picture of the author of the *Wāqeāt-ō-Hādesāt*, or should we say the 'authors'. For it is necessary to stress the unusual nature of this 'history', which appears very much in the form of a collective catalogue. Quite unlike the practice of the standard 'histories' we have become used to since colonial times,[41] there is no attempt here to authenticate the chronicle that is presented. The narrative, it appears, requires no 'proof'. It is the inherited knowledge of the qasba, or at least those sections of it that for Ali Hasan represented the qasba. In the sole instance of direct authorial intervention found in the manuscript, which comes in the prefatory statement referred to above, it is stated that the idea of putting together this chronicle arose out of a conversation in the Middle School at Mubarakpur, when someone remarked that the bloodshed of 1813 had been unprecedented and unrepeated, and Gada Husain asked Ali Hasan to undertake this task as 'a labour of love' (*Wāqeāt*, p. 1). It is important to look at the construction of this narrative, then, not simply as the product of a single authorial voice, but rather to carefully consider its different constitutive aspects. For this reason it may help to dwell a little longer on the *Wāqeāt*'s perception of some of the wider changes that came with colonialism.

The Wāqeāt *and the British*

Where the *Wāqeāt* refers directly to these changes is in the area of administrative control, and here it appears at one level to share the perspective of the colonial authorities. The importance of having good local officials is stressed (see N1 and N2 in Table 1). There is implicit recognition of the strength of British rule: thus when writing of how groups of men from Sikhthi, a village adjoining Mubarakpur, joined in the plunder of 1857 the author remarks that they had not

[41] Cf. the discussion regarding 'shifters' and authorial intervention in R. Barthes, 'Historical Discourse', in M. Lane (ed.), *Structuralism: A Reader* (London, 1970).

stopped to consider what would happen to them afterwards (*Wāqeāt*, p. 61).[42] Again, Ali Hasan expresses much admiration for individual British officials—'Penny',[43] who emerges as the hero of 1857–8, fighting bravely and successfully against very great odds, or Tucker, Officiating Magistrate at the time of the 1842 outbreak in Mubarakpur who was 'a very worthy (capable) Englishman' (*Wāqeāt*, p. 36). We have indeed a formal acknowledgement of 'the greatness of British rule'. In the incident listed as N1 above, when a cow's head was placed on a chauk in the qasba, the thanadar, Mirza Karam Ali Beg apparently handled the situation with efficiency and tact. He assured the inhabitants that what had happened in the 'Rikhai Shahi' of 1813 would not happen again, that no one from the countryside would be allowed to invade Mubarakpur, and that they should not panic and flee. He also sent an urgent message to the District Magistrate, who came with a troop of sepoys and camped in the qasba for several days. Thus 'a riot was averted'. 'All this was the greatness of British rule'. (*Wāqeāt*, pp. 22–3).

Yet in spite of this sympathy for the British and their administration, it is, as we observed in the last section, the differences in perception revealed by the two accounts that really stand out. We may obtain a better appreciation of this if we pursue some of the above points of similarity further. While Ali Hasan recognizes the importance of having fair-minded and experienced officials appointed by the state, he emphasizes also the wisdom and influence of local leaders which is recognized only obliquely in the colonial account. Writing about Event I, a clash between Shias and Sunnis in the qasba, he accuses the Nawab's *amil* of favouring the Shias because he was, like the Nawab himself, a Shia. But Shahab Mehtar, the head of the Mubarakpur weavers, 'wise and respected', 'the like of whom is not to be found in

[42] What happened afterwards is described by Ali Hasan himself in the following words: 'The people of Mubarakpur, especially the Nurbaf [weaving] community, *on behalf of the Government and at the orders of both Penny Sahib and the Tahsildar of Muhammadabad*' took a prominent and profitable part in the loot of Sikhthi; *Wāqeāt*, p.69. Emphasis added.

[43] This name refers almost certainly to Mr Pennywell, Deputy Magistrate of Azamgarh in 1857, but Ali Hasan appears to have confused his story with that of the European indigo planter, E. F. Venables. It is the latter who appears as hero and saviour in British accounts of the Mutiny in Azamgarh and it was he—not 'Penny', as Ali Hasan believed—who was fatally wounded in an encounter with the forces of Kunwar Singh in April 1858; S. A. A. Rizvi (ed.), *Freedom Struggle in Uttar Pradesh, Source Material, Volume IV* (Lucknow, 1959), pp. 5–6, 77, 85, 139–40, 466.

our times', who had had to journey to Lucknow before the nawabi officials agreed to act at all, now saved the situation and restored amity between the sects (*Wāqeāt*, p. 5). At the time of Event II, another Shia-Sunni conflict, Shahab Mehtar 'who was still alive' again intervened, unravelled a complicated court case and obtained the release of the innocent men who had been arrested by the police of the Muhammadabad thana. (*Wāqeāt*, p. 7).[44] In 1857–8, to take just one more instance, it was in Ali Hasan's view the determination and foresight of the zamindars and *sardars* (leaders) of Mubarakpur that was responsible for the maintenance of peace in the qasba. In the British official's view, we may recall, this achievement was credited to the tahsildar of Muhammadabad, Mohammad Taqi. If 'Penny Sahib Bahadur' had lived, Ali Hasan comments, the local zamindars and sardars would certainly have been rewarded and decorated (*Wāqeāt*, p. 73)—a notable example of the acceptance of colonial standards and colonial aspirations by the 1880s.

But that this was not always how the Muslims of Mubarakpur, or even their zamindars and leaders, had responded to the colonial power is amply demonstrated by local actions in the aftermath of the Hindu-Muslim fight of April 1813. Then the intervention of the colonial power had produced a quick closing of ranks and a display of considerable suspicion and hostility towards the new regime by both Hindus and Muslims of the region. Eight months after the 'riot' the Gorakhpur magistrate reported his failure to obtain the kind of evidence that was required in spite of the transfer of two sets of officials suspected of being insufficiently energetic in the pursuit of their enquiries. He felt that further delay in the commitment of the trial was pointless. In part this was because both sides, 'having been guilty of great outrage', were afraid to come forward. More significant however was his observation that 'the parties have now mutually agreed to adjust their grievances'. Further:

> The accounts existing between the Muhammadans and Hindoos which were destroyed by the fire or otherwise have been re-adjusted and new bonds and agreements have been entered into by the parties concerned, and I am of the opinion that a considerable quantity of property plundered must have been restored or that an understanding exists between the parties that it shall be when an opportunity offers . . .[45]

[44] We may note in passing that the earliest detailed report on Mubarakpur to be found in the colonial records acknowledged the influence of Shahab Mehtar: See p. 258 below.

[45] MG4, Judl. Series I, Acc. 169, Vol. 168, magistrate's letter 17 Dec. 1813, paras 7–8.

By the 1880s some of this had changed and the change is reflected in the pages of the *Wāqeāt*. A particular class of Muslims speaks to us here at (need I add?) a particular time: these are men from an impoverished zamindari background, acquainted with Arabic and Persian and Islamic theology, beginning to pick up elements of a 'modern' English education, having to reckon with the wealth of moneylender-traders and other 'upstarts', sometimes sharing a belief which was gaining ground in certain quarters that British power alone could defend their positions and their culture. Ali Hasan now emphasized the importance of 'Muslim' tradition and 'Muslim' unity, and with these the 'benefits' of British rule. He harked back to Shia-Sunni conflicts that are supposed to have plagued the qasba of Mubarakpur both before and immediately after the establishment of the colonial power (Events I and II). One wonders whether this does not have more to do with the Shia-Sunni and other sectarian differences that were coming to the fore in the later nineteenth century than with the state of affairs as it existed in the last years of nawabi administration.[46]

Shahab Mehtar, 'the like of whom is not to be found in our times', and 'the greatness of British rule' is a curious juxtaposition. Yet it is not quite so curious if one bears in mind the overall perspective of the *Wāqeāt-ō-Hādesāt*. What is honoured in Ali Hasan's chronicle is a body of traditions, customs and values that were for him the life of the qasba. There is a fundamental consistency here. British rule is saluted, as is the memory of Shahab Mehtar, for both served (or might serve) in their different ways, more or less efficaciously, to uphold these traditions and the position of the class that was above all responsible for creating them.

---

[46] For the later nineteenth century developments in Muslim public affairs, see F. Robinson, *Separatism Among Indian Muslims. The Politics of the United Provinces Muslims, 1860–1923* (Cambridge, 1974), Chs. 2 and 3; R. Ahmed, *The Bengal Muslims, 1871–1906. A Quest for Identity* (Delhi, 1981). The implications for the Muslim élite at the local level are spelt out in Bayly, 'The Small Town and Islamic Gentry in North India' and his *Rulers, Townsmen and Bazaars*, pp. 354–8. The 'Village Crime Register' for Mubarakpur, Pt. IV, entry for 1909 or 1910, notes that the qasba was inhabited by Muslims belonging to four sects: Sunni, Hanfi, Wahabi (which is inaccurately identified with Ahl-i-Hadis) and Shia. 'All these sects have their own separate mosques. They do not pray in one another's mosques. All take part together in the *taziadari* [at Muharram] but the Ahl-i-Hadis do not participate in this at all'. Qazi Atahar's researches also indicate that Shia-Sunni and other sectarian differences among the local Muslims became significantly more pronounced in the later nineteenth century; see his *Tazkara-i-ulema-i-Mubarakpur* (Bombay, 1974), pp. 30–3.

A Weaver Speaks

To what extent did the other, lower-class Muslims of Mubarakpur—
in particular the weavers who constituted by far the largest segment
of the population—share Ali Hasan's perspective and entertain the
same hopes, fears and expectations? The available records do not
enable us to give a definite answer to this question. They do however
indicate some of the elements of one.

There was without doubt an important area of beliefs and concerns
shared by these different classes. We get some idea of this from a
comparison of the *Wāqeāt* with the 'notes' (or diary) kept by Sheikh
Abdul Majid (c. 1864–193?), a weaver of *muhalla* Pura Sofi in
Mubarakpur. Abdul Majid writes some time after Ali Hasar, his
'notes' dating mostly from the 1910s and '20s, but he pays similar
attention to disputes between Hindus and Muslims of the qasba.
Thus Event XVIII in Ali Hasan's chronicle, the dispute over the
temple built by Manohar Das in 1877, is remembered and described
by Abdul Majid in a note headed *Mubārakpur kā wāqeā* ('An event
in Mubarakpur').[47] The '*balwa*' ('riot', 'insurrection') of 1904, the
latter part of which at least was witnessed in person by the diarist, is
traced to its 'root'—Mian Khuda Baksh, son of Fateh Kalandar,
zamindar of Mustafabad (a hamlet near Mubarakpur), who planted a
pig's head in a masjid in the hope of using the commotion that would
ensue to settle scores with a rival zamindar. In a reaction reminiscent
of Ali Hasan's when he wrote of the baseness of Faqruddin in the
'Faqruddin Shahi' (Event XVI), Abdul Majid remarks on Khuda
Baksh that this '*kam-zāt*' ('base person', 'of low origin') was behind
all the trouble.[48] At a certain level 'Muslim unity' is accepted as
natural and essential in this weaver's diary as in the *Wāqeāt*. Hence
the Muslim police official, during whose time in 1906 Hindus of
Mubarakpur were first permitted to blow *shankhs* (conch-shells) at
prayer, is accused of having taken a bribe from the Hindus.[49] And as
Ali Hasan had written of the Muslims who gave evidence against
other Muslims after the 'riot' of 1842, so Abdul Majid comments on
Muslim witnesses against Muslim 'accused' during the Non-Co-
operation Movement of 1921–2: 'These Musalmans are responsible
for having sent other Musalmans to jail'.[50]

[47] The diary of Sheikh Abdul Majid, c. 1864–193? is retained at the house of his
descendant, Sheikh Wazir Ahmad, Muhalla Pura Sofi, Mubarakpur. The date of the
above dispute is given as 1875–6 in the diary.

[48] Entry headed 19 May 1904. For details of this incident see Pandey, 'Rallying
Round the Cow'.   [49] Entry headed 29 June 1906.   [50] Entry headed 19 June 1922.

Other evidence indicates that Abdul Majid's outlook was not a departure from the views of the local weavers in the nineteenth century. Members of the weaving community had taken a leading part in raising contributions for and supervising the work of repair and construction of the mazār, Jama Masjid and Imambarah in the 1860s and 1870s.[51] The concluding sentences of Ali Hasan's chronicle expressed the hope that the system of public subscriptions organized by the weavers would within a short time enable them to buy land to be bestowed as *waqf* (charity) on the masjid, and the prayer that God may grant the weavers of Mubarakpur such favour that they would 'with their abilities and determination forever maintain this system of subscriptions' in the service of religion.[52]

In 1842 there was a striking demonstration of local Muslim unity in the face of an insult to their faith. On the occasion of the 'Bicchuk Shahi' (Event IX in Ali Hasan's list), the 'simultaneous attack' by several thousand Muslims 'headed by old offenders' on the houses of five Hindu merchant-moneylenders was so swift—it was launched 'within fifteen minutes' of the carcass of a pig being found on the imambarah at day-break—that the Magistrate saw in it evidence of 'design, unanimity and previous arrangement . . . throughout'.[53] Yet even if the dead pig was planted on the imambarah as a pretext (a suggestion that the weavers and other Muslims of the town indignantly rejected), the evidence speaks unmistakably of a large number of angry Muslims gathering by the imambarah to discuss their course of action. Bearing in mind the obstacles deliberately thrown in the path of the tazia procession by Bicchuk Kalwar and his associates at the Muharram for several years prior to this, we may infer that the 'unanimity' observed here was one of emotion rather than of 'design' or 'conspiracy'.[54]

---

[51] *Wāqeāt-ō-Hādesāt*, pp. 87–9. [52] Ibid., 89.

[53] COG, Judl. Azamgarh, Vol. 68, File 47, Craigee-Morrieson, 25 March 1842.

[54] Cf. India Office Library: Home Misc., Vol. 775, Report on Benares City by W. W. Bird, 20 Aug. 1814, para 12, which notes: 'The inhabitants by the most simple process imaginable can assemble in multitudes at any given spot on the shortest of notice. The method by which they do this bears a striking affinity to the practice of "gathering" in the Highlands of Scotland, and to a similar practice in Scandinavia. Swift and trusty messengers run full speed all over the City proclaiming in a single word the place of rendezvous, and invoking infamy and eternal vengeance on those who do not at the appointed hour repair to it. From the City the alarm is spread over the country. The first messenger conveys the symbol, which is a Dhurmputtree or paper containing a mystic inscription to the next village, and that to the next, till all know where, when, and wherefore they must meet. This practice is common not only among the Hindoos but the Mahomedans [here too, chiefly weavers] also, and in the disturbances of 1809 and 1810 was the means of collecting together an innumerable multitude at one spot in the space of no more than a few hours'.

In 1877 it was a general body of Muslims at prayer (*namaaz parhne wale*) who, on noticing the *trishul* at the top of Manohar Das's recently completed shivalaya went to ask of Gada Husain whether he had given permission for the building. The Hindus, they remonstrated, would sound the shankh and bells in the temple morning and evening; these and the *bhajans* would disturb the namaaz. And it was the threat of violence which weighed heavily with the Collector when he decided to order the dismantling of the shivalaya.[55]

Similarly in 1904 it was some weavers of Pura Sofi who discovered that a small unenclosed mosque which was being constructed by them in the open fields outside the qasba had been desecrated with the carcass of a piglet. They returned immediately to raise the matter in one or two mosques in their muhalla. A party went out to consult the zamindars of Sikhthi, in whose estate this section of Mubarakpur fell. An attempt was also made to get the local police to take action and then a deputation of weavers went out to Muhammadabad to report the matter at the police station there. Barring the brief consultation with the zamindars of Sikhthi, which was followed by further discussions in their own muhalla, the weavers appear to have acted on their own—gathering a large crowd at the defiled mosque by the sound of a drum, marching north to Gujarpar where the temple was defiled by the killing of a cow seized on the way, and then marching back to the town and through it (inviting 'neighbours and friends' to join them) onto the Mubarakpur temple which lay just beyond its southern extremity, where a cow belonging to the priest and a calf confiscated on the way south from Gujarpar were slaughtered and the images smashed.[56]

In 1813 too the investigating magistrate had observed that 'Shah Mahter, the Surdar of the Musulmans' (this refers to Shahab Mehtar, the head of the weavers) was at the time of the outbreak absent in Gorakhpur: 'had he been present the act [that set off the violence] would probably not have been committed'.[57] The sequence of events leading up to this outbreak is described in the *Wāqeāt-ō-Hādesāt* as also in a petition presented to the Gorakhpur court in 1813 by Shahab Mehtar and four other weavers of Mubarakpur, and a comparison of these is instructive.

[55] *Wāqeāt-ō-Hādesāt*, p. 78, records that the magistrate warned Manohar Das that he was creating the conditions for a riot.

[56] Gorakhpur Commissioner's Record Room, Dept. XIII, File 63/1902–5, 'Judgement' in Mubarakpur Riot Case, forwarded by Magistrate Azamgarh, 5–1–1905, esp. evidence of Bechu, Julaha of Pura Sofi.

[57] UPRAA: MG4, Judl. Series I, Acc. 169, Vol. 168, magistrate's letter, 17 Dec. 1813, para 3.

It is said in Ali Hasan's narrative and in the weavers' petition that the merchant-moneylenders were becoming arrogant, 'puffed up by their earnings' and 'drunk on their wealth'. According to the former it was roughly around the time of the construction of Rikhai Sahu's thakurduara that Angnu Kalwar, another prospering mahajan, also built a shivalaya in the middle of Mubarakpur and all the Hindus of the town began to worship there. Adjacent to the shivalaya was a chauk (or platform) on which tazias used to be kept during the Muharram: and the Hindus, out of consideration for their Muslim neighbours, used to suspend the singing of bhajans and the playing of music during prayers for the ten days of the Muharram. Thus four or five years passed in peace. Then, writes Ali Hasan, some among the Hindus argued that they should not have to suspend their worship for 'ten to twelve' days: 'Islam reigns over us for that period'. So 'the mahajans of the town, puffed up with their earnings', had a wall built around the Muslim platform—and this was the immediate cause of the 'famous Rikhai Shahi', the 'biggest', bloodiest and most fearful Event of all.[58]

The petition by Shahab Mehtar and other representatives of the weavers ('representatives of those who have suffered') puts the matter in a slightly different and broader historical context. It observes that Hindus and Muslims had lived together in amity until then, with tolerance and respect for one another's religious practices and customs; but 'since the Hindus have gained *amaldari* [from *amil—* important government official] the killing [*sic*] of Muslims has begun'.[59] The petitioners quote Devi Dube and Rikhai Sahu as saying to the panchayat, when the Muslims brought the question of the extension of the boundary wall before it, that they would spend a lakh of rupees if necessary on the shivalaya and 'leave not a trace of you people [the Muslims]'. In addition they explain the slaughter of a cow on the chauk in front of Angnu Kalwar's shivalaya in terms of a religious necessity.

Among Muslims and among 'the lower castes of other religions', says the petition, there is a practice of doing a *minnat* (prayer for a particular blessing) at an imambarah, masjid, Qadam Rasool or any

---

[58]   *Wāqeāt-ō-Hādesāt*, p. 8.

[59]   *Arzi ba Adalat Gorakhpur, ba silsila-i-jang Mubarakpur* (Sat. 17 April, AD 1813) Signed by Sheikh Shahabuddin and four other nurbafs on 7 June 1813, Introduction and para 2. Qazi Atahar made a copy of this petition from a copy he found in a rather poor condition with the late Maulvi Hakim Abdul Majid, Bakhri, Mubarakpur, and very graciously translated for me from the Persian.

dargah, [60] and sacrificing a cow or performing some other act of piety when the prayer is answered. Just so, 'someone' (a weaver called Boodhan, according to the Magistrate's report), had done a minnat at this chauk, and promised the sacrifice of a cow if his wish was fulfilled. Now, seeing the boundary wall of the shivalaya being extended to enclose the chauk, a step that would end his chances of making the sacrifice there, he had killed a cow at the spot 'to fulfil his minnat'. There may be no truth in this story; for a petition submitted after such destruction and murder as occurred in 1813 to a court that will determine the punishment to be meted out to the petitioners or their friends, has good cause for exaggeration and fabrication. But the fact that Boodhan, when arrested soon after the 'riot', confessed his deed and explained the killing of the cow in similar terms[61] lends some credence to it. What in any case is significant in the present discussion is the fact that such an argument was put forward at all in defence of the act.

Thus far the evidence points to substantial agreement among the Muslims of Mubarakpur. Yet it would be surprising if there were no variations in outlook. There were after all marked differences of status among both the Muslims and the Hindus of the qasba. The distinction between the *sharif* (or *ashraf*, the 'respectable' classes) and the *razil* (literally 'base', the labouring people) was well established. And Ali Hasan revealed his perception of these distinctions of community and birth in his peculiar interpretation of the Mubarakpur people's anger on receipt of Rajab Ali's letter threatening an attack on the mahajans in 1857: how could 'this Rautara ('new Muslim' zamindar)' dare to contemplate such action?[62]

In spite of all the influence of their Mehtars and sardars, there was a difference between the weavers and other lowly classes on the one hand and the 'pure' or 'noble' Muslims of the upper classes on the other, which the weavers were not easily allowed to forget. As a maulvi of the town put it to me, until well into the twentieth century 'no one was willing to give them [the weavers] the sardar's position in public prayers' or indeed to sit behind them in the congregation.[63]

[60] Cf. W. Crooke, *Religion and Folklore of Northern India* (Oxford, 1926), pp. 166–9; E. A. H. Blunt, *Caste System of Northern India* (Delhi, 1969), p. 292; H. R. Nevill, *Bahraich: A Gazetteer, being Volume XLV of the District Gazetteers of the United Provinces of Agra and Oudh* (Allahabad, 1903), pp. 149–50.

[61] UPRAA: MG4, Judl. Series I, Acc. 169, Vol. 168, magistrate's letter, 17 Dec. 1813, para 3; *Arzi ba Adalat* (17 April 1813), para 3.

[62] *Wāqeāt-ō-Hādesāt*, p. 62.

[63] Interview with Maulvi Kamruzzaman, Mubarakpur.

There is a clear recognition of this division between those with wealth
and social standing and those without in Abdul Majid's comments on
the 'riot' of 1904: 'It occurred at the instance of the notables [*bade
log*, literally, big men]', he wrote in his diary. 'The lower classes
[*chote log*, literally, small or unprivileged people]' were taken
unawares. 'If the latter had known that they would in their haste
commit excesses and be punished for them [in place of the bade log
who had inspired the disturbance], they would certainly never have
taken such action'.[64]

In the later nineteenth and early twentieth centuries the weavers
struggled to close this gap between sharif and razil Muslims in a
movement that gradually spread across most of northern India. Their
caste appellation, Julaha, was in all probability of Persian origin
(from *jula*—ball of thread), but many commentators sought to derive
the word from the Arabic *juhala* ('the ignorant class'). The weavers
responded with the argument that it came from *jils* (decorated), *jal*
(net), or *ujla* (lighted up, or white), from which perhaps came one of
the other names that the community used for itself (the one that Ali
Hasan also employed) in the later nineteenth century—*nurbafs* or
'weavers of light'. By this time Muslim weavers in many places had
come to reject the name Julaha altogether, and insisted that they be
called Ansaris (after a claimed Arabic ancestor who practiced the art
of weaving) or Momins (i.e. 'the faithful' or 'people of honour').[65]
Yet it was to be a long and determined struggle before the community
of weavers could overcome the marks of social inferiority and
ignorance implicit in the 'impure' status, and indeed the very name,
ascribed to them: and even then the label would not come completely
unstuck.

The marked distinctions of caste and class noticed above were
bound to make for important differences of outlook among diverse
groups of Muslims in Mubarakpur, as elsewhere. One aspect of these
differences is highlighted by another comparison of Ali Hasan's
Wāqeāt with Abdul Majid's diary. What the advent of colonialism
meant for the people of Mubarakpur is perhaps not unfairly summed
up in the following terms: more rigorous administrative demands
and control following the establishment of a centralized colonial

---

[64] Entry headed 29 May 1904.

[65] W. Crooke, *The Tribes and Castes of the North-Western Provinces and Oudh*,
Vol. *III* (Calcutta, 1896), pp. 69–70; C. A. Silberrad, *A Monograph on Cotton Fabrics
Produced in the North-Western Provinces and Oudh* (Allahabad, 1898), p. 1.

power; improved communications, increased traffic and a significant change in the direction of the cloth trade; and higher prices of food and of the raw materials needed for the local cloth industry, at least for important stretches of time. Of these new trends however it is only the first that finds place in Ali Hasan's 'history'.

The fortunes of the cloth trade are a notable silence. For if it was the bazaar and the palace, the 'Islamized trader' and the 'Hinduized aristocrat' who in Geertz's phrase 'stamped (their) character' on the Indonesian towns of Modjokuto and Tabanan,[66] it was the weaving of silken fabrics and the Muslim Julaha that gave to Mubarakpur its distinctive figure[67]—as the above pages should have made clear. Large stocks of finished goods were lost by the weavers in 1857–8 (as we learn from a single-line entry in the colonial records). The miserable condition of the majority of the local weavers was testified to by officials who enquired into the region's industry and trade in the early 1880s. Large numbers of these 'workers in silk' were being forced by the later nineteenth century to turn to the weaving of ordinary cottons—a far less 'honorable' vocation.

Yet these occurrences feature nowhere in Ali Hasan's chronicle. 'Processes' are of course not expressed as 'public' Events in this particular 'history'. But what of the loss of substantial stocks by the weavers in 1857? We do not get any hint of the longer-term process or this sudden loss in the not inconsiderable space devoted by the author to 'Non-Events' or 'Near Events' either.

Abdul Majid's sketchy diary offers a sharp contrast in this regard. Everyday life figures prominently here—births, deaths ('natural' as well as 'unnatural'), marriages and scandalous affairs in the qasba.[68] And while this certainly has something to do with the fact that 'diaries' and 'histories', even 'local histories', are different genres, there is no understating the concern with the cloth trade and its progress—a concern that is entirely missing from the *Wāqeāt.*

---

[66] C. Geertz, *Peddlers and Princes, Social Change and Economic Modernization in Two Indonesian Towns* (Chicago, 1963), p. 18.

[67] This remains true to this day; thus a young educated Kayasth contractor who gave me a lift to and from the qasba on one occasion said to me that this was only his second visit to the place because *'mujhe to in lungi walon se dar lagta hai'* ('I am afraid of these *lungi*-clad folk'). The lungi was the dress of lower-caste Muslims in this region, cf. Raza, *Aadha Gaon,* p. 65.

[68] See ibid., *passim,* for a very rich 'anthropological' account which reveals very much the same kind of everyday concerns among other Muslim inhabitants in this region in a slightly later period.

The haphazard entries in the diary contain numerous detailed statements regarding the price of different kinds of cloth and of silk thread, as of grain and other necessities, and comments on their implications. Thus on 10 August 1919: 'This year the trade has been such that Mubarakpur has become prosperous [*aabaad*, literally, 'populated' or 'full of life']. Until this year there has never been such a (prosperous) trade—nor will there be (again) . . . . And this year as many as 142 members of our brotherhood have proceeded to Hajj-i-Kaaba from here'. Again in July 1920: 'This year the outlook for the trade is not so happy. Silk thread has become very expensive'.[69] Or on a different subject, referring to the soaring prices of goat-skins in November 1916, the price having touched Rs 3 and Rs 4 per skin by this time: 'Many of the big and wealthy Muslims have taken to trading in these skins'.[70]

The concern with the immediate problems of subsistence that is reflected here may be one reason why the weavers of Mubarakpur appeared on the whole somewhat more ambiguous in their response to British rule than the Ali Hasans of the 1880s. In respect of the cloth trade, colonialism had certainly not been an unmixed blessing. I have written at some length elsewhere about the hardships suffered by the weavers of eastern UP owing to the dislocation of their market and supplies of raw material, and the increased dependence on intermediaries and new trails of migration that developed.[71] Whether it was because of this experience of being buffeted about or because of Gandhian support for handicraft industry or some other local factors, we know that the weavers of Azamgarh were, with most of their community throughout the rest of UP and Bihar, supporters of the Congress struggle for independence long after the emergence of a Hindu-Muslim schism at the level of provincial and 'national' politics.[72]

---

[69] Both these entires appear under the date, 10 Aug. 1919, but the second is clearly an addition made in a new paragraph.   [70] Entry for Nov. 1916.

[71] See Pandey, 'Economic Dislocation in Nineteenth-Century Eastern UP', section VII. There appears to have been a wave of migration from Mubarakpur and other such places to Malegaon and other cloth-producing centres in western and central India during the rising of 1857–9, Hafiz Malegumi, *Nakūsh* (Malegaon, 1979), pp. 70, 72, 116. (I owe this reference to Maulvi Kamruzzaman).

[72] National Archives of India: Govt. of India, Home Dept., Political (I) Branch, File 31/1/41, 'D.I.B's report on the political situation in Bihar' (Memo. by D. Pilditch, 15 Jan. 1941); Rajendra Prasad Papers, File XV/37, Col. I, tlg. Hakim Wasi Ahmad, Pres., Bihar Jamiat-al-Momineen to Rajendra Prasad, received 12 July 1937; Raza *Aadha Gaon*, pp. 252–4; interviews Maunath Bhanjan, Mubarakpur and Banaras.

Abdul Majid's own evidence on this is somewhat paradoxical. At more than one place in his diary he refers to the death of some distinguished British personage—Lord Kitchener or the wife of the Lieutenant-Governor of UP—and expresses a feeling of deep sorrow: 'The subjects [of the Lieutenant-Governor] were deeply grieved and they mourned for four days, and whatever we could give as charity we gave'.[73] Again, referring to the boycott of the Prince of Wales on his visit to Calcutta in December 1921, he writes: '*Afsos! Sad afsos!* [Shame! Undying shame!]. As far as my understanding goes, we cannot obtain Suraj [Swaraj] by such means'.[74]

But we know from other sources that Abdul Majid was very close to the police and local offcials: 'Abdul Majid, resident of Pura Sofi, although he is an ordinary person [i.e. of no great wealth or distinction], always informs police officers of any secret—[meetings?] in the qasba that he comes to know about'.[75] It is probable that this relationship had something to do with the opinions he formed. In addition it is not entirely clear what significance one can attach to this reverence for (or fear of) distant overlords like Lord Kitchener, the Lieutenant-Governor's wife and the Prince of Wales. For not only does the diarist add to the above comment on the Prince of Wales' visit: 'Yes, if God wills it, then there can be Suraj'.[76] He also condemns those Muslims who were responsible as prosecution witnesses for sending other Muslims to jail for their part in Non-Co-operation activities.[77]

In any case the weavers of Mubarakpur seem to have taken an active part in the Non-Co-operation Movement. Abdul Majid records meetings of the 'panchayat of twenty-eight' (referring to the twenty-eight *muhallas* of Mubarakpur) and of the '*chaurasi*' (or 'eighty-four', which drew in the leaders of the weavers from a considerable number of villages and qasbas to decide on matters of

---

[73] Entries dated 12 July 1914 & June 1916.

[74] 'Note' on Congress, Nov–Dec. 1921.

[75] 'Village Crime Register', Mubarakpur, Pt. IV (entry dated 1909 or 1910).

[76] 'Note' on Congress, Nov–Dec. 1921. Cf. also his note on Shibli Nomani, a Muslim 'unequalled in Hindustan' who had had dealings with 'great rulers all over the world'. The 'great rulers' here would seem to be on a par with those 'omniscient' and 'just', faraway and unseen rulers who provided the inspiration for numerous peasant uprisings in Russia, India and elsewhere in the eighteenth and nineteenth centuries; D. Field, *Rebels in the Name of the Tsar* (Boston, 1976); I. J. Catanach, 'Agrarian Disturbances in Nineteenth-Century India', *Indian Economic & Social History Review*, III, 1 (1966).

[77] Entry for 19 June 1922.

importance) that were called to enforce the boycott of foreign cloth.[78] It is also clear from his evidence that the leaders of the Khilafat Committee in Mubarakpur were mostly members of the weaving community[79]: the Sheikh zamindars of the qasba appear to have maintained a low profile during this period.

We have in all this some glimpses of the Mubarakpur weavers' outlook on the nineteenth-century world. This outlook differed in certain significant respects from that of the élite Muslims of the qasba but shared with it an important area of common concern. In common with exploited classes elsewhere in pre-capitalist societies, the weavers of Mubarakpur appear to have been further removed than their economically or culturally more privileged neighbours from direct political dealings with the colonial bureaucracy, and are consequently somewhat more hazy about their relations with their rulers. They were more ambivalent too in their response to the putative 'Muslim' community; more concerned about the bare problem of survival; yet in some ways more 'independent' with their reliance on the panchayat[80] and their faith in the power of 'tradition'; and at the same time deeply concerned about the honour of the community.

---

[78] Entries for 12 Dec. 1919, 8 Feb. 1920 & July 1921. L. S. S. O'Malley, *Census of India, 1911, Vol. V. Bengal, Bihar & Orissa & Sikkim. Pt I. Report* (Calcutta, 1913), pp. 462–3 explains the *Chaurasi* as follows: The lowest unit of caste government was the *chatai*, i.e. the right to sit together on a mat (or chatai) at a caste council meeting. Each chatai had a headman and other functionaries, and its area depended on the strength of the caste locally: there could be several chatais in one village or one chatai for several villages. These chatais were sometimes grouped into larger unions called Baisi or Chaurasi (consisting of 22 and 84 Chatais respectively). A Baisi could cover 10–15 miles, a Chaurasi 40–50. 'The jurisdiction of the Panchayat is necessarily local, but the combination of different Chatais helps to make its sentence effective over a considerable area'.

[79] Entry for 19 June 1922.

[80] O'Malley, *Census 1911, Bengal, Bihar & Orissa, Pt I*, p. 461, notes that an organized system of caste government existed among most of the lower castes in Bihar but not among the higher castes. He comments further that 'none of the Musalman groups approach so closely to the Hindu caste system with its numerous restrictions as the Jolahas'. The Julaha panchayat, headed by a sardar assisted by a *chharidar*, covered 10–50 houses, its sphere usually being coterminous with a village but sometimes covering several villages (p. 489). (In Mubarakpur there appears to have been a panchayat, headed by a *mehtar*, for each of the muhallas of the qasba). See also F.H. Fisher, *Statistical, Descriptive and Historical Account of the North-Western Provinces, Ghazipur* (Allahabad, 1883), pp. 56–7; and n. 54 & n. 78 above.

'*Ham log wahan maujud the. Yah dekhkar nihayat dil dukha'.*
Translation: 'We were present there [when the Inspector of
Police, Mohan Singh, trampled a copy of the *Qoran* underfoot
during searches after the 'riot' of 1904]. We were deeply wounded
by this sight'.

'*Bade-bade logon ka ishara tha, aur chote logon ne yah samjha ki
sarkari intazam ki vajah se kuch nahin hoga'.*
Translation: 'It was at the instigation of 'big men' [that the 1904
outbreak occurred]; the 'smaller folk' thought that nothing
would happen because of official precautions'.

'*Inke intakāl ka hamare badshah ko bahut bada ranj hua. Aur
hamko bhi bahut bada gam hua'.*
Translation: 'His [Lord Kitchener's] death caused very great
grief to our King. It also caused us very deep sorrow'.

'*In logon ne Musalman hokar Musalman ko qaid karaya'.*
Translation: 'These people who are Musalmans are responsible
for having sent other Musalmans to jail'.[81]

What is indubitably represented in these extracts from Abdul
Majid's diary is a consciousness of the 'collective'—the community.
Yet this consciousness of community was an ambiguous one, straddling
as it did the religious fraternity, class, qasba and mohalla.[82] Here, as
in Ali Hasan's account, the boundaries of the collective shift all the
time. It is difficult to translate this consciousness into terms that are
readily comprehensible in today's social science—Muslim/Hindu,
working class/rentier, urban/rural—or even to argue that a particular
context would inevitably activate a particular solidarity. What is clear
is that Ali Hasan is quite untroubled by the problems that confound
the modern researcher as he moves from one notion of the collective
to another through the eighty-nine pages of his manuscript.

I have suggested above that there is nonetheless a certain basic
consistency in Ali Hasan's stand. In Abdul Majid's random notes too
it is possible to discern a similar consistency; for what they speak of is
a fight on several fronts for self-respect and human dignity.[83] Honour

[81] These quotations are taken from Abdul Majid's diary, entries headed 29 May
1904 (first two quotations), June 1916 and 19 June 1922.

[82] For the importance of muhalla loyalty in the politics of Muslim weavers elsewhere, see J. C. Masselos, 'Power in the Bombay 'Moholla', 1904–5', *South Asia*,
No.6 (Dec. 1976).

[83] Dipesh Chakrabarty has pointed out to me how the semiotics of insult (honour/
shame) carries over from this region to the industrial city, reproducing an identical
structure of riots in the Calcutta mills in the later nineteenth and earlier twentieth
century.

(*izzat*) was inextricably linked as we have seen with certain kinds of worship, certain ritual practices; and any insult to these was unacceptable. But honour was also tied up by the later decades of this century of dislocation with the assertion of the rights of the chote log, the shedding of the degrading label of razil, and full acceptance in the equal fraternity of Islam that the Wahabis had propagated and other 'learned' Muslims now so often talked about.[84] If the positions of all men, high and low, seemed increasingly insecure in a fateful world, these were not fates that men and women, high or low, would accept without a struggle.

---

[84] For a different but relevant example of the importance attached to izzat by the peasants of this region, see K. Mukherjee and R. S. Yadav, *Bhojpur* (Delhi, 1980).

The Conditions and Nature of Subaltern Militancy: Bengal from Swadeshi to Non-Co-operation, c. 1905–22

SUMIT SARKAR

I

'If we sit idle, and hesitate to rise till the whole population are goaded to desperation, then we shall continue idle till the end of time . . . Without blood, O patriots! Will the country awake?' *Yugantar*, 26 August 1907.[1]

'The events of the first quarter of 1922 confirmed the fear that the movement had got beyond the control of the leaders . . . The spirit of violence and contempt of all authority, which now began to show its head, was not of the leaders, but of the masses.' Confidential official report on Non-Co-operation and Khilafat in Bengal, 1924.[2]

The quotations with which I begin indicate an interesting contrast between the Swadeshi movement in Bengal (1905–8) and the Non-Co-operation-Khilafat upsurge in the same region (1919–22) from the point of view of the nature, extent and consequences of 'subaltern' participation in nationalist politics. During the anti-Partition agitation the masses appeared irritatingly inert to the more radical activists, for despite the formulation of a theory of 'extended boycott' or 'passive resistance' which demanded popular participation and often anticipated

[1] Report on Native Papers (Bengal), hereafter *RNP (B)*, week ending 28 August 1907. West Bengal State Archives (hereafter *WBSA*).

[2] *Government of Bengal, Political (Confidential)*, hereafter *GOB Poll (Conf.)*, F.N. 395 i–iii/1924: History of the Non-Co-operation and Khilafat Movements in Bengal, p. 13, *WBSA*.

the methods of Gandhism,[3] the movement in practice seldom went beyond the confines of *bhadralok* groups. The politics of mass contact consequently soon became transformed into revolutionary-terrorist activity by a handful of educated youth. Non-Co-operation-Khilafat in sharp contrast revealed a picture of masses outstripping leaders, particularly in the winter of 1921–2, and popular initiative eventually alarmed leaders into calling for a halt. C. R. Das may have been unhappy about the timing of Gandhi's Bardoli retreat[4] but Calcutta and district newspapers had become nervous about the radical social implications of the upsurge months back.[5] The *Amrita Bazar Patrika*, a newspaper with a radical-nationalist reputation, explicitly praised the clauses in the Bardoli resolution which gave assurances to zamindars as helping to remove the misunderstanding 'that the movement of Mahatma Gandhi is aimed at the destruction of the rights of all property-owners.'[6]

I am using this contrast as the entry-point into an analysis of the conditions and nature of subaltern militancy in the anti-imperialist movement. Certain preliminary points about concepts and methods require clarification here. The categories of 'élite' and 'subaltern' have aroused some misgivings as allegedly assuming a simplistic two-fold division of society, and as a departure from the familiar digits of Marxist class-analysis. Judging from the theoretical explication

[3] This was developed above all in Aurobindo Ghosh's famous articles in *Bande Mataram*, 9–23 April 1907, later reprinted as *Doctrine of Passive Resistance* (Pondicherry, 1948). See also *Sandhya*, 21 November 1906: 'if . . . the chaukidar, the constable, the deputy and the munsiff and the clerk, not to speak of the sepoy, all resign their respective functions, feringhee rule may come to an end in a moment. No powder and shot will be needed, no sepoys will have to be trained . . .'. *RNP(B)*, 1 December 1906. *WBSA*.

[4] A compromise on favourable terms, possibly including a Round Table Conference to discuss more constitutional concessions, had been blocked in December 1921 by Gandhi against the wishes of Das and others. Reading to Montagu, telegrams of 15, 17 and 18 December 1921 (*Reading Collection*, India Office Library, hereafter *IOL*, MSS Eur. E.238/4).

[5] '. . . once the masses raise their heads, we do not know what will happen to us Babus'. *Nayak*, 3 September 1921. The *Hitavadi* of 25 November 1921 warned of the 'grim shadow of Bolshevism' due to 'the manner in which the swarajists are exciting the labourers.' The *Nayak* of 1 December 1921 complained that 'in Dinajpur it has become difficult to maintain zamindaries' and the *Tippera Guide* of Comilla of 24 January 1922 and the *Rarh Dipika* of Rampurhat of 8 February 1922 sounded similar notes of alarm. *RNP(B)*, weeks ending 10 September, 3 December, 10 December 1921 and 4 and 18 February 1922. *WBSA*.

[6] *Amrita Bazar Patrika*, 25 February 1921.

given by Ranajit Guha in the first volume of this series, this was very far from the intentions of the group responsible for the introduction of this Gramscian concept into modern Indian historiography.[7] There is surely a danger of prejudging the existence of distinctly-articulated and self-conscious classes in a largely pre-industrial society, and we do need some omnibus terms for such situations. 'Subaltern' is no more free of ambiguities and problems than its rough equivalents (for example 'popular', 'mass', 'lower-class'); it does have the advantage however of emphasizing the fundamental relationships of power, of domination and subordination. Nor does the subaltern concept exclude more rigorous class-analysis where the subject or material permits it.

I am employing the term 'subaltern' as a convenient short-hand for three social groups: tribal and low-caste agricultural labourers and share-croppers; landholding peasants, generally of intermediate-caste status in Bengal (together with their Muslim counterparts); and labour in plantations, mines and industries (along with urban casual labour). It will be obvious that we must expect considerable over-lapping, indeed conflicts, between these groups as well as sub-divisions. This is because the subaltern category includes exploiters as well as exploited—the *jotedars* for instance, or even fairly poor peasants employing agricultural labourers or getting their land cultivated by share-croppers. The fundamental rationale for using an omnibus term also constitutes one of the principle arguments of this article: that the subaltern groups so defined formed a relatively autonomous political domain with specific features and collective mentalities which need to be explored, and that this was a world distinct from the domain of the élite politicians who in early twentieth century Bengal came overwhelmingly from high-caste educated pro-fessional groups connected with zamindari or intermediate tenure-holding.

Charges of conceptual inexactitute apart, a serious problem in some 'subaltern' writing has been the tendency to concentrate on moments of conflict to the relative exclusion of much longer time-spans of subordination or collaboration—a trend it may be argued which really goes against Gramsci's own emphasis on the control exercised over such strata by more or less hegemonic dominant

---

[7] See Ranajit Guha, *On Some Aspects of the Historiography of Colonial India*, in Guha (ed.), *Subaltern Studies I* (Delhi, 1982), pp. 5, 8, for passages emphasizing 'the diversity of . . . . social composition' of subaltern groups as well as the ambiguities inherent in the concept as applied to the concrete realities of colonial India.

classes.[8] Subaltern groups normally enter the world of conventional historical sources at moments of explosion, consequently breeding a tendency either towards an assumption of total passivity or an opposite stereotype of heroic revolt. What one needs to keep in mind is a vast and complex continuum of intermediate attitudes of which total subordination and open revolt are only the extreme poles. James M. Freeman's fascinating 'life history' of Muli, an untouchable Bauri living in what is now a suburb of Bhubaneswar, provides important data in this context. 'Muli's ambivalent responses reflect respect for, affection for, resentment of, and rebellion against the same person.' That the acquiescence of this Bauri pimp to his superiors did not mean that he accepted his lot[9] is indicated by his attitude toward upper-caste men to whom he supplied prostitutes.[10]

So far we have talked only about the formal aspect of subaltern attitudes; in practice subordination/rebellion and all that might lie in between would naturally always develop in relation to specific issues, grievances, and social relationships. Here the essential point requiring emphasis and explanation is the coexistence and complex inter-penetration of extremely varied types of consciousness and activity: caste, communal, class, regional or national. One might recall here the first item in Gramsci's six-point programme for studying subaltern classes: '. . . the objective formation of the subaltern social groups . . . and their origins in pre-existing social groups, whose mentality, ideology, and aims they conserve for a time.'[11] The worker active in a strike might well have participated in a communal riot before and might do so again; the interpenetration of issues logically very different but in practice almost indistinguishable is even more evident in peasant movements; and similar complexities or contradictions are

[8] Guha's preface to *Subaltern Studies I* quotes Gramsci's well-known comment that 'subaltern groups are always subject to the activity of ruling groups even when they rebel and rise up' (p. vii), but this aspect tends to get somewhat neglected in the text of the volume and even in Guha's own paper.

[9] James M. Freeman, *Untouchable: An Indian Life History* (London, 1979), pp. 54, 384.

[10] 'To keep their prestige, they avoid us in public, but in private they screw our women, 'hu hu', panting like dogs', ibid., p. 22. And Muli does in the end become 'the first untouchable of his village to publicly challenge and insult a Brahman' (p. 354) over a harvest dispute.

[11] Antonio Gramsci, *Notes on Italian History*, in Hoare and Smith, (ed.), *Selection from the Prison Notebooks* (New York, 1971), p. 52.

apparent often in the politics of the élite, too.[12] Some of the East India
Railway workers who were to go on a massive strike in February-
March 1922 following an alleged assault by a white driver on an
Indian fireman had gone on strike in January of the previous year
demanding an end to cow-slaughter.[13] Swami Biswanand, extremely
active as a pioneer labour organizer in the Non-Co-operation days
and again in the late 1920s, preached cow-protection in Purulia in
August 1921[14] and was prominent in the Calcutta communal riots of
1926.[15] Stephen Henningham's valuable study of anti-zamindar and
anti-British peasant movements in north Bihar, which pays very little
attention to caste or communal conflicts,[16] consequently appears so
much less comprehensive than Satinath Bhaduri's novel *Dhorai
Charitmanas* located in a part of the same region. Bhaduri has
described in vivid detail the complex (and very far from unilinear)
development of the consciousness of Dhorai in relation to the lowly
casual labour Tatma community of Purnea into which he was born
and the Koeri share-croppers of Biskandha, the village to which he
migrated. The rumour of the coming of 'Gandhi-bawa', a holy man
with wondrous powers, leads on to efforts at self-purification and
'Sanskritizing' caste-upliftment among the Tatmas, conflicts with the
neighbouring Dhangars (as well as with a Muslim hide concern) are
occasionally sharpened, and yet in the end Civil Disobedience, anti-
landlord struggle and Quit India all impinge vitally on the life-history

[12] Bepinchandra Pal's concept of 'composite patriotism' leading up to a 'federal'
India with religious communities as its units clearly attempted a kind of combination
between nationalism and religious-communal affiliations. See my *Swadeshi Movement
in Bengal, 1903–1908* (New Delhi, 1973), pp. 422–4. A biography of Chittaranjan
Das, to take another example, repeatedly emphasizes his loyalties towards Vikrampur
as well as pride in being a Baidya. A Baidya Sammilani was held in 1914 by Das in his
house at his own cost. (Hemendranath Dasgupta, *Deshbandhu-Smriti* (Calcutta, 1926,
1959), pp. 24, 27.) And the novelist Saratchandra Chattopadhyay has recorded how the
face of the architect of the Bengal Pact paled 'at the thought of what will happen ten
years from now' as the percentage of Muslims went up further. *Swadesh o Sahitya*
(Calcutta, 1933), pp. 50–1. I owe this reference to Partha Chatterji.

[13] *Mussalman*, 10 February 1922, 7 January 1921. The January 1921 strike took
place at Adra Junction with cooks, butlers, and sweepers of the town joining railway
menial staff in a demand for an end to cow-slaughter and closing down of the local
slaughterhouse.

[14] Ibid., 26 August 1921.

[15] Kenneth McPherson, *The Muslim Microcosm: Calcutta 1918 to 1935* (Wiesbaden,
1974), Chapter 5.

[16] There is only one reference to communal conflict (on p. 15) in Stephen Henningham,
Peasant Movements in Colonial India: North Bihar 1917–1942 (Canberra, 1982).

of Dhorai and his community.[17] Bhaduri's Dhorai was based on a
real-life figure but there are still obvious dangers in reading-off too
directly the attitudes of the rural poor from a text composed by an
upper-class patriotic novelist with a strong social conscience. The
author in fact admitted later that he had somewhat exaggerated the
'positive' features of his hero as well as the extent of change in peasant
consciousness.[18] *Dhorai Charitmanas* is valuable therefore not for
providing additional data about exploitation or dawning patriotic
awareness, but precisely because it does focus to a considerable
extent on 'negative' or contradictory dimensions—elements which
the novelist had no reason to invent or over-emphasize.

A final methodological point emerges as a corollary from the above
discussion. Subaltern participation in anti-imperialist struggle is a
sub-set within the broader theme of subaltern awakening: the one
does not automatically lead to the other without a variety of complex
mediations in which the specific socio-economic structure of a region,
historical traditions, efforts at mobilization by the élite—nationalist
groups and ideologies—and British strategies all play a part. The
distance or otherwise of a specific subaltern group from the white
overlords is rather crucial here. Thus the Patidar landholding peasants
of a raiyatwari area like Kheda paying revenue directly to the colonial
state could gravitate much more easily towards nationalism than their
Baraiya subordinates who often proved more militant but were
seldom consciously anti-imperialist.[19]

I intend to put two types of questions before a selection of the
available data concerning subaltern attitudes and activities in early
twentieth century Bengal. In the first place I feel that a comparative
study of Swadeshi and Non-Co-operation can provide a useful test
for the relevance or otherwise of some of the existing explanations of
popular entry into nationalist politics. The 'Cambridge' assumption
that factions explain everything since local 'patrons' have a kind of
inherent and automatic capacity for mobilizing their 'clients', as well
as the standard nationalist interpretation in terms of mobilization

[17] Satinath Bhaduri, *Dhorai Charitmanas*, 2 vols. (Calcutta, 1949–51), *Satinath
Granthabali*, Vol. II (Calcutta, 1973), pp. 25–34, 36, 62–4 and *passim*.
[18] 'I completely suppressed certain major defects in Dhorai's character . . . The
traditional values of the Dhorais have not changed—not as much as had been hoped for
or as depicted in the book.' *Satinath Granthabali*, Appendix, pp. 495, 498. My
translation.
[19] David Hardiman, *Peasant Nationalists of Gujarat: Kheda District, 1917–34*
(Delhi, 1981), pp. 45–50, 65, 110–13.

from the top by patriotic leaders or ideologies share in common a serious underestimation of the extent of popular initiative. A point brought out by much recent research on other regions and periods, this is abundantly confirmed by the data from early twentieth century Bengal. Nor can popular outbursts be explained by immediate economic factors like price-fluctuations alone. What needs to be questioned is the central assumption underlying all these approaches: that subaltern groups lack any relatively autonomous culture or mind of their own, and only respond mechanically to economic pressures or are mobilized through initiatives from the top.

But mere reiteration of the fact of subaltern autonomy together with an emphasis on the interpenetration of its diverse forms do not take us very much beyond the level of pure description. The second, much more speculative and provisional but to my mind more important, part of my analysis consists of an attempt to utilize data to explore some of the dimensions of collective mentality underlying apparently very different forms of popular militancy in the period under study. Certain recurrent patterns do seem to emerge, whether we study mass participation on a national issue or a communal riot or a caste movement or an apparently pure 'economic' struggle. Something like a very tentative 'structure' of popular mentality can be reconstructed in the Lévi-Straussian sense of an implicit, perhaps largely unconscious logical system lying beneath the surface of myths, beliefs, values and activities.[20] One must hasten to add that reconstruction on the basis of militant outbursts alone cannot but be extremely provisional and incomplete and needs to be followed up by much deeper research, not attempted in this paper, into popular cultural and religious traditions. Revolt as I have already argued is only an extreme and exceptional pole in the continuum of subaltern attitudes; it provides a convenient starting-point only because it tends to be so much better documented.

In attempting the difficult but vitally necessary adventure of exploring popular consciousness, historians need to develop a fruitful dialogue with other social sciences, particularly perhaps with social

---

[20] Claude Lévi-Strauss, 'History and Anthropology', in his *Structural Anthropology*, Vol. I (Harmondsworth, 1979). 'Structure' has been used in a very different sense in the more narrowly empiricist British anthropological tradition, for example, as 'an arrangement of persons in institutionally controlled or defined relationships . . . a system of social positions'. A. R. Radcliffe-Brown, *Structure and Function in Primitive Society* (1952; reprinted London, 1976), p. 11.

anthropology in a country where mass illiteracy makes first-hand
documentation of the world of the subaltern so very limited.
'Structural' analysis has often been accused, not unjustly perhaps at
times, of underestimating the importance of change in the quest for
synchronic patterns. But structure to my mind certainly does not
exclude variations, both vertically in relation to the different strata
coming under the omnibus subaltern category, and horizontally over
time. Reconstruction of structures may indeed pose interesting
problems for diachronic analysis. In my concluding section I raise
certain questions regarding the extent to which mass movements
from the 1920s of a more 'modern' type (the Gandhian Congress in
its later, more organized and disciplined form, or kisan and trade
unions under Left and particularly Communist leadership) were able
to bring about significant modifications in the collective mentality-
patterns I have tried to trace on the basis of early twentieth century
data.

II

Down to 1919 the autonomy of the subaltern domain found expression
through two distinct forms: general passivity vis-a-vis efforts at
patriotic mobilization from the top, and a variety of more-or-less
militant actions distant from and sometimes directly opposed to the
nationalism of the bhadralok.

Despite much talk about the need for mass awakening, the Swadeshi
movement of 1905–8 seldom got beyond the confines of Hindu
upper caste bhadralok groups—students, journalists, teachers,
doctors and lawyers who very often had a link with rentier interests
in land in the form of zamindari or intermediate tenure-holding. The
main centres of the upsurge reveal a strong correlation with the
presence of large numbers of educated upper caste Hindu gentry:
Barisal (Backergunj), Madaripur, Vikrampur, Kishoreganj, the
Brahmanbaria subdivision of Tippera, as well as of course Calcutta
with its heavy bhadralok concentration.[21] The peasant seldom if ever
appears in Swadeshi plays:[22] the volunteers in Mukunda Das' *jatra*
Palli Seva declare that they all have some land and hence do not have to

[21] For details about the location of the Swadeshi movement, see my *Swadeshi Movement*, pp. 26, 72, and Chapter 7.

[22] A good example would be Amritalal Bose's play *Sabash Bengali*, in which Pashdanga village never becomes quite as real as the scenes of Calcutta life, no peasant appears on the stage and the village movement is presented as a matter of school-boys led by their patriotic headmaster, ibid., p. 300.

worry about 'mere rice and *dal*'[23] and police statistics about the social origins of Samiti members in Backergunj firmly establish the link with intermediate tenure-holding.[24] A few Calcutta lawyers with nationalist affiliations did develop an interest in the labour movement, and Aswinikumar Dutta's Swadesh Bandhab Samiti could briefly acquire some kind of mass base in Barisal villages through sustained humanitarian constructive work. Yet the limits remain very evident, particularly in comparison with Non-Co-operation-Khilafat days. The strikes led or unions formed were mainly of white-collar employees of printing presses and railways or of Bengali (and seldom Hindustani) workers in jute mills. The plantations and mines were entirely unaffected and, with the exception of something like a hartal on 16 October 1905, there were no instances of political strikes.[25] Even Barisal village samitis consisted 'of the bhadralok of the village'[26] and an Anushilan militant turned Communist has recalled in his memoirs how peasants were occasionally mobilized for swadeshi meetings, shy and silent participants in loin cloth roped in by the well-dressed babus to prove Hindu-Muslim unity.[27] And evidence about the considerable use of caste, religious and class pressures by the patriotic Hindu gentry to enforce the boycott in the countryside is really far too extensive to be dismissed as official or Muslim propaganda.[28]

Yet subaltern passivity can be overemphasized, and I now feel that I erred somewhat in that direction in my earlier work on Swadeshi Bengal. So far as labour is concerned nationalist leadership generally entered the scene well after 'spontaneous' initiative had led to a strike. Patriotic barristers like Aswinikumar Banerji or Apurbakumar Ghosh began their brief careers as labour leaders only when in the autumn of 1905 arrested clerks and tram workers sought legal help.[29]

[23] Ibid., pp. 358–9.

[24] Thus in Sarupkhati police station of Backerganj 'nearly half the volunteers are said to be talukdars, that is to say, persons with a tenure-holding interest in the land'. *Government of India Home Political Deposit* (hereafter *GOI Home Poll Dep.*) October 1907, No. 19. *National Archives of India* (hereafter *NAI*), quoted in ibid., p. 72.

[25] For details, see *Swadeshi Movement*, Chapter 5.

[26] Resume of Affairs in Backerganj for 1907, para 27, *GOI Home Poll A April 1908*, No. 24. *NAI*.

[27] Satis Pakrashi, *Agni Diner Katha* (Calcutta, 1947), recollecting his boyhood days in a village in Dacca.   [28] *Swadeshi Movement*, Chapters 6, 7 and *passim*.

[29] As when Banerji and Ghosh in September 1905 defended a clerk arrested for assaulting a strike-breaker at Burn Company. Next month they were reported as appearing for two tram conductors in a similar case, ibid., pp. 201–2.

In many cases Swadeshi involvement never came into the picture at all.[30] The fact that the bulk of the working class in Bengal was employed in foreign-owned concerns and that a Bengali industrial bourgeoisie hardly existed, permitted, however, considerably greater nationalist interest and sympathy in labour affairs than could be seen on questions of rent or rural indebtedness. Surendranath Banerji's *Bengalee* on 13 May 1906 for instance did praise Rabindranath for giving rent-remissions and loans to his tenants at Shelaidaha due to the prevailing scarcity—but it apparently saw no contradiction when, a fortnight later, it stoutly defended the zamindars of Muktagaccha for rejecting a petition complaining about a new fifty per cent *abwab* (cess). The Muktagaccha landlords had argued that 'lately the ryots of this quarter have conceived an idea that their rents will be reduced and that their representation will be favourably considered by the government', and the *Bengalee* found in this evidence that Fuller, the strongly anti-Swadeshi Lieutenant-Governor of East Bengal and Assam, had 'demoralized the Mussalman ryots of Mymensingh.'[31] That peasant protest could be construed as demoralization is a revealing comment on the class inhibitions of bhadralok nationalism in Bengal.

The scattered and limited data available on lower-class unrest during the Swadeshi years indicate the existence of three strands, distinct in logic though much less so in practice. In the first place rumours about conflict between the government and patriotic gentry seems to have led peasants to feel that the time was suitable for some action on their grievances concerning rent or cesses. An official report noted in November 1906 that zamindars 'in some cases . . . are afraid to appear before their tenants in definite opposition to government lest this should endanger their collection of rents'.[32] An enquiry in February 1908 by the SDO of Jamalpur in Mymensingh district about the relations between the well-known Swadeshi zamindar Brojendrakishore Roychaudhuri and his tenants produced similar consequences: 'As a result of these enquiries Brojendra Babu's tenants have got it into their heads that he has somehow become an object of official displeasure . . . . Those of the tenants who had agreed to pay an enhanced rent are now refusing to do so'.[33]

[30] A four-month-long strike at Hooghly Jute Mill by 4,000 workers, for instance, apparently aroused no nationalist interest at all, ibid., pp. 230–1.

[31] *Bengalee*, 13 May, 27 May, 30 May 1906, quoted in ibid., p. 334.

[32] Fortnightly Report, E. Bengal and Assam, No. 1331, 23 November 1906, *GOI Home Public A December 1906*, No. 311. *NAI*.

[33] *Daily Hitavadi*, 11 February 1908, *RNP(B)* for week ending 15 February 1908,

Over large parts of East Bengal the discontent of the largely Muslim peasantry found articulation in the form of communalism, with Hindu gentry, traders and moneylenders as the principal targets. The *Charu Mihir* of Mymensingh started complaining from early 1906 onwards that 'illiterate low class cultivators' were harbouring 'wild ideas' that 'they should pay rents at the low rates which obtained years ago', while Muslim sharecroppers were 'refusing to work under Hindus, and cultivate lands of which the latter are proprietors.'[34] Destruction of debt-bonds, attacks on landlord houses and desecration of images constructed through an *Iswar-britti* cess figured prominently in the riots at Iswargunj in Mymensingh district in April–May 1906, in Brahmanbaria sub-division of Tippera in March 1907 and in the Jamalpur region of Mymensingh in April–May 1907. Some of the complexities of the situation were revealed a few months later at Sherpur in Jamalpur sub-division where a Muslim crowd attacked a contingent of additional police posted there in the context of earlier riots; no Chinese wall evidently separated 'communal' disturbances from an anti-government outburst.[35] Manifestations of lower-class discontent took place mostly in the countryside, but there were certain urban parallels too. In the looting of Hindu shops in Comilla town in March 1907 Muslim '*gariwallas* who earn a large part of their living by driving Hindus of the better classes' were very prominent.[36] In Calcutta during 2–4 October 1907, following a clash between the police and a Swadeshi crowd at Beadon Square, the Bengali bhadralok found themselves being beaten up and their property looted by what a non-official enquiry committee described as 'large numbers of low-class people, such as mehtars, dhangars, sweepers, etc.'[37] The standard nationalist explanation for all such incidents in terms of official-cum-Muslim communalist instigation from above ignored pre-existing structures of exploitation and social envy without which divide-and-rule methods could have made little headway.

WBSA. The SDO of Jamalpur in 1908, interestingly enough, was A. K. Fazlul Huq. Humaira Momen, *Muslim Politics in Bengal: A Study of Krishak Praja Party and the Elections of 1937* (Dacca, 1972), p. 37.

[34] *Charu Mihir*, 23 January, 27 February, 13 March 1906, *RNP(B)* for weeks ending 3 February, and 10 and 29 March 1906. *WBSA.*

[35] For details, see *Swadeshi Movement*, Chapter 8.

[36] Chittagong Divisional Commissioner Luson's Report, 11 G, 15 March 1907, *Home Public A May 1907*, No. 163. *NAI.*

[37] 'Report of the Unofficial Commission of Inquiry into the Riots in Calcutta on the 2, 3 and 4 October 1907.' The Commission, headed by the Moderate politician Narendranath Sen, examined 173 witnesses, including 72 shopkeepers, 29 clerks, 19 merchants, 10 zamindars—but only 4 'menials'. *GOI Home Poll A January 1908*, Nos. 75–80. *NAI.*

If Islam provided the key vehicle for Muslim peasants in the expression of their socio-economic grievances, one could expect caste movements to perform somewhat similar functions for rural Hindu society.[38] The first two decades of the twentieth century in fact witnessed a large number of 'Sanskritizing' caste movements and association in Bengal. The most significant among these were the movements among the Mahishyas of Midnapur, Howrah, Hooghly and 24 Parganas, the Rajbansis of Jalpaiguri, Rangpur and Dinajpur and the Namasudras of Jessore, Khulna and Faridpur—the three major castes below the level of the bhadralok in a province otherwise marked by unusually great fragmentation among intermediate and low castes.[39]

The Mahishyas of Midnapur and the Rajbansis of north Bengal included large numbers of gentry and jotedars as well as peasants. The Namasudras in contrast were overwhelmingly cultivators or sharecroppers subordinate to bhadralok zamindars or tenure-holders.[40] The movements organized by the Bangiya Mahishya and Rajbansi Kshatriya Samitis consequently remained confined to claims to higher caste status and 'Sanskritizing' changes in surnames or social customs; agrarian issues were hardly ever raised.[41]

Among Namasudras of Jessore however a conference in 1908 which discussed educational and social improvement and set up a structure of village, union and district committees financed by weekly rice collections was followed up the next year by moves 'not to work

[38] In a recent article Partha Chatterji has made the interesting point that East Bengal Muslim landholding peasants behaved in many ways like intermediate castes in other parts of the country, with the difference that religion permitted easier extensions of the movements both upwards and downwards to include Muslim gentry and the Muslim landless or poor peasants. 'Caste and Politics in West Bengal', in *Teaching Politics: Special Number on Land, Caste and Politics in Indian States* (Delhi, 1982).

[39] See Chatterji, 'Caste and Politics in West Bengal'. See also *Census of India 1931 Volume V (Bengal and Sikkim) Part I*, Statement XII–10, giving the district-wise number per mille of the five most numerous Hindu castes: Brahman, Kayastha, Namasudra, Mahishiya and Rajbansi.

[40] The proportion of Brahmans, Kayasthas and Baidyas per mille of the Hindu population in 1931 was 184 in Faridpur, 141 in Jessore, 118 in Khulna—but only 71 in Midnapur, 51 in Rangpur, 28 in Dinajpur and 27 in Jalpaiguri. *Census 1931*, Chapter 12, Statement XII–8.

[41] Hitesranjan Sanyal, 'Congress Movements in the Villages of Eastern Midnapur, 1921–1931' in *Asie du Sud: Traditions et Changements* (Paris, 1979). For information about Rajbansi caste movements I am indebted to Ranajit Dasgupta's unpublished 'Nationalist and Left Movements in Bengal: Jalpaiguri 1905–1947'.

as menial servants' in upper-caste houses in Narail sub-division and a refusal to cultivate lands of the latter in Magura. The Jessore Namasudras got some support from Muslim cultivators occupying a similar socio-economic position, and in 1909 Muslims in a village of Sadar sub-division 'combined not to cultivate the lands of their Hindu landlords, unless the latter agreed to allow them to retain a two-thirds share of the produce instead of a half-share'—fascinating evidence of an anticipation of the *tebhaga* demand of the 1940s.[42] A Madaripur pleader in June 1909 reported similar refusals to cultivate *barga* lands and render menial services on the part of the Namasudras of Faridpur.[43] At Telak village near Khulna town in May 1908 a Namasudra-Muslim combination allegedly challenged Brahman control over the local festival of Kali in a conflict which quickly led to a confrontation with the police on the Sherpur pattern. Three years later, in a contrast which once again reveals the interpenetration of diverse issues, Namasudras and Muslims along the Jessore-Khulna border came into conflict with each other, with riots and looting affecting eighteen villages. Details of both incidents unfortunately do not seem available.[44]

A Government of India unpublished 'Note on serious disturbances and political trouble in India from 1907 to 1917' provides interesting confirmation of the distance of mass upheavals from the world of organized national politics during this entire period. The section on 'political disturbances' is confined virtually to a survey of revolutionary-terrorist activity, while the only incidents with something like a mass character included in the list for the Swadeshi years in Bengal are the Mymensingh riots of April-May 1907 and the Calcutta clashes of October 1907. For the years from 1908 to 1917, apart from

[42] O. Malley (ed.), *Jessore District Gazetteer* (Calcutta, 1912), pp. 50, 83. Tanika Sarkar in her unpublished thesis has already drawn attention to anticipations of *tebhaga* in 1909 and again in the 1920s, see 'National Movement and Popular Protest in Bengal, 1928–34' (Unpublished thesis, Delhi University, 1981), pp. 111–21.

[43] Binod Lal Ghosh (Pleader, Madaripur), 'What can be Done for the Namasudras', *Modern Review*, June 1909. Ghosh pleaded for better treatment by upper caste Hindus of Namasudras on the social plane, as well as efforts to start schools and dispensaries, but remained characteristically silent about remedies for agrarian tensions.

[44] There are very brief references to both incidents in *GOI Home Political Deposit February 1918*, No. 31. The *GOI* files on the 1908 affair are not available, that on the Namasudra-Muslim riots of May 1911 (*GOI Home Poll B July* 1911, 76–83, *NAI*) are not particularly illuminating. See also *RNP(B)*, week ending 6 June, 13 June and 20 June 1908 for some scattered information about the Telak village incident. *WBSA*.

the two Namasudra disturbances already mentioned, the only other Bengal reference is to a communal riot at Titagarh and Serampore on the occasion of Bakr-Id in January 1909.[45]

Our sample for the years separating the decline of open Swadeshi politics from the beginning of the 1919–22 upsurge must include the Kamariarchar peasant conference in early 1914. The conference, organized by Khan Mohammed Sarkar of Jamalpur sub-division in Mymensingh with the help of some Calcutta-based Muslim leaders (Fazlul Haq, Abdul Kasem, Muhammed Akram Khan, Moniruzzaman Islamabadi) raised a number of specific demands of the upper stratum of the tenantry vis-a-vis the zamindars[46] and marked the beginning of what came to be called the Praja movement in Bengal. We have to note also the development of Pan-Islamic sentiments in Calcutta which had acutely alarmed the government already by early 1913,[47] and the Calcutta riots of September 1918 in which lower-class Muslims clashed bitterly with the police and army and looted houses and shops of Marwari businessmen in Burra Bazar.[48]

The two recurrent and salient features seem to be the potential strength of peasant solidarity in East Bengal and of mill hands and casual labour in and around Calcutta, and the extreme volatility of popular sentiments and actions. The Praja movement throughout its history would combine in ever-varying proportions anti-zamindar class sentiments with appeals for Muslim solidarity, and the Kamariarchar conference presaged both aspects by its expression of purely agrarian demands though a meeting in which all the speakers were Muslims. In the riots of January 1909, following a clash over cow-slaughter at Titagarh, 'Muhammadan emissaries' were able 'to get their co-religionists in all the mills on the right bank of the Hooghly to march together and cross the river to wreak vengeance on the Hindus', while 'a large number of Muhammadan workers in the Calcutta mills as far south as Garden Reach struck work and commenced to march in various bands on Titagarh'.[49] In 1913 however, in the context of the Balkan wars, Pan-Islamist agitators like

[45] *GOI Home Poll Dep. February 1918*, No. 31. *NAI*.

[46] Jatindranath De, *The History of the Krishak Praja Party in Bengal 1929–47* (Unpublished thesis, Delhi University, 1978).

[47] *GOB Poll (Conf.) F.N. 66/1913: Mohammaden Feeling in Bengal. NMML* microfilm.

[48] Kenneth McPherson, Chapter 3.

[49] Officiating Chief Secretary, Bengal to GOI Home, 4 January 6 January, 9/10 January 1909, *GOI Home Police A February 1909*, Nos. 149–55. *NAI*

Ismail Husain Siraji, Mujibur Rahman, Moniruzzaman (all three with Swadeshi backgrounds, incidentally) and Muhammed Akram Khan were co-operating actively with extremist veterans like Krishnakumar Mitra and Shyamsundar Chakrabarti, and some radical Hindus of Telinipara and Chandernagore were allegedly employing an agent named Hyder 'to preach a regular Jehad against the British . . . among all the Mussalman mill hands belonging to the mills on both sides of the river between Hooghly and Calcutta.'[50] The September 1918 riots again saw 'the coolie class . . . giving trouble . . . a large crowd of coolies made incessant attempts . . . to break through from Garden Reach and obtain entry into Calcutta.'[51] Though ultimately directed against Marwaris, the riots had been preceded by bitter anti-British propaganda in the course of which Fazlur Rehman, one of the principal non-Bengali agitators involved in the affair, had even 'eulogized the action of Kshudiram Bose and other revolutionaries'. Governor Ronaldshay in his diary juxtaposed the provocation offered by the alleged insult to the Prophet in the Anglo-Indian journal *Indian Daily News* with memories of the Shahabad riots of 1917, the 'misfortunes of Turkey, the internment of Indian Muhammaden leaders, and the high price of cotton cloth leading during the past winter to a considerable outbreak of *hat*-looting . . .' as causes of the riots.[52]

The reference in Ronaldshay's diary to cloth-prices is a reminder that economic-determinist explanations of popular outbursts have been fairly common. They have been put forward by contemporary officials and later historians alike as supplements to or sometimes alternatives of the interpretation in terms of mobilization from the top alone, and pride of place in such analysis has usually gone to price-fluctuations. British officials often tried to relate bhadralok involvement in Swadeshi and terrorism to the impact of the post-1905 price-rise cutting into relatively inelastic and sometimes in-adequate incomes from fragmented zamindaris, tenure-holdings and services, while the link with the labour upsurge of 1905–8 appeared obvious. The indifference of the peasantry to Swadeshi agitation was

[50] Extracts from Intelligence Branch Secret Reports for weeks ending 12 March, 30 April, 23 July 1913; Chief Secretary, Bengal to Presidency and Burdwan Divisional Commissioners, 8 February 1913, *GOB Poll (Conf.) F.N. 66/1913*.

[51] Bengal Diary of Governor Ronaldshay, entries for 10 September 1918, *Zetland Collection, IOL* MSS Eur. D. 609, *NMML* microfilm.

[52] Bengal Diary, undated, ibid.

conversely sought to be explained by the alleged benefits for agriculturists from high prices of foodgrains and jute, while landless labourers it was argued also did not suffer since they were paid mainly in kind.[53] A closer look compels numerous qualifications. I have argued elsewhere that sheer economic distress fails to explain bhadralok unrest in the Swadeshi age.[54] Allegedly beneficial high prices did not prevent considerable agrarian rioting during 1906–7, and an alternative economic explanation of this in terms of a less optimistic view of the impact of price-rise on the peasantry does not go all the way either. The objectives of the Mymensingh rioters included such 'non-economic' aims as the 'rescue' of Muslim prostitutes, and as for labour strikes the Swadeshi data indicates that an assertion of human dignity against racist insult was a not unimportant element in their causation.[55] Narrowly economic interpretations are of no help at all in understanding the multiplicity of types of subaltern activity and their interpenetration.

With the Rowlatt upsurge of April 1919 we are at first sight in a very different world. The multitude of mass initiatives in the immediate post-war years, most of them combining briefly into an anti-imperialist torrent, seems to bear ample witness to the success of the nationalists in breaking through to and effectively mobilizing the masses. An economic explanation also appears attractive. Price-rise equals labour unrest once again, and though a slight inconsistency might be noted in relating high prices this time to rural upheaval (the official argument in 1905–8 had been just the reverse), an escape-route for the economic-determinist is provided by the fact that industrial prices rose much faster than the agricultural. Such interpretations abound in contemporary archival documents[56] and have been echoed by recent historians like Judith Brown and Rajat Ray.

[53] *Swadeshi Movement*, pp. 25–6, 510–12. The *Annual Report on the Administration of Bengal* (1906–7) noted that there had been 'no serious agrarian disturbances during the year . . . strained relations . . . are the exception rather than the rule.' The 'real sufferers' from the abnormally high prices were the 'so-called bhadralok'. pp. v, 4.

[54] *Swadeshi Movement*, pp. 510–12.

[55] Ibid., Chapter 5.

[56] 'Economic pressure supplies a background of unrest: the high cost of living has caused suffering and discontent and the sufferers . . . are inclined vaguely to attribute their misfortunes to Government or their employers, who in the case of the concerns employing large bodies of industrial labour, are mainly European firms.' Chief Secretary, Bengal to GOI Homes, D.O. 2087P, Calcutta, 19 February 1921 *GOB Poll (Conf.) F.N. 39 (1–2)/1921. WBSA.*

The two assumptions, political and economic, are fairly easily combined: élite-politicians successfully manipulated an economic con-
juncture favourable for agitation through 'sub-contractors' or
organization-cum-propaganda to bring into existence a mass
movement.[57]

Yet the correlation between price-rise and popular militancy was
by no means exact even in 1919–22. At the all-India level Judith
Brown's figures show prices to have started *declining* by 1921–2, the
climactic year for Non-Co-operation-Khilafat.[58] In Bengal the price-
rise was most acute during the lean pre-harvest months of 1919—but
Ronaldshay was reporting at that time that 'apart from a certain
amount of *hat*-looting which has been due entirely to economic
causes, the situation in Bengal continues satisfactory'.[59] In very sharp
contrast a contemporary official report noted the winter of 1921–2 as
being marked in Bengal by a slow recovery from the post-war
economic crisis, with a bumper rice crop and raw jute prices recovering
after six lean years[60]—and yet it was precisely during these months
that the 'mufassil . . . [was] . . . seething with unrest',[61] and that the
upsurge in the countryside attained its point of climax. On the
micro-level too at least one official report related rural militancy to
the relative *absence* of economic distress: 'The inhabitants of Contai
thana are capable of bearing the cost . . . [of punitive police] . . . There
has been a very good rice crop and the people are generally
well-to-do.'[62]

As for mobilization from the top, a very significant though seldom
noticed feature of the Non-Co-operation-Khilafat days was in fact
the distance between the expectations, political methods, and frames
of reference of the patriotic intelligentsia leading the movement, and
what really happened lower down the social scale and ultimately

---

[57] Judith Brown, *Gandhi's Rise to Power 1915–1922* (Cambridge, 1972); Rajat Ray,
'Masses in Politics: the Non-Co-operation Movement in Bengal, 1920–22', *Indian
Economic and Social History Review*, December 1974. Ray for instance begins with a
brief discussion of economic pressures, but his account of the whole movement is
heavily coloured by the assumption that leaders manipulate the masses.

[58] Taking 1873 as 100, the price level went up to 281 in 1920, but fell to 236 in 1921
and 232 in 1922. Judith Brown, p. 125.

[59] Ronaldshay to Montagu, 24 September 1919. *Zetland Collection.*

[60] *Report on Administration of Bengal*, 1921–2, pp. iv.

[61] Ronaldshay to Montagu, 26 January 1922. *Zetland Collection.*

[62] L. Birley, ADM, Midnapur, to Burdwan Divisional Commissioner, 27 January
1922, *GOB Poll (Conf.) F.N. 87 (1–9)/1922. WBSA.*

provided the upsurge with most of its real momentum. In Bengal the collective mentality of this intelligentsia was still very largely set in the mould constituted during Swadeshi years. There was considerable continuity at this level in personnel, methods and social inhibitions.

Though the two top leaders of 1905–8, Surendranath Banerji and Bepinchandra Pal, now played very different roles (and Aurobindo Ghosh had retired from politics into mysticism), Chittaranjan Das and his barrister-friends had provided considerable financial and legal support to earlier extremism. Shyamsundar Chakrabarti, Das' 'Gandhian' rival in 1920, had been deported in 1908 and Das built up the Congress organization from 1921 onwards, relying heavily on released terrorist detenus. Among Khilafat leaders Azad later claimed some vague terrorist connections in youth, and Akram Khan, Mujibur Rahaman, Moniruzzaman Islamabadi and Ismail Hussain Shiraji had been noted for their Swadeshi sympathies.[63] It needs to be emphasized further that very many of the Gandhian forms: boycott and swadeshi, national education, arbitration courts, populist calls for village reconstruction and work in the countryside, an anti-industrial and anti-urban mood, peaceful violation of laws through a 'satyagraha' not perhaps all that different from the 'passive resistance' creed of Pal and Aurobindo—were much less of a novelty in Bengal than in provinces like Gujarat, UP or Bihar which had been untouched by extremism. Official attitudes were equally conditioned by memories of 1905–8 and subsequent terrorism. Though 'revolutionary crime' virtually disappeared from the scene between 1919 and 1924, Ronaldshay in June 1919 had to express alarm for the 'mental balance' of a top police official who was busy deciphering from the pages of the *Amrita Bazar Patrika* a terrorist code based on Conan Doyle,[64] and the Non-Co-operation-Khilafat volunteer movement for a long time excited alarm largely in terms of its alleged terrorist connections.[65] As for social inhibitions, Das' famous Bhowanipur address (1917)

[63] Maulana Abul Kalam Azad, *India Wins Freedom* (New York, etc., 1960), pp. 5–6; Muhammad Waliullah, *Yuga-Bichitra* (Dacca, 1967), pp. 272–7.

[64] *Bengal Diary*, 29 June 1919. *Zetland Collection.*

[65] A fear greatly enhanced by the undoubted role of revolutionaries in building up the Congress and volunteer organizations in the districts following Das' agreement with them in late 1920. Thus Madaripur sub-division in Faridpur, an old Swadeshi and later terrorist base, excited much official alarm in the spring and summer of 1921 due to its regular drilling of volunteers headed by ex-revolutionaries. Intelligence Branch (Bengal) reports for weeks ending 7 April, 7 July 1921, *GOI Home Poll 327/V/1922. NAI.* And yet popular violence, as we shall see, generally developed in 1921–2 in areas very different from Madaripur or other strongholds of the bhadralok.

had combined passionate pleas for village work with total silence about rent issues or zamindari exploitation, and a scheme of village organization announced in January 1921 by Das, Azad and other Congress and Khilafat leaders was marked by a similar silence.[66]

On the eve of the Rowlatt satyagraha in Calcutta Ronaldshay found the scene at a Town Hall protest meeting 'redolent of the anti-Partition agitation', but was assured privately by Das and Byomkesh Chakrabarti that 'provocative language' would be avoided, shops would not be closed, and that passive resistance to specific laws 'was not favoured' in Bengal.[67] The actual course of events in April 1919 proved startlingly different from Swadeshi patterns and leadership expectations alike. In the disturbances in Calcutta on 11–12 April following the news of Gandhi's arrest, educated Bengali Hindu youth, so prominent in 1905, were much less in evidence than Muslims and Marwaris whose 'fraternization' so soon after the September 1918 riots naturally appeared 'mysterious' and 'disconcerting' to Ronaldshay.[68] Except for this brief flare-up Bengal was much less affected by the Rowlatt satyagraha than Delhi or the Punjab, and in general the Khilafat-Non-Co-operation movement took a rather long time to get off the ground in the province. Bengal extremists now led by C. R. Das resisted Gandhi's plunge into Non-Co-operation till the Nagpur Congress of December 1920. The Khilafatists were more enthusiastic and active, calling for hartals (not very successfully) on 19 March and 1 August 1920, helping to make boycott of elections very effective in Muslim-majority districts and bringing a large number of Muslim students out of government schools by November-December 1920. Yet Khilafat leaders too had their inhibitions, indicated for instance by the announcement on the eve of the 19 March hartal 'that the coolie class was not to cease work . . . for more than a hour at the time of midday prayer.'[69]

[66] Both the address of April 1917 and the January 1921 statement talked about co-operative banks and grain-stores (*dharmagolas*), sanitation, drainage and medical efforts, arbitration courts, relief work, and reduction in jute acreage. R & B. K. Sen, *Deshbandhu Chittaranjan Das* (Calcutta, 1926), contains the text of the Bhowanipur address; *Mussalman*, 28 January 1921.

[67] *Bengal Diary*, 21 March, 4 April 1919. *Zetland Collection.*

[68] The Governor sought to explain it by alleged Marwari expectations of a Muslim quid pro quo (giving up cow-slaughter), veneration for Gandhi as 'a supporter of orthodox Hindu aspirations', and Marwari resentment about the excess profits tax. Ronaldshay to Montagu, 19 May 1919, ibid.

[69] *History of the Non-Co-operation Movement in Bengal—GOB Poll (Conf.) F.N. 395 1–3/1924. WBSA.*

Even during 1921–2, it was precisely the forms of agitation sanctioned by Gandhi and well-integrated with the Swadeshi memories of the intelligentsia which proved surprisingly ineffective in Bengal. At times their impact seems to have been even less than in 1905–8. A numerically small but culturally very significant part of the intelligentsia headed by Rabindranath Tagore was openly hostile to Gandhian Non-Co-operation, and it is significant that the flood of patriotic songs which constituted such a notable feature of the Swadeshi era found no counterpart in 1919–22. Boycott did evoke a somewhat greater response from trading groups now, with sections of the Marwari community in a new patriotic mood, swayed by Gandhi and no doubt influenced also by the sharp fluctuations in the rupee-sterling exchange ratio which made the keeping of contracts with Lancashire often a hazardous business.[70] But boycott was reported to be 'lukewarm' in Bengal in August 1921, and by November some of the Calcutta Marwaris who had promised Gandhi not to indent foreign cloth for six months (till February 1922) had started breaking their pledge.[71] In sharp contrast to 1905 there was no spurt this time in indigenous entrepreneurship, while *charkha* propaganda was officially described as not very successful 'except in fashionable non-co-operation circles in Calcutta.'[72] What caught the popular imagination and alarmed the authorities was not the concrete economic impact of boycott or Swadeshi but the mass courting of arrest in November-December 1921 through token sales of khadi by a cross-section ranging from the wife of C. R. Das to mill hands and boatmen. As for the educational boycott, Das' spectacular gesture of January 1921 did for a time produce a real exodus from government colleges and schools.[73] but the emphasis was now on youth abstention from

[70] Sabyasachi Bhattacharya, 'Cotton Mills and Spinning Wheels: Swadeshi and the Indian Capitalist Class 1920–22', in K. N. Panikkar (ed.), *National and Left Movements in India* (New Delhi, 1980).

[71] Viceroy to Secretary of State, 25 August, 9 November 1921, *Reading Collection*, MSS Eur. E.238/4, *IOL*.

[72] *History of Non-Co-operation Movement in Bengal*, p. 5.

[73] By March 1921, 11, 157 out of 103, 107 attending government or aided institutions had left, though about one-third rejoined later on, ibid., p. 4. The statistics of student enrolment given by Vice-Chancellor Asutosh Mukherji to the Calcutta University Senate may be more complete: he reported a 23 per cent fall in recognized schools and 27 per cent decline in colleges in July 1921 as compared to July 1920. *Mussalman*, 30 September 1921.

education for a year, not the starting of alternative national schools.[74] Arbitration courts were more successful, totalling 866 in all for the period from February 1921 to April 1922; at their height in August 1921 'they considerably outnumbered the Government courts.'[75] The other major plank in the official Non-Co-operation-Khilafat rural programme, a campaign among peasants against jute cultivation, had once again Swadeshi precedents in theory if not practice.[76] Started in February 1921 it did have some impact for a time, but had to go against the economic fact that raw jute prices though unusually low in 1921 were still higher than that of paddy. The later official survey makes the interesting point that the one significant result of the anti-jute agitation 'was to make the cultivator think of other methods in which he might improve his position and to prepare the way for the no-taxes and no-rent movement . . .'[77]

Official files and private papers make abundantly clear that what really alarmed the authorities and made of Non-Co-operation-Khilafat a movement vastly different from that of 1905–8 was the large scale adoption of such 'other methods' through popular initiative and not anything deliberately worked out by Gandhi or the Calcutta leaders. The vast range of such initiatives extended from sporadic hat-looting[78] through a massive labour upsurge to jail-breaks, resignations by policemen, non-payment of chaukidari and Union Board taxes, hostility to settlement operations, no-rent, and virtually total disavowal of British authority by peasants fired by a conviction that Gandhi raj was coming or even already in existence.

Among all these forms, haat-looting was the one most directly related to economic distress. The high price of cloth led to one such outbreak in the winter of 1917–18.[79] In August-September 1919 a

---

[74] Hirendranath Datta, veteran of the 1906 national education movement, issued a notice in January 1921 proposing a revival of Arts and Science departments in the Bengal National College provided 150 students were available. An Education Board was set up under Jitendralal Banerji to conduct 'national examinations', and we hear of a Kalikata Vidyapith with Subhas Bose as Principal. *Mussalman*, 28 January, 11 February, 23 September 1921. National Schools were set up in nearly every district in early 1921, but most of them quickly withered away. *GOB Poll (Conf.) 395 1.3/1924*, p. 4. *WBSA*.   [75] Ibid., p. 6.

[76] *Swadeshi Movement*, p. 270.

[77] *GOB Poll (Conf.) 395 1.3/1924*, p. 4.

[78] 'Haat'—the indigeneous term for village or small town markets, usually held on a specific day in the week.

[79] Bengal Diary, undated entry describing the Calcutta riots of September 1918. *Zetland Collection*.

very sharp rise in rice prices (due to large scale exports from Bengal to feed other famine-striken areas) was accompanied by eighty-two cases of haat-looting.[80] The available extremely scanty data unfortunately provide no information about the climate of popular opinion which conditioned such haat-looting; we have no information for instance as to whether the food rioters were animated by any definite conception of a 'just price'.[81] Haat- and fish-pond looting by Santals in north-west Midnapur and Bankura in 1922 and 1923 however was clearly part of a broader upsurge and had more to do as we shall see with rumours of a crisis in authority than economic distress alone.[82]

Throughout 1920 and even part of 1921 the correspondence of the Governor of Bengal indicates that labour unrest evoked maximum official concern, followed by the Khilafat agitation (itself connected with the presence 'of a very large Muhammadan labour force employed in the jute mills');[83] specifically Gandhian Non-Co-operation came as a poor third.[84] In a telegram to the Secretary of State, Chelmsford attributed the unprecedented countrywide strike wave primarily to economic factors: soaring prices and the 'general shortage of industrial labour' due to post-war industrial expansion and the influenza epidemic. But he also mentioned as contributory elements the growing awareness 'that capitalists, millowners in particular, are making very large profits', the impact of 'world-wide political unrest . . . frequent reports of labour trouble in England and Europe', and 'to some extent' encouragement 'by political agitators in India'.[85] The Bengal Committee on Industrial Unrest listed 137

[80] Ronaldshay to Montagu, 24 September 1919; Ronaldshay to King George V, 30 September 1919, ibid., *Annual Report on Administration of Bengal, 1918–1919*, pp. 15.

[81] There are references to crowds enforcing lower prices (and not just looting) in north Bihar in 1921 and parts of Bengal in 1931–2. See Stephen Henningham, Tanika Sarkar.

[82] *GOB Poll (Conf.) 87 1–9/1922, 181/1923. WBSA.*

[83] The 'proximity' of this labour force to Calcutta, Ronaldshay argued, was 'the chief danger', for the Muslim worker 'if aroused is capable of serious rioting as our experience in September 1918 showed.' Ronaldshay to George V, 12 May 1920. *Zetland Collection.*

[84] 'Gandhi's non-co-operation movement still falls flat in Bengal' (Ronaldshay to Montagu, 5 July 1920). 'Apart from the activities of Kalam Azad and half a dozen of his tools in Calcutta, the situation in Bengal is entirely satisfactory', ibid., 19 July 1920. An earlier letter to Montagu (6 April) had identified some of these 'tools' with 'the group of Calcutta pan-islamists which gave us trouble in September 1918'—yet another indication of the interpenetration of logically very different forms of political activity.

[85] Telegram from Viceroy to Secretary of State, No. 8C, 25 October 1920, in reply to a query from the Secretary of State dated 16 October, *GOI Home Poll B November 1920*, No. 281. *NAI.*

strikes in the province in the nine months starting from July 1920, while the annual administrative reports chronicle 150 strikes involving 265,000 workers in 1921 and 91 strikes involving *c*.160,000 next year.[86]

Comparison with Swadeshi labour unrest is again illuminating. Trade unions were far more numerous, though still often somewhat ephemeral, than in 1905–8: an Intelligence Branch list recorded forty 'labour unions and associations' in Bengal in 1920, fifty-five in 1921 and seventy-five in 1922.[87] Barristers with nationalist connections were once again fairly prominent, men like I. B. Sen, S. N. Haldar or N. C. Sen, all three close to Chittaranjan Das. But the government was much more worried by the activities of Khilafat agitators like Muhammed Osman, trying 'to spread disaffection on religious grounds among the mill coolies',[88] and recruiting volunteers from jute labourers via contacts with sardars.[89] The spate of swamis or 'political sanyasis' also made officials nervous. As in 1905, strikes, unions and nationalist barrister-connections were at first most noticeable among white-collar employees of printing presses and mercantile firms, along with railway clerks and tramway men.[90] But the upsurge in the jute mills far outstripped Swadeshi precedents, plantations and the coal belt were affected for the first time, and among mill hands, tea garden coolies, miners and railway menial staff alike a more 'religious' style of leadership was apparent. Apart from Muhammed Osman, Swami Iswar Das from Chapra was active among jute mill hands. Swami Biswananda (Rasul Singh), Swami Dinanada (ex-professor of Sibpur Engineering College) and Swami

---

[86] *Report of Committee on Industrial Unrest* (Calcutta, 1921), p. 2; *A Report on Administration of Bengal, 1920–1*, p. xi and *1921–2*, p. xi.

[87] *List of Labour Unions and Associations in Bengal 1920, 1921, 1922* (Bengal Government confidential publication) I am grateful to Rajat Ray for giving me access to these documents.

[88] *History of Non-Co-operation Movement in Bengal*, p. 1, GOB Poll (Conf.) F.N. 395 1.3/1924. WBSA.

[89] Officiating Chief Secretary Bengal, to GOI (Home), No. 16410 P of 17 November 1921—*GOB Poll (Conf.) F.N. 333 11–26/1921. WBSA.*

[90] Thus an Employees Association of merchant office clerks was set up in August 1919, with Sachindranath Basu, son of the Swadeshi labour leader Premtosh Basu, an office bearer. The Journalists and Press Employees Association of January 1920 had C. R. Das as President and Bepin Pal, Jitendralal Banerji, I. B. Sen, S. N. Haldar, Hemantkumar Sarkar and Maulavi Akram Khan among its office bearers. Tram workers went on strike repeatedly during 1920 and 1921, and N. C. Sen and S. N. Haldar figured among the office bearers of the Tramway Employees Union set up in October 1920. See *List of Labour Unions and Associations in Bengal.*

Darshanananda figured prominently in strikes in the coal belt in the winter of 1920–1 as well as in the Assam-Bengal rail and steamer strikes of mid-1921 and the EIR strike of early 1922. Official reports attributed the exodus from tea plantations in the Chargola valley partly to the preaching of sadhus like Bisamber Das Guru of Central Provinces and Siyaram Das of Ajodhya.[91]

Initiative from below however remained far more important than organization through outsiders in the strike wave of 1919–22. The Committee on Industrial Unrest statistics reveal the striking fact that labour unrest was at its height in the last quarter of 1920,[92] i.e. before the Non-Co-operation-Khilafat Movement really got into its stride in Bengal. Political agitation and labour militancy followed parallel but largely separate paths, intermingling only on two occasions: the East Bengal railway and steamer strikes following the belabouring of tea garden coolies at Chandpur in May 1921, and the use of mill hands as volunteers courting arrest in Calcutta in December 1921–January 1922. Yet statements that leaders like J. M. Sengupta 'brought off'[93] the East Bengal strikes grossly oversimply a more complex reality. These began really as a more-or-less spontaneous protest against Gurkha atrocities taking place 'before the very eyes of the railway employees'.[94] The strikes were no doubt encouraged by the Bengal Congress decision to provide 'advice and financial help',[95] but they continued mainly on the basis of specific labour demands for strike pay and recognition of the Assam-Bengal Employees Union.[96]

[91] Notes by Intelligence Branch, CID, Bengal, 9 July 1921, 7 November 1921, and by CID, Assam, 21 October 1921, *Reports on activities of political emissaries disguised as sadhus and fakirs. GOI Home Poll 118/1922. NAI.*

[92] Of the 137 strikes listed by the Committee on Industrial Unrest, 11 per cent took place in the third quarter of 1920, 65 per cent in the last quarter of the same year, and 24 per cent in the first quarter of 1921. Quoted in Sanat Bose, 'Industrial Unrest and Growth of Labour Unions in Bengal 1920–24', *Economic and Political Weekly*, Special Number, November 1981.			[93] Rajat Ray, p. 367.

[94] Statement of J. M. Sengupta at Chandpur, 14 July 1921, *Mussalman*, 22 July 1921. Following the Gurkha attack on the night of 20 May, sympathy strikes began among Chandpur and Laksham railway staff on 24 May; the decision for a general strike was taken by the Chittagong-centred Assam-Bengal Railway union next day. The steamer strike began on 27 May, following the arrest of the Secretary of the Sarangi Association, Abdul Majid. *Indian Annual Register, 1922*, p. 144.

[95] 'Each station staff should go to the nearest Congress Office for advice and financial help.' Statement by J. M. Sengupta, *Mussalman*, 17 June 1921.

[96] J. M. Sengupta's statement of 14 July pointed out that the railway employees were 'holding out on three points'—strike pay, no break in service, recognition of their Union (of which Sengupta was President). *Mussalman*, 22 July 1921.

It is interesting that Das' defence of the railway strike was more than a little embarrassed.[97] The use of mill hands to court arrest did bring about a startling though shortlived change in the social composition of the Calcutta agitation.[98] But even if we disregard repeated official charges that the labourers were no more than mercenaries hired through Khilafat funds,[99] one does get the impression that the politicians were really using the proletariat as cannon-fodder at a time when student and bhadralok enthusiasm for going to jail was fast ebbing.[100] There was little or no nationalist interest in the major East India railway strike of February-March 1922, and certainly no effort at all to co-ordinate it with the civil disobedience programme.[101] And

[97] C. R. Das in a statement at Chandpur on 12 June declared that the strikes were 'not labour or political strikes . . . they are national', examples of 'spontaneous non-cooperation' similar to the hartal by lawyers of Comilla, Chittagong and Noakhali courts following news of the Chandpur incident. 'If it had been a labour strike, a mere question between the employer and the employed, I should have certainly discouraged it from the Congress point of view. I mean I would not have allowed it to interfere in any way with the ordinary work of the Congress.' *Mussalman*, 17 June 1921.

[98] Of the 349 arrests in Calcutta during the week ending 5 January 1922, only 39 were students. '123 were mill hands from Telipara, Metiabruz, Kankinara, Champdeney, Barrackpore, Shamnagore, Khurda, Kamarhatty, Gondalpara and Bhadreswar. The remaining persons arrested were boat manjhis and low class Muhammedans from the suburbs'. Calcutta Police Commissioner to GOB Chief Secretary, 5 January 1922, *GOB Poll (Conf.) 14 (1–20)/1922. WBSA*. It would be difficult to imagine a greater contrast with Swadeshi days.

[99] The volunteers courting arrest were mostly students till 17 December, Ronaldshay noted in his diary, 'but since then nearly the whole has been millhand, paid for the purpose.' Bengal Diary, 20 December 1921, *Zetland Collection*. The *Amrita Bazar Patrika* of 21 December 1921 tried to refute the charge of the *Englishman* that millhands were being paid by the Khilafat Committee—'Our information is that the millhands raised money by subscription among themselves . . .' Court reports of statements by arrested millhands and boatmen carried in the same issue were somewhat ambiguous. Some stated 'they were volunteers, but they could not say what was the object of the organization of the hartal on 24th. An elderly mill coolie said that his conscience told him to organize hartal on the 24th and so he was preaching this among his countrymen.'

[100] The difficulties in recruiting middle class Bengali volunteers are recalled in Hemendranath Dasgupta, pp. 218–19.

[101] There was a brief strike of the EIR menial staff from Mughal Sarai to Asansol in early January 1922, following alleged high-handedness of a foreman. A bigger strike began on 2 February 1922 after a case of assault by a white on Indian firemen at Tundla at a time when civil disobedience had not yet been countermanded by Gandhi, *Amrita Bazar Patrika*, 3, 5, 6 January 1922; *Mussalman*, 10, 24 February 1922. The *Servant* of 24 February 1922, the Calcutta journal closest to Gandhism, commented apropos of the EIR strike 'that it is an unpardonable mistake to suppose that labour strikes are either necessary or can in any way avail to advance the cause of non-cooperation'. *RNEP(B)* for week ending 4 March 1922. *WBSA*.

Gandhi himself as is well known denounced the East Bengal strikes,[102] while in December 1921 the arrest of Biswanand evoked from him the following hasty telegram to the Jharia coal belt: 'Coolies must not strike. They may discard foreign clothes in earnest of their devotion. They must be absolutely peaceful.'[103]

Though most strikes took place on specific economic demands, other dimensions were not entirely absent. Racist insults and assaults at Jhajha and Tundla provided the immediate occasions for the two EIR strikes in early 1922. At Kumardhubi in January 1921 the men left work after a similar incident, and when the management tried to lay off some of them declared 'that they would either go back to work in a body or not go back at all.'[104] In November 1921 in a striking demonstration of working class solidarity tramwaymen were 'joined by mill hands from neighbouring mills' in picketing Belgachia depot (north Calcutta) and in subsequent clashes with the police.[105] 5,000 Calcutta dock labourers went on strike on 14 December after an officer had removed a man's Gandhi cap; they demanded the immediate release of C. R. Das and the right to 'shout Gandhi Maharaj Ki Jai while working on board.'[106] And in a fascinating combination of patriotic millennial rumours and hardheaded collective bargaining jute mill workers in the last week of December 1921 demanded an end to the common practice 'to keep three days wages in hand while paying a week's wages. The reason of such a demand is, we are told, that the workers are in the belief that they will get Swaraj on the 24th.'[107]

The rumour of imminent swaraj in fact worked wonders repeatedly during 1921 and early 1922. Apart from the famous exodus of 6,000–7,000 coolies from Chargola tea estates in May 1921,[108] the most

[102] 'In India we want no political strikes'. *Lessons of Assam, Young India*, 15 June 1921.

[103] Telegram to G. K. Gadgil, *Amrita Bazar Patrika*, 28 December 1921.

[104] Swami Biswanand in his speech to Kumardhati and Kulti workers at Barakar on 17 January 1921 emphasized this dimension: '. . . although there was need for food in this world, there was also need for honour . . .', *GOI Home Poll Dept. February 1921*, No. 5. *NAI*.

[105] Viceroy to Secretary of State, 14 November 1921, *Reading Collection*.

[106] *Mussalman*, 16 December 1921.

[107] *Amrita Bazar Patrika*, 23 December 1921.

[108] The Chargola labourers demanded large pay increases 'with shouts of Gandhi-Maharaj ki jai', and then left the plantations in a body. Viceroy to Secretary of State, 21 June 1921, *Reading Collection*. The *Sanjivani* complained on 7 July that the tea coolies were rejecting offers for agricultural employment in Bengal . . . 'unfortunately the idea has become rooted in their minds that Gandhi has become king of their province and that his Raj is free from sorrow and want. They are not therefore prepared to go anywhere but their native villages.' *RNP(B) for week ending 16 July 1921. WBSA.*

anywhere but their native villages.' *RNP(B) for week ending 16 July 1921. WBSA.*

spectacular instance was probably the jailbreak by 669 prisoners from Rajshahi on 24 March 1921. This had been preceded by rumours that Gandhi was coming to Rajshahi on 25 March to end the British raj. The prisoners before breaking out 'bound *rakhis* or threads on their wrists as a sign of unity', thus reviving the symbolism of 1905 in a totally different context, and marched openly in a body through the streets of the town after overpowering their guards.[109] Smaller jail-breaks occurred or were attempted at Sirajganj, Netrokona, Dinajpur, Rangpur, Midnapur and Barisal.[110] Even more serious from the government point of view was large scale disaffection among the police with thirty Calcutta Muslim constables and head-constables resigning after a Maidan meeting of 200 policemen on 13 November 1921, pro-Non-Co-operation sentiments among upcountry constables in Howrah, and reports of police unrest flowing in from Noakhali, Rangpur, Mymensingh, Khulna, Bogra, and 24 Parganas.[111] A Hindi newspaper quoted a moving statement by one disaffected constable: 'We shall all go home giving up our service and till land and spin charkha and pass our days happily. Mahatmaji has opened our eyes.'[112]

Turning to more specifically rural movements, one might perhaps distinguish three strands. The very successful anti-Union Board agitation in Contai sub-division of Midnapur and the boycott of settlement operations in Bogra and Birbhum were organized and controlled movements under local nationalist leaders (Birendranath Sasmal in Midnapur, Jitandralal Banerji in Birbhum), taking up grievances which were specific, occasionally long-standing,[113] and

[109] Official account of the Rajshahi jail-break, published in *Mussalman*, 20 May 1921.

[110] *Report on Administration of Bengal, 1920–21*, p. x

[111] Reports on Political Situation (Bengal), *GOI Home Poll 18/November 1921, 18/December 1921*. Note by D.I.G. Intelligence Branch, 31 December 1921—*GOB Poll (Conf.) 39/137/1921*. In February 1922, two Nepali women were reported as spreading disaffection among Gurkha armed policemen in Calcutta. 'I beg to point out that it is now impossible to deal with these women', complained the Deputy Commissioner of Police. *GOB Poll (Conf.) 14/21–30/1922. WBSA.*

[112] *Hindustan*, 16 November 1921—*RNP(B) for weak ending 26 November 1921. WBSA.*

[113] Thus the introduction of Union Boards into Contai meant a possible seven-fold increase, from Rs 12 to a maximum of Rs 84 in a chowkidari tax which a Bengal Chief Secretary had admitted way back in 1908 as falling 'too heavily on poor communities which really cannot afford wholetime chowkidars'. B. N. Sasmal's report on the Contai movement, *Mussalman* 7 October 1921; *GOB Poll (Conf.) 187(1–2)/1908.* As for settlement operations, there were widespread fear that these would affect the standing crops, already rather poor in Birbhum in 1921.

above all without divisive potential so far as the rural community was
concerned. Barring an isolated assault on a white settlement officer in
Bogra[114] such movements were both united and remarkably peaceful.
Thus at Contai tahsildars were invited by villagers to attach their
property 'amidst shouts of Haribole and blowing of conch-shells',
'labourers and cartmen . . . refused everywhere to carry the attached
moveables',[115] and Union Boards had to be withdrawn from Midnapur
district as it was 'impossible to realize Union board rates by distraint,
since no one will come forward to bid at the sales.'[116] In the four
northern police stations of Birbhum centered around Rampurhat
(J. L. Banerji's home-town), settlement operations 'almost completely
stopped' in November 1921 due to social boycott of officials. It was
'impossible to procure coolies locally for the work' and moves by the
authorities to get zamindar support failed: 'the resident landlords are
for the most part petty and would be unable even if they were willing
to put a stop to the opposition of the people.'[117] The dominant
Swadeshi pattern of patriotic zamindars rallying their tenants had
clearly been reversed to a considerable extent.

But it would be a serious mistake to assume an extension of the
Contai pattern everywhere or to think that Gandhian restraints and
social harmony could be maintained always in 1921–2. The Bengal
Congress leadership in general remained as always very allergic to the
raising of rent issues. The most 'radical' leadership statement was
probably that at the Barisal Provincial Conference in April 1921, and
even this limited itself to requesting zamindars not to levy abwabs
and to limit the filing of rent suits 'even at a sacrifice.'[118] Some
newspapers in the Non-Co-operation period did give greater coverage
to zamindari exploitation than at all common in Swadeshi days, but
most of these journals tended to be somewhat aloof and at times
positively hostile towards the political movement.[119] A special case

[114] Report on Political Situation (Bengal), GOI Home Poll 18/November 1921.
WBSA.   [115] See B. N. Sasmal's report.
[116] See Report on Political Situation.
[117] Report on F. W. Robertson, Settlement Officer, Bankura-Birbhum to F. A.
Sachse, Director of Land Records, Suri, 17 November 1920, GOB Poll (Conf.)
347(–1–5)/1921. WBSA.
[118] The Conference went a bit further on labour issues by extending 'cordial support
to the movement for organising labour unions . . . while deploring the necessity for
strikes', Mussalman, 1 April 1921.
[119] Of the three newspapers giving noticeable coverage to agrarian disputes, the
Raiyat clearly warned that 'the raiyat movement will be stifled if it is mixed up with
politics' (3 September 1921). The Navyug was edited in part by the future Communist

was presented however by the Midnapur Zamindari Company, a white-owned concern with extensive estates in central Bengal as well as in Midnapur. Newspapers carried frequent reports about the oppressive ways of this company, and more particularly of its branches at Bilimaria in Rajshahi and Shikarpur at Nadia[120]—areas where tensions had been sharpened by a bid to revive indigo cultivation taking advantage of the wartime elimination of German synthetic dye competition. Das privately encouraged Someswarprasad Chaudhuri, a young medical student who had joined the educational boycott, to try and organize peasant resistance to the company along the Rajshahi-Pabna-Nadia-Murshidabad border, though he made it clear that the Congress formally could give no support as the movement could very well adversely affect Indian zamindars who followed not dissimilar practices. Someswarprasad's autobiographical account gives vivid and fascinating details about the pattern of initial contacts (through Marwari traders and village *pramaniks* or headmen) and the forms of struggle (mass recording of grievances followed by a *dharmaghat* or collective refusal to do *begar* or work for the company)—as well as about the inevitable social problems when no-rent spread to the neighbouring estate of the zamindar of Rifaitpur in Nadia, in whose house a top Congress leader happened to be staying just at that time.[121]

While the central Bengal peasant agitation still retained a somewhat tenous link with the Congress leadership through Someswarprasad's personal connections with and loyalty to C. R. Das, more elemental

leader Muzaffar Ahmed, but its owner was A. K. Fazlul Huq who opposed Non-Co-operation. At least some of its articles could be frankly communal, as when it accused Khilafatists of trying to submerge 'Musalmans as a race . . . into the community of idolators' (25 November 1921). The *Hitavadi*, which had earlier carried a lot of news about zamindari oppression, changed its line abruptly around November 1921 to warn about the 'grim shadow of Bolshevism' and the danger that 'swaraj would mean Khilafat raj' (25 November 1921) *RNP(B)* for weeks ending 10 September and 3 December 1921. *WBSA*.

[120] *Raiyat*, 16 April and 3 September 1921; *Nava Yuga*, 24 May 1921; *Hitavadi*, 24 June, 8 July, 15 July, 19 August, 26 August, 2 September and 16 September 1921, *RNP(B)* for relevant weeks. *WBSA*.

[121] Someswaraprasad Chaudhuri, *Nilkar Bidroha* (Calcutta, 1972) pp. 6–8, 9–10, 16–19, 22–4, 29–43, 48–62. There are some clear parallels with the Champaran movement of 1917, where too the Indian trading element resented white planter rivalry and collective recording of grievances played an important role. See Jacques Pouchepadass, 'Local leaders and the intelligentsia in the Champaran satyagraha (1917); a study in peasant mobilization', *Contributions to Indian Sociology*, 1974.

and uncontrolled movements had started developing in the winter of 1921–2. There is considerable evidence that what frightened the authorities most were not movements of the controlled Gandhian variety of which Birendranath Sasmal's Contai is the best-known prototype, but the 'great wave of lawlessness which swept over the affected areas of east and west Bengal' in which the authority of district Congress Committees was 'rapidly lost' and there was a drift toward 'civil disobedience', though no leader had ever sanctioned it.[122] Ronaldshay reported to Montagu in real alarm on 9 February 1922: 'it is being widely stated in the villages that Gandhi raj has come and that there is no longer any necessity to pay anything to anybody. They are consequently not only refusing to pay rent and taxes but also repudiating their debts!'[123]

British officials had repeatedly warned local Congress leaders with land who were heading the movement for non-payment of chowkidari taxes that 'the next step the people will take will be the refusal to pay rent'.[124] Despite a formal statement by the publicity board of the Provincial Congress warning the districts against no-rent,[125] reports of such movements were flooding in by the winter of 1921–2 amidst a general collapse of authority in a number of regions. The four areas principally affected were Midnapur, parts of Rangpur and Jalpaiguri, Chittagong, and Tippera—mostly outlying regions it is interesting to note, relatively distant from the metropolis. We also hear of incidents in Mymensingh where a Kishoreganj Marwari trading firm with extensive landed property became the principal target, and Noakhali where zamindars were reported by the District Magistrate to be in terror of their own tenants.[126] Peasants in Mymensingh district were said to have declared 'that they live in the land of God and are His creation and they are not to pay anything to anybody in the world.'[127]

In Midnapur the district Congress urged paying up of chowkidari

---

[122] *History of Non-Co-operation movement in Bengal*, p. 13.

[123] *Zetland Collection*.

[124] Notes by Midnapur Sadar SDO, Manicharan Bose, 13 January 1922, and by Midnapur A.D.M. L. Birley, 16 January 1922, *GOB Poll (Conf.) F.N. 87(1–9)/1922. WBSA.*

[125] Report on Political Situation, Bengal, 2nd half of January 1922, *GOI Home Poll F.N. 18/January 1922. WBSA.*

[126] Report of Mymensingh District Magistrate, 1 January 1922, *GOB Poll (Conf.) F.N. 14(21–30)/1922.* Report of Officiating District Magistrate, Noakhali, 28 December 1921, *GOB Poll (Conf.) F.N. 39 (118–128)/1921. WBSA.*

[127] *GOI Home Poll F.N. 18/January 1922. WBSA.*

taxes once the Union Board had been withdrawn in December 1921, but there were still widespread refusals in regions like Contai, Panskura in Tamluk, Daspur in Ghatal, Debra in Sadar, and Gopiballbhpur in Jhargram sub-divisions. The SDO of Ghatal reported that 'the masses absolutely refuse to listen to' local Congress committees, using the argument that payment to the Swaraj Fund exempted them from all other claims, while Santals of Gopiballavpur claimed 'that the chaukidari tax had been abolished by Gandhi Maharaj's order'.[128] Meanwhile in semi-tribal north-west Midnapur (Jhargram sub-division) Santals and Mahatos (Kurmis) went about looting haats, destroying liquor shops amidst shouts of 'Gandhi Maharaj Ki Jai', searching for foreign cloth but taking 'all kinds of cloth indiscriminately', and forbidding the export of paddy but (interesting evidence of some sort of underlying 'moral economy') not 'taking any away'. . . . 'everyone at Silda, including the non-co-operators, was very much afraid', and there was panic in Jhargram town on 29 January. The Santals had been inflamed also by a dispute with the Midnapur Zamindari Company over 'wood for houses and agricultural purposes.' No additional police was ultimately required for Contai but Jhargram had to be pacified by a route-march of the Eastern Frontier Rifles.[129] There was also a spate of dacoities, thirty-three in Midnapur district in January 1922 out of a total of 111 in the province that month.[130]

At Madarihat in Jalpaiguri district on 21 February, following a market quarrel between a Marwari shopkeeper and a Santal coolie, police attempts to arrest some Santals led to an attack by a crowd wearing Gandhi caps which 'demanded the release of the prisoners, shouting all the time that they were immune from bullet wounds as they were wearing Gandhi Maharaj's caps.'[131] Three Santals were killed in police firing. No-rent movements developed in neighbouring Rangpur, affecting the estates of Maharaja Manindra Nandy of

[128] L. Birley to Divisional Commissioner, Burdwan, 27 January 1922, pleading for additional punitive police for Contai and Daspur thanas, *GOB Poll (Conf.) F.N. 87 (1–8) 1/22. WBSA*. It is interesting that many of these areas were to figure very prominently in later militant movements—Daspur in 1930 (the Chechuahat incident—see Tanika Sarkar, pp. 212–17), Contai and Tamluk in 1942, Debra and Gopiballavpur in the Naxalbari days.

[129] L. Birley to Burdwan Divisional Commissioner, 28 January 1922; A. W. Cook, District Magistrate, Midnapur, to Burdwan Divisional Commissioner, 1 February 1922, ibid.

[130] *History of Non-Co-operation Movement in Bengal*, p. 15.

[131] *Mussalman*, 10 March, 1922.

Kasimbazar in Kurigram sub-division.[132] Marwari and Shaha merchants and moneylenders became principal targets along the Rangpur-Assam border, and in Batashan pargana the District Magistrate persuaded the zamindar to give concessions to his tenants as there was 'some danger that that Raiyats' Samiti might be captured by the non-co-operators.'[133]

In Chittagong there was widespread violation of forest laws in Banskhali, Satkania, and three police-stations in Cox's Bazar sub-division. A ten day permission to collect building material after the cyclone of May 1921 was extended indefinitely by popular action, eight out of twelve forest offices burnt in Cox's Bazar, and 'until about May 1922 the Forest Department might have been said to have ceased to function . . . . This widespread looting was not the work of volunteers, but of ordinary villagers out to help themselves . . .'[134]

In Chaudagram police station of Tippera, a part of the district untouched by previous organized agitation (unlike Brahmanbaria or Chandpur), the rural police system had collapsed by November 1921: 'No taxes were being paid, and no agricultural rents collected . . . the agitation was entirely Muhammaden, but not religious. The people were simply out to assert themselves . . .'. Efforts to restore authority led to five clashes with the police in February-March 1922, culminating in a confrontation on 9 March in which three villagers were killed. An official report noted that 'volunteers tried to restrain the mob but without effect', and that educated nationalist reaction to the firing was much less evident than after Chandpur in May 1921 'where the amount of force used was very much less.'[135] Rural Tippera incidentally would again witness a powerful agrarian movement with a nationalist content during Civil Disobedience.[136]

It is noteworthy that unlike more organized movements, popular outbursts of this sort went on happening even after Non-Co-operation had been abruptly called off by the Congress Working Committee at its Bardoli session on 12 February 1922. In April 1923 for instance there was a wave of looting of fish-ponds and violation of forest

[132] Additional Superintendent of Police, Rangpur, to Deputy IG of Police, Intelligence Branch, Bengal, 12 February 1922—*GOB Poll (Conf.) F.N. 14(21–30)/1922. WBSA*.
[133] Reports of Rajshahi Divisional Commissioner 13 August, 18 October 1921, *GOB Poll (Conf.) F.N. 333 (30–46)/1921. WBSA*.
[134] *History of Non-Co-operation Movement in Bengal*, p. 15.
[135] Ibid., p. 14. See also *Mussalman*, 31 March 1922.
[136] Tanika Sarkar, pp. 301–6.

rights over an area of 200 square miles extending from Jamboni and Gopiballabhpur (Jhargram sub-division, Midnapur) westwards to Ghatsila (in Singhbhum district of Bihar) and northwards through Silda and Binpur to Raipur police station in Bankura district. The situation was aggravated in Jamboni by a dispute between the local zamindar and his rival Pratap Dal of Dhalbhum, and in Silda by the activities of the local Congress leader Sailajananda Sen—very different types of politics producing interestingly similar results. However the real roots lay not in any outsider instigation, but in the encroachment on traditional Santal rights to free use of forests by the Jamboni Raj and the Midnapur Zamindari Company once the construction of railways had made timber commercially profitable. Crowds of upto 5,000 consisting of Santals as well as low caste Bengali peasants looted fish-ponds in daylight, asserting what they felt was a natural right. The Santal, an official reported, 'will tell you how in his father's time all jungles were free, all *bandhs* (ponds) open to the public . . . Sometimes he is right.' On one memorable occasion they made Additional District Magistrate Peddie flee for his life: 'It is the first time I have had to run away and I did not like doing so—but there was nothing else possible.'[137]

Agrarian conflicts of various types—tenant-zamindar disputes over rent and tenure, *bargadar* claims to a two-thirds share of the produce—in fact remained a major feature of Bengal life in the mid-1920s, particularly in the context of the rumours and debates which preceded the passage of the Tenancy Amendment Act of 1928.[138] But the link with nationalist politics, always a bit tenuous, had once again broken down—a rupture made blatant by the Swarajist pro-zamindar stance in the 1928 Assembly discussions.[139] Peasant movements consequently tended to revert back to their Swadeshi or post-Swadeshi pattern, finding articulation through forms of communalism or caste.

Thus the abrupt withdrawal of Non-Co-operation and the break-down of Hindu-Muslim unity at the top with the abrogation of the

[137] Fascinating details about the whole affair are given in *GOB Poll (Conf.) F.N. 181/1923. NMML* microfilm.

[138] For details see Tanika Sarkar, Chapter 2, and Partha Chatterji, 'Agrarian Relations and Communalism in Bengal 1926–1935' in R. Guha (ed.), *Subaltern Studies I.*

[139] A detailed analysis of this significant episode has been made in Partha Chatterji, *Agrarian Relations and Politics in Bengal: Some considerations on the Making of the Tenancy Act Amendment 1928* (Centre for Studies in Social Sciences, Calcutta, Occasional paper No. 30, 1980).

Bengal Pact after C. R. Das' death did have serious repercussions on
the world of the subaltern. Relative autonomy is very different from
total disjunction and, as Peter Burke has recently argued, 'peoples'
history', however crucially important, has to be seen as part of a
more all-embracing 'total history'.[140] An example of such interaction
is provided by intelligentsia reactions to the spectacle of mass
awakening in 1919–22. Characterized in the main by panic and
retreat, the same years also saw the beginnings of constructive work
in scattered village centres (Tamluk-Contai, Arambagh, Bankura,
Comilla, etc.) along Gandhian lines leading up to the gradual
formation of more stable peasant bases for the national movement.[141]
It is not a coincidence furthermore that the first Communist groups
emerged in Bombay, Calcutta and Madras in the wake of Non-Co-
operation and its Bardoli anti-climax.

   An unpublished diary written by a young man who would develop
later into a pioneer Marxist teacher and intellectual can be used to
illustrate my point about the far-reaching impact of popular militancy
on the intelligentsia. A Presidency College student named Susobhan
Sarkar, immersed throughout much of 1921 in the poetry of Tagore
and the internal quarrels of the Sadharan Brahmo Samaj, quite sharply
critical of Gandhi along the lines worked out by Tagore in his *Call of
Truth*, was yet sufficiently stirred by the spectacle of thousands
courting arrest in the streets of Calcutta in November-December
1921 to start wearing *khadi* for a while as a token of protest, and to
give up once and for all earlier plans formed under family pressure to
take the ICS examination. What was breaking down above all under
the pressure of mass militancy was the legitimacy of foreign rule, its
acceptance as sacrosanct even by groups otherwise very distant from
nationalist politics and affluent enough to be personally untouched
by economic distress.[142]

   Conversely it is again in terms of a weakening of the legitimacy or

---

[140] Peter Burke, 'Peoples' history or total history', in Raphael Samuel (ed.), *Peoples'
History and Socialist Theory* (London, 1981).

[141] Hiteshranjan Sanyal, 'Arambage Jatiyatabadi Andolan' (*Anya Artha*, Calcutta,
1974–5) and 'Dakshin-Paschim Banglay Jatiyatabadi Andolan' (*Chaturanga*, Calcutta,
1976–7).

[142] Sarkar's diary says nothing about price-rise, is generally very non-political, and
incidentally reveals no awareness as yet of the significance of the Bolshevik Revolution.
All the more interesting, however, are the references to the September 1918 riots, the
Rowlatt disturbances, Chandpur, the hartal of 17 November 1921, and subsequent
mass courting of arrest.

hegemony of the existing order that we can best understand the impact of certain phases of nationalist agitation on the world of the subaltern. In 1919–22 direct organizational or ideological mobilization was still rather minimal; as one official report put it, the 'particular form of lawlessness, which depended on organization and a constant supply of speakers, was shortlived.'[143] What was crucially important was the spread of rumours, potent in their very vagueness about the impending collapse of British rule and the coming of 'Swaraj' or 'Gandhi raj' within a year. The predominant rumour in the Swadeshi period in contrast had been that the babus were quarrelling with the government, and not that the sarkar itself was going down. An understanding of the impact of such things requires something in the way of an analysis of the 'structure' of popular mentality underlying the multifarious forms of militancy we have been studying so far.

III

Taking our sample of popular movement as a whole, I think it is possible to construct a system of correlations and oppositions, structures of collective mentality conducive to rebellion or its opposite. The impact of economic pressures and middle-class political movements can best be understood in terms of their impinging on and activizing such pre-existing structures.

Central to most of the popular outbreaks of our period is a concept of *breakdown*, real or more often rumoured, in the pattern of coercion/hegemony which 'normally' keeps the subalterns in their place despite misery and exploitation. Oppression in 'normal' times is cloaked by a certain legitimacy which makes rebellion seem not only too dangerous in view of the force at the command of the dominant classes and the state, but also morally wrong. A rumour of breakdown is needed to weaken this hegemonic control. Breakdown again can have two dimensions: a more-or-less sudden change in the conditions of life (predominantly, though not necessarily solely, economic) of the oppressed, and rumours of weakening of authority structures due to external threats to or divisions within the dominant strata. In colonial India war or rumours of war with Afghanistan, Russia, Germany or the Ottoman empire repeatedly sparked off such developments, and the early impact of middle-class nationalism was perhaps not qualitatively different.

The first type of breakdown is obviously related to the economic

---

[143] *History of Non-Co-operation Movement in Bengal*, p. 13.

pressures we have been talking about: price-rise and/or poor harvests bringing in their train haat-looting, dacoity and labour unrest, and contributing to communal riots with a significant economic dimension as in Mymensingh in 1906–7 or Calcutta in September 1918. It is a characteristic feature of such disturbances that relatively 'new' oppressors, or at least people considered for various socio-religious or cultural reasons to be 'outsiders', tend to become the principal targets. Thus Hindu landlords and Shaha and Marwari traders-moneylenders, felt to be outside the moral community of a pre-dominantly Muslim peasantry, became objects of attack in parts of eastern and northern Bengal in 1906–7 and again in 1921–2—though there must no doubt have been equally oppressive Hindu zamindars, jotedars, and usurers exploiting Hindu peasants in other parts of the province. Partha Chatterji has recently argued that a Muslim element was by no means unimportant even among rentier groups in East Bengal.[144] Bargadar movements seem to have developed earlier in Jessore, Khulna, or Faridpur, where Namasudras confronted upper caste jotedars, then in Midnapur where Mahishya caste ties helped to keep the countryside more united for a time. In north-west Midnapur in 1923 the Santals blamed newcomer 'Bengalis' for their troubles and displayed a loyalty towards the dispossessed Pratap Dal in preference to the zamindar of Jamboni who had recently taken over the Dalbhum estate from the former.[145] As the protests were usually against what were felt to be new developments, evocations of earlier norms tended to be extremely common, at times developing into golden-age myths. Peasant rioters in Mymensingh in 1906 recalled an old pargana rate of rent,[146] while Santals in 1923 'believed that they were simply carrying on an old tradition', bringing back a 'golden age' when 'all jungles were free'.[147] A nice sense of discrimination was sometimes displayed in actions conditioned by such memories. Thus Gurusaday Dutt, the

[144] Partha Chatterji, 'Agrarian Relations and Communalism in Bengal, 1926–1935'.

[145] Bengal Chief Secretary to GOI (Home), 10 May 1923, enclosing extract from report of Deputy Commissioner, Singhbhum to Chief Commissioner, Chota Nagpur, 28/29 April 1923, *GOB Poll (Conf.) F.N. 181/1923. NMML.*

[146] Before and during the Iswarganj riots of May 1906, there were 'wild and extravagant expectations' that rent would be reduced to Rs 3–6 as per *ara* (a local unit of about five *bighas*). An identical demand had been raised in the same area way back in 1882–3, and the Dacca Commissioner felt that this was 'a reminiscence of a former pargana rate.' *Swadeshi Movement*, p. 458.

[147] Report of Deputy Commissioner, Singhbhum, *GOB Poll (Conf.) F.N. 181/ 1923. NMML.*

District Magistrate of Bankura, reported in 1923 that Santals freely admitted looting of fish-ponds to be illegal, but 'they considered tank-raiding might act as an inducement to zamindars to concede their old customary rights over jungles'.[148]

Yet for resistance to develop, a change for the worse in the conditions of exploitation is often less important than rumours of breakdown of the second type: Santals of Jhargram and Bankura after all had been losing their forest rights for decades. Within the concept of breakdown of authority, I think it is useful to distinguish further between a less and a more 'extreme' form. In the first the rumour is that of a conflict among the superiors: the zamindars or the babus have quarrelled with the government, the latter's officials consequently would be more sympathetic towards our grievances (or conversely the immediate superior would help us in our struggle). The more extreme variety is that *all* existing authority is collapsing, usually through the emergence of a new symbolic power-centre like the Gandhi raj of 1921–2.

Examples of the first type include the refusal of enhanced rent in the Swadeshi period by tenants of patriotic zamindars like Brojendra-kishore Roychaudhuri of Mymensingh, the Muslim attacks on Hindu gentry in 1906–7 fired by rumours that officials were on their side, and the beating-up of Swadeshi babus by plebian elements in Calcutta in October 1907. In the Sherpur incident of September 1907 we meet the alternative version too: the Muslim crowd attacking the police shouted 'that the nine-anna zamindar [a Hindu, and quite a 'well-behaved' one] had ordered them to beat the police and loot their quarters.' The local Superintendent of Police drew 'a rather apt parallel between the shouting of the crowd and the cry of the Musalman rioters in the Dewanganj and other looting cases that the Government and the Nawab [of Dacca] had ordered them to loot the Hindus. It is quite probable that the mob had as little foundation for the one cry as for the other . . .'.[149] In the Midnapur Santal rising of April 1923 the dispossessed Raja, Pratap Dal, was rumoured to have given permission to take wood and fish freely, and so there was a

---

[148] Report from District Magistrate, Bankura, enclosed in report of Divisional Commissioner, Burdwan, to Chief Secretary, GOB, 11 May 1923, ibid.

[149] Telegram from Commissioner of Dacca Division, Jamalpur, 24 September 1907; letter of District Magistrate, Mymensingh to Commissioner, Dacca Division, 10 October 1907, *Government of Eastern Bengal and Assam, Poll (Conf.) F.N. 513(1–22)/1907. WBSA.*

'genuine belief by 90% of the crowds that they were doing nothing illegal.'[150] Some corroboration of the significance of this kind of conflict of authorities in triggering-off peasant movements comes from Satinath Bhaduri's *Dhorai Charitmanas*: Dhorai tells the share-croppers of Biskandha that the time for action has come, since the 'babusaheb' has lost the support of the officials as his son has joined the Congress.[151] There may well be insights worth exploring here for historians of the Kisan Sabha movement which acquired such strength in Bihar immediately after the Civil Disobedience years.

Glimpses of the myth of an alternative power-centre displacing the existing structure can be seen on a few occasions even in the Swadeshi period, in the appeal of Muslim peasant rioters to the alleged authority of Salimulla, the Nawab of Dacca. A Muslim communal leaflet, *Nawab Sahaber Subichar*, portrays the Nawab as taking over, in fact conquering, large parts of Bengal from the British.[152] A fantastic and ludicrous vision, for Salimulla in reality was a notorious sycophant of the British, and yet the emphasis on conquest is surely an interesting pointer to certain subterranean structures of popular mentality. Such dimensions rose to the surface in an incomparably more massive and direct manner during Non-Co-operation-Khilafat with its dominant myth of the coming of Gandhi raj.

A crucial feature of the concept of breakdown of authority in its more extreme form is its predominantly magico-religious character, natural and indeed inevitable in a peasant society which has not undergone the process of 'disenchantment of the world' partially brought about in the West in the post-Reformation era. Religion in such societies, as Marx emphasized in a magnificent passage of which only the last sentence is commonly remembered, 'is the general theory of that world, its encyclopaedic compendium, its logic in a popular form, its spiritualistic *Point d' honneur*, its enthusiasm, its moral sanction, its solemn complement, its universal source of consolation and justification.' 'The *protest* against real distress' con-sequently also takes on the alienated form of religion.[153] In a world

---

[150] See *GOB, Poll (Conf.) F.N. 181/1923.*

[151] 'Why should we be afraid any longer? The *daroga, hakim*, and *chaukidar* are all against the *babusaheb* now.' *Satinath Granthabali*, II, p. 173. My translation.

[152] The Nawab, the pamphlet claimed, has conquered Assam, Sylhet, Chittagong—and, Allah permitting, he might conquer the whole world some day. For details, see *Swadeshi Movement*, pp. 456–7.

[153] Karl Marx, *Contribution to the Critique of Hegel's Philosophy of Law, Intro-duction* (1844), in Marx and Engels, *Collected Works*, Vol. III (Moscow, 1973), p. 175.

largely untouched by secular creeds of progress, total breakdown involves a change of such magnitude that it can usually be conceived only in supernatural terms. I feel that the religious dimension is vital for an understanding of at least four crucial features of popular movements in the early Gandhian era: the nature and significance of rumour, the ethical norms and ritual obligations imposed by the emerging cult of Gandhi, the mood of renunciation and sacrifice evoked by the Mahatma, and the persistence of faith in him despite repeated instances of hopes deferred or frustrated.

Religion, particularly at its more popular levels, may promise the magical removal of specific ills; occasionally at moments of high excitment it can also hold out the apocalyptic vision of an immediate total transformation. Thus Max Weber distinguished between 'the massive and archaic growth of magic' engulfing 'the masses . . . everywhere', and the occasional 'prophetically-announced religion of redemption'.[154] Brian Wilson in his recent comparative study of primitive and Third World religious protest movements has attempted to conceptualize this distinction through the categories of 'thaumaturgical' and 'millennial'.[155] To him these are variants of what he calls, not very happily perhaps, 'deviant' religious forms as distinct from religious orthodoxies which try to absorb both removal of specific ills and hope of salvation into a basic sanctification of the status quo. Catholic orthodoxy for example has always sought to maintain a priestly monopoly over magic[156] while relegating the hope of redemption to the life after death or a safely distant Second Coming. 'Deviant' movements, however, naturally take over many forms and symbols from the orthodoxy prevalent in the concerned area, and sects in their 'introversionist' phase, as Peter Worsley shows in detail for Melanesian cargo-cults,[157] can once again emphasize a purely internal or distant salvation and so contribute to passivity.

---

[154] Max Weber, *Social Psychology of the World Religions*, in H. H. Gerth and C. Wright Mills (eds.), *From Max Weber: Essays in Sociology* (London, 1967), pp. 274, 277.

[155] Brian Wilson, *Magic and the Millennium: A Sociological Study of Religious Movements of Protest among Tribal and Third World Peoples* (London, 1973), Chapters 1, 2 and *passim*.

[156] Keith Thomas, *Religion and the Decline of Magic* (1971; reprinted London, 1980), Chapter 2 and *passim*.

[157] Peter Worsley, *The Trumpet Shall Sound: A Study of Cargo Cults in Melanesia* (2nd edn., London, 1970), *passim*.

Among Calcutta mill workers the story was current that British soldiers threw a bomb at Gandhi but 'it melted like snow as soon as it touched his person'.[164] The miracle-worker is able not only to preserve himself from every danger but (along occasionally with close associates like Muhammed Ali) also gives miraculous gifts to his devotees. Gandhi and Muhammed Ali 'possess heavenly bread which when hung up by a pious maulvi in a Mosque is found to have doubled itself on the following Friday and also to have produced holy water which is a panacea for all disease.'[165] But Gandhi also 'possesses the power of turning people to stone by breathing on them'[166]—an indication that the new deity can also punish those who do not accept him. The theme of punishment is very noticeable in Shahid Amin's collection. I would expect further research to unearth much more data on this in Bengal too, for the reward/punishment syndrome is always very common in stories about the rise of new deities. One might recall the medieval Bengali myth of Mansa the serpent-goddess who establishes herself through inflicting a series of disasters on Chand-Saudagar, while her devotees prosper.

Rumours of this first type present Gandhi alone, or at most a colleague like Mohammed Ali who is also a national figure, as miracle-workers. At a second level, however, thaumaturgical power may pass on to the followers or minor local leaders too. Someswarprasad Chaudhuri has recorded how at the height of the movement against the Midnapur Zamindari Company peasants started acknowledging this young ex-medical student as their '*guru*, whose *mantra* is *dharmaghat* [strike]'. The accidental death of Panja Pramanik, a powerful village headman who had opposed the movement, led to Someswar's orders being considered to be the commands of 'Khoda or Iswar'.[167] And by February 1922 as we have seen Santals of Madarihat in Jalpaiguri had come to believe that they were immune from bullets 'as they were wearing Gandhi Maharaj's caps'.[168] A recurrent feature in tribal and peasant uprisings both in India and in other parts of the world has been the belief that bullets turn into

---

[164] Ronaldshay to George V, 1 June 1921. *Zetland Collection.*
[165] *Bengal Diary*, 11 July 1921, ibid.
[166] Ronaldshay to George V, 1 June 1921, ibid.
[167] Someswarprasad Chaudhuri, *Nilkar Bidroha*, pp. 74, 111.
[168] *Mussalman*, 10 March 1922.

water.[169] One notices once again the characteristic pattern of inversion: red-hot bullets or bombs turn into innocuous water or snow, for the world itself is being turned upside down. And the Gandhi cap has become the equivalent of the amulets or the sign of the cross of more conventional religions, or of the protective water of the Maji-Maji rebels.[170]

In rumours of the third, so to say highest, type, it is this theme of sudden miraculous *total* transformation or reversal, as distinct from supernatural removal of specific personal ills, which predominates, and the transition from thaumaturgical to millennial is accomplished. In May 1919 Ronaldshay was informed about an Islamic prophecy that loss of Constantinople to the infidel would be followed by the coming of the Mahdi to restore Islam.[171] Throughout 1921 Gandhi's promise of Swaraj within a year led to dates being predicted repeatedly when a total transformation would come about: 25 March at Rajshahi, leading to the jailbreak,[172] 26 July among Darjeeling tea labourers,[173] 24 December among mill hands in and around Calcutta.[174] And the content of this Swaraj as we have seen went on broadening, embracing by early 1922 visions at times of a total repudiation of taxes, rents and interest payments.

A cult usually imposes ethical and ritual obligations on its devotees, and the existence of a strong religious dimension in many of the popular movements we have been considering is indicated also by the fact that the actions undertaken often went beyond the removal of the

[169] A few scattered examples out of many: the movement led by Korra Mallaya in the Vizagapatnam Agency in 1900 promised 'that he would arm his followers with bamboos, which should be turned by magic into guns, and would change the weapons of the authorities into water.' E. Thurston and K. Rangachari, *Castes and Tribes of South India*, Vol. III (Madras, 1909), pp. 350–3. In the revolt headed by Enoch Mgijima in South Africa in 1920 the expectation was that 'Jehovah would protect them and give them victory, turning the bullets of the soldiers to water'. In the much bigger Maji-Maji rebellion in German Tanganyika in 1905–6 the rebels used a 'protective water' which they believed 'changed bullets into water'. Brian Wilson, pp. 62, 244.

[170] One might be permitted a brief speculative aside on the significance of the Gandhi cap as a possible counter-symbol to the sahib's hat, Western attire has become much more widespread in India after independence, but the hat—better suited to a hot climate than suits or ties—seems to have disappeared completely.

[171] *Bengal Diary*, 17 May 1919. *Zetland Collection*.

[172] *Mussalman*, 20 May 1921.

[173] Ronaldshay to Montagu, 2 August 1921. *Zetland Collection*.

[174] *Amrita Bazar Patrika*, 23 December 1921.

specific concrete grievances which underlay them in a purely material sense. Thus agrarian tensions were certainly very important in the Mymensingh riots of 1906–7 but the objectives included the 'rescue' of Muslim prostitutes, the withdrawal of menial services to Hindus, and at places a general destruction of images. As a contemporary official report pointed out about the Iswarganj riots of 1906, 'the object of the mob was not plunder, but what, according to the maulvis, religion demanded of them.'[175] A strong note of internal moral purification was very prominent in Gandhian movements. The Tatmas of *Dhorai Charitmanas*, converted to the new cult by the miracle of 'Gandhi-Bawa's face appearing in a pumpkin, decide to give up meat, fish and tobacco, wash every day, and stop working on Sundays in the houses of the babus'—and only the last decision had any possible 'economic' connotations.[176] Gandhi's anti-liquor campaign did hit British revenues, but there can be little doubt that much of its appeal lay in its purificatory 'Sanskritizing' role. An early report of Non-Co-operation meetings in Rajshahi, for instance, describes how 'Mehtars, Doms and Chamars . . . promised in a body to give up drinking', after which the local Congress leader Provash Lahiri publicly embraced a sweeper.[177] Similarly the symbolic value of things like *khaddar* and *charkha* far outstripped the rather limited material gains villagers could be expected to derive immediately from a revival of archaic crafts. The *Dhorai Charitmanas* interestingly enough refers to a song which identifies the charkha with the *Sudarshan-chakra* with which Krishna destroyed enemies in the Mahabharata war.[178]

Rumours and ritual obligations alike invariably centered around the image of Gandhi, and the most varied of popular actions were undertaken, all in his name. The historical problem then is really two-fold: the extraordinarily open nature of the 'reception' of the Gandhian message, the way in which it became what in Roland Barthes' terminology might be called a text without an author,[179] and the fact that at the same time a mythical 'authorship' is being constantly

[175] Deputy Magistrate Debendraprasad Roy to District Magistrate, Mymensingh, 25 May 1906, *GOI Home Public A, July 1906*, No. 124. See *Swadeshi Movement*, pp. 445–6, 458–9.

[176] *Satinath Granthabali*, II, pp. 28–34.

[177] *Mussalman*, 18 March 1921.

[178] *Satinath Granthabali*, II, p. 207.

[179] Roland Barthes, 'The Death of the Author', in *Image-Music-Text* (Glasgow, 1982).

imputed to the Mahatma. To take an example from another province, an Allahabad police report in early 1921 asserts that Gandhi was being revered by villagers mainly because he was supposed to have stopped *bedakhli* (eviction) in neighbouring Pratapgarh.[180] The peasants' own achievements under their local leader Baba Rama- chandra were thus being attributed by them to Gandhi: an example perhaps of the peasants' need for representation through a master, their dependence on a saviour from above which Marx talked about in his *Eighteenth Brumaire*.

As for the choice of Gandhi (and at a more local level of a large number of political sadhus like Ramchandra, Vidyananda in Darbhanga, Biswananda and Darshanananda among Bengal and Bihar workers, etc.), the religious dimension ('code' might be a better term) can once again provide part of an explanation. It is not sufficient here to talk about Gandhi's 'use' of religion in the abstract, or merely to emphasize his effective combination of 'modern', 'traditional' and 'saintly' political idioms.[181] Extremist leaders had also 'used' religion and sought to give to patriotism the colours of a Hindu revival. Yet no equivalent popular cult developed around Bepinchandra Pal or even Tilak, and Aurobindo's post-1909 mysticism led his devotees away from active politics. Perhaps the comparative method can again provide a hint towards an answer. The Swadeshi (and terrorist) identification of patriotism with religion emphasized the centrality of *puja*: Durga or Kali as the Motherland, a symbolism going back to Bankimchandra. Gandhi evoked rather the mood of renunciation, austerity and sacrifice: the giving-up of fashionable garments and the prospect of comfortable jobs through official education, going to jail, unflinchingly facing lathis and bullets without retaliation, the ritual of fasts so deeply ingrained in Hindu tradition. One might tentatively suggest that while the concept and imagery of puja is integrally bound up with social and divine hierarchy,[182] the path of *sanyasa* is open to all and might even represent a moment of controlled

[180] *GOI Home Political Deposit February 1921*, No. 13 (*NAI*). The report has been reprinted in Gyan Pandey, 'Peasant Revolt and Indian Nationalism: The Peasant Movement in Awadh, 1919–22', Appendix, in R. Guha (ed.), *Subaltern Studies I*.

[181] W. H. Morris-Jones, *India's Political Idioms*, in C. H. Philips (ed.), *Politics and Society in India* (London, 1963).

[182] Lawrence Babb, *Divine Hierarchy: Popular Hinduism in Central India* (Columbia, 1975), Chapter 2 and *passim*.

rebellion.[183] Dumont's reference to the contrast between the figures of the emaciated sadhu and the pot-bellied Brahman in the north gate of Sanchi[184] emphasizes the greater and wider respect that *sanyasis* have on the whole evoked as compared to priests. Muslims would not come near a puja, the presence of lower castes would pollute worship in temples or upper-caste households, but there have been innumerable holy men, local sadhus or *pirs*, devotion to whom has cut across barriers of caste and creed. Gandhi's link with the Muslim masses did remain tenuous, for the persistent use of Hindu imagery could not but be an irritant. But that problem still lay in the future in 1921, thanks to the close alliance of Non-Co-operation with a Khilafat movement which emphasized hostility towards the British as the prime religious duty of the moment.

As for the virtue of sacrifice in the context of Indian tradition, it is significant that the wealthy epicurean barrister Chittaranjan Das won enormous popularity and the title of Deshabandhu precisely by two such actions: giving up practice in January 1921 and going to jail along with women of his household towards the end of that year. The first evoked a storm of student withdrawal from colleges and schools; the second revived enormously the flagging enthusiasm for the courting of arrest.

It would be dangerous to press this point too far, for the path of renunciation in Gandhi's case obviously led not to an escape from the world but towards efforts at remodelling it. The religious dimension has to be placed alongside other aspects of the total Gandhian 'message'. In the context of 1921–2, however, I would still argue that the secret lay not so much in Gandhi's specific political programmes or techniques, organizational abilities, or the undoubted peasant appeal of his anti-industrial populism (relatively little-known before the spread of constructive-work centres in the countryside), but in the combination of his reputation for saintliness with two rather different elements. Gandhi was a holy man with an already-acquired reputation for effectively doing something about specific 'wrongs' (South African pass laws, Champaran indigo exploitation, Kheda revenue burdens), who was now promising a total change which

[183] 'With his negation of the world and his asceticism, he [the *sanyasi*] represents that very reversal of values which we expected to find in festivals . . . he is the safety-valve for the Brahmanic order'. Louis Dumont, 'World Renunciation in Indian Religions', in his *Religion/Politics and History in India* (Paris/Hague, 1970), p. 51.
[184] Ibid., p. 44.

enthralled by its very vagueness: 'Swaraj' within a year. If an analogy may be permitted from a very different milieu, the combination here of the particular (including mythical particulars like stopping bedakhli at Pratapgarh) with the general recalls Barthes' analysis of the subconscious codes underlying the efficacy of modern advertising.[185]

Part of the strength of a religious faith is derived from the kind of built-in explanation it tends to contain about failure. If the devotee does not obtain the specific benefits he has been praying for, the fault lies not in the deity but in himself. He has not observed the rites properly, or in the true spirit required of him. A millennial movement, once the flash-point of maximum hope in immediate deliverance has come and gone, can still survive therefore, though in a transformed, 'introversionist' manner, emphasizing internal salvation through self-purification. Returning to the Gandhian context the religious dimension can perhaps help us to understand why despite so many 'betrayals' Gandhi could retain so much more authority among the peasant masses than was ever enjoyed by his radical Left critics. Gandhi himself made ample and very effective use of this aspect of religious faith, fixing the responsibility for the retreats he so often ordered on the inadequacies of himself and of his followers with respect to issues like non-violence or untouchability. The explanation proved all the more effective because to a considerable extent Gandhi believed in it himself. This is indicated by his repeated expiatory fasts, and above all perhaps by that curious episode in Noakhali when the Mahatma risked a break with close followers and a public scandal by undertaking some very controversial experiments in sexual abstinence in order to develop in himself the moral power to fight back communalism and Partition.[186] Persistence of faith in a new cult despite the fading-away of millennial hopes because devotees blame themselves for the failure, corresponds to the survival of orthodox religious faith even though rituals, pilgrimages, bathing in the Ganges, etc. seldom obtain for the faithful the hoped-for boons. Popular explosions of the type we have been discussing consequently tend to have a sporadic and intermittent character, sudden brief explosions

[185] Jonathan Culler, *Barthes* (Glasgow, 1983), pp. 75–6.

[186] 'Ever since my coming to Noakhali, I have been asking myself the question, "What is it that is choking the action of my Ahimsa? . . . May it not be because I have temporized in the matter of Brahmacharya?" ' Gandhi's conversation with Thakkar Bapa, 25 February 1947, Pyarelal, *Mahatma Gandhi: The Last Phase*, Vol. I (Ahmedabad, 1956), p. 586.

alternating with longer periods of relative passivity without building up into continuous and really effective movements.

I would like to emphasize in conclusion that the structure of correlations and oppositions I have tried to set out is a very provisional one, not a definite statement but rather a starting-point for further research directed towards greater concreteness and the study of variations and change. I emphasize this precisely because 'structuralist' analysis does tend at times to overemphasize unchanging or 'synchronic' elements, leading to the absurdities so effectively pilloried by E. P. Thompson in his *Poverty of Theory*.

Five types of variations, I feel, would be particularly relevant for developing and concretizing the framework sketched out here. First, as I have already emphasized in my first section, subordination and revolt constitute only the extreme poles in a complex continuum of varying attitudes. 'Breakdown' in my model is related to popular explosions, as distinct from various forms of protest which may not be uncommon even in normal or 'stable' times. Isolation of specific elements underlying the extremes, however, may be of help precisely in analyzing this continuum, in exploring for example the range of religious attitudes, symbols, myths and norms lying between the opposite poles. What is needed above all is an ideal of totality: the study of popular movement in India has to break out of the confines of the narrowly economic and narrowly political alike, and develop into social history in the broadest sense of that much-abused term.

In the second place, regional differences: my data in this paper has been entirely from Bengal, but a study of popular movements in other provinces in the same period would no doubt bring out inte-resting and significant variations, particularly in the specific use of religious symbols and myths and their interactions in a complex pattern of continuity/inversion with the established structures of 'orthodox' popular religion. Thus Crooke has some valuable pages on the role of hero-cults in the popular religion and folklore of northern India,[187] and it may be interesting to consider the ways in which the cult of the Mahatma continued and/or deviated from the established patterns.

The third, and to my mind very important variation would be the modifications in the structure of beliefs, emotions and actions related to the differences among the varied social groups we have been

[187] Crooke and Enthoven, *Religion and Folklore of Northern India* (London, 1925), Chapters 5–6.

lumping together under the omnibus categories of 'subaltern' or 'popular'. I confess I find it difficult to go all the way with Partha Chatterji when he talks about a specific 'peasant-communal mode of politics',[188] both distinct and presumably more or less homogeneous. Attempts at dividing-up the peasantry into distinct strata are admittedly hazardous and quite often very mechanical. Yet the differences remain vital, and particularly, as I have tried to argue in another paper, the gap in Indian conditions between landholding peasants—usually of intermediate castes—and low caste, untouchable or tribal agricultural labourers often debarred by religious and social tradition from holding land even in land-surplus situations.[189] One might hazard a tentative hypothesis for instance that rumours of a conflict of authorities and movements with specific, limited goals would tend to be more typical among landholding peasants. Examples from an earlier period would include the Pabna and Deccan 'riots' of the 1870s, in both of which rumours were current that the ultimate superiors, the Queen or British authorities, were on the side of the peasants against zamindars and moneylenders, while the demands were quite specific and limited. Tribal movements in contrast were both more far-ranging, at times millennial in their aims, and often inspired by rumours that British rule itself was coming to an end. It may be important to explore whether such distinctions are also valid within Gandhian popular movements.

The relative role of material pressures and rumours of breakdown appears to be another possible social variable. Haat-looting, many forms of rural crime, and labour strikes seem to have a closer correlation with economic indicators like price-variations than peasant movements against their social or political superiors.[190] Crowds gather anyway on market-days, industrial labour is concentrated at the place of work, but the peasants in their scattered fields and villages may be more in need of the stimulus of a rumoured breakdown before they go in for large-scale action on issues like rent.

The limited data presently at my disposal also hint at some differences in the way apparently identical symbols and myths were used

[188] Partha Chatterji, 'Agrarian Relations and Communalism in Bengal, 1926–35'.

[189] Sumit Sarkar, *Popular Movements and Middle-Class leadership in late Colonial India: Perspectives and Problems of a 'History from Below'* (Deuskar Lecture, Centre for Studies in Social Sciences, Calcutta, 1983).

[190] David Arnold's study of Madras police records brings out marked correlations between food riots and dacoity and years or seasons of scarcity. 'Dacoity and Rural Crime in Madras, 1860–1940' in *Journal of Peasant Studies*, January 1979.

by peasants and industrial workers. Take for example the symbolism of the Gandhi cap. Santals of Madarihat were moved by a belief in the invincibility it was supposed to give to its wearers into what was after all a totally suicidal confrontation with the police. Industrial workers in contrast seem to have used the symbol as well as rumours of imminent Gandhi raj in a more hard-headed way, sometimes to further what amounted to trade-union unity in a fairly effective pursuit of specific objectives—as when Calcutta jute workers wanted an end to the practice of holding back wages on the ground that Swaraj was coming on 24 December 1921.

This brings us to the question of variations over time, which structuralist analysis at times tends to neglect or treat in a cyclical manner. Certainly any assumption of a unilinear development of popular consciousness in a 'progressive' direction has to be abandoned. In labour history oscillation between class struggle and communal strife remains all too evident, while the united peasant actions of the Non-Co-operation-Khilafat period gave way by the mid-1920s to agrarian-communal riots very reminiscent of 1906–7. Yet certain shifts can be seen, if we take a long enough time-span, and the greatness of Satinath Bhaduri's novel lies precisely in its comprehension of the complex development of popular consciousness in and through interruptions and retrogressions. The national movement had very far from a unilinear development, and yet the legitimacy of foreign rule was eroded over time. To take another example, the importance of Swamis in leading peasant and labour movements seems to have been an essentially time-bound phenomenon. Again the importance of rumours of breakdown as preconditions for popular militancy is probably not a universal phenomenon, but related to the stability attained by British rule in the post-Mutiny phase.

Finally the spread of Gandhian constructive-work cadres over the countryside, followed a little later by the penetration of Left-wing ideas and organizations, raises the problem of the extent to which the structure of popular mentality we have been analysing was modified by the entry of more 'modern' ideological—organizational patterns. The crucial differences once again would lie in the conception of breakdown. For a militant of a modern party, breakdown (or in less radical terms some kind of significant overall change) would be not the starting-point or presupposition for action but rather the objective aimed at, and sustained political work would attain priority over intermittent unorganized explosions interpersed with periods of subordination. One would also expect the religious dimensions to decline over time, along with the related dependence on outsider leaders conceived as deified masters rather than democratic representatives. Whether or to what extent such changes have actually taken place in India is a problem worth investigating.[191] We would certainly expect to find complex interactions between such theoretically distinct structures, most obvious in developed Gandhism with its combination of peasant-populist religious idiom with strong urban bourgeois links and hard-headed organizational discipline mastering and channelizing autonomous outbursts. In the historiography of Gandhian nationalism as well as occasionally in studies of Left movements the focus has recently been on a kind of spontaneity-consciousness debate, with leaders presented either as heroes or betrayers. A more systematic analysis of variations in structures of collective mentality might go some way towards enriching the subject and broadening its perspectives.

---

[191] Dipesh Chakrabarty in his contribution to the present volume has argued the case for continuity even within the Communist-led trade union movements.

Glossary

abkari	Excise duty on alcoholic drinks.
adivasi	A culturally distinct peasantry, normally living in the more remote areas of India, who are considered to be 'tribal'.
Ahirin	Wife of an Ahir, a middle caste of herdsmen and cultivators.
amil	Subordinate official.
asahyog	Non-co-operation.
atmashuddhi	Self-purification.
Baya	Mother goddess, associated in Maharashtra with smallpox.
bhadralok	Respectable person of middle-class origin.
bhajan	Devotional song.
bhajan mandali	Group which sings devotional songs.
Bhumihar	A caste of dominant landholders of eastern UP.
bigha	A measure of land, roughly equal to one-third of an acre.
brahmchari	A Hindu celibate, well-versed in religious texts.
cambu	Spiked millet *(Pennisetum typhoideum)*.
charkha	Spinning wheel.
chauk	Platform.
cholam	Great millet *(Sorgham vulgare)*.
choultry	A rest-house or feeding place for pilgrims and travellers.
darshan	Ritualized viewing of an image of a god or a god-like person.
daru	Country liquor.
Devi	Mother goddess.
dharmopdeshak	Religious preacher.
Dussehra	A Hindu festival.

faliya	Street, or—in adivasi areas—a separate hamlet of a village.
farman	Injunction.
Gaula	Shaman of the Dangs tract of South Gujarat.
gram	Village.
haat	A periodic village market.
hakim	From *hukm*: order; a master, used colloquially for district and tahsil officials.
Halwai	Confectioner.
ilaqa	Territorial domain.
imambarah	Place of worship for Shias.
jai	Victory.
jaikar	Shouting '*jai*': 'Long live . . .'
janta	People; public; masses.
Julaha	Weaver.
kaliparaj	'The black people'—a derogatory term for the adivasis of South Gujarat.
kanji	Gruel made from rice or miller.
kargah	Loom.
kargahi	Tax on looms.
karinda	A minion employed by a zamindar.
karkhana	Workshop; firm.
katcha	Makeshift, temporary.
khadi	Cloth which is hand-spun and hand-woven.
Kisan Sabha	Peasant Association.
kolhuar	Place where cane is crushed and raw sugar (*gur*) manufactured.
mahajan	Moneylender; trader.
marsia	Lamentations in verse concerning the tragedy at Karbala which is commemorated at Muharram.
masjid	Mosque.
Mata	Mother goddess.
mazar	Grave.
mela	Fair.
mohalla	A residential quarter or a ward in a town.
mufassil	Interior.
muhalla	See *mohalla*.

mukhtar	A category of legal practitioners who operate usually in sub-divisional courts.
Nagri	Hindi script.
naib-tahsildar	An influential officer in the sub-divisional revenue administration.
nilhe saheb	Indigo planter.
Panchali	A form of Hindu devotional music.
pannaiyal	Tied farm servant.
panwali	Female seller of betel leaves.
pargana	A sub-division within a *tahsil* (q.v.).
parja	See *praja*.
patiyal	Hired farm labourer.
patta	A land title.
pattadar	Holder of a land title.
pracharni	Devoted to the cause of propagation or propaganda *(prachar)*.
praja	Lit. 'subject'; used primarily to mean tenant cultivators, connoting their relationship of dependence on their landlords.
prasad	Food ritually offered to Hindu deities.
puja-paath	Ritual of worship and reading of sacred texts addressed to Hindu deities.
qasba	Small town; 'urban' manufacturing, marketing or administrative centre.
qazi	Judge trained in Islamic law; interpreter of Islamic law and injunctions.
ragi	A variety of millet *(Eleusine coracana)*.
raiyat	Peasant; peasant proprietor.
raiyatwari	Landholding system in which *raiyats* (q.v.) are immediately subordinate to the state.
raja dharma	A ruler's duty.
Ramlila	A folk festival which celebrates the career of the Hindu mythical hero Rama by dramatizing some of its principal episodes.
raniparaj	'People of the forest'—term for adivasis of South Gujarat used by Gandhian nationalists.
rausa	Notable. (Singular: *raees*).

razil	Base or uneducated people, especially those who do menial labour.
ryot	See *raiyat*.
sabha	League; association; society.
sahukar	Moneylender.
samskar	A sanctifying or purificatory Hindu ritual.
sardar	Headman; jobber; leader.
sarkar	Government; state.
sattu	Chick-pea flour, often used as food.
seer	A measure equivalent to 2.057 lbs.
Shakti	A goddess; the principle of female energy and power.
sharif	Respectable folk.
shivalaya	Small temple used for ritual worship of the Hindu deity Siva.
shuddhi	Purification.
suba	Baroda State official, equivalent of British District Collector.
tahsil	A sub-division within a district.
takia	Platform, often used for resting *tazias* (q.v.).
taluk	Administrative sub-division of a district.
tazia	Replica of the mausoleum of Imam Husain, carried in procession during Muharram.
thakurain	Wife of a *thakur*, member of a dominant landed caste in eastern UP.
thakurduara	Temple.
thana	Police station; area under the jurisdiction of a police station.
thanadar	Officer in charge of a police station.
updesh	A moral or spiritual discourse, advice or command.
vakla	Advocates. (Singular: *vakil*).
vratkatha	A sacred ballad or narrative recited on certain Hindu ritual occasions.
waqf	A religious endowment; an irrevocable settlement to safeguard the usufruct of property for charitable purposes.

Index